For Marie Louise
and David Bernal

Hoping you enjoy
this American view
of Swedish business.

Jerry Hagstrom

To Be, Not To Be Seen

The Mystery of Swedish Business

Forest
Agriculture
RUSSIA
Kiruna
Luleå
Gulf of Bothnia
Atlantic Ocean
Umeå
Östersund
FINLAND
Sundsvall
NORWAY
Gävle
Falun
BERGSLAGEN
Uppsala
Västerås
Gulf of Finland
Karlstad
Stockholm
ESTONIA
Örebro
Linköping
Skagerrak
Göteborg
Jönköping
Visby
Kattegatt
Gotland
LATVIA
Kalmar
Öland
North Sea
Karlskrona
DENMARK
Malmö
Baltic Sea
LITHUANIA
GERMANY
POLAND

To Be, Not To Be Seen

The Mystery of Swedish Business

Jerry Hagstrom

The George Washington University
School of Business and Public Management

Published by
The George Washington University
School of Business and Public Management

Copyright © 2001 by Jerry Hagstrom
All rights reserved, including the right of reproduction
in whole or in part in any form.

Produced and distributed by
SkanAtlantic Press
PO BOX 1191
Middleburg, VA 20118

ISBN 0-9709460-0-7

For
Ingrid Hagstrom Huber Brenneise
and her granddaughter, Sara Huber

CONTENTS

Introduction	11
From Ice to Iron 12,000 B.C. - A.D. 1721	25
The Development of Freedom- Political and Economic 1721-1867	49
The Age of Entrepreneurship I: The Bankers and Their Spheres 1856-1932	73
The Age of Entrepreneurship II: Great Corporations and Founders 1864-1932	95
Challenge to Capitalism and the Saltsjöbaden Agreement 1867-1938	129
Swedish Modern - the Golden Years, 1933-1973	177
Paradise on a Roller Coaster 1971-1999	219
The Empire and the Cottage - Sweden's Business Future	255
Acknowledgements	287
Biography of Jerry Hagstrom	289
Interviews and Conversations	291
Bibliography	295

Introduction

SWEDEN IS FAMOUS for so many natural wonders and social virtues—the grandeur of the Midnight Sun, the beauty of its women, the grace of its Olympic athletes, the glory of the Nobel prizes, the heroism of Raoul Wallenberg, and the success of its welfare state in maintaining one of the most stable societies on earth. Consumers all over the world know Sweden for the quality of products such as Absolut vodka, Volvo cars, Ericsson telephones, Electrolux vacuum cleaners and Orrefors crystal. Industrialists also recognize Sweden as the inventor of the self-aligning ball bearing and the source of some of the world's purest iron, precision steel, and the finest woods and paper. Sweden has also recently been recognized as the European center of information technology, particularly in wireless communications.

But mention of the phrase "Swedish business" is likely to provoke stares and questions such as, "Isn't Swedish business a contradiction in terms?" and "Doesn't the government own the industry in Sweden?"

In fact, Sweden has many reasons to claim a special place in the world capitalist community. The Volvo car and truck, the SKF ball bearing and other Swedish products are all manufactured and marketed by private Swedish enterprise. The origins of Stora, the mineral and forest products company, can be traced back to the 13th century, and Swedes say it is the world's oldest joint stock company. One of the poorest countries in Europe in the 1860s, Sweden began to industrialize in the 1870s and for the next 100 years enjoyed a higher economic growth rate than any other country in the world except Japan. In the 1930s, '40s and '50s, when France, England and other countries were nationalizing industry or starting state-run companies, Sweden kept almost all of its private sector private. For many years, Sweden has had more firms on the Fortune list of the 500 largest international industrial companies than countries with populations much larger than its 8.9 million. In 1996, a study by the *Financial Times and Economist Intelligence Unit* showed Sweden to be home to 33 of the 500 largest companies in Europe and that among the industrialized nations had the highest number of large corporations per 1,000 residents.

Created mostly in a great burst of invention and entrepreneurial activity between 1860 and 1930, Sweden's industrial giants such as SKF, Volvo, Electrolux and Atlas Copco would make any country proud. In addition to their roles as producers of high-quality goods and creators of wealth, Swedish companies today are ahead of most of their competitors in addressing environmental issues. That a country so small in population and so remote from centers of population and commerce should be so successful in worldwide industry is a remarkable accomplishment in itself. That the country has kept its business community almost a secret is a peculiarly Swedish phenomenon.

This book, written to shed some light on Sweden's business tradition and future, has its origins in a reporting trip I made to Sweden in 1991 to observe the general elections. I thought it a natural part of political reporting to find out how Swedish business leaders viewed the economic programs of the country's multiple political parties and candidates—in particular because polls showed that Swedes were then inclined to throw out the Social Democrats, who had run the country almost continuously since 1932, in favor of a nonsocialist coalition government.

I quickly discovered that Swedes considered my line of inquiry very odd. The Swedish Foreign Ministry paraded every imaginable labor and social interest group leader in front of the foreign press. But the ministry presented the reporters no business leaders except Count Ian Wachtmeister, a candidate of the New Democracy Party, a populist political movement that won seats in the Riksdag that year but has since fallen apart.

The Swedish political reporters whom I met had no plans to interview business executives, and the industrialists whom I insisted on meeting seemed alarmed at the prospect that their political views might receive a public airing. My questions, I was told, were "very un-Swedish."

On a series of research trips to Sweden between 1992 and 1998, I discovered that Swedes are uncomfortable discussing the history of their business community, because the reality of that story conflicts with the vision they have of their society as one run by and for a single mass of people. Swedish business is the story of nobles, Jews, village geniuses and members of non-Lutheran Protestant "free churches," all of whose characteristics as individuals and as subgroups in Swedish society have propelled them to be inventive and entrepreneurial.

The Swedish discomfort with people who "stick out" the way inventors and entrepreneurs invariably do goes back much further than the rise of the Social Democrats in the late 19th century. There are several theories about why Swedes feel this way. Ulf Olsson, a Stockholm School of Economics professor who is the semi-official biographer of the Wallenbergs, Sweden's most powerful business family, says that Sweden is part of a "collectivistic, northeastern European tradition" in which the group is still more important than the individual.

Others point out that a majority of Swedes have lived in cities only since World War II and say that they still have strong memories of rural life, in which people had to cooperate and conform to survive. Carl Johan Westholm, former president of Sweden's Confederation of Private Enterprises, a small-business lobbying group, says that Swedes still suffer from the religion of fear and suppression in the old villages described by Aksel Sandemose, the early-20th-century Danish-Norwegian writer, in his novel *A Fugitive Crosses His Tracks*. Sandemose wrote that in a typical Scandinavian village (he called the one in his novel Jante), there were 10 rigid laws to keep people down. The first was "Thou shalt not believe thou *art* something." Scandinavian intellectuals have long criticized the "Jante law" for discouraging personal and artistic expression, but Swedish business leaders told me repeatedly that the "Jante" way of thinking also discourages young people from pushing themselves to become entrepreneurs and the society from giving the entrepreneur his or her proper due.

The reasons for Swedish business's invisibility at home and abroad go back to the Great Depression of the 1930s, when the reputation of capitalism worldwide was at its nadir. In 1932, the Social Democrats won control of the Swedish government. Swedish industrialists were able to resist efforts over the next few years to nationalize their companies, but after that battle, all Swedish business decided that the safest way to survive was to adopt the motto of the Wallenbergs: *Esse non videri*, "To be, not to be seen," taken from the Prussian King Friedrich II (1712-86).

Swedish business's visibility abroad was diminished by the 1936 publication in the United States of Marquis Childs's *Sweden: The Middle Way*. The point of the book was, in fact, that Sweden had developed a model society halfway between capitalism and communism, but Childs devoted much more attention to the way Sweden spent its money to improve the living standards of its people than to how it created its wealth.

As Childs acknowledged in a 25th-anniversary edition of his book, Swedish business leaders had complained that he exaggerated the roles of the government and producer and consumer co-ops in Sweden's mass prosperity. But their private grumbling could hardly compete with a book that became a national best-seller in the United States, was read in many other countries and led the world to think of Sweden as a social democratic utopia. It is an image that lingers to this day.

An Un-Swedish Story

With all these cultural impediments, how did Sweden develop such a successful business community? Sweden had the advantage of iron and copper deposits so rich and accessible that even the earliest settlers could remove them from the earth and export them. The Viking raids brought Sweden into contact with Russia and other countries to the east—and perhaps most important, established a spirit of adventure that is taught to every schoolchild to this day. The Thirty Years War (1618-1648) took a terrible toll on the Swedish people, but Sweden's involvement in it also intensified the country's contacts with European culture. Sweden was not an early center of technological innovation, but its kings, nobles and burghers imported European and British technology to improve mining operations. Sweden adopted the Protestant Reformation and therefore could accept scientific ideas more easily than Catholic countries mired in conflicts between religion and modern science. The Lutheran Church's practice of identifying the most intelligent and talented boys in each village and educating them to become priests also allowed the country to bring the "best and brightest" of its common people into the upper levels of society. Although Swedes often say that these boys and their male descendants went from "peasant to priest to civil servant in three generations," many of the priests' sons and grandsons became scientists and businessmen.

In the 1700s, Sweden established its own Academy of Sciences, made science an important subject of study in its universities, and sent its talented young men abroad to study or take apprenticeships, often at government expense. When Swedes didn't have the skills the country needed, the government brought in engineers from other countries and encouraged them to settle there. From the late 1700s on, Jews were allowed to settle, and they went on to play a crucial role in the development of trade, banking and textiles. Sweden has always "recognized talent and helped talent to help itself," noted Michaël Hammarskjöld, the former director of Sweden's House of Nobility and a nephew of the late U.N. Secretary General Dag Hammarskjöld. Sweden's earliest nobles were landowners and warriors, but in the century before ennobling ceased in 1902, Sweden honored artists, scientists and merchants by adding them to the ranks of the nobility.

The Swedish people were better prepared for modern times than many of their European neighbors. Sweden has a democratic tradition of assemblies and peasant rights that goes back to prehistoric times and, compared with the continent, was never very feudalistic. During the Middle Ages, the proportion of peasants who were landowners was much higher in Sweden than in other European countries; in the 1600s, when the nobles attempted to enserf them, they protested bitterly, eventually succeeding in reversing the trend. Swedish nobles elected the country's kings from among their peers until Gustaf Vasa made the monarchy hereditary in his family in 1544. A number of Sweden's kings tried to institute an absolute monarchy, but the nobles always resisted. The story of Swedish politics dominated by the nobles before the constitutional monarchy of 1809 is its own unheralded tale.

Historians have traditionally viewed Sweden as a poor country that industrialized late, but they are revising that view, according to industrial historians Kersti Morger of the Swedish Central Board of Antiquities and Marie Nisser of the Royal Institute of Technology and Uppsala University. In the late 18th century, Sweden was already producing handicrafts of a very high standard, and the agrarian revolution, with its land reclamations, systems of crop rotation and better drainage, created the capital for the transformation of small workshops into the first factories, according to Morger and Nisser. Earlier scholars had contended that industrialization destroyed rural crafts such as wire making, clock making, carpentry, glassblowing, and spinning and weaving, but Morger and Nisser write that these "protoindustries" laid the foundation for the development of Sweden's manufacturing and rapid growth in the 19th century.

In 1842, inspired by American ideas of progressive education, the Swedish government established primary schools throughout the country, and when manufacturing began in the 1870s, the industrialists had the advantage of taking their workforce from a population that could read and write. They also had plenty of workers from whom to choose because high agricultural productivity, the introduction of modern medicine—primarily the smallpox vaccine—and cultivation of the potato had led to fast growth in the Swedish population in the l9th century. The rapid population growth could have caused social chaos, but Swedish industry developed under relatively peaceful conditions, in part because more than a million Swedes emigrated to the United States between 1865 and 1914.

Without the United States as a "safety valve," Sweden might have been more subject to the turmoil and revolution that plagued neighboring countries.

Business and the Social Democratic Era

While the new industries created great wealth, they did not reduce the gap between the rich and poor or improve working conditions. The labor union movement, then growing throughout Europe, gained enormous popularity in Sweden, and in 1898, the Swedish trade unions set up a central organization called *Landsorganisationen* (Swedish Trades Union Congress), known by its Swedish acronym LO. Private companies tried individually to deal with the unions, but in 1903, they set up the *Svenska Arbetsgivareföreningen* (Swedish Employers' Confederation), known as SAF, to negotiate as a group with LO. In 1907, the Federation of Swedish Industries was established to represent big Swedish companies on other issues.

During the first quarter of the 20th century, while Conservatives and Liberals still controlled the government, the right to vote was extended to all Swedish men and women, basic pension and medical care programs were established, and the workday was shortened to eight hours. In the early 1930s, however, the world economic crisis brought record levels of unemployment in Sweden and started a new political age. The spectacular failure of industrialist Ivar Kreuger's Swedish Match Co. in early 1932 seemed to confirm growing sentiment in Sweden that capitalism itself had failed—and that some other economic model would be better suited to organizing the country's resources and production capabilities.

The Social Democrats promised to end unemployment with a program of public works paying full wages, to be financed by high taxes on upper-income people. In the fall of 1932, the Swedes gave the Social Democrats the largest number of their votes in the general election, though not enough for a majority. The Social Democrats entered into a coalition with the Agrarian Party, which demanded agricultural subsidies as the price of their cooperation. The change of government didn't stop Sweden from going through bitter strikes and disputes between 1932 and 1934, and some analysts feared Sweden might go Communist or fascist. Swedes proved, however, that they were more interested in reform than revolution. In 1938, Swedish industrialists and labor leaders signed the Saltsjöbaden Accord—the key document of modern Swedish economic life—and agreed that labor and management would both abide by negotiated contracts. For many years, labor also ceased its calls for nationalization or worker takeover of industry.

The Great Depression proved to be shorter in Sweden than in most other countries, and economists and political scientists all over the world began to view what became known as the Swedish Model of economic intervention and labor-management agreements as one of the few bright spots in a darkening world. It would be many years before economists would conclude that, while the interventionist economic policies did stabilize the country, Sweden's sales of iron and other raw materials to Germany, which was then building up for World War II, were also crucial to that recovery.

Sweden's great period of business formation ended when the Social Democratic era began. Sweden became a country where people would rather tax the rich than become rich. While the Social Democrats tolerated the existing companies, they were not enthusiastic about capitalism, small business or the growth of small companies into medium-sized or large concerns. One family, the Wallenbergs, came to control 40 percent of the shares on the Stockholm Stock Exchange—a concentration of economic power that sociologists might have noted was similar to that in the Latin American banana republics if they had not been so busy extolling Sweden's social virtues.

Because it seems contradictory that Swedes would profess such a spirit of equality and yet allow one family to influence and not want to create the conditions for other Swedes to become wealthy, I asked a Swedish diplomat why Swedes allowed this situation to continue. "The Wallenbergs are tolerated because they are at a distance and they create jobs," the diplomat replied. "If the man down the street gets rich, then the average Swede has to ask himself, 'Why did he get rich and I didn't?' and he doesn't want to face that question."

The problem with this attitude is not so much that the Wallenbergs controlled so many companies, but that so few new companies have been formed. Of the Swedish-origin companies on the Fortune 500 list in the 1990s, the only two formed after 1932 were Tetra Pak, the juice and milk carton maker, and IKEA, the furniture retailer.

World War II and the Postwar Era

When World War II broke out, Sweden managed to continue the neutrality it had established after the Napoleonic era. Sweden maintained economic relations with all countries as long as possible, but after the Skagerak channel between Norway and Denmark was mined in 1940, almost all of Sweden's trade was with Germany and the countries it controlled. As the tide turned against Germany, Sweden was in greater danger of becoming a battleground, but it avoided being invaded by allowing Hitler's troops stationed in Norway to travel through Swedish territory in sealed trains on their way to Germany for home leave and through Swedish air space to the Finnish front. After the war, Sweden had the only intact industrial plant in Europe, and it boomed. Some critics have said that Sweden had an almost unfair advantage in the war and early postwar years because it made money first on sales to Germany and then on the postwar reconstruction of Europe. But the fact is that Sweden could not have done either if it had not industrialized several decades earlier.

The '50s, '60s and early '70s were a period of extraordinary prosperity for Swedish companies and for the Swedish people. Swedish exports increased steadily, the number of jobs and the level of wages soared, the welfare state grew ever broader and both Swedes and foreigners came to look upon Sweden as paradise on earth. Under the surface of this perfect image, however, big problems were looming. In the 1960s, it became evident that some older, heavy Swedish industries such as shipbuilding could not survive world competition from Third World countries with cheaper labor. Small-business owners found that tax laws made it more lucrative for them to sell their companies to larger ones or to simply shut down than to grow bigger or pass their businesses on to the next generation. Sweden was also suffering a brain drain of some of its most talented, entrepreneurial people, who sought greater opportunity and less regulation and taxation in the United States and other countries.

In the postwar era, Sweden became one of the world's most generous donors of foreign aid, and therein lies a great tragedy of the Swedish business story. Sweden, in fact, had pioneered export-led development. But its diplomats and development "experts," many of whom disapproved of capitalism, never taught Sweden's highly successful capitalist model to the rest of the world. The Republic of China on Taiwan, South Korea and other Asian countries took up the export-led model after World War II, however, and when they succeeded and centrally planned economies (some of them encouraged by Sweden's development agencies) failed, economists in international organizations and officials in poor countries began to recommend export-led development. By the

1990s, nearly every Third World country was trying to increase its wealth through exports and international competition, but the credit for the model went to the Asian tigers, not Sweden, which had originated it nearly a century earlier.

Finally a Crisis... and Action

Throughout the '50s, '60s and early '70s, Swedish business leaders remained remarkably passive in the face of increasing taxation and regulation. Some Swedish business leaders say that the Social Democrats and their masterful prime minister, Olof Palme, beat them, while others say that they were too busy developing and running profitable multinational business empires to devote too much attention to Swedish governmental affairs. There may, however, be deeper explanations. Sweden never had a revolution, and its industrial community was grafted onto a preindustrial society whose elite—the monarchy, the nobility, the military and the state Lutheran Church clergy—occupy special places in Swedish society to this day. In conversations about economic and tax policy, Swedes of average backgrounds tend to lump the old aristocrats and the business elites together, making no distinction between those policies that may maintain the privileges of inherited wealth versus those policies that may encourage job creation and new business formation. Upper-class Swedes, meanwhile, often give the impression they feel lucky that their ancestors were not beheaded or exiled like the French or Russian aristocrats and believe that they have maintained whatever position they hold by being discreet and using behind-the-scenes manipulation rather than taking a role in public life. I asked an upper-class Swedish woman why Swedish business had not stood up for itself more on issues of taxation and regulation during the years of Social Democratic domination. She looked at me sternly and said, "You know what would have happened."

By the late '60s, Swedish business began to pay for its lack of participation in politics and government. Wages rose faster than productivity, making Swedish products less competitive on world markets. The left wing of the Social Democratic Party, which had been campaigning for greater control of industry for years, finally prevailed in establishing "wage-earner" investment funds, which were intended to bring companies under a higher level of employee control. The overall political atmosphere encouraged these trends. The image of the Vietnam war as an effort to maintain U.S. capitalist hegemony in the world made business less respectable in Sweden, and the sons and daughters of Swedish executives were among those youth who took up radical leftist rhetoric and led or participated in Swedish miniversions of the student protests that rocked Paris in 1968.

The Swedish Employers' Confederation, which had been criticized by the owners of smaller companies for not doing more to improve the image of business in Sweden, decided in 1968 to take a more aggressive position. In 1970, Marcus Wallenberg brought together the high-ranking managers of companies the Wallenbergs controlled, and they decided to become more active in convincing Swedes that the country needed pro-business policies. This evolution was overshadowed, however, by the 1973 world oil crisis, which revealed Sweden's dependence on expensive imported oil and made its products even less competitive internationally. In 1976, Curt Nicolin, president of Asea, a Wallenberg-controlled company whose business included construction of nuclear power plants, was elected chairman of the Employers' Confederation. Nuclear power had become the hottest political issue in Sweden in the 1970s, with business executives arguing that the country needed a guaranteed domestic source of energy and critics charging that disaster could result. In a 1980 referendum, after a campaign in which Nicolin vigorously defended nuclear power, Swedish voters decided by a small majority to continue nuclear power into the early 21st century, but to get rid of it eventually.

The wage-earner funds remained such a threat to management control of private enterprise that in 1983, Nicolin adopted the tactics of the labor unions by leading a march in the streets of Stockholm. More than 100,000 Swedes showed up to demonstrate their solidarity with Sweden's tradition of keeping private business ownership private. The wage-earner funds were not eliminated completely, however, until a nonsocialist government took power in 1991.

Toward the 21st Century

Sweden enjoyed a new phase of prosperity in the 1980s, but the good times turned out, as in many other countries, to be based on devaluations and a real estate bubble. The 1990s began a new era for Sweden on many fronts. With Communism's fall in the Soviet Union and Eastern Europe, Sweden's foreign policy of nonalignment with either the Communist East or the democratic, capitalist West was rendered meaningless. The reaction against big government everywhere in the developed world finally gained a foothold in Sweden, and in 1991, the country elected its first nonsocialist coalition government since 1982 and the first since the 1930s with a strong agenda. The nonsocialists reduced taxes and attempted other reforms but were plagued with a recession that sent unemployment soaring from nearly zero in 1991 to 14 percent in 1993. For the first time since the start of the welfare state in the 1930s, the Swedish government could not afford to create jobs, and the percentage of the population receiving unemployment or retraining benefits remained in the double digits until 1999.

Swedes' enthusiasm for nonsocialist rule faded quickly. In the 1994 elections, Swedes returned to normalcy, putting the Social Democrats back in power. The "new" Social Democratic era is different from times past, however. With the European Union a much more powerful and cohesive economic force, it became crucial for Sweden to join the Union or miss out on export sales and investment opportunities. The Social Democrats, who had opposed membership in the Union since the establishment of its predecessor, the European Economic Community in the 1950s, had reversed their position in early 1991. In a 1994 referendum, Swedes voted by a slim margin to join the EU. As the nearby Baltic countries, which had been part of the Swedish empire in the 16th and 17th centuries, emerged from Communist rule, the Swedish government also made stronger business relations part of a massive foreign aid effort to help those countries toward stability.

Following a devaluation of the krona, Swedish exports and stock prices skyrocketed in the mid-'90s. Swedes have not felt the benefits of this business success as strongly as they would have in the past, however. Swedish companies have shifted some of their production abroad, both to save labor costs and to be closer to their markets. And the Wallenbergs, eager to be competitive on a global scale, have repeatedly told the financial press that they want to be considered Europeans, not Swedes, and that they will diversify their own portfolio to include more non-Swedish companies.

The Wallenbergs often make statements critical of the Social Democratic governments, but they do not appear to have given up on the country. Jacob Wallenberg, who became head of the Skandinaviska Enskilda Banken at 41 in 1997, said in an interview for this book that he hopes that Swedish government and industry can have a more "constructive dialogue" in the future. "Here industrialists don't have a clue what it means to run a country from a political viewpoint, and politicians have very little understanding of the industrial side." French business leaders and politicians and their counterparts in other members of the Organization for Economic Cooperation and Development (OECD) move back and forth between business and government service and have a "greater appreciation of the circumstances" under which both work, Wallenberg said. "I hope we can improve on this dialogue [so that] there is an understanding of professionalism and an exchange of views."

Changing economics have caused Swedes to recognize that, while the big Swedish companies will continue to be an important part of the economy, the country has—and needs—other assets as well: small businesses with growth potential, a stable society that can attract international companies and a new generation of inventors and entrepreneurs.

Sweden has long had a community of small businesses that the Stockholm-based government, corporate and labor union establishments have always dismissed as inferior to large enterprises. Many of them are located far from Stockholm. The biggest concentration of these businesses is in Jönköping, otherwise known as Sweden's Jerusalem because it is home to so many of the free churches, such as the Pentecostals, the Baptists and the Methodists, that challenged the state Lutheran Church's supremacy in the 19th century. Many of the businesses were started earlier in the century by free church members who broke with the hierarchical Swedish mind-set and started firms making tools and wooden items. Entrepreneurship among these poor country folk became so strong that Swedes gave it its own name, the Gnosjö spirit, after a county near Jönköping. Today, descendants of the small companies' founders have built the businesses into stable firms that are suppliers to bigger firms in Sweden and elsewhere in Europe, and the area in and around Jönköping has the lowest unemployment rate in the country. One of the brightest signals of the Swedish government's attitude toward business was the decision to establish a business university in Jönköping that will attempt to teach the Gnosjö spirit and to provide small entrepreneurs with more-sophisticated business skills.

On the big-business end of the spectrum, Bert-Olof Svanholm, chairman of Volvo at the time of his death in 1997, had another dream: to make Stockholm and Gothenburg the launching pad for non-European companies that want to do business in Europe. "If I were an American or a Japanese company and my work had to do with design and data processing, I would conquer Europe from Sweden," Svanholm said in an interview. Svanholm probably faced a more difficult task in convincing his own countrymen of the wisdom of this idea than he did in attracting branches of major foreign companies. Even after companies such as Microsoft, Intel, Nortel Networks, Oracle and IBM located research and development operations in Sweden, Swedes ask why anyone would want to move to cold, distant Stockholm with its high taxes and difficult language when he or she could live in a world capital such as London or Paris. They forget that the same kind of crime and cost-of-living problems that have led many American executives and their families to prefer Minneapolis, St. Paul and

Seattle over New York City and Los Angeles may lead others to prefer Stockholm over London, Paris, Frankfurt and Brussels.

Svanholm's dream can be taken a step beyond attracting foreigners. Just as Seattle was able to lure back hometown boy Bill Gates, the founder of Microsoft Corp. and now the richest man in the United States, Sweden, as these pages tell, has attracted back from the United States young business leaders such as Laurent Leksell, president of Elekta, the company that makes the world-famous Gamma Knife used in brain surgery. Others, such as Jonas Birgersson, the founder of Framfab, an Internet consulting company, have taken pride in starting global companies at home. Swedes often say—sometimes with humor, sometimes without—that they want "capitalism without capitalists." But more and more Swedes now recognize that capitalism must remain dynamic if it is to work, and that they no longer have any choice about encouraging new business—even if it does lead to unequal wealth and ostentatious living.

Some Swedes believe that the environmental and other social movements in their country are so strong that Sweden will evolve into a center for "ecotourism" with little industrial production. Sweden's unemployed, who would benefit from a new round of entrepreneurship and wealth creation, have history on their side. From the Viking era to the Gustavian period, from industrialization in the 19th century to the creation of the welfare state in the 20th, Sweden has met the challenges of each new age. The process may have fits and starts, but there's every evidence Sweden is using its abundant natural resources and human talent to reinvent itself once again.

1

From Ice to Iron
12,000 B.C. - A.D. 1721

"SWEDEN IS A FOREST," says a Swedish businessman who lived in the United States for many years, "and the Swedish people are standing on the edge of the forest looking out at the rest of the world."

That a Swede could make such a statement in the 1990s sounds almost treasonous, but it is not surprising. Sweden is located on the northeastern edge of Europe and since the 1930s has seemed to prefer its own rarefied welfare state. But by focusing on Sweden's isolation, the businessman is conveying only half his country's history and spirit. From time immemorial, Swedes have been travelers, traders, adventurers and warriors paving the way for their country's industrialization and role in today's global society.

The first settlers in the south and east of Sweden were immigrants. As one modern Swedish historian has envisioned the scene, soon after Scandinavia began to emerge from the Arctic ice cap—about 12,000 B.C.—tribes of nomadic hunters from what is now Denmark came "squelching through the icy slush and spied through the swirling mists a land that was eventually to be known as Sweden." By 8,000-6,000 B.C., all of what is today Sweden was occupied—though sparsely—by people using simple stone tools. About 2,000 B.C., another wave of immigration occurred, this time from the east. (As the settlers from mainland Europe moved further and further into the interior, they came into contact with the Sami people, who historians say had probably originated in the interior of Asia and had migrated to the northerly parts of Sweden, Norway, Finland and Russia in prehistoric times. Relations between the Swedish majority and the Sami, whose ancestral economy revolved around the reindeer and fishing, remain difficult to this day.)

Life in this cold northern land was harsh, of course. Sociologists say the image of "The Silent Swede" has its origins in the necessity of "doing" rather than "talking" during the short growing season and that the Swedes' invention of so many practical tools was also a survival technique. By 1500 B.C., Scandinavian chieftains were rich enough to import bronze from across the Baltic to fashion axes, spears, swords and jewelry. But Scandinavia's real break from primitive life came about 500 B.C., when its own people began to extract iron from the bog ore formed at the bottom of lakes to make their own tools and armaments from their own natural resources. The Scandinavians first showed up in European literature in A.D. 98, when the Roman historian Tacitus, in his *Germania*, described a people he called the Suiones—assumed to be the Svear, who lived around Lake Mälaren in central Sweden—as rich in warriors, arms and fleets.

The Viking Model, circa A.D. 800-1066

Scandinavia's contact with the rest of the world was intermittent until about A.D. 800, when the Vikings—as the Swedes, Danes and Norwegians were then jointly called—began journeying as far away as Western Europe, North America, Constantinople and the caliphate of Baghdad on raids that would be described for centuries to come with the words "rape, burn and pillage." Lars Romert, press secretary at the Swedish Embassy in Washington in the late 1980s, has wryly described the Swedish Vikings as business travelers who ran into people "who didn't want to do business." Although it's unlikely that the English, French, Russians and others who were party—or victim—to these "negotiations" would accept that description, modern-day scholars are softening history's attitude toward the Vikings. Archaeologist Else Roesdahl wrote in *The Vikings* that "the classic image of the Vikings appearing on foreign shores in their ships, sword in hand, performing bloody deeds, plundering churches, extorting money, engaging in battle, murder and abductions is a one-sided picture, created by contemporary clerics in Western

Europe, who tended to record only violent events, and elaborated by medieval storytellers and historians, among them the Icelandic saga writers, in their search for a dramatic national identity. But the Vikings were not just warlords. Their kings were engaged in complicated international politics, engineers built fortresses and bridges, merchants traded over vast distances."

The pertinent questions today about the Vikings are why they started their travels and why they stopped. There are no precise histories of Swedish society in Viking times, but it is known that although Viking societies were ruled by kings and included aristocrats and slaves, they were predominantly made up of free people, who had the right to speak at the *Ting*. The *Ting*, or assembly, was the forum at which the people discussed and reached decisions on issues. Most of the free people made their living through agriculture, but many were servants, craftsmen, merchants and professional warriors. The kings' income came from owning land (often seized from adversaries), levying customs duties, minting coins and granting licenses for piracy. Though there is no question that Viking kings gained their power with weapon in hand, historians say that many maintained their positions by leading their people ably and by rewarding good service.

Poems and legends tell us that Viking Swedes traveled a lot and far—to local and national *Ting* and to religious festivals, to family celebrations and to markets, to trade centers and to war. Vikings walked, and they rode horses. In the harsh winters, the snow and ice, rather than deterring Sweden's development, advanced it by making the frozen lakes and uneven ground passable. But the Vikings considered water voyages safer and faster than going through uninhabited territory. Historians say their conquests were so successful in part because their sailing ships were comparatively easy to carry over land and because they could surprise the people they encountered. A poem about King Magnus the Good (who died in A.D. 1047) recounts that when the king let the ships "run across the sea," it was just as if "the Heaven-Lord's crowd of angels were floating together across the waves."

Even before the time of the Vikings, northern people were trading across the Baltic, selling slaves, skins and furs, walrus tusks, iron, whetstones and soapstone cooking pots. The Vikings' decision to embark on far-flung journeys may have just been a benefit of better ships and sailing skills. The Belgian historian Henri Pirenne has suggested that wars along the Mediterranean coasts in the seventh and eighth centuries A.D. had created a trade and communications gap between Western Europe and the Orient, and the Vikings filled the void. Some clerics and historians have suggested that the journeys may have been encouraged by overpopulation (in the words of one cleric, "outrageous union with many women" producing "innumerable progeny"), endless quarrels over property, and poverty. Others suggest that nearby societies were so weak they were easy marks for plunderers.

Whatever the motivation, the Danes, Norwegians and western Swedes focused on Germany, England, France, Ireland and America, while the eastern Swedes looked east. Some trolled the coasts of the Baltic and the rivers that stretch deep into present-day Russia, establishing trading stations and short-lived principalities such as that of Rurik at Novgorod. Others, traveling via the Black and Caspian Seas, made it all the way to Byzantium and the caliphate of Baghdad. The journeys were hazardous, but the rewards were vast quantities of silver, gold, magnificent artwork—and fame. The "trade" was not only one-way, however. The Swedes left behind amber and fine pelts that they brought from the far north—and, as has been famously documented, their genes.

Most historians close out the Viking Age in 1066, the year that England's King Harold Godwinsson defeated the Norwegians at Stamford Bridge. Scandinavians still like to note that both Harold and William the Conqueror of Normandy, who defeated him in the Battle of Hastings, had Scandinavian blood coursing through their veins. The Viking era left Sweden enriched with foreign loot, but perhaps more important, with its own trading centers, such as Birka on an island in Lake Mälaren and Visby on the island of Gotland, and a literature filled with inspiring tales that has enhanced national pride and identity for generations. A rune stone at Gripsholm Castle in Södermanland describes the fate of a Viking expedition to Russian territory by the chieftain Ingvar the Far-Traveled in the mid-11th century: "In manly mood they sought gold afar and gave eagles food in eastern lands. They died in the south in Serkland."

Christian Times

In the years immediately following the Viking era, Sweden appears to have lapsed into stagnation. But Scandinavia was already in the process of Christianization, which would bring the region into continuous contact with Europe, linking it to the continent economically as well as culturally. The impact of Christianization was so great that the Nordic style of animal ornamentation in art was superseded by medieval European pictorials—a phenomenon art critics say marks the time Swedish art ceased to be distinct from the European.

During their bronze age, the Swedes had come to believe in a clan of gods called the Asar. Odin, the war god, was head of the Asar, and at his side were Tor, the god of virility, thunder, lightning, rain and crops, and Fray, the goddess of fertility and peace. The first Christian apostle with permission to preach to the Swedes was Ansgar, who had come from Denmark to Birka in 830. But Christianization progressed slowly in Scandinavia. Denmark did not become officially Christian until around 960, Norway followed early in the 11th century and Sweden later in the same century. Christianity had its natural appeals. Vikings who had been on missions had already seen the awe-inspiring cathedrals on the continent, and the existence of these extraordinary structures convinced the travelers that the Christian God was a good helper. The Church preached equality, urged peace and mercy toward others, freed prisoners of war and slaves and looked down on blood feuds. Some historians say it was these Christian values that caused the Vikings to end their raids.

Scandinavian kings saw, however, their own reason for becoming Christian: a chance to break the old order and establish more-centralized power. The English Beowulf saga and archaeological evidence have led historians to conclude that Sweden may have had a king as early as A.D. 800. The early kings apparently commanded the fleet, but the country was really a federation of the provinces in the central part of present-day Sweden, each with its own laws. "All they had in common was the king and the sacrificial festivals at the heathen temple at Gamla (Old) Uppsala," historian Alf Åberg has written.

It is probably no accident that Sweden's first powerful king was also its first Christian king, Olof Skötkonung, who was baptized before A.D. 1000 and ruled over the Götar and the Svear at the beginning of the 11th century. Between 1150 and 1250, two powerful clans, the Sverkers and the Eriks, struggled violently for political control of the country. But the more significant story of these years was the formation of a kingdom out of the "old" provinces such as Västergötland, Östergötland and Uppland; the development of the forestlands of Småland, Värmland and Dalarna; the settlement of Finland; and the establishment of a socioeconomic order that would last for centuries. The kingdom was divided into counties, each taxed and administered from a nearby fortress or castle. A royal Council was established to aid the king, with a lord chief justice in charge of the law, an earl marshal in charge of the army and a chancellor in charge of administration.

The Church emerged as a truly powerful institution and large landowner. In the 1150s, Erik Jedvardsson, later to be canonized St. Erik, led a "crusade" to Finland to baptize the Finns. In 1164, the first archbishop of Sweden was installed at Uppsala on the site of the by-then-demolished heathen temple. Historians say the papal bull establishing this bishopric is the first written evidence that Sweden was an independent realm ruled by a single king. By the mid-13th century, it became legal to bequeath land to the Church and its institutions.

In 1250, Valdemar, nephew of the last king of the Erik clan, was elected king of Sweden; but he was a minor, and power passed into the hands of his father and guardian, Birger Jarl. Valdemar ascended the throne in 1266, but there was a revolt against him, and his brother Magnus Ladulås assumed the throne in 1275. In 1280, under the Alnsö Decree, Magnus Ladulås rewarded the men who had served him and supplied him with horses and weapons by creating a national secular nobility similar to that in the German states. The decree exempted from taxation "all those men who serve under the king with their own war-horse." The bishops blessed Magnus Ladulås's coronation, and the next year, he waived all royal taxes and levies on the Church's property and declared that all fines imposed in connection with ecclesiastical matters would be paid to the Church, in effect, creating an ecclesiastical nobility. Soon, nearly 50 percent of Sweden's land was nontaxable—5.6 percent belonging to the crown, 21.3 percent to the Church and clergy and 20.7 percent to the nobles—and the burden of supporting the nation fell to the mostly peasant owners of the other 52.4 percent, which was taxed.

When Magnus died in 1290, his son Birger was still a minor, and power fell to the earl marshal, Torgils Knutsson, who completed the annexation of Finland started by Erik Jedvardsson and established Sweden's border with Russia at the Neva River. A power struggle broke out between Birger and his two brothers, and in 1317, Birger invited them to a banquet at Nyköping, where he had them assassinated. In 1319, Birger himself was put aside in favor of his 3-year-old nephew, who was crowned Magnus Eriksson. In exchange for absolute fealty to the king, the secular and ecclesiastical nobles insisted on a Letter of Privilege that has been called Sweden's Magna Carta and first constitution. In the letter, the king promised

—Not to impose new taxes without the consent of the Council
—Not to appoint any foreigner counselor or castle bailiff
and, finally,
—To govern by law and not imprison anyone, whether rich or poor, without due examination and judgment in process of law.

In 1350, abiding by the above principles, Magnus Eriksson replaced provincial codes with a national code of laws. He also enjoined cities north of Stockholm and Finnish cities north of Åbo (Turku) from direct trade with the regions south of these two staple cities. In 1356, tailors in Stockholm were granted a charter for an organization that created a guild system for artisans. The guilds set standards, trained members and limited competition for the next five centuries. Thus Sweden established the framework for a full medieval social order and soon had all the trappings of chivalry and courtly poetry. But Swedish peasants always resisted the idea that the nobles deserved a higher place in society than they did. In southern Sweden, peasants avoided being enserfed, although they were "bonded" to the land by annual employment contracts that allowed them to quit only on the anniversary date of their contracts. In the north, which was a frontier remote from European society, the medieval order never did have much of an impact. Swedish nobles and peasants in the central part of the country did develop a strong sense of each other's class standing, but trade through the Hanseatic League and the exploitation of the copper reserves at Falun in the province of Dalarna soon created the conditions for a challenge to the old order and for the establishment of modern business.

The Hanseatic League

Despite the history of Viking exploits, foreign trade was insignificant in Sweden in the Middle Ages. The only import that mattered to the mass of the people was salt, which could not be found at home. Sweden was still a "storage economy" in which no food—animal or vegetable—was eaten fresh, except at weddings and funerals. Subsistence agriculture dominated the economy, and the people lived in constant fear of a grain shortage.

Historians write that most medieval people, including the Swedes, viewed importing and exporting only as a means to obtain otherwise unavailable goods. Trade got a tremendous boost, however, in the 12th century with the development of the Hanseatic League, a confederacy of German cities and German merchant settlements in other countries around the Baltic Sea. The league started in the German city of Lübeck, which had been chartered by Henry the Lion of Saxony in 1158. The German merchants developed a central trading place in the old Viking trade town of Visby on the island of Gotland in the Baltic, and it became Sweden's chief commercial center in the 13th century. Acquiring commercial rights and privileges from various monarchs and then protecting their convoys and caravans from competitors and pirates, the Hansards by the 14th century created the first integrated economic region in Northern and Northwestern Europe.

From Visby, the German merchants expanded to Riga, Latvia and Reval (today's Tallinn, Estonia) and Novgorod in European Russia. Visby dominated trade from the Rhine to the Baltic, and the league extended all the way to Bruges and London. The Hansards exported Swedish iron, copper, hides and timber, but the league's records show that in the 1360s, butter, which had a high value to volume ratio, was the number one Swedish export, followed by iron and copper. European Catholics needed fish for days of abstinence, and herring from Norway and Skåne in southern present-day Sweden was exported as far south as Prague, Vienna and northern Italy. In exchange, the Hansards brought salt, cloth, beer, wine and luxury crafts to Sweden.

Trade had its dangers, however. In 1349, an English ship arrived at Bergen, Norway, with its crew dead on board. The ship's rats jumped ashore, spreading the Black Death throughout Scandinavia and ushering in a period of economic and population decline that didn't stop until the latter part of the 15th century, when iron production began to make the Swedish economy more prosperous.

The fact that the Swedish language assimilated a lot of German words displays how weak the structure of Swedish society was in the 14th century. The Swedish economic historian Eli Heckscher has written that Sweden was not involved in the great commerce of the Mediterranean or the Atlantic. Rather, Heckscher wrote, "the Swedish share consisted in the crumbs that fell from the table of the Hansards."

Eventually the Hanseatic League inspired resentment against Germans and the rise of Swedish nationalism. In the 1460s, a critic wrote, "The Master of the Mint is a German, the Collectors of Duties and Tolls are Germans, the Collector of Taxes is a German, so that for Swedes no office is left or open but that of executioner and of gravedigger."

Bergslagen and the Stora Story

Archaeological evidence indicates that prehistoric Swedes dug iron ore out of the peat bogs and raked it up from the bottom of the lakes in the southern part of the country, reducing it to wrought iron in small hearth-like furnaces. Analysis of ore and slag found at Visby dates iron mining from rock deposits to the first half of the 13th century. The ore did not come from Gotland, however, but rather from the Stockholm archipelago. By the second half of the 12th century, the area of Sweden that has become known as Bergslagen—Värmland, Västmanland, Närke and southern Dalarna—was yielding iron, copper and silver. In the early days, any peasant could mine ore, when he wasn't busy with farming or working in the forest, and produce iron in a bloomery. But the *bergsmän* also became members of mining and furnace companies, which employed miners to extract the ore and bring it to the surface. The extraction technique, called firesetting, involved lighting a fire against the rock and dousing it with water until the rock cracked and the ore it held could be removed. The ore was processed in a furnace built beside a watercourse, with a waterwheel to power its bellows. By 1250, Swedes were exporting across the Baltic so-called osmund iron, a term that referred to pieces cut to weigh half a pound. According to tariff records, Swedish iron commanded a price 50 percent higher than that of German iron in the Middle Ages, presumably because the quality of the ore and the processing was higher.

The Bergslagen region also took on its own mythology and culture that form the background of the novels of the early-20th-century Nobel prize-winning author Selma Lagerlöf. Industrial historians Marie Nisser and Kersti Morger wrote in an essay in *Technology & Industry: A Nordic Heritage* that "the Nordic light gave [Bergslagen] a mysterious appearance, with distant blue mountains that hid the ore, deep and dark forests that provided fuel for the blast furnaces and forges, glittering waterfalls that gave the power to run the bellows. The small industrial units were in remote and sparsely populated areas. The colorful owners who often ran them developed their own cultural and economic milieu."

There are records of attempts to improve the organization of the Bergslagen iron mines in the 13th century, but the iron story is dull compared with the fabulous tale of Stora Kopparberg—the Great Copper Mountain—at Falun in the province of Dalarna. Legend holds that in the days of King Solomon, Swedish miners working at Stora Kopparberg provided copper to ornament the temple of Jerusalem. That story is probably fanciful, but the best Swedish research indicates that Stora Kopparberg started operations somewhere between A.D. 850 and 1000, toward the end of the Viking Age.

What makes Stora Kopparberg unique in world business history is that it can claim to be the world's oldest joint-stock company. That claim derives from the records of a meeting called by King Magnus Ladulås in 1288 at which the cathedral chapter of the bishopric of Västerås recquired an eighth share in the mine, which its bishop, Peter Elofsson, had earlier transferred to his nephew to pay part of the cost of his installation as bishop. The records are most important for revealing that the mine's ownership was divided and that the diocese considered the investment so good that it was willing to give the nephew a farm, including mills, arable land and meadowland, pasture, fishing rights and forest land, in exchange for the one-eighth share. By the mid-1300s, the aristocrats had transferred control of the mine to a group of master miners who would become Sweden's first miner-entrepreneurs.

Scandinavian Union and Breakup 1397-1521

In the 14th and 15th centuries, political events slowed down the development of Sweden's minerals. In addition to being ruler of Sweden, Magnus Eriksson had inherited the crown of Norway from his maternal grandfather and the Danish province of Halland from his mother. He also purchased the southernmost provinces of Skåne and Blekinge from the Danes. Magnus constantly tried to assert the power of the crown over the nobles and was eventually forced into exile. Albrekt of Mecklenburg was elected to the Swedish throne in 1364, but the nobles decided they wanted Margareta, queen of Norway and Denmark (and the widow of Magnus Eriksson's son Håkan), and her son Olof, a minor, to jointly take the throne. Olof died in 1387, and Margareta was recognized as the ruler of all three Scandinavian countries. The three nations' relationship was formalized in 1397 in the Union of Kalmar.

Margareta promised not to interfere with Norway's and Sweden's traditional laws and to fill all-important positions in each country of the Union with natives of that country. She soon abandoned the latter promise, appointing her own confidants to key posts. Her son Erik of Pomerania assumed the throne before she died in 1412. During his reign, he tried to free himself from the economic power of the Hanseatic League by going to war with the North German cities, but he succeeded only in disrupting Sweden's commercial links and crippling the Bergslagen mining district. Angry that they could not export their iron, people in the province of Dalarna revolted against Erik in 1434. The rebellion was led by Engelbrekt Engelbrektsson, a member of a wealthy mining family, and the nobles elected him captain-general. To gather support for his movement, Engelbrektsson in 1435 called the first Parliament (*Riksdag* in Swedish) on the European continent. Historians say the Riksdag, the Icelandic *Althing* and the English Parliament were the only parliamentary bodies then existent in Western civilization. The Swedes, however, took the idea of parliamentary government one step further than the other countries by including representation of all classes. By the 1460s, a Riksdag of four estates—nobility, clergy, burgher and peasantry—was firmly established.

In 1440, Engelbrektsson was murdered. The nobles elected another nobleman, Karl Knutsson Bonde, as protector of the realm. A power struggle ensued between the Swedish nobles and the Danish-based monarchy, but Erik's nephew Kristoffer of Bavaria managed to hold on to the crown and technically preserve the Kalmar Union. Karl Knutsson served several times as king, but the Danish kings regained power. In 1471, after a renowned battle at Brunkeberg, the Swedish regent Sten Sture the Elder defeated the Danes. His reign is notable for the establishment, in 1477, of Uppsala University, Sweden's first institution of higher education.

In 1517, Kristian II of Denmark managed to capture control of Stockholm and had himself proclaimed king of Sweden. In 1520, he ordered the execution of 80 of Sweden's most prominent men, mostly nobles, in Stortorget, the main square of Stockholm. This event, which became known as the Stockholm Blood Bath, paved the way for Gustaf Vasa, a young nobleman who had escaped the massacre, to rise to power.

The Reign of Gustaf Vasa, 1523-1560

Gustaf Vasa escaped to Dalarna, the center of discontent, where he raised a peasant army to renew the struggle against Kristian II, who still held Stockholm. Gustaf then went to Lübeck, where he got the support of the Hanseatic League and returned to capture the Danish-held castles, be crowned king in 1523 and liberate Stockholm.

Conveniently for Gustaf's ambitions, word of Martin Luther's criticism of Catholic doctrine had reached Sweden. In 1527, only four years after his coronation, Gustaf summoned a Parliament that authorized him to confiscate most of the Catholic Church's estates. He later broke off relations with Rome, established the state Lutheran Church, which made him—rather than the Pope—God's representative on earth, and built castles at Uppsala and Vadstena to symbolize that he had more power than the clergy. The confiscation dramatically changed the land ownership structure of Sweden. When Gustaf Vasa took power, the crown owned 5.5 percent of the land, the state Catholic Church 21 percent, the nobility 21.8 percent and the peasants 51.7 percent. When he died, the crown owned 28.2 percent of the land, the state Lutheran Church nothing, the nobility 22.4 percent and the peasants 49.4 percent.

Gustaf Vasa's unilateral confiscation of the Catholic Church lands and the establishment of the state Lutheran Church with himself at the head were only the beginning of his actions to centralize power within the monarchy and its bureaucracy. Gustaf Vasa gave Swedish cities the same economic powers that their continental counterparts had, awarding them the exclusive right to the so-called urban industries—commerce, shipping and handicraft. But these powers, which had emerged in Germany "from below" as the logical result of a series of economic events were imposed in Sweden "from above" through deliberate policies of the central government—a manner of governing that has continued in Sweden to this day.

Gustaf Vasa's treatment of the province of Dalarna illustrates his determination to centralize power in himself and his monarchy. The people in Dalarna assumed they had a special status because Gustaf had sought refuge there before he became king, and they rose up in a series of protests between 1524 and 1531 against poor goods, poor coinage, high taxes and their forced conversions to the Lutheran Church. In 1525, the people's county council wrote him a letter reminding him that he had once wandered around in the forests of Dalarna, an outlaw, "like a squirrel in the pines," until he was rescued by the men of Dalarna. The council members also threatened to take away their loyalty if he did not reduce the price of grain. Annoyed because he was preoccupied with what he considered bigger problems, Gustaf Vasa summoned the people of the mountain to a meeting in February 1533. On the advice of their master miner, Måns Nilsson, the people of Dalarna said the king should have to ask them for safe passage in their region—further enraging him. Gustaf Vasa ordered the execution of the leaders of the uprising and brought others to Stockholm, where they met the same fate. "When the king revisited the mountain in 1542, he was greeted by an audience of highly attentive subjects," Sven Rydberg wrote in the official history of the modern Stora company.

Gustaf Vasa changed Sweden dramatically. He encouraged Finnish peasants to settle the forests in Värmland and young Swedes to move to the northern frontier. He also encouraged expansion and modernization of mining. There had been a series of collapses at the Stora Kopparberg copper mine, and Gustaf Vasa brought in German engineers to construct hoisting devices and improve the mine's efficiency. The Sala silver mine had been discovered between Uppsala and Falun in 1510, and although its production never exceeded 11,000 pounds per year, it made Sweden one of Europe's main sources of silver in those years just before Spain exploited the vast reserves in Mexico and Peru. Gustaf Vasa hoarded the silver produced at Sala, and it was said that Swedish authorities loved silver so much that the government spent more money searching for silver than it made selling it. Gustaf also brought to Sweden German iron experts, who constructed forges and who promoted the refinement of iron into bars. The price paid for iron shaped into bars was about twice that paid for osmond iron. Gustaf Vasa tried to make the production of osmond iron illegal, but the *bergsmän* resisted.

Gustaf Vasa also made a long-term contribution to Swedish economic life by striking the *daler,* a coin that had the same value as many foreign coins, and keeping its value stable. Coins had first been minted in Sweden during the reign of Olof Skötkonung, but the value of Swedish coins often deteriorated and for long periods of time foreign coins were used as a medium of exchange. Individual provinces also developed their own currency systems. By the Middle Ages, the coin that was accepted throughout Sweden was the mark, which had a weight of 210.6 grams (somewhat less than seven Troy ounces). In the late 16th century, the *daler* was made equal to four marks and it floated. But the old *daler* coin was renamed the *riksdaler* and maintained its value for centuries. (Sweden was so remote and trade such a small part of its economy that the European inflation following the influx of silver from Mexico and Peru in the 16th century did not affect Sweden until the early 17th century.)

Swedes call Gustaf Vasa's reign the Age of Bliss because the country was both peaceful and prosperous for the first time in many years. In the words of the 19th-century Swedish poet Erik Gustaf Geijer, the peasant "could till with his blood-sprayed hands." But historians and economists are less kind to Gustaf Vasa, saying that he did little to move Sweden beyond the medieval age. Historian Jörgen Weibull has written, "He ran the realm as if it were one big farm."

Gustaf Vasa arranged construction of the first paper mill in Sweden and had the Bible translated into Swedish. Considered a linguistic masterpiece, the Gustaf Vasa Bible remained in use, with few revisions, until 1917. But in the course of reducing the power of the Church and the clergy, Gustaf Vasa nearly destroyed the country's intellectual life. Fledgling Uppsala University had already closed when he came to power, but rather than reestablish it, he took the cheaper option of sending a few students abroad to study.

Historians fault Gustaf Vasa for not doing more to promote a Swedish role in navigation, communication and commerce, which were expanding at the time. Between 1534 and 1536, Gustaf Vasa sided with Denmark in a war with Lübeck, gaining peace with Denmark and relief from the trade credits that Lübeck had held ever since it helped him rise to power. Gustaf Vasa transformed the Swedish navy from a mercenary organization in private hands to a state-controlled operation by creating state-owned shipyards at naval ports. By the time he died in 1560, there were 56 ships in the military navy and 60 in the merchant navy. But only late in life did he show interest in promoting commercial shipping, and trade in Swedish ports continued to be conducted by foreigners. When the Hanseatic League left, its traders were replaced by the Dutch and the Scots.

In 1544, Gustaf Vasa achieved the ultimate in Swedish power when the Riksdag agreed to replace the monarchy elected by the nobility and declared it hereditary in the Vasa family. For his sons, Erik, Johan and Karl, Gustaf Vasa created dukedoms, and in Sweden the title of duke is reserved for royal children to this day. When Erik XIV became king in 1560, he was dissatisfied with Denmark's control of the Baltic. He gained Estonia as Swedish territory, setting the stage for creation of Sweden's Baltic empire, but he bankrupted the country fighting a losing war with Denmark. During Erik's reign, the nobility—whose previous generation of leaders had nearly been decimated in the bloodbath that preceded Gustaf's rise to power—reasserted itself. In an attempt to get the nobility on his side, Erik made some nobles Sweden's first counts *(grevar)*, but in 1568, the nobility deposed Erik and imprisoned him for life, placing his brother Johan III on the throne. In his own attempt to get along with the nobles, Johan III created another titled rank, the barons *(friherrar)*. There were still tensions between him and the nobles throughout his reign, however, because they wanted to rule in collaboration with him and he refused. When Johan III died in 1592, the third brother became King Karl IX. But the nobles preferred Johan III's son, Sigismund, who was also king of Poland. Sigismund was crowned king of Sweden in 1592, but because he lived in Poland, he entrusted the Swedish government to Karl.

Sigismund and Karl had a falling-out, and in 1598, Sigismund invaded Sweden with Polish forces. He was defeated, however, and the Riksdag dethroned him in 1599. Karl declared himself Protector of the country, had the leading nobles executed in the Linköping massacre of 1600 and ascended the throne as Karl IX in 1604.

Sweden's Century as "A Great Power"

Karl IX died in 1611, leaving the throne to his 17-year-old son, Gustaf II Adolf, who ushered in what is known as Sweden's "Great Power" period. Before Gustaf was crowned, the nobility obliged the young king—who is better known to the world by his Latin name, Gustavus Adolphus—to agree that he would not make laws, declare war or form alliances without the consent of the Parliament and the Council. He further agreed not to impose taxes without consulting the Council and to reserve all high administrative positions for nobles. Gustaf II Adolf moved the capital from Uppsala to Stockholm and, in effect, ruled Sweden in concert with Axel Oxenstierna, his chancellor of the realm and the nobles' leader. Gustaf II Adolf and Oxenstierna, who like many nobles of that period was educated in Germany, made a powerful team, the king bold and the chancellor cautious. During the early part of Gustaf II Adolf's reign, Sweden successfully concluded a war with Russia, won Latvia from Poland, gained control of customs duties in the Baltic and established the country's munitions industry.

Gustaf II Adolf was determined to make Sweden less dependent on foreigners and continental universities. Karl IX had reopened Uppsala University at the time of Gustaf II Adolf's birth, and Gustaf II Adolf put the institution on a firmer financial footing by endowing it with estates. He also increased the number of its professorships and extended its curriculum beyond theology and philosophy to include medicine, politics and law. Just as important, Gustaf II Adolf established the *gymnasia* as the link between elementary school and the university. Most Swedish students at Uppsala were still from noble families, but talented peasant boys were admitted and raised money for their fees by spending the summer touring the country begging and singing.

In 1619, Gustaf II Adolf resolved to deal with one of Sweden's most annoying problems: the weakness of its only stronghold on the west coast. The Danes had captured the Älvsborg fortress on the estuary of the Göta River a number of times, and when they took it in 1612, only a year after Gustaf II Adolf became king, they demanded one million *riksdaler*—23 tons of silver—to return it. Determined to establish a fortified and Dane-proof town, Gustaf II Adolf decided to build a new city from scratch. In 1619, he established the city of Gothenburg, which was destined to become Sweden's second city and its seaport to the Atlantic. From the beginning, Gustaf II Adolf knew he was building a commercial city. He called in Dutch experts on draining and urbanizing swamps and put them to work forging a city on the river's edge. When he gave Gothenburg its royal charter in 1621, he invited Dutch merchants to settle there so that they would buy Swedish iron and timber, which could easily be shipped down the river.

The Thirty Years War between Catholic and Protestant countries broke out in 1618. After Denmark was defeated in 1625, Sweden was threatened and Gustaf II Adolf decided to intervene. To finance Sweden's involvement in the war and a propaganda campaign to create public support for it, Gustaf II Adolf sold copper, iron and tar. In 1625, he even introduced a copper standard for money, a move he hoped would increase demand for copper and make it scarce and more expensive in foreign countries. Gustaf II Adolf was so successful in battle that Sweden became the principal Protestant power in Northern Europe, with territory in Norway, Denmark, the Baltic and northern Germany. The "Lion of the North," as Gustaf II Adolf became known throughout Europe, died on the battlefield at Lützen in 1632. He was succeeded by his daughter, Kristina. Because she was only 5 years old, Oxenstierna set up a regency government and was the de facto ruler of Sweden for 12 years until Kristina was declared of age in 1644.

Colonies - America and Africa

Aware that Spain, France and England were busy colonizing the rest of the world, Sweden, the Great Power of the 17th century, didn't want to be left out of the action. In 1638, only 18 years after the *Mayflower* had landed in Massachusetts, Oxenstierna granted Peter Minuit, a Dutchman, official support for a Swedish expedition to the New World. The expedition was to a large extent financed by Dutch capitalists, who apparently wanted to compete with the Dutch East India Company, which the Dutch government had helped establish in 1602 to trade with Asia. Minuit, who had spent several years in the service of the Dutch in North America, had bought land from the American Indians near the Delaware River and hoped, by establishing a Swedish-Dutch company, to corner the market on beaver skins. Two Swedish ships, the *Kalmar Nyckel* and the *Fågel Grip*, sailed from Gothenburg and arrived in Delaware in March 1638, proceeding up a river they renamed the Kristina in honor of Sweden's queen. Minuit died that year in an accident on the return voyage of the *Kalmar Nyckel*, and the colony he had established, New Sweden, languished until five years later, when Johan Printz, a Swede, became its governor.

The Swedish settlers sent large shipments of skins back to Sweden, but the colony was not much of a financial success. The Dutch investors, who were uncomfortable about competing with the Dutch East India Company, sold their interests to Sweden in 1641. About 10 years after it was established, the colony had about 200 inhabitants. Many of them were descendants of the Finns whom Gustaf Vasa had brought to Värmland 100 years before to settle the forests. With the native Värmlanders charging that the Finnish settlers were ruining the forests, Swedish authorities coerced them to immigrate to the New World.

In 1654, another 350 colonists arrived, but in 1655, Peter Stuyvesant, the governor of New Amsterdam (later New York) laid siege to Fort Christina, New Sweden's strongest bastion, ending the Swedish ruling class's dream of a North American colony. The Dutch took over, later losing the colony to the English. Most of the Swedes stayed in the New World. One of their descendants, John Morton, signed the U.S. Declaration of Independence in 1776. Less than a century after that, the knowledge of unoccupied land and freedom in the United States would inspire Swedish emigration on a mass scale. Some Swedes also looked enviously upon other countries' profits in the slave trade, and in the 1650s, the Swedish-African Company built a fortress called Carlsborg near the Bight of Guinea on the west coast of Africa. This business venture was short-lived, but Sweden apparently has been so ashamed of its countrymen's participation in the slave trade that scholars rarely mention it. Vilhelm Moberg, author of a series of novels on Swedish immigration to the New World, wrote that he sought in vain for any information on this episode in "our own histories."

Louis de Geer - Father of Swedish Industry

In economic terms, the longest-lasting benefit of Gustaf II Adolf's warring was the development of the Swedish munitions industry. To obtain loans to finance his early wars, Gustaf II Adolf used the services of Louis de Geer, a Liège-born Walloon nobleman who had established himself as a merchant in Amsterdam. Trying to collect his debts, de Geer traveled to Sweden, where he recognized the great potential of Swedish iron mining and manufacturing. In 1620, Gustaf II Adolf put him in charge of the crown's arms factories.

De Geer expressed his admiration for Swedish armorers, but he brought in Walloons to improve the Swedish techniques. The Walloons settled in Uppland and Östergötland and brought many contributions to Swedish life, including an element of religious diversity. Mostly Calvinists, the Walloons for several generations lived in close-knit separate communities, where they were comfortable practicing their own faith rather than the official state religion of Lutheranism.

De Geer was granted a monopoly on the production of cannon, which became the foundation of his business empire. De Geer is considered the father of Swedish industry and is credited with creation of the *bruk*, or ironworks communities that formed the backbone of the Swedish economy for 200 years. Iron bearing a stamp from his Leufsta Bruk fetched a premium price. De Geer also owned the Finspång Bruk in Östergötland, the center for cannon making, and had ironworks in Västmanland and Värmland. He also had interests in paper, cloth and flour mills and has been described as "one of the shrewdest and boldest of foreign agents in the markets in the 1620s." De Geer's technique was to buy minor amounts of his own products through straw men, thereby creating a market expectation of a price rise that enabled him to sell the bulk of his supplies at high prices. He became a Swedish citizen, was ennobled in 1641 and established a family that is distinguished to this day.

De Geer was not the only *bruk* owner of this period, however. The introduction of more-advanced iron-making techniques, in particular the replacement of timber and earth furnaces with brick blast furnaces, made continuous iron production possible. These more elaborate production facilities required more capital to buy modern equipment for the plant, more forestland to produce charcoal and more farmland to raise food for the workers.

The *bruk* became the first "capitalist" undertakings in Sweden, and the system continued more or less intact for 300 years. Värmland, for example, had about 60 *bruk*. Two of them, Uddeholm and Munkfors, founded in 1668 and 1670, respectively, by rival members of the same family, remained in separate operation until 1829, when they merged; in 1869 Uddeholm became the first Swedish ironworks to become a joint stock company.

The *bruk* were often in precarious financial straits. Foreign importers, mostly Dutch, made advances to export merchants in Stockholm and Gothenburg who, in turn, provided credit to the ironmasters, who then used the money to pay their workers. The distance between lender and ironmaster in this system of investment and finance was so great that the line between principal and interest began to blur. Eventually, however, iron-bar forging created the Swedish bourgeoisie. Some of the ironmakers *(brukspatroner)* were nobles; but others were not and they and exporters in Stockholm and Gothenburg were the first secular group outside the nobility to acquire the wealth and social standing that made them upper-middle-class. Many Swedish companies have the word *bruk* in their names, an indication that their origins were in iron making.

The Thirty Years War increased the demand for iron and weapons in Europe and secured Sweden's reputation as a munitions supplier. Sweden had a rich supply of ore and, just as important, rich forests that could supply charcoal for the forging process at a time when forests on the continent were depleted. The province of Värmland became the leading iron-producing region in Sweden, turning out in 1695 a full 22 percent of the nation's iron. The young city of Gothenburg became Sweden's main shipping port.

The Swedish iron industry achieved a reputation for meticulous precision and was particularly noted for its Dannemora steel and for the Carolean sword favored by many armies. Holland was a particularly good weapons customer. Historians attribute the Swedish iron and steel industry's reputation for quality to the high standards set and enforced by the guilds and the fact that Swedes were so distant geographically from their customers that they worried constantly about losing business.

Kristina's Reign - Paper Money and Banks

Most accounts of Queen Kristina's short and colorful reign ignore her impact on Swedish economic history. Taking power on her 18th birthday in 1644, Kristina established a world-renowned court, issuing invitations to notable thinkers, including the French philosopher and mathematician René Descartes. She is most remembered for refusing to marry her cousin Karl Gustaf, abdicating in his favor in 1654, leaving the country, converting to Catholicism and settling down in Rome, where she is buried in St. Peter's.

While these actions have made Kristina a glamorous historical figure, she and her advisers made other decisions with longer-lasting consequences for the Swedish economy. Her regents established the Board of Mines in 1637. Her regents also became worried that the forests that provided the charcoal for the furnaces in the old mining region would disappear. In 1647, she established a forest statute, the first of its kind in the world, which banned the burning of woodland unless it was to permanently clear land for crops or pasture. The legislation also prohibited overcutting in the neighborhood of the blast furnaces and mines. This law is the reason that ironworks sprang up in rather isolated locations scattered over the forest districts of central Sweden and other areas—a pattern that gave Swedish industry a spatial character different from the continent's and that continues in the Swedish iron and steel industry to this day.

In 1651, Kristina set up the Board of Trade, which would make loans for technological innovations. In 1651, she ennobled Johan Palmstruch, the son of a trader from Riga who had assisted Gustaf II Adolf in his wars. Palmstruch was granted the right to create a bank modeled after those in Amsterdam. Stockholm Banco, as the institution was named, charged customers for deposits and granted loans. Because the copper money that Gustaf II Adolf introduced was so heavy, Palmstruch came up with the idea of issuing paper bills in fixed amounts. Banks were opened in Gothenburg, Falun and Åbo, Finland, but more bills were printed than there were deposits to support their value. Palmstruch went bankrupt, lost his title and was sentenced to death, although he was later pardoned. Out of the ashes of Stockholm Banco, the Riksbank, or Swedish central bank, was created in 1688.

The Great Power Crumbles

The world Kristina abandoned in 1654 was already beginning to fall apart. Kristina was able to manipulate the nobles into accepting her abdication and Karl X Gustaf as king because the country was in economic crisis. Oxenstierna's foreign policy leadership was often brilliant, and Sweden continued to win more territory, including most of Pomerania. But on the domestic side, his position as chancellor undoubtedly contributed to the nobility's quest for greater power and privilege.

The nobles who had the double advantage of being estate owners and occupants of the high government posts that Gustaf II Adolf had reserved for them became wealthier and wealthier, and the distinction between them and their rural cousins was becoming greater. In 1627, the statutes of the House of Nobility formally separated the members into the "higher" nobility of counts and barons and the "lower," untitled, nobility. In 1634, two years after Gustaf II Adolf's death, the higher nobility succeeded in introducing a new constitution, which placed all administrative authority in the hands of five high state officials who, of course, had to be nobles.

Another problem was the growing size of the privileged class. As late as 1600, the Swedish nobility was a small group of people; adult noble males numbered only 440. To staff his officer corps, Gustaf II Adolf had imported German, Scottish and English soldiers and ennobled them. To reward the officers for their services, he and Kristina made gifts of the land that Gustaf Vasa had taken from the Church and other property that he had bought. Kristina raised the number of counts from 3 to 20 and the number of barons from 7 to 34 and included in her grants lands that had been set aside for the fleet and the cavalry. During the Thirty Years War, the government—at Oxenstierna's urging—also sold lands to the nobility to get money. By the middle of the 17th century, 600 noble families owned 72 percent of Sweden's land, leaving only 28 percent of the nation in the hands of the crown or the peasants. Nobles also had power to tax peasant-owned land located near their own. Many of the military officers returned from the continent with enormous quantities of booty, and—as the nouveau riche of their time—began building Italian-, Dutch- and French-inspired palaces. Oxenstierna's own personal palace was called Tidö.

Both the lesser nobility and the peasants bitterly resented the upper nobility's privileges and their own rising taxes. In the Riksdag of 1650, the peasants protested bitterly saying, "We are aware that in other lands the country folk are thralls. We fear that the same fate may befall ourselves, although we were born freemen." Kristina said she sympathized with the clergy, burghers and farmers who favored a land reform, but after obtaining approval for her abdication, she refused to take any action.

The problems of maintaining Sweden's far-flung empire and dealing with the country's economic crisis were left to Karl X Gustaf. He concentrated his efforts on war with Poland and Denmark and in 1658 succeeded in regaining from Denmark the southern Swedish provinces of Skåne, Blekinge, Bornholm, Halland, Bohuslän and Trondheim (now part of Norway). Karl X Gustaf began the process of "reducing" the nobles' holdings in 1655 by reclaiming "forbidden places" such as forts and mines, which under Swedish law the crown should never have given away or sold. Karl X Gustaf ruled only six years, however, dying on a trip to Gothenburg in 1660 after a brief illness and leaving his 4-year-old son Karl XI to cope with worsening problems. During the 12-year regency that began his reign, the nobles expanded their power and wealth, while the peasants suffered more than ever, paying the taxes that supported the country in war.

In 1660, after another war with Denmark, Sweden gave Bornholm and Trondheim back to the Danes, and eight years later, in a move to make the people of Skåne feel they were part of their new country, it established a university at Lund. But the Danes were still determined to get the other provinces back. The Danes did not succeed, but during the Skåne War (1675-79), the Swedish government was so short of money that Karl XI agreed with the Riksdag to force the nobles to return to the crown lands that earned more than 600 dalers in income. In the Great Reduction of 1680, the nobles retained their ancestral estates, but the nobility's share of land dropped from 72 percent to 31.5 percent, while crown ownership increased to 35.5 percent. Peasant ownership increased to 31.5 percent—all of it taxable. By 1700, only one noble in three was a landowner, and the nobility was transformed from a class of landowners into a bureaucratic class obedient to the king's will. "In essence," historian Franklin Scott has written, "the reduction was a revolution—political, social and economic—that broke the political power of the greater nobles and curtailed their economic base." (The nobles who remained the largest landowners were those with the richest land, particularly in the southern, formerly Danish province of Skåne, who could afford to buy back the land that was confiscated and to purchase other lands. Swedish business leaders today say that the Skåne nobles are the only ones who could maintain a noble lifestyle without going into government or commerce, but in fact the Skåne nobles also were leaders in the modernization of Swedish agriculture and the development of agribusiness.)

As an adjunct to the reduction, Sweden established a new system of recruiting and maintaining its military. During its wars, Sweden's armies had fed and clothed themselves by plundering the countries they crossed. But in the last 20 years of the 17th century, the empire was in a state of relative peace, and Sweden faced the problem of feeding its troops. Between 1680 and 1690, Karl XI set up the *indelningsverket,* a system to support soldiers that lasted unchanged until 1901. Commissioned and noncommissioned officers were given, in lieu of salary, some of the recently reclaimed crown lands on which they were supposed to support themselves when they were not at war. The peasants were divided into recruitment units called *rotar*, each of which was required to recruit and equip one soldier. Karl XI also built a new navy, invited British naval architects to work at the state-owned shipyards and in 1680 established a naval base at Karlskrona.

Defending an empire that stretched from Finland to northern Germany turned out to be more than Sweden could handle. In 1697—the same year Karl XI died, leaving the crown to his 15-year-old son, Karl XII—the Latvian aristocracy obtained the support of Poland against Sweden. In 1700, Denmark, Poland and Russia formed an offensive alliance against Sweden, initiating the Great Northern War (1700-21). Karl XII was declared of age, and in alliance with the British and the Dutch, he led his troops to stunning victories in Denmark, Poland and Russia. But in 1709, Karl XII was disastrously defeated at Poltava in the Ukraine. He fled to Turkey, where he remained for five years. He returned home in 1715, determined to continue his military exploits, and in 1717 managed to capture Kristiania (Oslo). But on November 30, 1718, Karl XII was killed outside the Norwegian castle of Frederiksten by a bullet that may have been enemy fire or the act of an assassin. Over the next two years, under the leadership of Karl XII's sister Ulrika Eleonora and her husband, Prince Fredrik of Hesse, Sweden lost its German territories and most of its colonies on the other side of the Baltic, although it still held on to Finland.

Sweden's losses of territory were only one indication of the country's general decline. By 1700, Stora Kopparberg was a shadow of its former self. Its copper production had reached its zenith in 1650 at 3,000 tons. In the last two decades of the 17th century, copper prices rose markedly to the relief of Karl XI, who needed the exports to finance his armies and wars. But in 1687, this "excessive and predatory exploitation," as one historian has called it, led to a cave-in. In 1690, a mining expert wrote that Sweden was "as a mother" in copper, but production was still in decline. In 1693, Christopher Polhem, a mechanical genius, became a mining engineer at Falun and over the next 16 years developed a series of innovations for Stora Kopparberg. But after Polhem left in

1709, his successors neglected to maintain his innovations in favor of more-traditional methods of ore extraction.

Sweden had been at war 75 of the 120 years between 1600 and 1720. But the country also developed during that time. Stockholm had grown from 9,000 to 50,000 people, and the newer sections of the city had orthogonal rather than narrow, winding, medieval streets. In all, 32 Swedish cities had been founded in one century, including the northern coastal outposts of Umeå, Piteå and Luleå. The postal system had been improved with better links to the continent; the first newspaper, *Ordinarie Post Tijdender*, had been established in 1645; and Erik Dahlberg's *Suecia Antiqua et Hodierna,* a book of engravings and drawings of Swedish cities that records Sweden's point of greatest glory, had been published. In the coming centuries, Sweden would be able to capitalize on these advances, but for now it was a poor, purely agrarian economy except for some small ironworks and the copper mine at Falun.

Historian Weibull maintains that at the beginning of the 18th century, "Sweden was again a minor state." But even worse than the country's loss of its stature among nations was the Swedes' personal agony. As a Dutch traveler wrote in 1719, "Nowhere in Sweden did I see a single young man between 20 and 40 years of age, only soldiers. The cruel war had swept away almost the entire youth of this unhappy realm. . . . The whole kingdom to an unbelievable degree [was] run to seed. Often, arriving at an inn, we found neither people nor horses."

2

The Development of Freedom-Political and Economic 1721-1867

WHEN THE RIKSDAG assembled in Stockholm in 1719, a year after Karl XII's death, its members had had enough of absolute monarchs, their wars and whims and refused to give the throne to his younger sister and closest heir, Ulrika Eleonora, or her husband, Prince Fredrik of Hesse, until she renounced all claims to absolute power. After she agreed to abdicate in favor of her husband, he was crowned Fredrik I. In 1720, a new constitution placed power in the hands of the Council, in which the king had only two votes, and gave the Riksdag control of the state's finances and legislation, a voice in foreign policy and the right to intervene in the administration of government and the judiciary.

Sweden's loss of empire proved to be a liberation. Instead of defending far-flung territories, its people began a process of economic and political modernization that set the stage for industrial development. The impact was swift. Within 50 years, historian Jörgen Weibull has written, Sweden went from being a "small, poor country on the fringe of civilized Europe" to attaining "the same level technically, commercially, scientifically and culturally as the leading countries of Western Europe."

The old upper class resisted, but by the 1860s, Sweden had in place all the institutions and laws for industrialization to take off.

Land Reform and the Beginning of Industry

The transition to a more modern society was eased by good harvests in the 1720s and '30s. The peasants began buying the lands the crown had reclaimed from the nobles under the reductions, and between 1700 and 1800, the portion of the nation's land base owned by tax-paying peasants rose from 30 to 50 percent. Between 1757 and 1762, the crown began a land reform with the goal of ending the medieval practice under which each peasant owned and tilled a narrow strip in each field according to a common plan in favor of a system in which each farmer controlled a larger, single unit. This new land arrangement made it possible for individual farmers to experiment with different cultivating techniques and eventually increase productivity.

After suffering great loss of life on the battlefield and seeing their empire dwindle, the Swedes had changed their thinking about who contributed the most to the society. Martial arts ceased to be the virtue prized above all others and the likeliest reason a man would be raised to the nobility. Instead, the greatest honors began to go to those who expressed ideas about how to develop the country economically. In 1730, a Swede named Andreas Bachmanson, who had been a merchant in Sundsvall and had lived in England, published a book arguing that as long as Sweden was a poor country, Swedish students should not start their studies by reading philosophy or the classics, but economics. After they understood economics, Bachmanson argued, they should proceed to other useful disciplines, such as physics, mathematics, mechanics and navigation. Only when the country became wealthy, he said, should students take up philosophy, literary criticism and other "adornments." Bachmanson credited the wealth of England and the Netherlands to their emphasis on what he called "utilitarian studies." Bachmanson's ideas caught on. In 1743, he was ennobled under the name Nordencrantz and became active in politics.

In the early 18th century, the Industrial Revolution was beginning to transform Great Britain, and a few young Swedes who had traveled there had already begun to bring home proposals for encouraging manufacturing. Jonas Alströmer, the son of a poor townsman in Alingsås, became a bookkeeper in London and eventually worked for a company that was exporting textiles to Sweden. Alströmer decided to start a Swedish textile industry to minimize the expensive imports of woolen cloth. After a study tour of textile factories in England, Germany and Holland that really amounted to industrial espionage, Alströmer managed to buy some textile machinery in Holland. Because export of such equipment was illegal, Alströmer dismembered the machines before shipping them to Gothenburg and Alingsås.

Alströmer's plans for a large-scale textile manufacturing plant so excited the Riksdag that it not only gave him financial support in 1724, it exempted the young men of Alingsås from military service so that the budding industrialist would not experience any shortage of manpower. But Alströmer ran into the same problem that afflicts many start-up protected industries: His goods were inferior. Both the manufactured British woolens preferred by the Swedish elite and the cloth woven at home by the peasants surpassed his textiles in quality.

Facing a lack of market for the products of Alingsås Manufakturverk, Alströmer then did what generations of protected industrialists all over the world have done: He went to the nation's capital and lobbied the government for more support. The company was never very successful, but Alströmer was so good at convincing the members of the Riksdag to continue backing a project in which they had made a political as well as financial investment that it stayed in business until 1824.

Another young Swede who also worked in London and brought home innovations in this period was Mårten Triewald. When his appointment as a secretary to a businessman ended, Triewald became superintendent of one of the first steam engines at Newcastle-upon-Tyne. Theorizing that steam engines could be used to drain mines, he returned to Sweden in 1726 to build a steam engine and convinced the mine owners at Dannemora to back him in his enterprise. Triewald managed to construct his engine, but it never worked very well. Like Alströmer, Triewald eventually came to prefer intellectual and political life in Stockholm to trying to get his machines to work in remote Dannemora. Alströmer and Triewald did not quite succeed, but they inspired others to form enterprises that have lasted. The Rörstrand porcelain company, which was started in 1726, survives to this day at Lidköping.

The Swedish East India Company

Meanwhile, Gustaf II Adolf's idea of developing Gothenburg as a commercial trade city had succeeded, perhaps beyond his wildest expectations. By the second half of the 17th century, Gothenburg was sending England and Spain record amounts of Swedish wood, tar and iron. Sweden was missing out, however, on the large-scale Far Eastern trade, in which London and Amsterdam were making fortunes. This trade was conducted almost exclusively through government-sanctioned companies set up for that purpose—the English East India Company, founded in 1600, and the Dutch East India Company, founded in 1602.

The idea of Sweden conducting its own trade with other parts of the world had been proposed to the Swedish government by both Swedes and foreigners in the 17th century, but those proposals had come to naught. In 1626, William Usselinx, a Dutchman, received a 12-year charter to establish a Swedish company to trade with Asia, Africa and North and South America. But the Thirty Years War prevented that company from being organized. In 1718, a representative of pirates on Madagascar succeeded in obtaining a charter to conduct Sweden's trade with the East Indies as well as a commission for himself as the Swedish governor general over those areas that he could conquer. But when Karl XII died shortly thereafter, the plan could not proceed. In 1719, Daniel Niclas von Höpken, the permanent secretary for foreign affairs, proposed chartering a Swedish company for trade with the Far East, but the Riksdag rejected the idea as too expensive. In 1729, Henrik König, a merchant and commissioner in Stockholm, applied for a permit for two ships to trade with East Asia. It, too, was denied.

Despite all the setbacks, the dream of increasing trade persisted, particularly in Gothenburg, which had begun outfitting its own privateers in 1710. The idea of a Swedish East India trading company emerged from one of those chains of events and series of happy coincidences that are so often behind the world's most successful business ventures. Nils Persson Sahlgren, a Gothenburg tradesman and councilman with roots in Uddevalla, had close ties with trade and shipping in Holland, England and Spain. In 1717, he sent his son Niclas Sahlgren to Holland, where he worked for six years for a firm that did business with the Dutch East India Company. Niclas Sahlgren returned to Sweden, but in 1728, on a trip to Ostend in present-day Belgium, he met Colin Campbell, a Scottish nobleman who had worked for the Ostend Company, an Austrian East India company that had been forced to cease operations. In comparing notes, Campbell and Sahlgren decided that Sweden could develop a great advantage in world trade. The Chinese would accept only silver in payment, and Sweden was already sending exports to Cádiz, the city in southern Spain where silver arrived from the Americas and its price was the lowest. Campbell and Sahlgren theorized that Sweden could sell wood, iron and tar for silver in Spain, take the silver to Canton and buy tea, porcelain, mother of pearl and silk and bring them back to Gothenburg to sell them throughout Europe at an enormous markup.

Campbell, knowing that the Swedish Riksdag was unlikely to give a foreigner a charter for such a venture, took his idea to König, who was of German ancestry but was Swedish-born and well connected politically. Many members of the Riksdag feared that a Swedish East India company would squander the nation's most valuable resources. But König managed to refute these objections by explaining the importance of the Dutch East India Company to Holland's economy and pointing out that the imports could be reexported at a profit. On June 14, 1731, the government granted a 15-year "privilegium" to "Hindrich König & Compagnie" for shipping and trade in the East Indies. The charter forbade all other Swedes from engaging in direct or indirect trade with the East Indies. It also said that the company's ships were to depart from—and return to Gothenburg—and that the cargo was to be sold at public auction as soon as possible after the ships' arrival home. The charter also created a kind of "free-trade zone" because it said the goods could be sold within Sweden or abroad without paying taxes.

König was granted the monopoly, but the charter also called for two other native-born or naturalized Protestant Swedish citizens to "control and direct" the trade. Campbell, who became a Swedish citizen and nobleman on the same day the charter was issued, was one of the other two directors. Sahlgren did not initially become a director, but joined the board a few years later. König died in 1736, and Campbell and Sahlgren became leaders of the company.

Between 1731 and 1806, the Swedish East India Company undertook 130 voyages, all but three of them to Canton. The profits made from the China trade were enormous. The value of a single ship's cargo could reach one or two million riksdaler, and the net profit ranged from 30-80 percent. A total of 37 ships sailed in the company's service, including the *Götheborg*, which ran into a well-known underground rock in the Gothenburg harbor on September 12, 1745, and sank with its cargo of tea, spices, silk and porcelain. In 1984, members of the Marine Archaeological Society of Gothenburg discovered the ship, and in 1985, its cargo of porcelain was recovered for museum display.

Economic historian Eli Heckscher has called the Swedish East India Company "Sweden's most successful trading economy . . . an exotic plant in the not-exactly-colorful herb garden of Swedish commerce." The Swedish East India Company, Heckscher said, "spoke to the Swedish imagination of the time," and indeed it did. The company built a grand structure (now a museum) in Gothenburg as its headquarters, and for a time, the western seaport threatened to overwhelm Stockholm as Sweden's most important city. The merchants associated with the Swedish East India Company—some of them immigrants—started a tradition of private philanthropy that outshone Stockholm and other Swedish cities. Sahlgren, for example, established a Gothenburg hospital that still bears his name.

The China trade was the greatest single source of Swedish venture capital in the 18th century. Because the charter said the company could buy only Swedish ships, it also boosted the Swedish shipbuilding industry. Even though most of the cargo was exported, Sweden, like the rest of Europe at the time, became "rampantly Sinophilic," as historian Sverker Sörlin has written. King Adolf Fredrik, Fredrik's successor, built a little China palace in the royal gardens at Drottningholm outside Stockholm for Queen Louisa Ulrika in 1753, and many upper-class homes built during the period bear Chinese decoration.

The Swedish East India Company's charter was renewed twice, but business declined when trade patterns changed. To the everlasting sadness of Gothenburg, the company was liquidated in 1813.

The Hats - Sweden's Mercantilists

The Riksdag's original reluctance to charter the Swedish East India Company stemmed from the recently defeated country's inherent conservatism in this period. From the 1720s-1730s, the Council was led by its lord president, Arvid Horn, a cautious noble who emphasized good relations with Russia and Great Britain and neutrality in conflicts among the great powers. The 1719 Riksdag had done away with the distinction between the higher and lower aristocracy, giving the more recently ennobled and landless members much more political power. By the 1730s, the younger members of the newly ennobled families united with two goals in mind: to avenge Sweden's embarrassing loss in the battle at Poltava and to industrialize the country. Horn's opponents became known as the Hats, and Horn's defenders as the Nightcaps, supposedly because they were as timid as "little old ladies in nightcaps."

The economic policy of the noble Hats was mercantilist; they favored increasing exports and reducing imports by subsidizing manufacturing. The policy also won support from a majority of the burgher estate of the Riksdag. At the 1738-39 Riksdag, the Hats forced Horn to resign and replaced him with their own leader, Carl Gyllenborg, who would push Sweden into an age of subsidized economic development and new wars.

Modern economists are very critical of mercantilism. But in those years before Adam Smith revolutionized economics, mercantilism was considered an advance that brought together advocates of the development of the nation's resources. In this spirit of cooperation between Hat politics, mercantilist economics and technological development, the Riksdag set up a Manufacturing Office in 1739. The Hats helped the ironmasters organize themselves into an association in 1747 and secure a royal charter to establish an Iron Office, which regulated industry to keep prices high, granted loans to ironmasters to undertake experiments in innovation and gave students grants to study abroad. In 1769, the Iron Office became independent of Riksdag control. Historians say it possessed more autonomy from state control than any other organization in Sweden.

The Hats' basic interest, however, was not economics, but glory for the Swedish state. When the War of Austrian Succession broke out in 1740, the Hats took the Swedes into the war on the side of France against Russia. The war ended in defeat, with Russia occupying Finland and, under the 1743 Peace of Åbo, keeping the southeastern part of the country. Fredrik I was childless, and the Russians insisted that the Swedes accept their candidate for king, Adolf Fredrik of Holstein-Gottorp. Adolf Fredrik was the grandson of Karl XII's elder sister, but Russian comfort with him was just as important to his selection as his ancestry.

Despite these defeats at the hands of the Russians, the Hats did not lose power immediately. Economic growth was simply too strong, and the ideas of the French Enlightenment too popular, to stop the trend. But after the Hats' alliance with the French involved Sweden in the Seven Years War against Prussia from 1756-63, they lost control of the Riksdag to the Caps, who went on a rampage of reversing Hat policies. The Caps' "oracle," Uppsala University professor Sten Carlsson, has written, was Bachmanson, who had moved away from the Hats' mercantilist pro-manufacturing policies toward a recognition of the need to develop agriculture and to allow people other than privileged nobles and government officials to participate fully in the economic system. The Caps restricted credit and protection for manufactured goods and replaced Sweden's treaty with the French with one with Great Britain. They also made overtures to Russia. The Cap policies caused such deflation that their regime lasted only four years (1765-69) before the Hats returned to power and put their mercantilist policies back into place. The Caps had one great accomplishment, however: the 1766 passage of Sweden's first law guaranteeing freedom of the press.

Establishment of the Royal Academy of Sciences

On June 2, 1739, a group of six prominent men met at the House of Nobility in Stockholm to create the Royal Swedish Academy of Sciences. Neither the establishment of the academy nor the presence of the noted Swedish botanist Carl Linneaus (Carl von Linné), was surprising. Scientific academies had already been established in Italy and in London, Paris, Berlin and St. Petersburg. Linneaus was already world-famous for exploring Lappland and for *Systema Naturae*, his monumental classification of the three realms of nature. What was unusual about the meeting was the other men who were present and the thinking behind the academy's creation. Besides Linneaus, the other founders were three Hat politicians and Alströmer and Triewald, the dreamer-entrepreneurs. All Europe was obsessed with the emerging field of science in the 18th century, and Sweden, although less advanced, was no exception. Uppsala University had upgraded its scientific education, and members of wealthier families were traveling abroad to study. Anders Celsius was appointed a professor of astronomy at Uppsala in 1730 and in 1742 would reveal the thermometric scale scientists use today. Linneaus, a minister's son who declined to follow in his father's footsteps because he was so fascinated with birds and flowers, had studied at Uppsala. In 1732, a royally chartered scientific society in Uppsala had sent him to Lappland. In 1735, he went to Holland, where he earned a degree in medicine. Linneaus won patrons in Holland and stayed abroad for several years. When he returned to Sweden, he settled in Stockholm and was appointed a professor of medicine at Uppsala, where he continued his botanical and zoological research.

What brought Linneaus, Alströmer, Triewald and the Hat politicians together was their common view that Swedish science needed to be moved beyond academia and made a national concern. The Swedish Academy of Sciences would eventually become an institution dedicated to pure scientific research, but its purpose in the beginning was very practical—or, to use the word that was then in vogue, "utilitarian."

The academy "was anxious to be part of the learned community in Europe," Tore Frängsmyr, research professor in science at Uppsala University, has written in the academy's official history, and it encouraged the translation of the work of Swedish scientists into more widely read languages. But, as Frängsmyr notes, the academy decided that its own publishing would be in Swedish, which came to benefit the mass of the Swedish people. The frontispiece of the first volume of its

Proceedings showed an old man digging a hole to plant a tree "For Posterity." Subjects in its early issues included how to exterminate pests, how to tar roofs, how to improve the harvest with new tools and methods, and how to draw beer and wine from barrels in a cellar.

In 1747, the academy was granted the exclusive right to publish the Swedish Almanac, which contained such basic information as the times of sunrise and sunset, weather predictions, the dates of the year's fairs and details about the fairs. Each edition also included a short essay for the edification of the public; the first, written by Linneaus, was about ale and its uses and abuses. The academy printed 135,000 copies of the almanac the first year, and by 1785, the annual number of copies had risen to 294,000. It was said that every village in Sweden had at least one copy.

Through its writings on astronomy, health and sickness, and perhaps most important of all on the improvement of agriculture, the Swedish Almanac brought science into the lives of the Swedish people. The potato, which had been brought from the Americas to Europe by the Spanish conquistadors, had been planted in an Uppsala botanical garden in 1658. Alströmer is credited with popularizing the potato in Sweden, and the almanac urged its cultivation as well as the spreading of manure on fields, the planting of certain crops, the development and use of plows and beekeeping. (The academy's official history acknowledges that "unkind observers" have noted that promotion of the potato also made Sweden part of "the aquavit belt.")

The founders had no reservations about inviting aristocrats who could pay for the academy's research to join the working scientists as members. The very first year, at Linneaus's suggestion, the founders appointed to the board a cargo officer of the Swedish East India Company. Linneaus hoped to secure for researchers the right of annual free passage to China on the company's ships. He never convinced the East India Company to be quite that generous, but many Swedish scientists did travel on the ships and were able to pursue purely scientific, not commercial, research. Sverker Sörlin, the assistant director of the academy's Center for the History of Science, has written that Magnus Lagerström, the company's first secretary in the 1750s, had such a passion for science that he coordinated the interests of the company with the academy "always to the advantage of the latter." (The academy was also remarkably feminist for its time. Invoking the precedent of Voltaire's mistress, Madame Chatelet, the academy in 1748 elected to membership Countess Eva Ekeblad, who had submitted a short article on the production of starch and powder from the potato. Countess Ekeblad's husband, Claes Ekeblad, was councilor of the realm and a member of the academy. His high position may have played a part in her election, but the inclusion of a woman is still notable for its rarity in scientific societies of the period.)

Members of the academy also became advocates of modern enterprise. In his address at the end of his presidency of the academy, Alströmer told his fellow academicians that, as a native of the sparsely populated Swedish forests, he had been amazed to see people "teeming like ants" in England, Holland and other countries on the continent. The reason there could be so many people and so few beggars in those countries, Alströmer said, was "the restless spirit of enterprise, the unhindered concentration on useful work."

The early members of the academy were men of their times, however, and reflected the fact that economics as a discipline was not as advanced as the hard sciences. Alströmer and other 18th-century Swedish advocates of industrialization believed that population growth would provide the key to the nation's development. Anders Berch, who held the first chair in economics at Uppsala University, believed that machines should perform only those functions that humans could not perform as well.

The utilitarians were highly nationalistic. "The ultimate goal of all utilitarian activity was to make Sweden strong," Gothenburg University professor Sven-Eric Liedman wrote in 1989 in the official history of the Royal Academy of Sciences. "Sweden was to attain a respected position in the world for its trade, its national wealth and its armies and navy; also for its good morals, its flourishing agriculture and its manufacturing; and last, but not least, for its science. It was the Swedish state that was to glitter in the eyes of the surrounding world," Liedman wrote. And the Swedish "state," he continued, "should not be seen here as an abstraction. It was in a very concrete sense the political institutions, particularly the estates of the Riksdag, and the government offices. The state was the top-ranking figures in the government, who were also, during the regime of the Hats, the leading people in economic life."

Berch advocated the state's keeping the majority of the population at a "steady and appropriate level of poverty" so that they would work hard. But because he considered promotion of trade to be the consummate demonstration of utility to the country, he said that those engaged in foreign trade should be given as much freedom as possible.

Despite their interest in international scientific research, some of the utilitarians did have a xenophobic side. Christopher Polhem, the 18th-century inventor, said in old age that learning should be communicated only in the native tongue and that students sent abroad should be closely supervised. Polhem also advocated censorship of foreign books In general, members of the academy in the 18th century agreed with the mercantilist theory that manufacturing was a greater source of value than agriculture and should receive government promotion. But the Riksdag's support of Alströmer's textile manufacturing venture was highly controversial and divided some members of the academy on the issue of which enterprise the government should emphasize. Polhem, for example, said that rather than promoting industries based on imported raw materials, all Swedish manufacturing should be based on Swedish raw materials. Iron,

Polhem said, is "the master key to the welfare of many."

The question of agriculture versus manufacturing led to a division between Linneaus, who believed that economics meant agricultural economics, and Berch, who believed that manufacturing was superior in economic terms to agriculture. Chairs in economics set up at the universities in Lund and Åbo, and a second chair in economics at Uppsala, financed at Linneaus's suggestion by a Värmland ironmaster, all became posts for Linnean disciples.

By the late 1700s, these chairs became posts for botanists, while the Berch chair came to be occupied by a legal scholar. That there were no objections to this trend was symbolic of the end of the first great period in Swedish science. The Swedish elites from King Gustaf III down had become bored with science and technology and preferred lighter, more glamorous pursuits, ranging from the opera and the ballet to occultism and mysticism.

The End of "Freedom" and the Gustavian Age

Swedes call the period between 1719 and 1772 the "Age of Freedom" because the monarchy had relatively little power and foreign governments often subsidized the Hat and Cap parties. For many years, Swedes viewed the Age of Freedom negatively because it was a period of foreign influence, but more-modern historians have come to view it as key to the development of Swedish democracy. During this period, two members of the peasant estate, Olof Håkansson a Hat from Lösen in Blekinge, and Joseph Hansson, a Cap from Mossebo in Västergötland, became speakers of the peasant estate and pillars of their respective parties. According to Carlsson, no other peasant politicians in Europe achieved such a high position in the 18th century. Håkansson and Hansson managed to improve the lot of peasants by restricting nobles' privileges in hunting and property ownership, but campaigns failed to place peasants on the Secret Committee, the central governing body of the Riksdag, which was composed of 50 noblemen, 25 clergymen and 25 burghers under the chairmanship of the speaker of the House of Nobility and controlled public finances and foreign policy.

When Gustaf III ascended the throne in 1771 at the age of 24, the issues of democracy and equality prevalent throughout Europe had arrived in Sweden. The clergy, the burghers and the peasants all wanted an end to the nobles' privileges. They were supported by the Caps when they retook power in the Riksdag in 1772. In the midst of a threat of famine, Gustaf III, on August 19, 1772, obtained an oath of loyalty from his guards, locked up the members of the Council, dismissed the Riksdag's Secret Committee and carried out a bloodless coup. He imposed on the Riksdag a new constitution, which gave the king the exclusive right to rule and reduced the Council to advisory status. Parliament retained power over taxation.

Thus ended the "Age of the Freedom" and began the Gustavian Age (1772-1809), which also includes the rule of Gustaf IV Adolf, who succeeded his father in 1792. It proved portentous that Gustaf III was visiting Paris when his father, King Adolf Fredrik, died. Impressed by the French capital's intellectual and political accomplishments, Gustaf III turned into an enlightened despot, who spent his reign trying to bring the French Enlightenment to Sweden on his own terms.

The Gustavian period was not without technological or economic advancement. Gustaf III built up the navy and in 1781 appointed Fredric Henric af Chapman, a Swede of English parentage and author of *Architectura Navalis Mercatoria,* a world-famous 1768 book on ship architecture, to be director of the Karlskrona shipyards. Perhaps the most practical invention to come out of the Gustavian period was the *kakelugn*, or tiled stove, developed in 1767 by Carl Johan Cronstedt, a pupil of Polhem's. But Gustaf III is much better known for his cultural legacy. He was a patron of individual artists, and his reign is remembered for the songs of Carl Michael Bellman, the sculpture of Johan Tobias Sergel and the paintings of Carl Gustaf Pilo. Gustaf III founded the Royal Theater, which housed drama and opera, the Swedish Academy of Literature and the Royal Academy of Fine Art. The inspiration for the period was French, but the furniture, silver and crafts of the period were so uniquely Swedish in their design that they are called Gustavian.

The arts aside, the Gustavian period is also noted for political intrigue and war. Gustaf III's nearly absolute monarchy started out with great public support. The peasants hoped he would favor them, and the nobles hoped he would prevent a revolution. Gustaf III quickly imposed some of the new French ideas. In 1781, Sweden introduced religious freedom for foreigners and, in 1782, passed special regulations permitting Jews to settle and practice their religion in all the major towns. Gustaf III also permitted civil servants to retire at 70 with a pension.

Gustaf III took a great interest in international affairs. Swedes served in the American Revolutionary Army, and in 1783, Gustaf III became the first neutral monarch to recognize the new nation of the United States. He had also paid a courtesy call on Catherine the Great in St. Petersburg in 1771, but failing to secure a nonaggression treaty with her, decided to seek a military alliance with France. He traveled to Paris in 1784, where he arranged a subsidy for the Swedish military and also made arrangements for Sweden to take over the small West Indies island of St. Barthélemy. The island was to be used as a shipping point for Swedish iron and other products to the Americas, and a Swedish West Indies Company was formed. Before Gustaf III left Paris, Louis XVI warned his ambitious friend, "Peace, that kind of glory which is after your Majesty's heart, is much to be preferred to the deceptive splendor which invests princes who yearn for conquest."

Gustaf III disliked dissent, however, and in 1774 restricted freedom of the press. By 1786, members of the Riksdag were tired of Gustaf III's autocratic ways and used their powers of the purse to cut back on grants to the crown. Finns chafing under Swedish rule were talking about declaring themselves a principality and believed they could get Russia's support.

In 1788, trying to regain his popularity, Gustaf III took Sweden to war against Russia in the most dramatic fashion imaginable. Dressed like Gustaf II Adolf, he sailed out of Stockholm harbor toward St. Petersburg. In Finland, Swedish troops, dressed in Russian uniforms that had been sneaked from the Royal Opera's wardrobe, burned and looted a Swedish village. Some Swedish noble military officers considered Gustaf III's aggression against Russia unconstitutional and demanded peace negotiations.

The noble rebellion backfired. Popular once again, Gustaf III assembled all four estates of the Riksdag, upbraided the nobles and ordered them out of the room. The nobles were infuriated, but followed the royal command. In what historians say was the first time a Swedish king addressed a session of commoners only, Gustaf III announced that all appointments to future high office would be based on merit rather than birth and that non-nobles could buy noble lands. He also gave himself the power to declare war without consulting the Council of the Riksdag. To the delight of the other estates and the nobles' intense frustration, Gustaf III declared all his proposals accepted.

In 1790, Gustaf III won his war with Russia and came home triumphant. But the French Revolution of 1789 had emboldened nobles and army officers who opposed the absolute monarchy. On March 16, 1792, Johan Jakob Anckarström, an army officer, shot and killed Gustaf III at a fancy dress ball in his beloved opera house. The assassination became the basis for Verdi's opera *Un Ballo in Maschera*.

Napoleon, the Loss of Finland and Union with Norway

The death of Gustaf III did nothing to end Sweden's political chaos. As Napoleon rose in power in France, the situation worsened. Upon Gustaf III's death, his son, Gustaf IV Adolf, age 13, became king. Gustaf IV's regents continued his father's appreciation for the French Enlightenment by establishing the Royal Institute of Technology in 1798. But Gustaf IV hated both the French Revolution and Napoleon, and when he became of age, he joined Sweden to Russia and Denmark in a pact of armed neutrality. Russia broke the alliance and Sweden joined Russia, Austria and England in a coalition against Napoleon. French troops overran Swedish Pomerania, and in treaty negotiations, France and Russia insisted that Sweden join a commercial blockade against Britain. Sweden refused. In 1808, Russian troops attacked Finland. In 1809, Sweden lost Finland to Russia and a group of military officers forced Gustaf IV Adolf into exile in Switzerland, where he died in 1837.

Following agreement on a new constitution, which clearly defined the authority of the monarch and the Riksdag, Gustaf IV Adolf's uncle succeeded him as Karl XIII. Because Karl XIII was old and childless, the negotiations for his successor began immediately. The Riksdag elected a Danish prince, Kristian August of Augustenborg, as crown prince, but he died of a stroke in Skåne in 1810. There were rumors that he had been poisoned by Gustavian loyalists. Feelings were running so strong at Kristian August's funeral that Axel von Fersen, marshal of the realm, who had become famous for trying to help the king and queen of France escape during the Revolution, was attacked by a mob and torn limb from limb.

With Napoleon at the height of his power, the Swedes chose Jean Baptiste Bernadotte, Napoleon's marshal who had allowed Swedish troops to leave Pomerania unmolested in 1806, as crown prince. Bernadotte had encouraged the Swedes to think that his election would bring the favor of Napoleon. In fact, relations between Bernadotte and Napoleon were not particularly positive, partly because Bernadotte had married Napoleon's onetime fiancée, Desirée Clary. No sooner had Bernadotte arrived in Sweden and changed his name to Karl Johan, than he announced he would not try to regain Finland, but would attempt to bring Norway into a union with Sweden.

To avoid a confrontation on the seas, he also began secret negotiations with Britain. After France invaded Swedish Pomerania again in 1812, Karl Johan met with Czar Alexander at Åbo, Finland, to form an alliance. In 1813, Karl Johan took a Swedish army to Germany to fight against Napoleon. After Napoleon's defeat at the Battle of Leipzig, Karl Johan turned his forces against Denmark and forced it to sign the 1814 Treaty of Kiel, which ceded Norway to Sweden. The Norwegians, who wanted their independence, had already adopted a constitution and selected a king, but Karl Johan threatened war. The Norwegian Parliament was forced to accept a union with Sweden, but Karl Johan agreed to accept the Norwegians' Eidsvoll constitution, which granted Norwegians broader suffrage than Swedes would enjoy for more than 100 years. The treaty gave the Swedish king authority over Norway's foreign policy but called for Norway to manage its own domestic affairs with its own Parliament.

Upon the death of Karl XIII, Karl Johan was crowned Karl XIV Johan in 1818. The union with Norway would ultimately prove unworkable, but it was Karl Johan who decided that Sweden's alliances with the Great Powers had not served it well and promulgated the policy of peaceful but armed neutrality.

Constructing the Göta Canal

While Karl XIII and Karl XIV Johan and their courts were occupied with matters of war and foreign policy at the beginning of the 19th century, Swedes more interested in their country's economic modernization were following the canal building that was at the height of its popularity in Europe and the United States. A series of canals had been built across Britain for inland transportation of raw materials, coal and finished products, and these had attracted attention in Sweden. The Trollhätte Canal, which linked Lake Vänern with Gothenburg, had been completed in 1800. Shortly after the psychologically devastating loss of Finland in 1809, Sweden's greatest poet of the period, Bishop Esaias Tegnér called for "reconquering Finland within Sweden" by strengthening Sweden militarily and economically. Even before the end of the Napoleonic Wars, the Swedish government decided to construct a canal reaching from the east coast to the west coast of the country by connecting Lake Vänern with Lake Vättern and the Baltic. Swedes believed that inland waterways would make it possible to transport ships, munitions and manpower from coast to coast without going through Öresund, the sound between Sweden and Denmark, which could harbor hostile forces.

The Göta Canal, as it was called, was a military project led by a naval officer, Baltzar von Platen, although its promoters said it would be used for commercial purposes. Its construction was based on a theory of central defense: If Sweden were attacked from the east, the army would use a series of delaying tactics by withdrawing inland to the Karlsborg fortress on Lake Vättern to which the royal family and high government and central bank officials would retreat.

Von Platen invited Britain's foremost canal-builder, Thomas Telford, to Sweden in 1808 to analyze the practicality of the project. In 1809, the Swedish Riksdag granted a loan to the company that was to take charge of planning and constructing the canal. About 10 regiments of Sweden's army did the actual construction, which continued for 23 years. King Karl XIII opened the first section in 1813, and the final section of the "nation's ditch" was opened in 1832 by King Karl XIV Johan.

Taking a boat on the Göta Canal is a popular tourist adventure today, but it was never a military, industrial or financial success in the 19th century. The concept of central defense would eventually be abandoned in favor of protecting the country's frontiers, and railways, which would be introduced in Sweden in the 1850s, proved to be a much more efficient way to transport goods.

Although the Göta Canal did not turn out to be crucial to the nation's defense, its construction played a key role in the development of Sweden's engineering industry. It provided early work experience for John Ericsson, the inventor and emigrant whose propeller on the U.S. ship *Monitor*, which battled the Confederate *Merrimac*, would help the North win the American Civil War, and for his brother Nils (who spelled the family name Ericson), the man responsible for the state railway system.

For construction, von Platen bought a steam power dredger from Scotland and asked the manufacturer to send along someone to maintain it. The company sent Donald Fraser, who set up Motala Verkstad as a service and maintenance shop but soon expanded it to include a smithy, a carpentry, a machine shop and a foundry. Eventually, it began to make steamships. Motala needed more skilled craftsmen than it could find and set up a training school. Students at Motala went on to become some of the great leaders of 19th-century Swedish industry. They included Carl Bolinder, founder of Bolinders Mekaniska Verkstad in Stockholm, and Alexander Lagerman, who would invent machinery for the production of safety matches. Chalmers University professor Jan Hult has called the Göta Canal "Sweden's oldest and longest technical university." In addition to these industrial leaders, Hult notes, thousands of young men who worked on the canal brought technical knowledge back to their homes all over the country.

Economic Modernization - Agriculture, Iron and Textiles

The Göta Canal was only the biggest and most visible example of Sweden's adoption of technology and business methods from Great Britain and the continent in the first half of the 19th century.

Agriculture changed first. The 18th-century land reform under which individual farmers controlled larger pieces of village-owned lands had dramatically increased productivity. But when Rutger MacLean, a Swedish baron whose Scottish ancestors had come to Sweden to escape Oliver Cromwell, inherited Svaneholm, an 8,500-acre estate in Skåne in 1782, he took the reforms a step further, following the English and Danish model, by splitting up the farms on his estate and dividing them into single homesteads. In 1803 and 1807, after vigorous debates, MacLean pushed agricultural reforms through the Riksdag, first for southern Sweden and, beginning in 1827, for the entire country. Under the law called *laga skifte*, the old villages were split and the land was deeded to individual farmers. Thus, Swedish farmers began to leave the villages and established their residences on their farms, almost invariably painting the houses Falu red, a tint the Stora Kopparberg mine had begun making in the 1680s. Those provinces that participated in the land reform experienced gains in productivity, while the ones that resisted, particularly Dalarna, did not enjoy the same increase in their food supply. Swedes also began to cultivate what had been forestlands, and the number of arable acres tripled between 1810 and 1870. The government also signaled its approval of agricultural modernization by moving the scientific academy's agricultural research activities to a new Royal Academy of Agriculture established in 1812.

The increased productivity came at just the right time for the development of Swedish exports. The Industrial Revolution had enriched Britain, which began importing Swedish grain in large quantities in 1829. It was said in the middle of the century that the horses pulling the first trams in London were all eating Swedish oats. The grain boom would last until the 1860s, when Sweden experienced several years of poor crops and cheaper U.S. grain began flooding the world markets.

In Britain and on the continent, the movement of people from the countryside to the cities also created an unprecedented market for Swedish lumber to build housing for the new industrial workers. The large-scale export of timber from Sweden required opening up the vast virgin forests of Norrland, which extended to the Lappland tundra. There were already a few *bruk* scattered throughout the forests, and in the 1700s, some forward-

65

thinking *bruk* owners and merchants had begun ordering the clearing of logs and other debris from the northern streams and rivers so that logs could be floated downriver and exported from Gothenburg. Fine blade saws, which reduced the amount of sawdust and waste wood, first came into use in Norrland in 1740, but true exploitation waited until the 1840s, when the more accessible Norwegian forests had been depleted.

In 1823, the Riksdag decided to transfer many of the state forestlands to private hands. In Norrland, allotments as large as 16,000 acres were given to individual peasants.

Within the same decade, the Dicksons, a Gothenburg merchant family that was then cutting through the Värmland forest, began buying up Norrland forests at very low prices. The Dicksons did not create the only timber empire in Sweden, but theirs became the most notorious. The Swedish government had for centuries been concerned about overexploitation of the forests and had established quotas for the cutting of trees on crown lands. But the Dicksons considered the laws ridiculously antiquated in an era of worldwide free commerce and flouted them outrageously. The peasants who had sold or leased forestlands to the Dicksons became infuriated, and in 1843, the provincial authorities fined James Dickson, the head of the Norrland sawmills. After the highest court in the land reversed the verdict, provincial officials appealed to King Oskar I, who asked Dickson to take an oath of innocence. Dickson arrived at the courthouse in a fine carriage driven by three horses. When he left, the carriage was driven by only two horses, which prompted locals to say that only two horses were needed because Dickson had lost his soul in the hall.

James Dickson's son Oscar continued his father's practices. In 1867, when timber from crown forests showed up among the Dicksons' possessions, *"Baggböleriet,"* a reference to the Dicksons' town of operations in the north, entered the Swedish language as the equivalent of "robber baron." (Dickson's notoriety was not, however, enough to keep him from being made a real baron.)

The Dicksons and other timber owners had located their sawmills inland to be near the rapids or falls that drove waterwheels for the saws, but in 1845, Jean and Carl Bolinder, who had studied sawmill machinery in England and were alumni of Motala Verkstad, opened an engineering works in Stockholm that in 1847 built the first complete Swedish steam saw. The use of steam power to drive sawmills allowed the sawmill owners to locate their production operations close to the coast, where cut lumber could be moved directly onto ships.

In 1851, the Swedish government paid for a number of Swedish workers to attend the London Exposition, and some of them visited the woodworking factory at Woolwich and observed a variety of machine tools in use. The same year, a similar factory was started in Gothenburg, run by foremen who had worked in England. But in the following years, the "carpentry factories," as they were called, began spreading to other cities such as Jönköping and Kalmar, where they built on the handicraft tradition.

By the 1860s, wood products had replaced iron as Sweden's principal export, but that didn't mean the iron industries weren't trying to keep up. As early as 1767, Swedes learned that the British had figured out how to smelt iron with coal. The *brukspatroner* were too rich and comfortable to heed any early warnings about Britain's capability to produce its own iron, and the Napoleonic Wars postponed international competition in the industry. But by the early 1800s, the Swedes had to address both the decline in Britain's demand for Swedish iron and the threat of Russia's developing iron industry.

In addition, the British developed the rolling mill and "puddling iron," which increased efficiency, and the quality and quantity of their iron. To compete, the Swedes needed to use these new technologies. But they couldn't simply import the British equipment, because it ran on coal. Sweden had no coal of its own, and even if the Swedes had imported coal, they could not have transported it to the scattered *bruk* because they had not yet built railroads.

The Iron Office sponsored research trips to Britain and experiments during the 1830s, but it took until 1843 for Gustaf Ekman, a nephew of Count von Platen, to adapt the Lancashire process to the use of charcoal. Historian Eli Heckscher called Ekman's achievement "the most glorious page in Swedish iron handling." But as Ohio State University professor Carl Gustavson, author of *The Small Giant*, has written, Sweden's "long struggle to adapt more advanced technology . . . is filled with irony, no pun intended," because the government decided in 1854 to build railroads. Charcoal prices rose about the same time, and iron makers found it more practical to buy cheap imported coal and convert their *bruk* to its use as fuel.

The European iron and steel business was further transformed in 1856 when Henry Bessemer introduced his method for mass-producing steel in Great Britain. But steel producers in Britain and the United States found it impossible to make Bessemer's method work until Göran Fredrik Göransson, a Swedish businessman with no academic training, showed that Bessemer's experiment was a success when he—accidentally—used iron that didn't contain phosphorous. Swedish steelworks adopted the Bessemer method, initially using the purest Swedish iron in their works. Methods to take phosphorous out of iron were soon developed, allowing the vast deposits of less-pure iron ore in central and northern Sweden to be exploited for another prosperous period in the Swedish iron industry.

In 1863, Göransson and others founded Sandviken, an iron and steel mill. Sandviken was the first Swedish mill to use the Bessemer method, but historian Gustavson has noted that equally significant was the decision of its founders to locate the mill not near mines or forests but at Storsjön, a lake near the port of Gävle and on the railroad line between Gävle and Falun. "For the first time, a railroad emancipated a Swedish ironworks from the inflexible costs of old-time production," Gustavson wrote. Sandviken closed in 1866, when some of its founders went bankrupt, but Göransson bought it back and production resumed in 1868. Domnarvet, a division of Stora, bought Sandviken around 1900.

Protected by a postwar tariff established in 1816, the Swedish textile industry also expanded dramatically in the early 19th century. Its center was at Norrköping in Östergötland, which had become a center of textile industry precisely because it had the surging Motala River to provide the energy for production. In 1790, in what architect-author Gunnar Sillén has called "that blend of philanthropy and utilitarian thinking peculiar to the Industrial Revolution," a spinnery was built to provide employment for women in a nearby prison. The women were, of course, paid exploitive wages. In 1810, on the same site, Christian Lenning began manufacturing woolens on a large scale. The working conditions—dangerous, noisy machines, air thick with dust and water—were notorious. Another center of textile production developed near the city of Borås in southwest Sweden. Since the 1600s, the area around Borås had been a center of cottage spinning and weaving, whose goods were distributed by *gårdfarihandlare,* or farm peddlers. In 1834, Sven Erikson, the son of one of these traders, built the first cotton-weaving mill in Sweden at Rydboholm.

In the 1830s, the Swedish government began lowering the tariffs on textiles little by little, until by 1865, they were virtually eliminated. The pressure of competition from imports forced the Swedish textile manufacturers to go to ever-larger mass production, or die. Some textile manufacturers made fortunes in the 19th century. Wilhelm Röhss, a textile worker from Germany who shared his knowledge of a dyeing process with Grönvall & Co., a Gothenburg importer-exporter, in exchange for a partnership in the firm, went on to own a *bruk* and a sawmill and become an investor in Skandinaviska Banken and many other ventures. The names of Wilhelm Röhss and his brother August live on in a museum of design and crafts in Gothenburg. Based mostly on imported raw materials and imported machinery, the Swedish textile industry was not destined to last once Swedish wages rose in the 20th century, but as historian Gustavson has noted, its development played key roles in stimulating both the entrepreneurial spirit and market demand.

Liberal Economics and Politics

Along with imported technology and increased international trade came movements to free industry and business from government regulation, improve the lot of Sweden's common people and broaden political participation. Many of these liberal ideas were promoted by *Aftonbladet (The Evening Paper)*, founded in 1830 in Stockholm by Lars Johan Hierta, a noble who was influenced by French ideas about freedom of expression and journalism, and *Göteborgs Handels- och Sjöfartstidning (Gothenburg's Commercial and Shipping News)*, founded in 1832. *Aftonbladet* became Sweden's largest daily and developed national influence because half its circulation was outside Stockholm. Farmers who could not afford their own copies shared subscriptions. Hierta frequently offended officials, but he fought so vigorously against censors that in 1845 the government gave up trying to control the press. Hierta was also active in business and is credited with developing the candle industry in Sweden.

The idea that nations that allowed their economies to be "liberal" (meaning that they engaged in free trade) would be more prosperous than those that controlled their economies took hold among Europe's economic establishments, and Hierta and others campaigned for laws to make it possible for Swedish industry to develop with less government intervention. Pressure for liberal business and trade laws came, surprisingly enough, from some of the ironmasters, who viewed the old laws as discouraging technological innovation and sales. The heavily controlled iron industry was deregulated one step at a time. All trade in pig iron within Sweden was freed in 1835, but it wasn't until 1858 that all mining restrictions were removed. The guilds, which in their early years had helped craftsmen develop skills and preserve and add to technical knowledge, came to be viewed as nothing more than a way to maintain job security and keep out mass production. In 1846, the guilds were abolished in favor of professional associations. Between 1846 and 1860, the number of industrial workers increased by 41 percent, and in 1864, the professional associations were abolished, giving Swedes complete freedom of employment for the first time since the Middle Ages.

The economic chaos during the period of the Napoleonic Wars had destroyed the Swedish banking system. In 1824, private banks were allowed; and in the 1830s, Sweden began to reconstruct the private banking system, but with a goal of incorporating the middle- and lower-class savers and borrowers into the system. The government established a series of banking laws and, in 1848, passed the Limited Liability

Companies Act, which made it easier for companies to incorporate and acquire capital.

The man behind the dismantling of state controls on commerce was Johan August Gripenstedt, who began serving King Oskar I as a consultative minister in 1848 and later served King Karl XV as finance minister. Gripenstedt was a landowner's son who had an army career and married the niece of C.H. Anckarsvärd, a rebel aristocrat who had been part of the group responsible for the coup against Gustaf IV Adolf. Gripenstedt took over management of Anckarsvärd's estate at Nynäs and became interested in economic policy. He also formed an alliance with the railroad builders and helped get government approval for their projects. Under his leadership, Sweden reduced tariffs in 1857. In 1865, he negotiated a tariff treaty with France that signaled Sweden's acceptance of free trade.

The liberals, including the newspaper editors, did not limit their campaigns to economic issues, but pushed as well for other reforms they considered vital to a modern society: universal suffrage, improved education, freedom of religion and women's rights. King Karl XIV Johan turned into a rigid conservative, but his son, Crown Prince Oskar, used his own goodwill to push legislation for the benefit of the common people.

Only half the parishes in Sweden had elementary schools in the early 19th century, and they were for only half the population—boys. The farmers joined the campaign for better schools, and Bishop Tegnér declared that in a democracy "crudity was unconstitutional and ignorance was treason." Prince Oskar argued for the free election of local school boards, and in 1842, the Riksdag passed a law requiring each parish to establish a common school. The schools were primitive, and it took many years before poor students had the same opportunity as wealthy children to advance to higher learning; but by 1900 almost all Swedes could read and write.

Oskar assumed the throne upon the death of his father in 1844, and in 1845, with the king's assistance, the burgher, clergy and peasant estates in the Riksdag managed to establish women's inheritance rights. In 1858, the Riksdag also established an unmarried woman's right to become legally responsible at age 25. Oskar's social commitment extended to writing a book encouraging better treatment of prisoners. Oskar's book was translated abroad and helped establish Sweden's reputation as a socially conscious country.

Sweden's population had grown from 2.4 million in 1800 to 3.5 million in 1850, the result, as Bishop Tegnér summed it up of "peace, [the smallpox] vaccination and the potato." The land reform—or "rationalization" as it was called—had improved agricultural productivity, but it had also worsened the lot of landless people. From time immemorial, they had had access to grazing lands and had taken timber and firewood from the forests, but now found landowners more protective of their property. Farmers also tried to keep their new, individual farms intact by passing them on only to their eldest sons. This practice created an ever-growing class of landless, usually poor people. Many began immigrating to America, but in 1847, a Poor Law declared that "it was incumbent upon each parish and town to feed its own poor."

While the liberals—a loose coalition of farmers, business professionals and social reformers—had many successes in modernizing Swedish society in the first half of the 19th century, they had to campaign for nearly 50 years for another key goal: abolition of the four-estate Riksdag in favor of a bicameral institution. The liberals argued that the four-estate system not only preserved outdated privileges for the nobles and the clergy, but also left many people without representation, especially as the society industrialized. The peasants' estate, for example, represented small landowners, but workers on the nobles' lands were unrepresented and ineligible to run for election to the Riksdag. Conservative nobles, intellectuals and clergymen, who saw the way industrialization had transformed Great Britain and hoped to keep Sweden a simpler, agrarian society with a traditional power structure, opposed the change.

By the 1860s, the Riksdag had provided for the election of provincial and town councils, and finally in 1866, Minister of Justice Louis Gerhard de Geer, a descendant of the man who had brought the Walloon system of forging iron to Sweden, worked out a compromise on the parliamentary system that proved acceptable to all four estates. De Geer's new *Riksdag* consisted of two equal chambers. The councils selected members of the Upper Chamber to serve for nine-year terms. Candidates for the Upper Chamber had to possess a fortune or at least a large income. Members of the Lower Chamber were directly elected for three-year terms by Swedish men, but income and property restrictions limited voter participation to only about 20 percent of the male population. Women could neither vote nor be candidates.

The bourgeoisie considered the structure of the new Riksdag their triumph over the nobles. Johan Gustaf Schwan, speaker of the House of Burghers in 1862, told his chamber that the "bourgeoisie . . . is no longer alone and excluded," because now "the citizens' element, after long and tenacious resistance, has found its way to our benches. This constitutes the bourgeoisie's real triumph."

The two-Chamber Riksdag met for the first time in 1867, but the liberal reformers' joy was short lived. The Upper Chamber became dominated by the wealthy including many nobles and the Lower Chamber by the peasants. Agreement between the two chambers was often difficult, if not impossible. Olof Ehrenkrona, a speechwriter and chief of planning for former Prime Minister Carl Bildt, notes with irony that most of Sweden's liberal economic reforms took place under the old, supposedly backward four-chamber Riksdag when the debates were limited to the nobles and the burghers. In the two-chamber Riksdag, agricultural interests and later industry demanded and got protection from imports. Nevertheless, establishment of the two-chamber Riksdag was progress in the cause of equal representation and set the stage for the granting of voting rights to all Swedes after World War I.

3

The Age of Entrepreneurship I: The Bankers and Their Spheres 1856-1932

IN 1850, ANDRÉ OSCAR (A.O.) Wallenberg, a royal naval officer stationed in Sundsvall, decided to leave the navy and take the oath of a burgher so that he could enter the Riksdag. For a naval officer to reduce himself to the level of a burgher was "shocking" to the Swedish social order, Wallenberg's biographer, Göran B. Nilsson, has written. But, Nilsson noted, "it was also a symbol of the clash between the old and new social ideas." The 1809 Constitution officially had ended the privileges of the nobility, but Wallenberg realized that, as a non-noble, it would be almost impossible to make it to the top of the Swedish Navy. As a non-noble naval officer, he also had no right to vote or to be elected to the old four-estate Riksdag. And Wallenberg, who had traveled widely, knew that industrialization was coming to Sweden, and decided it would be his path to fame and fortune.

A Generation of Ambition

Wallenberg's decision to the leave the military was the first step in establishing a banking and investment dynasty that has become legendary. But Wallenberg could not have succeeded as a banker if it were not for an entire generation of knowledgeable and well-traveled young Swedish engineers, managers and bankers, mostly native-born but including some Jewish and other European immigrants, all of whom who were eager to make their fortunes. In the process, they turned Sweden into a rich, industrial country.

The story might have been different. In the second half of the 19th century, Sweden was like Southern Europe, Latin America, Asia, Africa and the southern and western United States—a wild frontier on the periphery of a world capitalist system based in London, Paris, Hamburg, Amsterdam and New York City. A primitive stock exchange for the trading of shares and bonds was established in Stockholm in the 1860s. It started out meeting once a month, but by 1895 was meeting once a week. Trading volume reached 1.5 billion kronor in 1918, a figure that in fixed prices was not surpassed until the 1980s.

In the early years of Sweden's Age of Entrepreneurship, London-based capitalists, some honest, others unscrupulous, invested in Sweden in much the same way as they did in their colonies and in Latin America, hoping to make fantastic profits. They mingled with ambitious, talented young Swedes of every class and character. Industrial enterprises sprouted like mushrooms, some dying quickly and others, such as Asea, the engineering firm; SKF, the ball bearing company; and Volvo, the car manufacturer becoming the industrial giants for which the country is known today.

Sweden quickly demonstrated that while its agricultural, timber and minerals-based economy was similar to those of Southern European, Latin American and Asian countries, it had strengths the others lacked. Sweden was independent, Northern European and Protestant, with its own scientific tradition, a strong legal system and a bureaucracy with a long history of honesty. Swedes with social standing and education had reason to become involved in business themselves rather than leaving it to foreigners. Swedish ironmasters had experienced tough international competition and had been forced to modernize their small *bruk* into larger enterprises to survive.

While upper-class people in some other countries could live on the rent from their lands, land reforms in Sweden had taken away most of the nobles' financial base, and they had to use their education and language and social skills if they and their children were to maintain their standard of living. As Olof Ehrenkrona, a member of a distinguished old Swedish family and a speechwriter for Prime Minister Carl Bildt in the early 1990s, put it, many nobles "had castles but no money to maintain them." The positions many Swedish nobles held in the civil service and the military provided status and power, but they did not pay very well. A Swedish count whose father headed a major Swedish company in the 1960s said that no one should be "too impressed" by the noble background of Swedish business executives because the motivating factors in their careers were the same as commoners: the desire to make money and the desire to extinguish embarrassing memories of childhood poverty. The son recalled that the most commonly repeated story at the family dinner table when he was growing up was of the day his grandfather, a military officer, got a promotion and invited his family to a Stockholm restaurant for a meal. His grandmother, who handled the family money, took a look at the menu and announced that she did not have enough money in her purse to pay for the meal. The family had to leave the table and walk out of the restaurant. Her son swore that, when he grew up, he and his family would never have to endure such an experience.

Protection from "A Thousand Troubles"

While Swedes accepted 19th century liberal economics by ridding themselves of outdated institutions such as the guilds, passing incorporation laws and signing free trade agreements, they also saw dangers coming from foreign control and acted to protect themselves. The first indication that Swedes were worried about foreign ownership and influence came early in the 19th century, when foreigners expressed heightened interest in exploiting Swedish natural resources. In 1829, the government prohibited citizens of other countries from buying real property in Sweden without permission from the king. A Swedish corporation owned by foreign interests could, however, make the purchase.

The second came in the 1850s, when construction of railroads became an issue. Sweden's slowness in accepting the railroad is one of the most notable aspects of its industrialization. By 1855, when Sweden began constructing major lines connecting Stockholm, Gothenburg and Malmö, Austria, France and Prussia already had long national lines. Historians and sociologists say it was because the Swedes were so used to water transportation that they had a hard time understanding how much rail lines could boost their economy. But behind the final delay in construction was also a national debate over the financing and control of the lines that was similar to debates about foreign investment in many countries today.

In 1845, Count Adolf Eugéne von Rosen, a noble of German Baltic origin who had worked with Baltzar von Platen on construction of Swedish canals and traveled widely, began a campaign to encourage railroad construction in Sweden. Farmers objected to the cost, and canal owners and shipowners to the competition. Critics also noted that Sweden did not have the reserves of coal with which to run the rails. But those criticisms turned out to be minor compared with the reaction to von Rosen's plan for British financing of the rails. No less a figure than J.A. Gripenstedt, who as finance minister in the 1850s and '60s would promote free trade, declared that "a few gentlemen on a street in London could bring about a thousand troubles and difficulties for us." The Riksdag of 1853-54 decided that the state would build the trunk lines, and private enterprise the smaller, connecting ones. Von Rosen's association with the British financiers made him so controversial that King Oskar I chose canal builder Nils Ericson rather than von Rosen to oversee construction.

While Swedes made their fortunes in exporting and endorsed free trade and liberal economics, they were not shy about seeking government protection from foreign competition and influence. After grain from Russia and the United States flooded European markets and depressed grain prices in the 1870s, Swedish farmers demanded and got, in the 1880s, protection from imports. In the 1890s, industrialists also got a measure of tariff protection.

While foreign ownership became dominant in other developing countries, only about 12 percent of Swedish industrial companies were foreign-owned in the 1890s, and only 2 percent of these companies were controlled by foreigners, University of Lund professor of international economics Bo Södersten wrote in *Diverging Paths,* a 1991 book comparing the development of Sweden and Latin America. As the pace of industrialization picked up, the issue of foreign control continued to arise. Banker Wallenberg presented a motion to the Riksdag in 1895 suggesting that to limit foreign ownership, shares be issued only to specific persons, and not anonymously. The Riksdag denied that motion, but the Swedish Companies Act of 1910 gave a corporation the option of regulating foreign ownership by limiting the right of foreign legal entities and certain Swedish legal entities to acquire its shares. The Swedish Companies Act also allowed the founder of a corporation and his or her heirs to prevent shares from being transferred to an outsider without family approval. In 1916, the Riksdag adopted a stronger law, under which foreign citizens and companies could acquire real estate in Sweden only with government permission and a Swedish company could acquire real estate only if it restricted foreign ownership to less than 20 percent of its shares or, if it had shares with different voting rights, less than 20 percent of voting power. The restriction was later changed to 40 percent of shares and 20 percent of voting power. The law remained on the books for more than 50 years. The Riksdag generally approved share purchases if it expected the purchaser to maintain long-lasting economic ties with the company, but did not approve portfolio investments.

The Swedish state took other actions that promoted economic development. In 1873, the Riksbank integrated the country into the world economy by switching from a silver standard to a gold standard. That same year, Sweden, Denmark and Norway (then in union with Sweden) formed a monetary union that remained in effect until the end of World War I. The transition to the gold standard went very smoothly, and the Scandinavian krona (crown) remained at a fixed rate against the other major international currencies until World War I. At the beginning of the 20th century, Sweden was still a net importer of capital for both private and public purposes; the state had also borrowed a lot of money abroad, particularly for the construction of the railroads. During the good economic times just before World War I, however, Sweden was becoming richer and creating its own capital base. When the war brought new wealth and inflation, the Swedish state paid off its foreign bonds cheaply.

The Swedish state also created institutions and transformed others in ways that aided business. New state agencies mapped and surveyed the country geologically, building up an infrastructure of information useful to mining and timber companies. As late as the 1860s, 20 percent of university students entered the Lutheran priesthood (the figure had been 70 percent in 1700), but in the 1870s, science replaced the education of teachers, bureaucrats and priests as the primary purpose of the state universities at Uppsala and Lund. Private technological universities were opened in Stockholm and Gothenburg, and in 1909, the Stockholm School of Economics was created as an advanced private business school. As Stockholm School of Economics professor Magnus Blomström and Chilean analyst Patricio Meller, the editors of *Diverging Paths*, note, this educational modernization was key to making Sweden's economic performance superior to that of the Latin American countries, where the universities continued to emphasize law and literature.

Sweden was never shy about compensating for its size by importing technological ideas from other countries. Sweden's upper classes had always looked toward France and Great Britain for cultural and economic inspiration, but in the 1870s, the country began to edge closer to Germany, which had been unified by Prussian Chancellor Otto von

Bismarck in 1871, and to the United States. King Oskar II, who succeeded to Sweden's throne upon his brother Karl XV's death in 1872 and was worried about instability in Russia and trouble in Sweden's union with Norway, encouraged a pro-German foreign policy. But Germany's reach soon went beyond military relations. Trade between Sweden and Germany grew, Swedish university students began to read German books, and Swedish military officers and officials began to look to their counterparts in the vibrant German government for ideas and direction.

It's well known that during this period, poor Swedes were immigrating to the United States and sending back letters describing conditions in the New World. But there were also many less publicized trips to the United States by Swedish students and business executives eager to learn from the growing technological prowess in the New World. Of the 8,000 graduates of the Chalmers Institute in Gothenburg and the Royal Institute of Technology in Stockholm between 1850 and 1929, 1,100 spent time in the United States studying or working. As Södersten points out, when a Swedish weapons factory received an order from the Swedish government, the owners would often send the manager and the leading engineer to the United States to learn the appropriate skills for production.

Money and Credit

Swedish banking was behind the rest of Europe by the mid 19th century. Private credit establishments called *diskonter* (discount banks) existed in Sweden in the late 18th century, but they failed in the economic chaos after the Napoleonic Wars. Swedish business banking after the 1810s was limited mostly to the merchant banking houses located in Stockholm, Gothenburg, Malmö and a few other cities. Technically only intermediaries for the export of iron and forest products, the mercantile firms began, in the absence of real banking facilities, to assume the banking function. Capital and credit were continual problems for the ironmasters and sawmill owners, who often had their money tied up in heavy equipment and goods that were transported over long distances. The merchants made loans to the ironmasters and sawmill owners as a service and, in return, controlled the sale of the borrowers' goods. The merchant bankers also imported so-called colonial wares—coffee, sugar and tobacco—and sold them in the towns near the ironworks. Through their export-import relationships, the merchant bankers developed Sweden's only private access to foreign credit. The Gothenburg merchants had their strongest relationships with banks in Amsterdam and London; the Stockholm merchants made their connections in Hamburg, the city from which they got most of their imports. Eventually, however, the Stockholm bankers also developed relationships with institutions in London and Amsterdam.

Swedish journalist Kurt Samuelsson has described the Stockholm and Gothenburg merchant houses as "the one main dynamic factor" in the Swedish economy in the 18th and early 19th centuries. The merchant houses often started as modest shops, entered the export-import business and eventually became owners of enterprises. The Tottie family, originally from Lancashire, England, arrived in Sweden from Scotland in 1688 and opened a tobacco workshop in Stockholm. Later, the Totties branched out to making snuff, playing cards, stockings and jerseys, and then moved on to shipping; exporting iron, tar and wood; and financing ironworks. The Totties formed a partnership with the Arwedsons, a family involved in Baltic and North Sea fishing, and by 1800, historian Carl Gustavson has written, Tottie and Arwedson was serving as agent for no fewer than 45 ironworks and was "probably the single most important merchant house in the capital city."

The Emergence of the Jews

Some of the merchant bankers were Jews whose ancestors had moved to Sweden from Germany at the end of the 18th century. Swedes had contact with Jews as far back as the ninth century, when the Vikings traded with the Khazars, a people that lived between the Black and Caspian Seas and practiced Judaism. The first known Jews in Sweden were physicians consulted by Gustaf Vasa in 1557 and Queen Kristina in 1645. Kristina also consulted the Texeira family of bankers who were of Portuguese origin but did business in Hamburg. In the 17th century, some Swedes began to recognize Jews for their skills in medicine, trade and business, but Jews who wanted to stay more than two weeks in Sweden had to convert to Lutheranism. In 1681, four Jewish adults and eight children were baptized in the German church in Stockholm in the presence of King Karl XI. In 1685, a small number of Jews who had settled in Stockholm were ordered to leave the country, and throughout most of the

18th century, hostility to Jews and opposition to their settlement existed in Sweden as it did in the rest of Europe.

Greater freedom of religion was one of the liberal ideas promoted by Gustaf III after his coronation in 1772. In 1774, Aaron Isaac became the first Jew allowed to settle in Sweden and practice his religion. In 1775, a Jewish congregation was established in Stockholm; the same year, the town of Marstrand near Gothenburg was made a free port, where foreigners could practice both free trade and their own religion. Sweden wanted only those Jews who would bring 2,000 riksdaler, however, and to Isaac fell the job of deciding which Jews Sweden would or would not accept.

In 1782, Gustaf III proclaimed a formal Jewish regulation that allowed Jews to settle, but only in Stockholm, Gothenburg, Norrköping and, later, Karlskrona, to engage in trade and manufacturing. After Gustaf III's proclamation, German Jews began moving to Sweden. By the time of the Napoleonic Wars, there were only about 800 Jews in Sweden, but in the economic crisis that followed the wars, Jews became scapegoats for the problems of the times, and the Riksdag restricted their immigration. In 1838, however, the Riksdag abolished most administrative restrictions on Jews' rights and, in 1870, granted them full civil rights.

Members of Sweden's small Jewish community engaged in many aspects of commerce, the export-import business, textile manufacturing and publishing as well as banking. In 1809, for example, Mendel Elias Delbanco, a member of the Leman family, established a branch agency for the Michael Leman merchant house of Hamburg. The Leman Gothenburg agency closed in 1815; but Delbanco later bought part of an oil works in Mölndal, a concern that would long dominate the industry in Sweden. It remained in the family until 1929. The Bonnier brothers—Adolf, Albert and David Felix—a Dresden bookseller's sons who moved from Copenhagen to Sweden between 1820 and 1830, opened bookshops in Gothenberg in 1827 and Stockholm in 1832. In 1837, the family started a publishing house in Stockholm that has become Sweden's largest media empire.

Many of the early Jews' financial ventures carried high risks. Two Jewish families from Germany, the Michaelsons and the Benedicks, started as court jewelers and expanded into banking in Stockholm. Michael Benedicks had connections with international financiers, including the Rothschild banking family, whose money he put at the disposal of the Swedish government. The story of Carl Benedicks, Michael's son, proved just how risky some of these early ventures were. Between 1824 and 1825, using the Benedickses as intermediaries, the Swedish government attempted to sell five old warships to Mexico or to Simon Bolívar, who was then trying to liberate South America from Spain. The Russian czar expressed such opposition to the prospect of aiding the Latin American rebels against Spain that King Karl XIV Johan canceled the deal. Tipped off early that the plan was falling through, Michael sent Carl, age 15, racing across Sweden to release the first two ships before the king's courier could reach them. They had already cleared Hälsingborg harbor when the courier arrived at the Karlskrona naval base. When the ships reached Cartagena in Colombia, the financial intermediaries of Bolívar refused to pay for them, and they sailed to New York City, where they were sold at auction. The adventure had turned into a financial failure for the Benedickses and, because it underlined Sweden's subservience to Russia, a humiliating setback for the country. The Benedicks' financial activities are but a footnote to Swedish history, but the name is still famous in Sweden. Michael Benedicks married a Swedish Lutheran woman, and their great-great-grandson Raoul Wallenberg, who was only one-sixteenth Jewish, would become an international hero for saving the lives of Jews in Hungary during World War II.

The Wallenbergs and the Development of Modern Banking

Historians say that Sweden's network of merchant banks functioned fairly well for the first half of the 19th century, but it did not encourage the accumulation of sufficient capital. Sweden's Riksbank, which dates back to 1668, making it the oldest central bank in Europe, did take some deposits and make loans, but only to the safest of borrowers. The Riksbank's major purpose was to act as an issuer and regulator of currency, and its managers did not have much interest in making it a receiver of household savings. Private banks were legalized in 1824, and eight private joint-stock banks were founded in eight provinces between 1830 and 1855. But they were small, and because the owners had unlimited personal liability for the banks' obligations, their managers were inclined to put deposits into government bonds rather than take risks.

Between 1834 and 1860, as Swedes became wealthy from sales of oats and timber, the number of local savings banks increased from 31 to 146, and their capital from 2.3 million to 29 million kronor. The first mortgage society was founded in 1836, and by 1850, most counties in south and central Sweden had their own. The mortgage societies became sophisticated enough to borrow abroad, and in 1858, out of a total bond liability of 72 million kronor, 52 million was owed to foreigners. But neither the local savings banks nor the mortgage societies provided the kind of commercial banking services that industrial business needed to expand.

The interest in building railroads and starting industrial enterprises made the accumulation of capital an issue throughout Europe in the middle of the 19th century, and several countries established institutions to try to encourage it. The French, establishing a network of limited liability banks, created the Société Générale de Crédit Mobilier to accumulate capital and then channel it into industrial development. It became a model for other countries. Scotland developed another system, which focused more on attracting the middle class as depositors and clients.

As A.O. Wallenberg's biographer Nilsson has documented, the battle over the modernization of Sweden's banking system in the 1850s was a major struggle between ideologies and political personalities. Nilsson has written that the banking issue reflected "the basic conflict between the old and new ways of viewing society. The old view was based on a vertical principle, according to which a hierarchically organized societal pyramid culminated with the monarch, who received his legitimacy from on high, while the new view was based on a horizontal, or individualistic, principle, according to which everyone was king." But, Nilsson continued, a reformist middle way in this conflict was suggested by "association liberals," who believed that "liberty for the individual was not only an end in itself, but was even more significant as a means for achieving the next step in the process of social development . . . solving problems that were too large to be mastered by individuals acting in isolation." These problems, the association liberals argued, could be solved by individuals joining together voluntarily. The association liberals not only struggled against state regulations and privileges that helped the well-born, the bureaucracy and the guilds, but also opposed the nearly unregulated private banks because they were dominated by aristocrats and bureaucrats who were not very interested in making loans to the growing and productive middle class.

The Swedish banking debate in the mid-1800s was further complicated by the fact that both the Riksbank and the private banks could issue banknotes. This peculiar practice had developed because, under the Swedish constitution, the Riksdag had control of the Riksbank, while the "government," consisting of the king and his bureaucracy, had the exclusive right to formulate "economic legislation." Without any direct interest in protecting the note-issuing monopoly of the national bank, the government had allowed the private banks to issue banknotes, which the Swedish people bought to pay bills. In 1846, the king's "government" established for itself the right to license private banks, but in 1848, the Riksdag recommended that private banks be discontinued. On a larger political scale, this disagreement was part of a constitutional conflict that would not be resolved until the early-20th century, when democracy and parliamentarism finally triumphed over the monarchy.

In 1850, A.O. Wallenberg entered the banking scene. The Wallenberg name was already known in Sweden. The first Wallenberg to rise to prominence was a Jacob Wallenberg, who went out as a chaplain on the Swedish East India Company ship, the *Finland,* in the 18th century and wrote a widely read account of his journey. A.O. Wallenberg, born in 1816, was the grandson of the chaplain's brother and the son of a bishop in Linköping. Historian Carl Gustavson has described Wallenberg as a mediocre gymnasium student who passed the naval officer's exam, went off to sea and, among other assignments, captained the propeller-driven *Linköping* on the Göta Canal. Gustavson has suggested that Wallenberg "may have discovered his true vocation while [he was] a sailor on American ships in New York and Boston, where he was fascinated by the bank crash of 1837."

Back in Sweden, Wallenberg began writing in newspapers and got involved in politics. France's February Revolution of 1848 scared even the most conservative Swedes into accepting political and economic changes that might allow the old institutions and themselves to survive, and Wallenberg became an advocate of modernization. His naval superiors were distressed by his outside activities, however, and in 1850, when he was 34 years old, they transferred him to Sundsvall, some 400 kilometers north of Stockholm. Wallenberg took the oath of a burgher in Sundsvall and resigned his commission as a first lieutenant the next spring. Returning to Stockholm, he joined the merchant firm of Lovén & Co., where he became a partner and treasurer and functioned as a private banker and broker. Wallenberg gained excellent experience at Lovén, but when he tried to interest the company in doing business in his home province of Östergötland, the internationally minded management declined. In 1851, Wallenberg got a second opportunity to push his ideas when he was elected to a private committee of wholesalers set up to study the question of establishing a commercial bank in Stockholm. According to Nilsson, the committee was formed because there was no private bank in Stockholm and businessmen were not satisfied with the limited banking services offered by the Riksbank.

In 1851, in an attempt to serve the middle class, the Riksdag created a system of private banks that did not have the right to issue banknotes, but had the advantage of subsidized credits in the Riksbank. They were called branch banks, a term that is not technically correct, because their ownership was independent of the Riksbank. Wallenberg managed to gather together the investors to open one of these branch banks, Stockholms Filialbank, in January 1852. That April, however, the government put an obstacle in the way by unilaterally reorganizing the branch banking system. Never one to stand idly by, Wallenberg, the same year, explored the possibility of establishing a limited-partnership bank with English capital, but that idea didn't go anywhere. Meanwhile, another group, which included Johan Holm, a Stockholm broker, and Pontus Kleman, a Swedish partner in the London firm of Hoare, Buxton & Co. who was well connected in both London and Hamburg, proposed establishing Svenska Handelsaktiebanken, a limited-liability bank that was to operate on capital obtained by selling shares, many of them to foreigners. Wallenberg criticized Svenska Handelsaktiebanken as unsound, and mobilized public opinion against it. He had also gotten elected to the Estate of the Burghers, and in the Riksdag of 1853-54, told the banking committee and members of the general body that they had to choose between the two banking systems quickly so that banks could expand. "Banks will be of little use until there are banks in everyone's neighborhood and until they are, like bakery shops, accessible for everybody," Wallenberg said.

The Riksdag, then still composed of four estates that often found it difficult to sort out complicated issues, didn't make a choice between the two banking systems and decided to respond to the threat of private banking projects in Stockholm by transforming the Riksbank into a commercial bank and appropriating a small amount of money for the establishment of new branch banks. Wallenberg won one of the appropriations and in the spring of 1855 returned to Sundsvall. He opened Sundsvall Filialbank in August of that same year. Wallenberg said his bank would be "like the old ones only in name," and he soon proved the point. Like the Scottish commercial banks, his bank sought out customers by offering a variety of deposit options. He also pioneered payments between different localities by reaching agreements with other banks to use bank money orders to pay off obligations. While Wallenberg introduced truly positive innovations, "this pretty picture," as Nilsson put it, "had its dark side" because the banker took the subsidies granted by the Riksbank for the bank's operations and bought obligation bonds from mortgage societies in southern Sweden. This produced quick profits, but in 1856, when the situation in the money markets deteriorated, Wallenberg had to resort to chancy discounting procedures to keep the bank afloat.

By 1856, both the Handelsaktiebanken crowd and Wallenberg were again trying to get government approval for competing bank projects. Holm and Kleman even tried to convince Wallenberg to get aboard Handelsaktiebanken, but he declined and instead organized another campaign of opposition against the project. Holm and Kleman had built a broader base of political support on their second attempt to establish their bank and had even gotten the approval of King Oskar I. But fate intervened on Wallenberg's behalf. Oskar I had planned to appoint one of the Handelsaktiebanken petitioners, Johan Gustaf Schwan, a prominent Stockholm businessman, to replace his minister of finance. But the State Council, which was dominated by noblemen, opposed Holm and Kleman's project and, because Schwan was associated with it, his appointment. Instead, Oskar I elevated Gripenstedt, the State Council's most liberal member, to finance minister. Gripenstedt told the king he would take the job only if the Handelsaktiebanken application would be set aside until the Riksdag could be consulted. Wallenberg abandoned his position that the government should not grant the right to issue notes to new private banks, and on July 1, 1856, his Stockholms Enskilda Bank (SEB) was granted a concession as a note-issuing private bank, but without the option to reorganize itself as a branch bank.

Wallenberg's memos from 1851-52 show that he already had in mind some of the innovations that made his bank a success. Although he had to charge higher interest than the state-owned Riksbank, he was able to compete for customers because the state bank had limited resources and lots of bureaucratic procedures. While he could not compete with private banks that paid 6 percent interest on deposits, he was able to convince public credit societies and charities to bank with him because he, unlike the Riksbank, paid interest. But his most important source of capital turned out to be the service his bank performed as a central clearinghouse for provincial banks. Swedish banking law required provincial banks to back a certain percentage of their notes with notes from the Riksbank and to exchange them for the notes of the Riksbank, which were legal tender, upon demand. The provincial banks employed a number of private bankers and brokers to handle this exchange of notes. The provincial banks earned nothing on these sums during the transaction period, and Wallenberg offered to place the provincial banks' money in interest-bearing accounts in his bank, which would act as a clearinghouse. Wallenberg also opened mutual bank money operations with the provincial banks. The Wallenberg bank got interest-free use of the money for the days until the individual would cash the money order. Each transaction was insignificant, but the volume proved enormous. Wallenberg also offered customers higher rates of interest for time deposits. It was the first time such accounts had been offered in Sweden since the 18th century, and they attracted another segment of middle-class depositors: maidens, widows, orphans and others worried about their money's safety. He also introduced the systematization of credit ratings for would-be borrowers. As required by his charter, Wallenberg gave the public the impression that Stockholms Enskilda Bank was a local institution, but Nilsson reported that he "began contacting provincial banks even before the opening" to offer them large credits.

Wallenberg had founded the bank in the midst of the Crimean War, a period of great prosperity in Sweden because Russian exports to Europe were cut off and Swedish grain prices were high. When the war ended, a liquidity crisis arose, and financial institutions such as Ullberg & Cramer in Hamburg, which was involved in the grain trade, and Hoare, Buxton & Co. and others in London, which had financed the transoceanic shipment of colonial wares such as tobacco and sugar to Sweden, found themselves overextended and stopped extending short-term credits to Swedish firms. The larger Swedish firms were able to handle the crisis, but more than 40 medium-sized ones were caught in risky financing. No fewer than 26 Stockholm firms collapsed, and more would have if Gripenstedt, the finance minister, had not secured Riksdag approval for a state loan of 12 million riksdaler, which he obtained from banks in Hamburg and Frankfurt. Meanwhile, people were stampeding to cash in the bank notes of the Skånska Enskilda Bank in the province of Skåne. Worried that the run on the Skåne bank would endanger his own institution, Wallenberg told Gripenstedt that the Riksbank itself might be in danger and procured a large loan on his own reputation and passed it on to the bank in Skåne, which survived the crisis.

Business historians now note that Wallenberg's bank did not initially possess limited liability and say that Wallenberg's greatest advantage in the early days was not his innovations, but his location in Stockholm, which allowed him to assemble a huge number of deposits and then extend credit to large enterprises such as railroads. Wallenberg also extended credit to the Norrland sawmill owners, who were then in the process of a massive expansion. The sawmill owners and some of his other clients became overextended, and Wallenberg had to intervene beyond his original intentions—and thus began the practice of both owning shares in companies and handling their banking needs.

From the time of the Stockholms Enskilda Bank's establishment in 1856, Wallenberg was its managing director and tried to dominate it by the force of his personality, but he was only one of 72 shareholders in the early years and held only 50 of the 1,000 shares. In 1871, however, when a dissident faction of shareholders broke away, he gained full control. (The dissident stockholders founded Stockholms Handelsbank [Svenska Handelsbanken after 1919], which wits, playing on *enskilda*, the Swedish word for "private," called the *frånskilda*, the "seceded bank." Handelsbanken became Sweden's second-largest bank, but to this day, its managers have to endure wags who call the Wallenberg bank "the bank" and Handelsbanken "the other bank.")

Bankers are rarely popular with the public, but whenever anything went wrong in Sweden from the 1860s to the 1880s, Wallenberg usually got the blame. He became known as an ogre, a symbol of unwanted change in the rapidly industrializing Sweden of the day. Wallenberg and newspaper editors were often on the same side in the promotion of liberal economic policies that led to the establishment of his banks, but as he rose in power, some of those papers became critical of him. A journalist named Carl Fredrik Lindahl, who wrote the Swedish newspaper column *Rikt Folk* ("Rich People") under the pen name Lazarus, said that on first meeting Wallenberg, a visitor was impressed with his good-naturedness and joviality, but if Wallenberg was crossed, "his mouth would tighten and his eyes turn mean." Lazarus wrote that Wallenberg lacked any sense of benevolence or nobility of character and that the "temple of Mammon on Lilla Nygatan was a gold mine for its owners, but a terror" for its borrowers, from whom the last *öre* was extracted.

Stung by the comments, Wallenberg tried repeatedly to gain control over a newspaper. He bought enough of Schwan's stock in *Aftonbladet* (Lars Johan Hierta's old paper) to control it, but the editor rebelled and secured sufficient help from Alfred William Dufwa, a banker who detested Wallenberg, to counter his moves. *Dagens Nyheter*, a Stockholm daily, ignored overtures, but Wallenberg finally managed to make another paper, *Nya Dagligt Allehanda,* his mouthpiece. Its editor had earlier written that Wallenberg's sole goal was to loan money for the shortest possible time at the highest possible interest, and he had an editorial tantrum when the banker received the rank of commander in the highly honorary Vasa Order from the king. It's said that Wallenberg later rescued the same editor from financial embarrassment while simultaneously taking over the paper. Wallenberg and Sven Hedlund, the editor of *Göteborgs Handels-och Sjöfarstidning,* carried on a long, memorable and mutually entertaining feud, the origin of which was supposedly not a business matter but the fact that in 1847, when Wallenberg was captain of the *Linköping*, he had officiously demanded that Hedlund, a student at the time, stop drinking on board ship.

Journalists were perhaps the least of Wallenberg's enemies. The Riksbank feared competition from the SEB, and when Dufwa headed the Riksbank from 1870-83, he used the power of the central bank to make life as difficult as possible for his rival. Lazarus commented that Dufwa (which means "dove") was no dove as far as Wallenberg was concerned. Wallenberg's worst public relations mistake may have been loaning money in 1862 to Hofors, a *bruk* midway between Gävle and Falun. Owned by the Petré family since 1680, Hofors in the mid-19th century ranked third in total iron production, after Uddeholm and Stora. Hofors was run for many years by Thore Petré, a skilled ironmaster who was also a radical liberal leader in the Riksdag. Thore's sons, Hjalmar and Casimir, took over when he died in 1853. They didn't have their father's business sense, however, and when Wallenberg lent them money, the loans went bad. In 1880, the Petrés were forced into bankruptcy and Hjalmar's wife and a sister of the brothers died within days of each other. Wallenberg became the scapegoat in the melodrama, with Lazarus writing about the "Wallenberg plundering of the colossal Petré properties." Wallenberg had his comforts, however. It was said that every day after breakfast, he would unlock a little casket, remove from it a teacup and saucer brought from China by his ancestor Jacob, sip a cup of tea, carefully wash the heirloom and replace it in the casket.

A.O. Wallenberg died in 1886, leaving behind a banking and industrial empire and a family dynasty. He was married twice, to Wilhelmina Andersson (1826-55), with whom he had two sons, and to Anna von Sydow (1838-1910), with whom he had five sons and six daughters. Two sons—Knut Agathon (K.A.), born in 1853 during his first marriage, and Marcus, born in 1864 during his second—succeeded him as the two most important bankers and business leaders in Sweden in the early 20th century. Torsten Gårdlund, a biographer of Marcus Wallenberg Sr. wrote that A.O. Wallenberg had a "program" for the education of his children, which included boarding school for both boys and girls. For the boys that meant a stint at an internationally oriented board school in Korntal outside Stuggart, Germany, to make sure that they understood foreign languages and cultures. He also sent his sons to the Royal Swedish Naval College, where the training included time at sea.

K.A. Wallenberg became a director of the bank in 1897 and was named chairman in 1911. Marcus Wallenberg Sr. was a deputy circuit court judge, president of the bank and chairman of a number of major industrial companies, including Atlas, Diesels Motorer, Hofors and Papyrus and chairman of the bank from K.A.'s death in 1938 until his own death in 1943. Knut and Marcus, who were said to distrust each other because they had different mothers, operated from a two-person desk at the bank's Stockholm headquarters. Both K.A. and Marcus Sr. took a great interest in international financial and diplomatic affairs. At K.A.'s initiative, "sister" banks—the British Bank of Northern Commerce and the Banque des Pays du Nord—were founded in Great Britain and France, respectively, with Scandinavian backing. From 1914-17, during World War I, K.A. Wallenberg was on "sabbatical" from the bank to serve as Sweden's foreign minister. In 1916-17, when Great Britain was blocking neutral Sweden's trade with the allies, Marcus Wallenberg Sr. headed a trade delegation to London, where, historian Franklin Scott has said, the allies granted Sweden trading terms more favorable than those for any other neutral country.

Wallenberg's Competition

Despite A.O. Wallenberg's extraordinary role in the development of Swedish banking, historians say that he must share the title of founder of modern Swedish banking with Theodor Mannheimer, a Danish Jew who was one of the founders in 1864 of the Gothenberg-based Skandinaviska Kreditaktiebolag, later known as Skandinaviska Banken. Skandinaviska was organized by a group of the most famous men in Swedish business at the time: Oscar Ekman, Oscar Dickson, Carl Benedicks and, briefly, A.O. Wallenberg. With the help of Carl Frederick Tietgen, a leading Danish banker, the group hoped to attract capital from the rest of Scandinavia and from Europe, but found that investors from other countries were not interested. The bank opened a branch in Stockholm in 1865 under the direction of Henrik Davidson and in Norrköping in 1868 under the direction of John Philipsons. Mannheimer, Davidson, Philipsons and Eduard Heckscher, another banker and the father of the economic historian Eli Heckscher, were all Jews. Mannheimer died in 1900, but under the leadership of Oscar Rydbeck, Skandinaviska Banken was considered the "most innovative and expansive bank during the 1920s," Stockholm School of Economics professor Ulf Olsson has written.

Stockholms Handelsbank, which had been formed by Wallenberg's dissident stockholders in 1871, came under the leadership of Louis Fränkel, a German-born Jew, in 1893, just as the Swedish economy was taking off. Fränkel, who had moved to Stockholm and made a success as a private banker before he became managing director of Stockholms Handelsbank, proved to be the man to grasp the opportunity. Fränkel's German background may have played a role in his banking style, because even after Swedish law forbade banks from owning shares in companies to which they provided financing, he emulated as much as legally possible the German banks, which were allowed to become involved in industrial operations. Already well acquainted with the Jewish financier Max Warburg, the managing partner of M.M. Warburg & Co. of Hamburg, and Sir Ernest Cassel, a London-based banker with interests in Sweden, Fränkel provided a high level of both financial and industrial advice to a small group of industrialists, who became known as the "Fränkelian circle." With his connections on the continent, Fränkel also played an active role in finding purchasers abroad for Swedish government and railway bonds. Bonds were a field in which Fränkel and the Wallenbergs sometimes overcame their natural competitiveness and cooperated.

"Gifted with a natural flair for business and an ever-ready receptiveness to new knowledge, topped off by a capacity for lightning-like decisions, Fränkel was able to pick and choose among his connections," Uppsala University economic history professor Karl-Gustaf Hildebrand has written.

Because Stockholms Handelsbank depended more on its own capital than on deposits to make loans, Fränkel had more freedom to take risks than some other bankers, and his bank became known for its willingness to make big loans to a relatively small number of customers. Fränkel also arranged mergers for clients such as Svenska Metallverken, a copper manufacturer, and helped L.M. Ericsson in its expansion into France, Austria and Hungary, but he was less involved in the growing engineering industry.

When Fränkel died of a heart attack in Germany in 1911, obituary writers noted that during his 18 years at the head of Stockholms Handelsbank, assets grew from 22 million to 150 million kronor. Historians say that the distinct role that Jews played in Swedish banking ended with Fränkel's death. The Jews remained in Sweden, but they assimilated so completely and intermarried so frequently that they became almost better known for intellectual and political roles than for business and banking. Magdalena Ribbing, a writer who is descended from several distinguished Christian and Jewish families, said in an interview that Swedes of partial Jewish ancestry ignored their roots for many years, but have begun to take pride in the role their ancestors played in their heritage.

The Spheres

To this day, foreigners find the most puzzling aspect of Swedish business life to be the close relationship between Swedish companies and their banks. Swedish law today separates the ownership of banks and the industrial companies that are their clients, but the Wallenbergs speak freely of their "sphere," which means their bank and the industrial corporations that they control through their investment companies, through their charitable foundations (which own stock whose voting rights they exercise), and through the stock that members of the family own personally.

There are two historical reasons for the close links between Swedish banks and businesses. Sweden was a country with a small population, a small capital base and a small group of bankers and capitalists when industrialization began, and it was almost impossible for the business relations of the bankers and the industrialists not to cross lines that are considered a conflict of interest today. Swedish banks first went beyond making commercial loans to companies by underwriting industrial bonds in the mid-19th century. Because the insurance industry, a major purchaser of bonds, was still small in Sweden, the banks often had to keep the bonds unsold. Equally important, the British and the Germans developed different banking practices. The Germans gave the commercial banks the authority to sell shares, while the British insisted that commercial banks be solely depository institutions and established separate merchant banks to specialize in share transactions and investments. In the late 19th century, when Swedish officials were writing banking laws, they were torn between the German and British types of regulation.

An 1886 law prohibited Swedish banks organized as joint-stock companies from trading or acquiring shares. Bankers found a way around the law, however, by allowing new companies to use their shares as loans for collateral. The banks also made loans to syndicates and consortia that bought shares. In 1899, the Wallenbergs founded AB Providentia as a holding company to administer their family's properties and to engage in the share trading in which the bank could not be legally involved.

In 1907, Handelsbanken's Fränkel formed a separate holding company, Svenska Emissionsaktiebolaget. It was supposed to handle industrial deals outside the bank's sphere, but the shareholders were, of course, members of his circle. "To a great extent," Hildebrand has written, Fränkel "acted by sovereign right, wielding a personal authority to which the board of the bank deferred without cavil. Borrowers who found favor would at times be accommodated with something approaching insouciance when it came to the formalities. Business secrets were shrouded in a pall of mystery that was often impenetrable both to high officials of the bank and to the governmental Bank Inspection Board, and the world at large was treated all along with a blend of patriarchal benevolence and autocratic choler."

In 1914, the Wallenbergs' Stockholms Enskilda Bank and Skandinaviska Banken established AB Emissionsinstitutet as an investment company. In 1915, Sveriges Privata Centralbank, a smaller institution, set up Centralgruppens Emissions AB, and when the Centralbank merged with Skandinaviska Banken in 1917, Centralgruppens Emissions AB became the largest investment company in Sweden.

In the freewheeling economy of the early 20th century, Swedish government officials were again under simultaneous pressures to assure the safety of depositors' money and to establish conditions so that Swedish companies could gain more access to venture capital. Swedish banks formed subsidiaries to buy and sell securities and real estate. Some of the new companies had very little equity, and their operations were funded by money borrowed from their parent companies.

The Swedish Bank Inspection Board, which was created in 1907, became worried that the commercial banks were jeopardizing the savings of ordinary people and proposed legislation limiting the ability of banks to own stock in companies to which they lent money. If a company in which a bank held an investment was failing, bank examiners asked, who would decide when to stop granting it loans? The situation, the examiners said, posed a conflict of interest and danger for investors in both the banks and the companies.

In 1911, a new law gave medium and large banks limited rights to purchase shares. In 1916, the Wallenbergs liquidated Providentia and transferred some of its stocks and those of the bank and Emissionsinstitutet into a new firm, AB Investor. The big difference between Investor and the Wallenbergs' previous holding companies was that while the Wallenbergs set up Investor to manage their long-term ownership interests in Swedish businesses, outside investors were allowed to buy shares in Investor, which was traded on the Stockholm Stock Exchange. The Wallenbergs still maintained control of the firm and the companies through a system of weighted voting shares that has come to be a hallmark of the Swedish economic system.

With the passing of the Fränkel era at Handelsbanken and the Mannheimer era at Skandinaviska, those institutions ceased to be identified with any single family or personality. But the Wallenbergs continued to control the Stockholms Enskilda Bank and the investment companies associated with it. In the 1920s, the Wallenbergs emerged as Sweden's most important banking and industrial family, even though Ivar Kreuger, the investor, industrialist and speculator who founded the Swedish Match Co., garnered more publicity at the time.

After the establishment of AB Investor in 1916, the Wallenbergs slowly modernized their portfolio. In 1917, a year after Investor was established, its holdings included the Göta Canal Co. and Halmstad-Nässjö Järnväg, a railroad company, both of which went back to A.O. Wallenberg's era, but the largest holding was SKF, valued at 18.6 million kronor. Other holdings included Atlas Diesel; Ostasiatiska Kompaniet, a shipping company; Papyrus, a paper company; the Stockholm-Saltsjöbad railway; Kopparberg-Hofors; Stora Kopparbergs Bersglag; AB Separator; and Scania-Vabis.

By 1924, the Wallenbergs and their investment companies, and the K.A. Wallenberg Foundation already controlled 26 percent of the voting rights in Atlas Diesel; 100 percent of Scania-Vabis; 50 percent of Astra; 14 percent of SKF; 3 percent of Stora Kopparbergs Bergslag; and

37 percent of Papyrus. The sphere also held stock in other transportation, trade, chemicals, forestry, banking and insurance companies.

The Wallenbergs had also been involved in the early development of Asea and sold their holdings at profit in 1926. But toward the end of the 1920s, they began buying shares again because Marcus Wallenberg Jr. had decided to go into business with Asea to form Elektro-Invest, a power holding company that bought electric generating utilities in other countries.

The Wallenbergs' outside investors were not always pleased with AB Investor's performance or their treatment. Investor's board of directors, controlled by the Wallenbergs, accepted the outsiders' money, but provided the outsiders with only that information stipulated by law. During Sweden's troubled economy of the 1920s, Investor did not pay a dividend for six years and its price dropped dramatically. Outside stockholders became so distressed about not being able to find out what was going on inside the firm that one told the board in 1927: "When Investor was established, the company was received with open arms, almost with divine adoration. Unfortunately, it has become something of a problem child, though one that's still very much loved, and that is why the stockholders are asking about the poor child's condition, whether it is helplessly lost or if it has prospects of recovering in the future and again becoming a child of joy." That round of criticism stopped in 1928 when the Swedish economy improved and Investor again paid a dividend.

During the late '20s and the '30s, the Wallenbergs also went in and out of foreign investments. In 1928, a Swedish tax law exempted corporations and cooperative associations from paying income tax on dividends received from Swedish companies. The change did not apply to banks, but it did apply to companies whose primary business was portfolio management. There was a new securities exchange in Luxembourg, and the Wallenbergs established Instor SA to manage Investor's and Plenum's portfolios. By giving Instor a "flexible" portfolio and leaving the long-term ownership interests in Investor's hands, the Wallenbergs ensured that Investor could retain its tax status.

In the '20s, the Wallenbergs were often in direct competition with Kreuger for investments and prominence. At one point, Skandinaviska controlled 17 percent of the voting rights in SKF (much to the annoyance of the Wallenbergs who controlled 9 percent and were not granted a seat on the SKF board). After a battle between 1927 and 1929 for shares in Stora, their stakes were roughly equal: in 1929, Kreuger owned 39,000 shares in Stora and the Wallenbergs 36,500. Marcus Wallenberg Sr. and Kreuger met on two occasions, and at one meeting, Marcus Sr. stated of Stora and two other companies: "I regard them as my children, and I would be reluctant to see them in another's hands."

Later, Marcus Sr. wrote Marcus Jr. that "I came away with the feeling that Kreuger is a peculiar fellow."

4

The Age of Entrepreneurship II: Great Corporations and Founders 1864-1932

THE WALLENBERGS, Louis Fränkel and Theodor Mannheimer and a handful of other capitalists, railroad builders and engineers come up so frequently in accounts of the formation of the major Swedish enterprises at the turn of the century that the story of Swedish business often seems like the tale of a very small cast of characters who owned everything and formed interlocking directorates. In reality, however, the bankers, railroad magnates and other capitalists were only creating the infrastructure to be used by the inventors and entrepreneurs to form the great corporations. The story behind each of these great Swedish companies is a saga in itself.

Nobel - Nitroglycerine AB, 1864
Bofors, 1894

The first of the Swedish inventions to achieve international significance was dynamite, which Alfred Nobel succeeded in making in 1864 by combining nitroglycerine with kieselguhr. The explosive material, which would be used both in war and for peaceful projects, such as building bridges, became the center of a business empire with production plants in Sweden, Germany, Scotland and other countries.

Alfred Nobel came from a family that was distinguished by its intellectual heritage and financial troubles. The family's founder, Petrus Olai, who was born about 1660, adapted the name Nobelius from the name of his parish in southern Sweden when he was a student at Uppsala University. Petrus Olai was of modest origins, but his musical talent brought him into the circle of Olof Rudbeck, the rector of Uppsala University and the leading Swedish intellectual of the time. In 1696, Petrus Olai married Olof Rudbeck's daughter Wendela. Of Petrus Olai and Wendela's eight children, only two sons survived, the younger of whom, Olof Pärsson Nobelius, was Alfred Nobel's great-grandfather. Olof, an artist whose scientific drawings were praised by Linneaus, never made much money. He and his wife, Anna Wallings, had seven children. Their youngest son, Immanuel, born in 1757, shortened the family name to Nobel in 1785. Immanuel Nobel never received a university degree, but practiced as a barber surgeon in Gävle and is said to have played a role in the introduction of vaccinations in Sweden.

In 1801, Immanuel's second wife, Brita, gave birth to a boy who was also named Immanuel and who was destined to become Alfred Nobel's father. Young Immanuel became a shipbuilding apprentice in Gävle and went into business for himself, but was forced into bankruptcy by a fire. Legend has it that two of his sons, Robert and Ludvig, sold matches on the Stockholm streets to help the family eke out a living before Immanuel moved to Finland and then to St. Petersburg. In Russia, he experimented with land and sea mines and, in 1842, started Nobel & Sons, an armaments factory. Aware of the ups and downs of the business world, Immanuel Nobel gave his sons the best education possible in Russia, and in 1849, he sent his third son, Alfred, to the United States to meet John Ericsson, the Swedish inventor. Nobel & Sons secured Russian government orders during the Crimean War (1853-56), but after the conflict was over, the orders stopped. Alfred, then 25, was sent to Paris and London to try to borrow money from their bankers, but he was turned down, and in 1859, the Nobels lost their factory and Immanuel returned to Sweden. Alfred and his brother Ludvig remained in St. Petersburg and went to two of their former teachers searching for new business ideas. One professor, Nikolaj Zinin, reminded them that a former pupil of his in Paris—Ascanio Sobrero—had combined nitric acid and sulfuric acid into an explosive called nitroglycerine, but had found it so unstable he could think of no practical use for it. As biographer Kenne Fant has written, Alfred Nobel became fascinated with nitroglycerine and how to "liberate its awesome power." One day, he tried mixing nitroglycerine with gunpowder and lighting the mixture with a fuse, and it exploded. He returned to Sweden and showed the experiment to Swedish defense officials. In 1861, after the Swedes declared the substance too combustible to use in battle, Alfred went again to Paris, where the Société Générale de Crédit Mobilier, which specialized in financing railroad construction, gave him a loan to develop a cheap explosive device. In 1862, he managed to detonate it under water in St. Petersburg and to continue his experiments. In November 1863, he succeeded in detonating nitroglycerine from a distance by placing it in porous coal and, in turn, placing the coal inside an iron pipe. The pipe was blown to bits, but no one was injured. He applied for a Swedish patent on January 10, 1864, on his new explosive, which he called "dynamite," but was too preoccupied with family and business affairs for the next two years to develop the experiment further.

Later in 1864, an explosion in a shed on the Nobels' Stockholm property killed several people, including Immanuel's fourth son, 20-year-old Emil Oskar. These sad events destroyed Immanuel's health, but Alfred continued his experiments. In late 1864, a representative of the state railroads declared that Nobel's explosive oil would be used in the construction of a tunnel connecting the northern and southern railway lines. After Nobel received this sanction for his work, he convinced J.W. Smitt, a Swede who had a made a fortune in South America, to form Nitroglycerine Aktiebolaget, a company to make dynamite, based in Stockholm. The original charter called for Alfred Nobel to be paid a fixed sum for transferring his nitroglycerine patent to the company; but apparently this plan was abandoned, because Nobel went on to become a director of Nitroglycerine and to found other companies throughout the world for manufacturing the explosive material. The company's first problem was that the Stockholm police prohibited the manufacture of nitroglycerine within a residential area; Nobel solved the problem by locating his factory on a covered barge that he bought and anchored in Bockholm Bay. In 1865, after Alfred invited Prince Oskar to a demonstration of nitroglycerine, the company received permission to build a factory on land at Winter Bay outside Stockholm.

Alfred's brothers, Ludvig and Robert, meanwhile, had returned to Russia, where they became major business figures. Ludvig started an engineering firm in St. Petersburg, where he manufactured rifles. Robert married a Finnish businessman's daughter who disliked living in St. Petersburg. They moved to Helsinki, where he started a petroleum business and set up a factory in 1865 to make nitroglycerine under Alfred's patent. But the czar of Russia, who feared that dynamite might be used in an assassination attempt against him, decided to prohibit the manufacture of explosives in the Grand Duchy of Finland as well as in Russia itself. In 1866, Robert came home to manage the Swedish factory.

Alfred was determined to make the detonating nitroglycerine safe, practical and useful. In 1866, he traveled to the United States to defend his invention against charges that nitroglycerine was dangerous and should be banned and to seek U.S. patents. Nobel spent four months giving lectures and meeting with reporters, but he could not stop the U.S. Congress from passing an anti-nitroglycerine law. On August 14, 1866, however, just after he had returned to Europe, the U.S. Patent Office granted him a patent on blasting oil. Realizing that nitroglycerine could explode too easily to win wide acceptance, he turned to the commercialization of dynamite, which could travel safely, and in 1868 got a U.S. patent on it.

Between 1866 and 1872, Alfred Nobel traveled constantly, opening factories around the world. He also continued his experiments, inventing blasting gelatin in 1875 and Ballistite (smokeless gunpowder) in 1884. He obtained 85 patents in all. He was often called "the richest vagabond in Europe." Family members said his only real homes were his laboratories in Paris, where he settled in 1873, and in San Remo, Italy. Alfred Nobel's health was delicate, he never married and he complained bitterly that some of his business partners were dishonest.

Robert Nobel, meanwhile had not proved to be a good manager of the Swedish factory and, in 1870, returned to St. Petersburg to become a partner in Ludvig's mechanical business. Ludvig also went into rifle manufacturing and sent Robert to the Caucasus to look for walnut wood for export. When he arrived there, Robert saw local people taking "Baku sludge" out of the ground and spent the money he had buying plots of oil-bearing land. By 1875, Robert was running the most important oil refinery in Russia. Ludvig then took charge of the enterprise, competing with John D. Rockefeller, the Rothschilds and Royal Dutch Shell for international supremacy in the oil business and becoming known as the "Oil King of Baku." When Ludvig died in Cannes in 1888, a French journalist mistakenly wrote an obituary of Alfred, calling him a "merchant of death." Already suffering from depression, Alfred Nobel was supposedly so upset by the denunciation that he determined his work and his wealth should amount to something more than a reputation as an armaments maker.

That determination did not, however, keep Alfred Nobel from buying, in 1893, a controlling interest in Bofors-Gullspång, a Värmland armaments factory, which in the 1880s had replaced the venerable de Geer family's Finspång Bruk as the great armament works of Sweden. The rise of Bofors had its roots in the decline of Finspång, the armaments factory the de Geers had bought from the crown in 1640 and presided over for more than 200 years. By the mid-1800s, they were primarily interested in political and cultural affairs and were neglecting the factory. In 1848, the family appointed Carl Edvard Ekman, 22, as Finspång's administrator, and eight years later, he bought the company.

Ekman set up a modern sawmill and acquired other ironworks, but Finspång's inability to keep up with the improved speed and strength of foreign competitors' cannon first became obvious at the 1867 Paris Exhibition. In 1876, the German Krupp firm, which had its own secret process for making cannon, defeated the Swedes in test trials, and in an 1878 test, the Swedish cannon burned out and its projectiles exploded in flight. By the next year, Finspång exports had declined dramatically and even the Swedish army began ordering Krupp artillery.

Bofors, a southeastern Värmland *bruk* started in 1846, had reorganized as AB Bofors-Gullspång in 1873. In 1883, after reports that Bofors had managed to produce steel whose quality matched Krupp's, the army asked Bofors if it could deliver to Finspång the castings for 44 artillery pieces. Bofors responded that it would deliver the *completed* artillery. Despite protests from Ekman, Bofors duly delivered its first order. It was on its way to becoming Sweden's premier major-armaments producer. (For 17 years, beginning in 1885, Bofors was under the technical direction of Baron Arent Silfversparre, who was mortally wounded in 1902 while watching the testing of cannon that was not made at Bofors and that he had advised against using. Swedish historians say he is one of the few Swedes in modern times to die for his country and therefore be certifiably entitled to enter Valhalla (the Swedish heaven in pagan times).

When news reached Sweden in the early 1890s that Nobel was looking for a company, Ekman hoped to see him and solve Finspång's financial predicament. Nobel decided that Bofors was a better place than his laboratory at San Remo for manufacturing cannon and conducting experiments on a large scale. At Bofors, Nobel and his associates experimented with new forms of gunpowder, blasting charges and mapping through photography by means of a camera shot up by a rocket and supported by a parachute.

In 1890, after a dispute with the French government, Nobel had retreated to San Remo, but in the autumn of 1895, perhaps anticipating his death, Nobel spent two months at his home in Paris rewriting his will. In the 1895 rewrite, Nobel dramatically reduced the size of bequests to 23 individuals so that he could leave the bulk of his estate to create a fund for the distribution of prizes "to those who, during the preceding year, shall have conferred the greatest benefit on mankind" in the fields of physics, chemistry, medicine, literature and peace. Nobel told no one the contents of the will, copies of which he placed in his home in San Remo and in the Wallenberg bank in Stockholm. His executor, Ragnar Sohlman, would later write that Nobel's "realization that his indefatigable work had at last found a goal" allowed him to overcome depression in the last years of his life even though he suffered from physical health problems.

Nobel died on December 10, 1896, in San Remo at the age of 63, and when the will was read, his nieces and nephews, the business world and the Swedish establishment were all shocked. Managers of Bofors, the Nobel Dynamite Trust Co. and the Nobel Brothers Naptha Co., in which Alfred Nobel's holdings had a decisive influence, were worried that their operations would be destabilized or disrupted. His brother Robert's widow and his nieces and nephews believed that they should have inherited all the shares in the family business.

The family eventually sued, but settled mostly for the right to buy the shares in various businesses at full price. Bofors went on to become one of Sweden's premier armaments firms in the 20th century. Ekman sold Finspång to W. Beardmore of Glasgow in 1902, causing a scandal because such a treasure was falling into foreign ownership. But Bofors bought its old archrival in 1905, returning it to Swedish hands. (The Nobel name retained its stature in business in the 1990s. Bofors, owned by Erik Penser, one of the high-flying Swedish investors of the 1980s, bought KemaNobel in 1984. In 1985, the whole concern changed its name to Nobel Industrier and in 1986 was bought by the Norwegian industrial concern Dyno Industrier. In 1994, the chemical manufacturing division of Nobel Industrier and Akzo, a Dutch company, formed Akzo Nobel. Nobel's defense division has become part of the Celcius company.)

One Swedish newspaper wrote that the only Swede to whom Nobel could be compared was King Gustaf II Adolf (Gustavus Adolphus), because the king had left his estate to Uppsala University and "ensured" the future of culture in Sweden. Some politicians criticized the will's provision giving the Norwegian Parliament the authority to award the peace prize, because the provision aided Norway in its quest to seek independence from Sweden. But the most interesting reaction came from Hjalmar Branting, leader of the Social Democrats.

In a letter headlined "Alfred Nobel's Will—Lofty Intentions, Lofty Blunders," Branting attacked Nobel for setting up a series of prizes that would most likely go to those who "already enjoy most of what our society can offer in material and spiritual terms." He said Nobel's decision to allow the elitist Swedish Academy to select the literature laureates meant that the works selected could not possibly be "idealistic" as the will said they should be. Branting also criticized creating a prize for peace, because, he said, "effective attempts to bring about world peace are never the work of a single individual."

In a statement that demonstrated the class cleavages that were developing in Sweden in the 1890s and would soon engulf the nation's politics, Branting challenged the whole social and economic system that made the prizes possible. "A millionaire who makes a gift of this kind may personally be worthy of respect—but we are better off without either the millions or the donations," he concluded. Branting did not, however, turn down the prize when it was awarded to him in 1921.

MoDo, 1865

One of the top three forest products companies in Sweden today owes its origin to the decision in the early 19th century of Carl and Henrik Kempe, two members of a Pomeranian merchant family that had held Swedish citizenship since the time of the Thirty Years War, to emigrate to Sweden.

The two brothers started out working in a sugar refinery in Stockholm. One day, Carl went swimming during work hours, and, when his employer got angry, quit his job. Carl almost returned to Pomerania, but, instead, he accepted an offer in a friend's father's firm in Härnösand, a northern seaport on the Baltic. Carl married the sister of the friend and, with his brother-in-law, founded a company that built ships and operated a fleet of vessels.

Carl Kempe became a partner in a water saw operation at Mo, inland from the Örnsköldsvik, a port north of Härnösand; he installed an ironworks and manufacturing shop at Mo and, later, a sawmill at nearby Domsjö. His son, Frans, added chemical plants and sulfite mills to create MoDo, today one of Sweden's largest cellulose producers.

Nydqvists & Holm (NOAB) 1847 and Atlas (Copco) 1873

The expectation of profits from the construction of railroad cars led to the creation of Nydqvist & Holm (NOAB), a venerable Swedish construction company, and Atlas Copco, today one of Sweden's premier engineering firms. The establishment of the state and private railroads gave a tremendous boost to the development of Sweden's machine shops, which had originated in the 1830s and '40s to produce agricultural equipment, mostly copied from British and American designs. The first locomotives came from Great Britain, and Carl Gottreich Beijer, chief of the state railways in Sweden, actually declared that no company in Sweden could make a locomotive worth buying. Beijer did not count on the determination of Antenor Nydqvist, a Stockholm doctor's son who had attended the Royal Institute of Technology; studied in Austria and Switzerland; worked with Nils Ericson on the Trollhätte Canal; and, in 1847, founded a firm called Nydqvist & Holm, which built water turbines. When his first potential customer, Count Sparre, the aristocratic owner of the private Uddevalla-Vänersborg railroad, told Nydqvist he would not dare take the responsibility for ordering railroad equipment from a Swede, Nydqvist responded, "But the honorable does not need to feel responsible. I will be responsible for it." Sparre reportedly decided that he liked Nydqvist's decisiveness and replied, "Oh, so, does the gentleman say that? Well, then it might as well go ahead."

By 1914, Nydqvist & Holm had built more than 1,000 locomotives; in 1916, it became a stock company and changed its name to NOAB; and, by 1920, it received the largest locomotive order in history—1,000 freight locomotives for Soviet Russia. The Soviets bought only half the original order, but made their payment in gold.

In 1930, after the Swedish government decided Sweden should manufacture its own aircraft engines for military purposes, NOAB started Svenska Flygmotor. The company manufactured nine-cylinder engines of British design until 1941. Because the Wallenberg family controlled both Svenska Flygmotor and SAAB, another aircraft manufacturer, the Swedish government decided control of this strategic industry was too concentrated and arranged the sale of Svenska Flygmotor to Volvo.

Back in 1873, the business for Nydqvist & Holm and other railroad car producers looked so good that A.O. Wallenberg; D.O. Francke, an owner of textile mills, sugar refineries and pulp mills, who vied with Wallenberg for the title of ogre in the Swedish press; and Eduard Fränckel, a Gothenburg merchant's son who had also worked for Nils

Ericson, joined together to found the firm Atlas to supply railroad equipment.

The founders of Atlas didn't realize that the railroad boom was already declining. In 1879, after heavy losses for investors, Wallenberg and his bank assumed control of the company and reorganized it as Nya AB Atlas. In 1917, it merged with AB Diesels Motorer, a firm founded in 1898 by Marcus Sr. and K.A. Wallenberg and others to make the diesel engine in Sweden. Atlas Diesel, which adopted the name Atlas Copco in 1955 because of its Belgian subsidiary, Companie Pneumatique Commerciale, has become one of the world's largest providers of compressor, construction and mining technology

Odhner 1874

One of the Swedish engineers who followed the Nobels to Russia was W.T. Odhner, a Värmlander who graduated from the Royal Institute of Technology in Stockholm in 1866.

Russia was then involved in an agrarian reform that required complex calculations to determine land holdings. While working in St. Petersburg for Alfred Nobel's brother Ludwig, Odhner began using his spare time to design an instrument that could handle the job. In 1874, he invented the world's first practical calculating machine. It used a pinwheel system: a simple disc with nine pins. Odhner patented his machine in 1878 and manufactured thousands of the calculators before his death at 60 in Russia in 1905.

During the Russian Revolution in 1917, the new government seized the factory where the calculator was being produced, but Karl Siewert, the managing director, had made blueprints and sketches of its design and sent them to Stockholm in a diplomatic pouch. Siewert and his family escaped from Russia by sleigh and reestablished the factory in Gothenburg as AB Original-Odhner. The word "original" was added to distinguish the Odhner product from its imitators.

In 1942, Original-Odhner joined the Facit Group, a maker of office furniture that in 1932 had begun manufacturing a 10-key calculator invented in 1930 by Viktor Rudin.

Euroc AB (Skånska Cement) 1871

Rudolf F. Berg pioneered the making of cement in Sweden with the founding of Skånska Cement in the Malmö area in 1871. In 1903, Ernst Wehtje, a deputy district judge, became Skånska's managing director. Ernst Wehtje's son, also named Ernst, joined the company in 1929 and remained until 1956.

Berg and both the first and second Ernst Wehtjes were all leaders of the Swedish Employers Confederation, and the Wehtjes have become closely associated with the Wallenberg family. The company changed its name in the early 1970s and has become a world wide leader in the manufacture of construction materials for bridges, airports, housing, sports complexes and roads.

L. M. Ericsson 1876

The story of Ericsson, today a worldwide telecommunications giant can be traced to the arrival of the telegraph in Sweden. Within a year of Samuel Morse's transmission of the first electric telegraph message from Washington, D.C., to Baltimore in 1844, Swedish astronomers and military officials proposed replacing the old optical telegraph system with an electric one. It took until 1853, however, for the promoters to convince Swedish officials that the king, who spent half the year in Norway; farmers, who wanted better weather reports; and newspapers, which were supposed to print *news*, could all benefit from speedier communications.

The telegraph became wildly popular in Sweden, with communities and business leaders agreeing to pay for the construction of lines. But because no one could figure out how to make a profit from the telegraph, a state Telegraph Service (Telegrafverket) was set up. Anton Henric Öller, the manager of the Uppsala telegraph station, from which the first message was sent to Stockholm in July 1853, was the most notable of several entrepreneurs who found it difficult to make money manufacturing telegraph equipment. Eventually, however, Öller would go down in Swedish history for hiring Lars Magnus Ericsson, a 20-year-old, self-educated poor peasant's son who had sharpened tools at a silver mine and worked in a *bruk* as a smithy.

Swedes apparently first learned of the existence of the telephone on September 30, 1876, when *Dagens Nyheter*, the Stockholm daily, reported on a speech by the British mathematician and physicist Lord Kelvin describing the telephone invented by Alexander Graham Bell, which he had seen at the Philadelphia Exposition that year. Less than a year later, J.S.K. Hopstock, a Norwegian engineer who became Bell's agent in Scandinavia, showed a telephone to King Oskar II.

One of the first practical people to take an interest in telephones in Sweden was former Öller employee Ericsson, who, after working in the telegraph shop for six years, had gotten a state stipend to study abroad and travel in Germany and Russia. Back in Stockholm in the spring of 1876, Ericsson borrowed 1,000 kronor to start a shop specializing in telegraph apparatus for police and fire departments and semaphores for the railroad. In 1877, he made two telephones for Henrik Cedergren, a jeweler who wished to communicate between his home and his office. To achieve the connection, a telegraph worker strung a telephone wire between the two buildings.

A group of Swedish investors, meanwhile, had gotten the U.S.-based Bell Telephone company's permission to open the Stockholm Bell telephone system. One of its first subscribers was Cedergren, who quickly decided its charges were too high. Annoyed that Stockholm Bell wouldn't listen to his complaints, Cedergren convinced acquaintances to join him in setting up the Stockholm General Telephone Co. According to historian Carl Gustavson, Cedergren, an 1875 graduate of the Royal Institute of Technology, thought he would never be able to use his engineering education because he suffered from ill health. But when no one else wanted to run the telephone company, he became one of Sweden's industrial pioneers.

Ericsson, meanwhile, had persuaded friends to invest 10,000 kronor with him to start a company making telephones. His wife, the story goes, wrapped the spools for his early phones and, for years, headed a division of the firm. By 1881, Ericsson was offering a telephone for sale and had installed a switchboard handling 50 telephones in Norrköping. Cedergren's Stockholm General started operations in 1883 and bought its phones from Ericsson. By 1885, Stockholm had more phones than either Paris or London and led the world in the percentage of homes and businesses with telephones. In 1886, Ericsson and Cedergren began selling an automatic switchboard they had developed. Smaller communities established co-operative phone services, and Ericsson also supplied their equipment. In 1881, in an event that has become part of Swedish folk history, the town of Gävle held a contest to determine whether Bell or Ericsson produced the world's best telephone equipment. At first Ericsson's telephone didn't seem to work, but then someone discovered that a pencil had been placed inside it. Gävle decided to adopt the Ericsson system, and other co-ops followed their example.

The state-owned Telegraph Service did not take these private enterprise initiatives lying down, especially after the telephone became more popular than the telegraph and phone lines began interfering with telegraphic connections. When Bell and Ericsson started operations, there was no law governing telephone companies, but in 1883, the Telegraph Service managed to get a royal order forbidding private telephone companies. The law was ignored, but the Telegraph Service began constructing its own telephone lines and even built its own factory to manufacture equipment. A Telegraph Service employee, Ansgar Betulander, well deserves his own place in history for patenting more than 300 telephone innovations. Agreeing that a government-owned phone company could provide better and more-standardized service, the Riksdag appropriated money for the Telegraph Service to buy local phone companies. Stockholm General held out until 1918. After the government bought it, almost all Swedish telephone service was in government hands.

Ericsson responded to the Swedish government's nationalization of the phone company by being inventive and seeking business abroad. In 1895, Ericsson patented his greatest contribution to the telephone industry worldwide: the handheld phone that combines the microphone and the earpiece. In 1896, he formally established L.M. Ericsson & Co. and, in the early years of the 20th century, built the phone systems in the cities of Moscow and Warsaw and a little later in Mexico, Spain, Turkey and many South American countries.

Ericsson was one of the first Swedish inventor-entrepreneurs to rise to the top of the business world without the advantages of either a noble or burgher family background or a university education. He retired to a country estate at age 50 in 1896, becoming, sadly, another Swedish prototype: the achiever who cannot enjoy success because he cannot overcome the inferiority complex that led him to strive so hard.

Ivar Kreuger, the Swedish "Match King" of the early 20th century, gained control of Ericsson & Co. during his rise, and when his empire began to collapse in the late 1920s, he sold 600,000 shares of the company to U.S.-based International Telephone & Telegraph (ITT), one of its biggest competitors. The Stockholms Enskilda Bank was one of Ericsson's largest creditors, and in the chaos, the bank increased its interest in the company. Marcus Wallenberg Jr. joined Ericsson's board in 1932, but it took until 1960 for the Wallenbergs to get ITT to sell its shares. Ericsson & Co. went on to become a world leader in all kinds of communications systems, most notably by the 1990s in mobile phones. Just as it had the highest level of telephone penetration in the 1880s, Sweden today has more mobile phones per capita than almost any other country. The vast majority of Ericsson's business is, as always, outside the country.

ASEA (ASEA Brown Boveri) 1883

The formation of the electrical engineering giant Asea (Allmäna Svenska Elektriska Aktiebolaget), took place in 1883, shortly after the introduction of electricity in Sweden. Ludvig Fredholm, a bookkeeper for his family's shipyard until it was sold, saw electricity in operation in England in 1880 and became the Scandinavian agent for the Anglo-American Electric Light Co. Fredholm organized a demonstration of electric light in Stockholm, where the technician in charge of making the lights come on was a scientifically minded young man named Georg Wenström. A short time later, in an attempt to interest ironmasters in electricity, Fredholm sponsored a public demonstration at Örebro. There he met Georg's brother Jonas, a student at Uppsala who had gone to the 1881 Paris Exhibition, where he'd been fascinated by the electrical exhibits. After Fredholm found that Jonas had built a generator, he ended his relationship with Anglo-American and together with Jonas founded the company Elektriska AB.

The Wenströms were typical of upwardly mobile scientific families of the era. Their father, Wilhelm Wenström, was a pastor's son who had served an apprenticeship with Gustaf Ekman at Lesjöfors *bruk*, studied at the Falun School of Mines and the Royal Institute of Technology and worked as a master builder and mechanic at various other *bruk*, where he devised water turbines to replace waterwheels. After growing up in this technically minded household, Jonas and Georg built upon their father's attempts to find alternative sources of energy for industry.

The company Fredholm and Jonas Wenström started was soon replacing fire-prone paraffin lamps with electricity in companies and installing town lighting systems. Georg, meanwhile, went traveling in France, Germany, Italy and Switzerland to study experimental approaches to long-distance transmission of current and then co-founded a company that worked on the generation and transmission of electricity. His company and Elektriska AB soon merged as Asea. In 1890, Jonas patented a transformer that used alternating currents to transmit power, and became famous as the "father of the Swedish high-tension current." Jonas's health was poor, however, and he died in 1893 at the age of 38.

Asea encountered intense competition from German firms, but after Asea electrified *Västerås Mekaniska Verkstad,* a maker of farm equipment, the owner became such an enthusiast of electricity that he helped find a location for a new Asea headquarters at Västerås on the shores of Lake Mälaren. With industry in Sweden electrifying as rapidly as possible in the 1890s, Asea prospered, but as soon as electrification was largely completed—around the turn of the century—it fell on hard times. By the early 1900s, the Wallenberg-controlled Stockholms Enskilda Bank was holding two million kronor in Asea bonds. In 1903, Marcus Wallenberg appointed J. Sigfrid Edström to head Asea and, with bank officials, to restructure it. Historians say Wallenberg's choice of Edström fulfilled his maxim, "No undertaking is so bad that it cannot be put on its feet by a competent man, and none is so good that it cannot be ruined by an incompetent man." A Gothenburg sea captain's son who had graduated from the Chalmers Institute and worked for Westinghouse in the United States, Edström (helped by government-sponsored construction of hydroelectric power plants in Scandinavia) returned Asea to profitability. Edström became famous in Sweden for helping stage the 1912 Olympics in Stockholm and long played a role on the International Olympic Committee.

The Wallenbergs sold their interests in Asea in May 1926 but by 1929 bought back a substantial amount of stock because the company was doing good business and because they didn't want either Ivar Kreuger or the U.S.-based General Electric Co. to gain a substantial stake in it. (Asea remained completely Swedish-controlled until it merged with Brown-Boveri, the Swiss company, to form ABB in 1987.)

AB Separator (ALFA-LAVAL) 1883

The development of the cream separator, which would transform the processing of milk throughout the world, started modestly enough in 1877 when a young engineer, Gustaf de Laval, was sitting with the other executives of the Kloster *bruk* in Dalarna eating dinner. Fredrik Lagergren, Kloster's *brukspatron,* noted that an article he'd read in the newspaper said that a German had invented a machine that could separate the cream out of milk by rapid rotation of the milk. De Laval, the descendant of a French officer in the Swedish army who was ennobled in 1646 and himself a graduate of Uppsala University and the Royal Institute of Technology who had also worked in Wilhelm Wenström's engineering office, announced self-confidently: "Centrifugal power no doubt works the same in Sweden as in Germany. I hope to prove that soon." The next morning he announced that not only could he make a machine that would separate the cream from the milk, but that his machine would make it unnecessary to skim off the cream by hand. A few days later, he quit his job and went to Stockholm to work on his invention.

De Laval offered his improved cream separator to W. Lefeld, a German inventor, hoping for a payoff or a royalty, but when Lefeld showed little interest, de Laval continued his own research. Creamery operators who used de Laval's separator said they had to stop the machine frequently in order to pour out the cream, so de Laval improved the separator so that the cream would be trapped in another container. His invention has become known as the continually operating centrifugal separator.

De Laval demonstrated that he had an exact understanding of the relationship between the inventor and the entrepreneur. "Briefly put, it is the personal acquaintance who exclusively drives through the affairs; otherwise it is impossible, no matter how good the thing," he wrote a friend. De Laval found a business manager in Oscar Lamm, a nephew of Jacques Lamm, the founder of Ludwigsberg, one of the biggest foundries in Sweden. De Laval and Lamm signed an agreement in February 1878 that led to the formation of AB Separator in 1883. In its first 15 years in business, AB Separator sold more than 100,000 machines, exporting more than four-fifths of them. The firm soon had a factory in the United States and sales offices throughout the world.

De Laval has been compared with Thomas Edison for the range of his interests and his love of self-promotion. He bought a *bruk* and began manufacturing turbines, and in 1894, he bought a light bulb firm whose output soon reached 3,000 light bulbs a day, the second largest among all such firms in Europe.

De Laval reached the zenith of his career and personal fame in 1897, when he provided the lighting for the Stockholm Arts and Industrial Exposition on the island of Djurgården. He went on to other ventures that did not work out and ended up owing millions of kronor to the Wallenberg bank and working in collaboration with Ernest Thiel, a Stockholm banker known for getting involved in risky ventures. In 1898, K.A. Wallenberg said of de Laval that "the pitcher is going to the well until it cracks" and "even de Laval is a human being." De Laval died on February 2, 1913, shortly after attending a demonstration of a new milking machine. He is remembered for his favorite saying, "Speed is the gift of heaven!"

AB Separator continued to prosper. In the 1920s, it bought up most of its Swedish competitors, and in 1927, the Wallenbergs acquired a major interest in the company. AB Separator changed its name to Alfa-Laval in 1963, honoring both de Laval and Alfa, the brand name of its top separator.

AGA 1904

De Laval played a key role in the life of another of Sweden's greatest inventors, Gustaf Dalén. A poor farmer's son, Dalén went to agriculture school, but at de Laval's suggestion, switched to a technical education, studying first in Gothenburg and later in Switzerland. AGA, a company founded in 1904 for production of dissolved acetylene, hired Dalén as chief engineer. He began a series of inventions, all related to the safe, commercial lighting of lighthouses. He invented the AGA mass, for storing and transporting gas in safety cylinders; the AGA flasher, a flashlight; the Dalén mixer, which combines acetylene and air for use with mantel burners in lighthouses; and a sun valve, a solar mechanism that turns on a beam of light when darkness falls and turns it off when the sun begins to shine.

Dalén was known as the Thomas Edison of Sweden, but Edison himself said of the sun valve, "It won't work." It did, of course, and Dalén became president of AGA in 1909. In 1912, he won the Nobel prize. The same year he lost his sight after being drenched with flaming acetylene gas during an experiment. Dalén continued to serve as president of AGA for another 25 years and, with the help of assistants, continued experiments that led to inventions such as the AGA stove, which is capable of running 24 hours a day on limited fuel. He also experimented with radio and sound film, making advances that were later used in the development of transistor radios, TV sets, stereophonic sound and communications equipment for the Swedish Air Force.

Dalén died in 1937, and in 1945, the Royal Swedish Academy of Sciences issued a medal in his name with an inscription in Latin that reads, "When the day vanishes, he bids darkness to light the beacon." In the years since, AGA has produced the Geodimeter, a surveying instrument that uses a reflected light beam to measure long distances with great speed and accuracy, and a heart-lung machine developed by Clarence Crafoord, a renowned Swedish heart surgeon.

STAL 1913

Both Alfred Nobel and de Laval played a role in the careers of Birger and Fredrik Ljungström, who are credited with the development of the alternate-flow turbine. The Ljungström brothers were the sons of the manager of a Stockholm workshop that manufactured surveying instruments. The father also invented instruments, some of which were displayed at the 1876 Philadelphia exposition. At age 16, Birger invented a bicycle and Alfred Nobel invested in a British firm which planned to manufacture it. The bicycle was a commercial failure, but Birger stayed on in Great Britain to develop a carbonic acid heat engine. Fredrik, an employee of Nobel, joined Birger in Great Britain after Nobel's death. The two brothers returned to Sweden and in 1903 went to work for AB Separator where Fredrik improved the milk machine.

De Laval, a visionary of extraordinary breadth, had also invented a steam turbine (a machine that converts the energy in a stream of fluid into mechanical energy by passing the steam through blades which rotate), began manufacturing it in 1890 and set up AB de Lavals Ångturbin in 1893. Birger saw De Laval's steam turbine and began making an improved version. In 1908, the brothers set up AB Ljungströms Ångturbin and in 1913 Svenska Turbin Aktiebolaget Ljungström (STAL) to manufacture steam turbines in a former artillery workshop at Finspång. Asea acquired a majority of STAL's stock in 1916. By 1932 STAL was building northern Europe's largest power installation at Västeras, Sweden, and went on to expand in the 1930s. Oscar Wiberg, STAL's design manager, won the gold medal of the Royal Swedish Academy of Engineering Sciences in 1930 and played a role in the company's development for many years to come. When Asea acquired its majority share, the Ljungström brothers set up a separate company, but STAL eventually acquired that company as well as de Laval's steam turbine company. Curt Nicolin, who played a leading role in Swedish public affairs, spent most of his career at STAL. He was appointed development manager in 1945, technical director in 1953, managing director in 1955, to the board of directors in 1961 and served as chairman of the board from 1968 to 1988. In 1959, STAL began development of a marine turbine with what became known as "advanced propulsion" and in 1982 developed the VAX turbine which is capable of generating previously unknown levels of power. Since the Asea-Brown Boveri merger in 1987, the firm has been known as ABB Stal AB.

The Reorganization of Stora Kopparbergs Bergslags AB, 1888

The Swedes' claim that Stora Kopparbergs Bergslags AB is the world's oldest joint stock company appears to be correct, but by the mid-19th century, the mine was way behind the times in both technical expertise and management.

After reaching a peak of 3,000 tons in 1650, copper production at Stora declined, and the company diversified into Falu red paint, iron and management of forest lands. Over the centuries, gold, silver, pyrite, sulfide of zinc, lead sulfide, ferric sulfate and other minerals were also found in the mountain at Stora, which some call the richest mountain in the world.

The Swedish crown always asserted rights to the mountain, but after the company's charter was granted in 1347, it was largely controlled by the active miners, whose shares gave them a right to take out ore for smelting in their own nearby hearths. The miners elected a council of 14 to run the mine and formed a guild to settle disputes. By the mid-1700s, the council consisted of the 24 "eldest" shareholders, and the head of Stora was called the *bergshauptmann*, the German word for the same position.

In the middle of the 19th century, the miners, like other *bruk* owners, had to face the demands of the new Industrial Age. In the 1850s, special assistance was given to those *bruk* with the best access to ore, water and transport and the best chance of survival. In 1862, the crown relinquished its claims to control of the mountain at Stora, and the owner-miners agreed to end the age-old form of management and the office of *bergshauptmann* in favor of a head director and three separate directors for its copper, iron and timber divisions. The man behind the changes was Gustaf Aldolf Lundhqvist, whose wife had inherited shares of the company stock. In June 1868, Lundhqvist, who has been described by historians as having the right mix of rebelliousness, naïveté and majesty to undertake the challenge of changing such an ancient enterprise, successfully sponsored a motion at the assembly of owners to appoint a committee to study a proposal to concentrate iron production in the most efficient locations. By the early 1870s, the members had decided to close several of the smaller ironworks and build Domnarvet, one large ironworks, at Tunaforsarna on the River Dalälven.

The ambitious venture, which called for four blast furnaces, two Bessemer converters and a total annual capacity of 43,000 tons per year, required massive amounts of capital for both the ironworks and the railroads, which had to be built so that Stora's production could be transported with modern efficiency. Lundhqvist formed an alliance with D.O. Francke, the Gothenburg capitalist and industrialist. The Gothenburg Commercial Co., an investment company established by Gothenburg merchants and industrialists in 1871, bought shares and also lent money for the construction of the railroad line from Falun to Gothenburg. A.O. Wallenberg, working with Francke, arranged a loan from his Stockholms Enskilda Bank.

In 1873, Lundhqvist and Francke gained control of Stora. They put four directors in charge and planned to run the company from

Stockholm. Construction began on Domnarvet in 1872, but because of rising costs and depressed demand, Erik Johan Ljungberg, who was appointed managing director in 1875, had to scale down the project. In 1879, amid a financial crash brought on by excessive private railroad construction, Francke went into bankruptcy. In 1888, the owner-miners of Stora exchanged each of their 1,200 old shares, called *fjärder*, for eight shares of stock worth 1,000 kronor each, and the enterprise became a full-fledged joint-stock company known as Stora Kopparbergs Bergslags AB, with its headquarters in Falun, not Stockholm. Ljungberg ran the company admirably for four decades. The company that had once stood for copper mining ceased mining it in 1895, but by 1900, it had become the largest iron and steel works in Sweden. Under Ljungberg, it also expanded its forest holdings and wood products output, which would ultimately be the core of its business. (Stora remains a giant company, but merged with Enso Oy of Finland in 1998 and has joint corporate headquarters in Helsinki and Stockholm.)

LKAB, 1890

Only the riches of Norrland ultimately proved too complicated for purely private enterprise. Swedes had known since the early 1700s that iron ore existed in the far north of the country near the Arctic Circle. A Lt. Karl Tingvall secured a royal concession in 1735 to mine at Gällivare in Lappland and to set up a *bruk* near the coast. In 1736, a royal commission had traveled even farther north, to Jukkasjärvi, to investigate rumors of iron ore riches. "We saw with wonder the imposing open seams of pure iron ore, both to the north and south . . . all of unusual height and completely unbroken by a gangue," the commission's report stated.

Primitive mining began at Gällivare, with the ore transported by reindeer-drawn wagons. In the late 18th century, the concession passed into the hands of Baron Samuel Hermelin, who was known for a time as the "King of Lappland." Eventually, he went bankrupt and is better remembered today as the founder of modern Swedish cartography. After a series of other owners found the far northern mines a losing proposition, King Karl XIV Johan bought the Hermelin properties. The land came in handy when Crown Prince Oskar asked Princess Josephine of Leuchtenberg to marry him and the Pope demanded that she be given the equivalent of the principality Napoleon had bestowed upon her when she was baptized. Once Oskar I ascended the throne, he sold what had become known as the "Principality of Gällivare" to a group of

113

Norwegians. A.O. Wallenberg became part of a partnership called Gällivare AB, but that, too, was troubled. In 1864, the company sold its assets to the Gellivare Co. Ltd., which also went bankrupt and was reorganized as the New Gellivare Co. Ltd., with mostly British investors. New Gellivare concentrated on timber, mining only enough to satisfy the concession. In 1887, the British built a railroad to Gällivare, but the rail ties were of such poor quality that the railroad had to be taken over by the Swedish government in 1891. That same year, Col. Carl Otto Bergman, a local man who had returned to the area after an army career and become the spokesman for the local residents disgusted by the foreign capitalists' inability to develop the mine, staked a claim to most of the ore with another man, Gustaf Broms. Their company was called AB Gällivare Malmfelt (AGM).

The northernmost reserves near Jukkasjärvi and Kiruna remained undeveloped. In 1875, a geological survey of Sweden estimated the amount of iron ore at Kiirunavaara (which means "the ptarmigan mountain") was 260 million tons, and at Luossavaara ("the salmon mountain") 27 million tons. In 1890, Luossavaara-Kiirunavaara AB (LKAB) was formed by Robert Schough, an employee of the New Gellivare Co., and K.A. Wallenberg. With no profits in sight until a railroad to Narvik was built, Schough and Wallenberg sold a lot of their stock to Broms—enough, in fact, that he gained control of LKAB as well as AGM. In his attempt to develop the mines, Broms borrowed so much money on the German bond markets and from German banks that it appeared a consortium of his German ironworks customers might take control of the mines.

Brom's troubles worsened, and in February 1903, Vollrath Tham, head of Trafikaktiebolaget Grängesberg-Oxelösund AB (Trafik AB), a competing iron and steel company, took an option on the majority of the stock in both AGM and LKAB. Tham portrayed himself as a savior, and it was true that Trafik AB's owners did not want the northern mines to come under German control because it would be bad for Trafik's business. But Trafik AB's control of LKAB was not a solution for the Swedes, because Trafik AB was also foreign-controlled. Behind its origins lay a twisting tale of corporate development. In 1869, Christopher Weguelin, a British financier, put together a consortium, called the Swedish Central Railway Co. Ltd., to build private railroads in Sweden. The consortium shortened its name to the Swedish Association and bought Kloten, a *bruk* that held shares in Grängesberg Stora Konstbolag, the supervising body of the Grängesberg ore field that straddles the provincial border between Västmanland and Dalarna. In 1875, the Konstbolag was reorganized, with shares passing into the hands of Carl Fredrik Liljevalch, a Swede who was a former employee of Weguelin in London; Tham; and Sir Ernest Cassel, the London-based financier. The shares in the Konstbolag controlled by Kloten were transferred to the Grängesberg Mining Co., owned by the Swedish Association, which was controlled by Cassel. In 1896, with help from the Warburg banking firm in Hamburg and Theodor Mannheimer, head of Skandinaviska Kreditaktiebolaget, the Grängesberg Mining Co. and three private railroads were put together into Trafik AB.

The fact that Trafik AB also had German creditors once again raised the question of foreign influence. Both the Conservative and Liberal political leaders had mixed feelings about state control, but in 1907, the state became half-owner of AGM and LKAB, with the right to take over completely in 1932 or 1942. The railroad was later electrified, and shortly after World War I, LKAB became a major ore supplier. By the late 1930s, it was supplying both Great Britain and Germany with ore, and it continued to be Germany's main supplier during the war years. The state takeover was delayed, but completed in 1957. Today, LKAB produces 2 percent of the world's iron ore, and the supply is expected to last another 100 years. LKAB's largest customer is SSAB, a Swedish steelworks at Luleå; but 85 percent of the production goes to Western Europe, and pellets for use in blast furnaces are exported as far away as East Asia.

ESAB, 1904

Just after the turn of the century, Oscar Kjellberg, a repairman of leaky ships' boilers in Gothenburg, began experimenting to improve the technique of arc welding. The influence of oxygen and nitrogen was causing the welded joints to be porous, and Kjellberg developed an electrode with a chemical coating which, during welding, was converted into a liquid slag that shielded the melted material. Kjellberg was granted a patent in 1904 and started Esab, which has become one of the world's largest welding companies. He formed his first foreign subsidiary, the Anglo-Swedish Electric Welding Co., in 1912 in London and by 1933 had established companies in Germany, Spain, Belgium, Czechoslovakia, Great Britain, Denmark, Holland, Italy and Norway. In more recent times, Esab's greatest notice has come from its contract to construct the Volga-Don Project, the largest manufacturer of nuclear power generating equipment in the Soviet Union.

ASTRA, 1904

With their strong scientific tradition, Swedes began developing a pharmaceutical industry at the beginning of the 20th century—a time when drugs were still being mixed by hand. In 1913, a group of investors, mostly pharmacists and physicians, that included Adolf Rising, a former production manager at Ciba in Basel, Switzerland, started a pharmaceutical firm called Astra, with plants at Södertälje in the Stockholm area. Astra did well manufacturing and selling pharmaceuticals and chemicals during World War I but, in 1918, made the mistake of joining in the formation of AB Svensk Färgämnesindustri, a company that made paint additives and ran into trouble. Hjalmar Branting, a future Social Democratic prime minister then briefly finance minister in the first Liberal-Social Democratic government, saw an opportunity to create a government pharmaceutical monopoly and successfully encouraged the government to permit Vin & Spritcentralen, the state-owned liquor authority, to buy Astra's plants. Astra continued to lose money, but in 1924, Erik Kistner, a medical supplies wholesaler, convinced banker and industrialist Jacob Wallenberg to make an investment in the company. A consortium financed by Stockholms Enskilda Bank bought Astra from Vin & Spritcentralen for one krona and assumed its debts of one million kronor.

In 1931, Astra began to invest in research and development of its own medications. Its first products included Hepaforte (for pernicious anemia), Nitropent (for heart ailments) and Sulfatiazol (for infections). In 1942, Astra bought a pharmaceutical factory in Hässleholm that had been started by a pharmacist named Paul Nordström in 1905, and the new firm became known as Astra Hässle AB. In the 1950s, research and marketing activities were moved to Gothenburg and manufacturing to Södertälje.

Astra Hässle's worldwide prominence would not occur until after 1967, when the company established a new research and development center at Mölndal and concentrated on medicines for cardiovascular and gastrointestinal diseases. In 1975, Astra Hässle would produce Seloken, the heart-selective beta blocker that has become one of the most widely used cardiovascular medicines in the world; and in 1988, Plendil, the calcium antagonist, and Losec, the acid inhibitor that some stomach ulcer patients have called the greatest invention of modern times. In 1999, Astra merged with the British firm Zeneca.

SKF, 1907

Today the Swedish textile industry is a shadow of its former self, but it still deserves credit for one of the most successful and profitable inventions ever, the self-aligning ball bearing.

The story began at the Gamlestaden textile mill in Gothenburg. A stationmaster's son who had studied at a weaving school in Norrköping and spent about half a year in the United States, Sven Winquist (1876-1953) was put in charge of the textile machinery at Gamlestaden. Winquist became annoyed by the frequent breakdowns of the mill's ball bearing installations, which came from a firm in Germany whose first priority appeared to be fulfilling the orders of bicycle manufacturers. Told after a breakdown in 1906 that his order for more ball bearings could not be filled for a year, Winquist is reported to have said that his factory couldn't wait that long and that he and his staff would make the ball bearings themselves using Swedish steel. His superiors didn't really care for this approach, but they gave him the chance to experiment in his spare time. Working nights and weekends, he designed a single-row ball bearing that proved to be many times more durable than the imported bearings. He and the Carlander and Johansson families that owned Gamlestaden formed the company Aktiebolaget Svenska Kullagerfabriken (AB SKF) to manufacture the bearing. Winquist wasn't satisfied with the design, however, and worked until he made the outer of the two bearings spherical in form, which permitted the inner circle to rotate freely and be self-aligning.

SKF's board quickly realized that Sweden was too small a market for such a marvelous invention and allowed Winquist, who was as good a salesman as he was a designer and worker, to travel to Europe, where he met with more than 100 potential customers in three months. SKF was exporting its ball bearings within the first year of production and by 1910 had established sales offices in France and Germany and was represented as far away as Australia.

In the early years, SKF faced formidable technical challenges in establishing worldwide production and markets. SKF initially imported the balls to make the bearings but began making its own balls in 1910, and in 1916 bought the Swedish Hofors works so that it could control completely the quality of the steel. In some countries, such as Great Britain, it had to establish domestic plants to protect its patent. Over the course of the 20th century, ball bearings would become a key item in virtually everything that moves, and SKF would make two-thirds of the world's ball bearings. History proved that SKF's first slogan was correct: "The Right Bearing in the Right Place."

Volvo, 1927 and Vabis, 1891
Scania, 1901 and Saab, 1937

Out of the success of SKF came the product for which Sweden today may best be known: the Volvo. The story behind the Volvo's development in the 1920s shows how much Swedish industry had matured by that point in time. Its development was led not by a noble or a peasant boy with native genius but by a well-schooled engineer and a business school graduate. The story of the car's development still retains the charm and simplicity of that era, however.

Contrary to popular impression, the Volvo was not the first Swedish car—though it was the first commercially successful one. The first Swedish car was developed by a predecessor of the current Saab company. In 1898, Vabis, a firm that had started in Södertälje in 1891 to make railroad cars, developed a vehicle with an internal combustion engine, and in 1901, a firm called Scania in Malmö built a private car with a water-cooled engine that was probably of French origin.

The future King Gustaf V was so impressed with the Scania that he ordered one that was delivered in 1904. Vabis and Scania merged in 1911 and produced 1,171 cars before the company experienced financial problems and fell into bankruptcy in 1921. (After reorganization, Scania-Vabis decided to concentrate on buses and trucks and, in 1969, would merge with Saab, which the Swedish government had encouraged the Wallenbergs and others to set up in 1937 to build aircraft. Saab began making cars in the 1940s.)

Back in 1920s Gothenburg, Assar Gabrielsson, who was the son of a tenant farmer and egg producer and who had been a member of the first class to graduate from the Stockholm School of Economics in 1911, started off on a brilliant career at SKF, the ball bearing maker. While serving as managing director of SKF in France and negotiating with the Soviets over an SKF plant confiscated in the Russian Revolution, Gabrielsson observed that Swedish ball bearings were cheaper than those of their competitors and decided that the cheaper bearing could be the starting point for the Swedes to produce a car that would compete in price and quality with the American cars that then dominated the world market.

Between 1917 and 1920, Gabrielsson worked with Gustaf Larsson, a farmer's son and 1917 Royal Institute of Technology engineering graduate who had come to SKF to work on various engine and carburetor projects. In 1920, Larsson accepted an offer in Stockholm to work for Galco, a manufacturer of carburetors, lubricators and farm equipment including the Agrippa binder. On Midsummer Eve 1924,

Gabrielsson was visiting Stockholm, probably to see his parents, when he ran into Larsson in a cafe.

"How pleased I am to meet you Gustaf. You have experience of car production, and I would like to discuss it with you," Gabrielsson said.

"Gladly, Assar. But I must rush off to catch the train. Perhaps we can meet again after the summer," Larsson replied.

The two men set no date, but a month later, on July 25, Gabrielsson was again in Stockholm. Staying true to the Swedish love for solitude, he decided that he wanted to eat a meal of crayfish alone. He headed for the Sturehof Restaurant. The same night, Larsson also felt the urge for a crayfish meal alone, went to the Sturehof and found Gabrielsson there, sitting behind a mountain of crayfish. The two decided to eat together. They dined sumptuously, neither man speaking of their joint interest until after they finished their meals.

Before the evening was over, however, the two agreed that Sweden should produce a car. Larsson began working at night in the children's nursery of his family apartment at Rådmansgatan 59 in Stockholm, an address that has become a shrine to Volvo enthusiasts. Larsson recruited young engineers from the Royal Institute of Technology to do the drafting and in 1925 hired Henry Westerberg to complete the drawings for 10 prototype cars. Larsson also hired Helmer MasOlle, a distinguished landscape and portrait artist, to draw the car, and he incorporated a number of features of his own 1914 French Voisin into the design of the first Volvo.

Gabrielsson, meanwhile, continued with SKF in Gothenburg, but on the side analyzed the economics of the car venture. SKF initially declined to get involved, and so Gabrielsson invested 150,000 kronor of his own savings. In 1926, however, SKF decided to invest 200,000 kronor and also to allow the venture to use the Latin name Volvo ("I roll"), which it had registered in 1915. The prototype cars, assembled at Galco's factory in north Stockholm in May 1926, included materials from several of the finest Swedish companies: the chassis frames from Bofors, the body shells from Svenska Stålpressings AB in Olofström, the engines from Pentaverken in Skövde and the bodies from Freyschuss. Westerberg, who remained with Volvo until 1980, told an interviewer late in his life that the alternators on two of the prototype cars were turned the wrong way so that on a drive to Gothenburg the electric power supply ran out and the cars ended up in a ditch. "No one was injured, but Larsson was very angry when he eventually returned to find us sitting on the footstep smoking calmly," Westerberg told the interviewer.

Galco did not produce the Volvo, though it would remain a supplier of parts. In October 1926, the newly formed Volvo company moved into the premises of a factory building that SKF owned on the island of

Hisingen in Gothenburg. On April 14, 1927, the first Volvos were driven out of the factory. The first car, however, had been assembled improperly and it set off backward, which caused Larsson to remark: "Fingal [the workshop manager] has really bridled up the horse back-to-front this time!"

European cars at the time were divided between the luxury vehicles such as the Rolls-Royce and the Hispano-Suiza and very small cars. The car Larsson had designed was intended for the growing middle class. The first model, the ÖV4 (an acronym for *Öppen Vagn*, or open car), was a highly functional four-cylinder, three-speed vehicle with an open top. It drove well, though fairly slowly in comparison with its competitors. But the open top turned out to be a mistake because of Sweden's climate, and MasOlle designed a new body with elegant oval side windows. The ÖV4 quickly became known as "the Swedish car," in part because of its logo, which was affixed with a metal stripe that ran diagonally across the radiator. The logo combined the figure of Mars, a symbol for Swedish iron, and the name "Volvo" written in Egyptian type.

Larsson and Gabrielsson aimed for the export market from the outset, and exported cars to Finland in 1928, to Norway and Denmark in 1930, and to Cuba in 1931. In the autumn of 1931, the krona was devalued in reaction to the Great Depression, and the Volvo became much cheaper to foreign customers. By 1932, Volvo was exporting to Palestine, Syria, Egypt, Morocco and shortly thereafter to Spain, Portgual and Romania. The success in Cuba led to sales in Brazil, Argentina, Uruguay and Chile, and the promotion of the car in South America included a trip over the Andes. Volvo also began making buses and, in 1935, sold 40 of them in Argentina. The first cars were not shipped to the United States—today Volvo's biggest market—until 1955. (Volvo would remain the brightest star in the Swedish constellation of companies for many years. Swedish stockholders rejected a Volvo merger with the French firm Renault in the mid 1990s, but in 1999 agreed to sell the car division to the Ford Motor Co.)

Aktiebolaget C. E. Johansson, 1911

C.E. Johansson invented the combination gauge block system, which has made modern precision measurement and assembly-line car production possible. Born in the province of Västmanland, northwest of Stockholm, Johansson built a miniature steam engine when he was 14 and, in 1882, at 18, made his first trip to the United States.

As the inspector in a rifle factory in Eskilstuna, he realized the importance of precision, especially in products with interchangeable parts. In 1894, as a member of an inspection commission that visited a German Mauser factory that supplied the Swedish government with rifles, Johansson noted that the company's measurement control system used thousands of gauge blocks and was clumsy. Determined to build a simpler, more accurate system of measuring, Johansson, his wife and several skilled assistants used an old sewing machine fitted with a cast-iron wheel for grinding to create a combination gauge block set in 1896.

With Johansson's set of 102 blocks in three series, it was possible to make 20,000 different measurements. The Swedish Patent Office denied Johansson a patent in 1899, but the English Patent Office gave him a patent in 1904 and a Swedish government patent followed not long after.

In 1911, he founded his company, Aktiebolaget C.E. Johansson in Eskilstuna. During World War I, the U.S. War Department adopted the Johansson system for all American arms production, and the "Jo-Blocks," as they were called, proved indispensable in the war effort.

Johansson had a warm, personal relationship with the American industrialist and pioneer automobile manufacturer Henry Ford, who hired him to work in Dearborn, Michigan, in 1923. Ford said that the mass production of automobiles would have been impossible without Johansson's measuring system. C.E. Johansson died in 1943, but his company continues to be a producer of precision instruments, including the Mikrokator, a versatile mechanical instrument capable of measuring the dimension of a shaft down to one-millionth of an inch.

Electrolux, 1919

In the midst of these inventor-entrepreneurs was one of the most uncharacteristic figures in Swedish business: Axel Wenner-Gren, a traveling-salesman-turned-self-promoter who developed the Electrolux vacuum cleaner. Wenner-Gren, born in Uddevalla in 1881, started out in business as a bookkeeper for a relative in Gothenburg, but after studying German, English and French, headed for Germany, where he begged for and finally got a job at AB Separator in Berlin. In 1908, he moved briefly to New York City, where he worked as a laborer for 15 cents an hour and as a chauffeur, but he was soon back in Europe seeking his fortune. In

Vienna one day, Wenner-Gren looked into a window, saw a Santo vacuum cleaner, a new invention from the U.S. city of Philadelphia, decided it was the perfect product to sell and got a job as Santo's general agent. After setting up a German sales network, he quarreled with his employers and returned to Sweden. A vacuum cleaner was already being manufactured jointly in Sweden by Elektromekaniska AB, which made the motors, and AB Lux, which made the suction tubes. Wenner-Gren suggested to the two companies that they make a cheaper and lighter model. They said they would consider it if he could deliver 5,000 orders. The orders came in so rapidly that AB Lux couldn't fill them fast enough. But by the end of World War I, Wenner-Gren had quarreled with these owners and formed his own company, AB Elektrolux (renamed Electrolux in 1957). Wenner-Gren's salesmanship became a legend, if something of an embarrassment to the staid and sober Swedish business community. He introduced door-to-door salesmanship in Sweden, telling his employees that there was "war at the door" and calling "every home an Electrolux home." Legend has it that his customers included the Pope (although no one has recorded that the Catholic leader made the purchase himself).

Meanwhile, Baltzar Carl von Platen and Carl Munters, two students at the Royal Institute of Technology, had patented a refrigerator that Wenner-Gren's company manufactured and sold by the millions in the United States under the name Servel.

Wenner-Gren would prove a controversial figure during and after World War II. On what he called peace missions, he met with both U.S. President Franklin D. Roosevelt and the German Nazi official Hermann Göring. But he was also accused of being a Nazi sympathizer. He moved his headquarters to the Bahamas in 1939, where his friend the Duke of Windsor (whom historians have also accused of Nazi sympathies), became governor. After the Allies put him on a black list, he moved to Mexico for the rest of the war years. Wenner-Gren was "rehabilitated" with an invitation to attend President Harry Truman's 1949 inaugural. Wenner-Gren had given a large block of stock to create the Wenner-Gren Foundation in 1937, and it has become a major international research center in Stockholm. Wenner-Gren died in 1961, but Electrolux went on under the leadership of Hans Werthén to become the world's largest manufacturer of household machines.

Svenska Tändsticksaktiebolaget (STAB), 1917
Svenska Cellulosaaktiebolaget (SCA), 1929
Boliden Mining, 1929

For sheer entrepreneurial lore, no other Swedish company can equal the tale of Ivar Kreuger and his role in the formation of the Swedish Match Co., SCA, the forestry conglomerate, and Boliden, the mining company.

It is said that the long, dark winters have always made Swedes obsessive about light. Some historians even attribute the boisterous celebration of Midsummer Eve, a rite that goes back to pagan times, to the lack of light in winter. Today, the number of Swedes who travel to Florida and Spain in the winter attests to the distances they will go to seek the sun.

It followed naturally that Swedish scientists, inventors and entrepreneurs would try to create light. Sweden's early contribution to the chemistry of matches came with Johan Gottlieb Gahn's discovery of calcium phosphate in bones and Carl Scheele's use shortly thereafter, in 1775, of sulfuric acid to release phosphorus, a key ingredient in matches, from bone-ash. The combination of Gahn's and Scheele's work made it possible for phosphorus to be produced in quantity.

The first matchsticks appeared in France around 1805, but they were poisonous and lit too easily. An English apothecary introduced successful friction matches about 1826, and by the 1830s, match factories had sprung up in Austria, England, France, Germany and the United States. Jonas Samuel Bagge, an instructor at the Royal Institute of Technology and later a professor at the Falun School of Mines, made Sweden's first matches in 1836. Matches were so combustible, however, that officials around the world opposed them, and some countries even banned them.

Gustaf Pasch, who had studied chemistry with J.J. Berzelius, the Swede who developed the system of chemical symbols, invented a safety match—one that would burst into flame only when it was struck against a specially prepared surface. He patented it in 1844 and had it made in Bagge's shop. Pasch's ingenious idea was to put the nontoxic, less chemically active red phosphorous on the striking surface of the box rather than on the match head.

Pasch's safety match didn't succeed commercially, however, until it was the subject of further experimentation by Carl and Johan (Janne) Lundström, sons of a prosperous Jönköping newspaper publisher and businessman, who were out to make their mark in the world. The

Lundströms' interest in matches started when Carl, who had studied technology abroad, wandered into a small match company in Malmö and observed the manufacturing process. He went back to his hotel and made drawings of the whole procedure, which he sent to Janne, who was known mostly for changing his program of study so frequently during his five years at Uppsala University that he never graduated.

Janne began experimenting with matches and, with the help of chemist Clemens Ullgren, improved the chemical combination of the igniting material. The first Lundström matches were sold on April 28, 1845, and the town of Jönköping was on its way to becoming the "match capital of the world." The Lundströms' development of the match industry in Jönköping is testament to what local entrepreneurs can do for a community. Located on the southern end of Lake Vättern, Jönköping possessed no particular advantages such as water power or raw materials, and it was distant from city markets. As historian Carl Gustavson has written, the Lundström brothers "started their match industry in Jönköping because they were known there and could borrow money in their home town; very probably it never occurred to them to go elsewhere."

Janne Lundström's match was different enough from Pasch's to garner its own patent, and the Lundströms began manufacturing their own safety matches in 1852. At the Paris Exhibition of 1855, the Lundströms won a medal for producing the best matches in the world. Their company grew rapidly, and as Gustavson has also written, the Lundströms demonstrated the importance of both the technical and business sides of a successful enterprise. "*Stickgubben* Janne ('the stick man Janne') was the thinker and experimenter, Carl the organizer and businessman," Gustavson wrote. "Without Carl to arrange for purchases and sales, the company would not have flourished, but without Janne, there would have been no company. Janne was the 'genial but restless pioneer type' who, once he had an enterprise running properly, would leave it to start another." In 1863, Janne sold his stock at three-fourths price to Bernhard Hay, the bookkeeper, and another man. Janne went on to add his technical expertise to several other enterprises, but ended up living on a modest pension. Some Swedes say Janne's quiet lifestyle is the reason he has become a more popular figure in Swedish history than Carl, who kept his stock and became rich.

Under Carl Lundström and Hay, the company—known as Jönköpings Tändsticks Fabriks Aktiebolaget—became a big business. Another inventor, Alexander Lagerman, enhanced the company's success by inventing a machine that automatically cut the matchsticks, and sulfurized, dried and packed them in containers in one mechanical operation.

By 1870, there were 34 match factories in Sweden employing 2,800 workers. Another company that was particularly successful was

Arenco AB, which manufactured and exported match-making machinery and, after 1920, automatic cigarette packers. In 1903, six of the largest factories merged into the Jönköping and Vulcan Match Co. Jönköping and Vulcan would look small, however, in comparison with the empire Ivar Kreuger would create.

Kreuger, who was born the son of a match factory owner in Kalmar in 1880, went off to America at the age of 20. After trying to sell real estate in Chicago, he worked in the New York City office of the Fuller Construction Co., which was using the latest methods to put up the Flatiron Building, Macy's department store and the St. Regis Hotel. After traveling to South Africa, India, London and the United States again, Kreuger, returned to Stockholm and in 1908 founded, with Paul Toll, the Kreuger and Toll construction company. The firm used the most-up-to-date American methods to build a stadium, the Norra and Södra Kungstornen buildings and the foundations of the Stadshuset.

In 1913, Kreuger merged 11 small match factories into the Kalmar Trust and, in 1917, merged the Kalmar Trust and Jönköping-Vulcan to create the Swedish Match Co. By this time, consumers all over the world recognized Swedish matches as the best; they remained usable in damp climates, and they were made of wood specially treated so they would extinguish quickly. Kreuger built a network of 250 branch offices in 43 countries, and two out of every three people in the world were using his matches. But Kreuger's attempt to create a match monopoly went (excuse the pun) up in smoke. Kreuger's company consisted of no fewer than 144 producing units in 33 countries, many of them owned by straw men. The cornerstone of Kreuger's empire was a knowledge of how to manufacture and sell matches, but the spectacular growth of his group was based on obtaining loans against the expected revenues from his match monopolies in many countries and a ruthless oligopolistic power play, scholar Ulf Olsson has observed.

Kreuger's empire building didn't stop with matches. In the 1920s, when many Swedish forestry companies got into trouble, Kreuger & Toll quietly began buying up 10 companies that owned forest lands and wood products plants and began assembling them into a company called SCA. Handelsbanken, meanwhile, had acquired several banks in northern Sweden and became the bank for a number of forestry companies on which it had to foreclose. In 1929, when Kreuger was at the height of his career, Handelsbanken attempted to reduce its exposure to the forestry industry by selling Kreuger 40 million kronor worth of stock in these companies so that he would have controlling interest. Handelsbanken historian Karl-Gustaf Hildebrand has written that the bank's managers hailed the deal "with profound satisfaction" because they believed that "in one swoop" they had rid themselves of slow-moving shares that provided them a continual source of anxiety. In 1931, the bank made Ytterstfors-Munksund, a big forest landowner and wood-processing company that had also gotten into financial straits, part of SCA. But Handelsbanken was in fact only getting into deeper and deeper trouble because it had also financed Kreuger's deals.

In 1929, Kreuger also bought from the Skandinaviska Banken the shares in two mining companies based on gold deposits that had been found about 40 kilometers west of Skellefteå. In 1931, Kreuger amalgamated the two companies into the Boliden Mining Company. Kreuger's paper empire couldn't withstand the Great Depression. On March 12, 1932, Kreuger committed suicide in Paris. The scandal helped the Social Democrats win the 1932 election that put them almost permanently in power. After Krueger's death, the revelation that more than 60 percent of the shares in his Boliden mining company were foreign-owned led to the passage of a law in 1934 forbidding foreigners to own more than one-fifth of the shares in a Swedish company. A "stooge law" made it illegal for Swedes to act as secret agents for foreigners.

The current generation of Swedish business executives and historians takes a more benign attitude toward Kreuger, arguing that, while he made mistakes, he assembled businesses that did well for the country in the long run. According to Olsson's research, Swedish Match at the end of the 1930s still consisted of 70 manufacturing units in 31 countries and accounted for 60 percent of Sweden's export of matches. The Kreuger empire was dismembered, but Swedish Match survives to this day, employing thousands of people around the world to make both matches and match-manufacturing equipment. About 98 percent of its Swedish production is exported to more than 100 countries. After's Kreuger's death, the Skandinaviska Banken had to resume ownership of Boliden. In 1952, Skandinaviska offered the majority of the Boliden shares to the bank's shareholders. In 1986, Trelleborg Ltd., a manufacturer of rubber items, acquired a majority of the shares and made Boliden Mineral, which processes copper, zinc as well as gold and silver, a subsidiary.

Kreuger's least internationally recognized legacy was his role in setting up SCA, today one of the biggest Swedish forestry conglomerates. In 1934, after a public auction revealed that no one was willing to buy SCA shares at a price close to their underlying value, Axel Wenner-Gren bought the shares at a price that was a bargain for him, but still seemed to Handelsbanken like the best deal it could get.

SCA did well for a few years, and Handelsbanken was glad to remain its banker. When World War II broke out, it became difficult to export pulp, and Wenner-Gren's decision to spend the war years in the Americas created management problems. In 1941, Handelsbanken had to write down the value of SCA shares to stabilize the company. In 1947, the bank bought out Wenner-Gren and, in 1950, sold the company without a loss. In his history of the bank, Hildebrand noted that the "end result was a remarkable piece of industrial development." In 1954, the individual companies held under the SCA name were merged into the single entity that continues to exist today.

While Swedish business executives have come to appreciate Kreuger's entrepreneurial skills, his spectacular rise and fall did great and seemingly permanent damage to the reputation of capitalism in Sweden. Per Albin Hansson, the Social Democrat who was catapulted to the prime minister's office in 1932 in part by the Kreuger scandal, said that Kreuger's way of doing business proved that "private enterprise and private initiative [should not be] allowed to run wild in the economic sector without any social control." It is a view many Swedes hold to this day.

5

Challenge to Capitalism and the Saltsjöbaden Agreement 1867-1938

ON MARCH 17, 1907, Stockholm banker Ernest Thiel and his second wife, Signe, celebrated the completion of their home and art gallery on the suburban island of Djurgården with a masked ball. For the occasion, every inch of wall space between the fine paintings was covered with roses.

Djurgården had once been a royal game park, and the fact that the royal family had granted Thiel, who was half-Jewish, divorced and remarried, permission to build a home there was a signal of how much Sweden had changed in the preceding half-century. One of the guests at the ball, Sven Lidman, a poet who would marry Thiel's daughter from his first marriage and later become a Pentecostal preacher, captured the poignancy of the moment, describing Signe Thiel as "moving like a vision in the palatial rooms, full of poetic phrases and practical wisdom, but constantly aware of and suffering under the ceaseless tug-of-war between shrewd calculation and indulgence."

Thiel's position and prestige were indeed a reflection of Sweden's transformation from an agrarian, Lutheran society to an industrial, cosmopolitan one. By 1907, the value of Swedish industrial output exceeded agriculture's; the industrial bourgeoisie dominated Swedish economic, political and cultural life; and unions had arisen as a reaction to the new elite. Over the next 30 years, the industrialists and the unions would be virtually at war before Sweden would achieve full democracy and the two sides would agree on what the world has come to know as the Swedish Model of cooperation between managers and workers.

The rise of the bourgeoisie was not quite a revolution in Sweden, but it definitely was an evolution. Just as the secular nobles superseded the ecclesiastical nobles after the Protestant Reformation in the 16th century and the *brukspatroner* had become more prominent than the landed nobles in the 18th century, now inventors, manufacturers, bankers, merchants and traders overwhelmed the *brukspatroner* and the remnants of the noble, clerical and military aristocracy. Because the new enterprises were just as dependent on minerals and forests as the old *bruk* were, industry in Sweden remained more spread out than it was in most other countries. But Swedish decision making—and the people who made the decisions—moved from the noble estates and the *bruk* to the cities. Stockholm, Gothenburg and Malmö grew rapidly, developing their own separate characters and, in fact, becoming quite competitive.

Industrialization made Sweden a much richer country, but for most Swedes, the 19th century was still a time of rural poverty, emigration to America or a rough transition to low-wage employment in the new industries. Most members of the new elite descended from the old noble and *brukspatroner* families or were the sons and grandsons of Lutheran priests or military officers. A few inventive village boys also managed to make a fortune, but government-kept statistics reveal that only 5 percent of Swedes could have been considered upper- or middle-class in 1900.

The working conditions in the forest industries, the mines and the factories were so abysmal and the gap between the rich and poor grew so great that the international socialist movement eventually held great appeal for the Swedish people. The conflicts in Swedish society at the turn of the century went far deeper than just a negotiation over wages and the differences between rich and poor. As University of Stockholm business professor Hans de Geer described the situation in his book *The Rise and Fall of the Swedish Model*, young people born in an agricultural society and forced by economic circumstance to work in industry encountered "fixed working hours, detailed control and a wretched working environment . . . close surveillance by foremen. . . . The individual worker was only a tiny cog in a vast wheel. And the greater their numbers, the wider the choice for the foreman; one 'hand' would do just as well as another."

It was not only the poor who had, at best, mixed feelings about the new industrial age. The late 19th century was a period of intense social criticism in Sweden. In 1879, author-playwright August Strindberg's *Röda Rummet (The Red Room)* appeared and forced Swedes to take a hard look at their lives and institutions. Strindberg was followed in the 1880s by a generation of socially realist writers, who described the miserable conditions of the common people. The mixed feelings that Swedes of all classes seemed to have about this harsh new world filled with factories, machines and international trade can be seen in Swedish art of the turn of the century. In the 1880s, Swedish artists had rebelled against the Royal Academy of Fine Art and its emphasis on formal, indoor portraits. Inspired by their travels to Italy and Paris and particularly by the French Impressionists, they began painting the natural landscape and scenes of the old and dying agrarian Sweden. Most of these romantic and nationalistic pictures found their way into the city apartments of the very bourgeoisie who destroyed that way of life.

Gothenburg vs. Malmö vs. Stockholm

Gothenburg in many ways was Sweden's leading city for business and new ideas in the second half of the 19th century. Bayard Taylor, a visitor in the 1850s, found Gothenburg "more energetic and wide-awake than Stockholm." As the western port, the city through which iron, grain and lumber were exported to Great Britain, and sugar, tobacco and cotton were imported, Gothenburg attracted many foreigners. So many of them were British that the people of Gothenburg liked to refer to their city as "Little London." Historian Carl Gustavson has said that many of the Swedes in Gothenburg were as much immigrants as the foreigners themselves. "They or their parents," Gustavson wrote, "had come from towns like Marstrand, Uddevalla or Vänersborg, drawn, like the British, by the location and opportunities of the young city."

The Swedes thought of all immigrants from Great Britain as English, but many of the famous names such as Campbell, Chalmers, Erskine and Carnegie were Scottish. Many of the immigrants had gotten into trouble of one sort or another at home. George Carnegie, for example, had fought at the Battle of Culloden on the side of Bonnie Prince Charlie in 1746 and supposedly fled to London disguised as a servant before taking a ship to Gothenburg, where he hung his sword on a wall in the export-import business he established. Whether English or not, the immigrants from Great Britain brought their business methods and technology, which were then the most modern in the world. And just as important, they brought their liberal political views, which favored a more democratic parliamentary system and, to use the phrase of the time, "rational economic thinking," which included abolishing guilds, lowering tariffs and creating conditions favorable for free trade.

Gothenburg managed to prosper in war and in peace, trading by lawful rules when that was possible and by smuggling when countries set up barriers. During the Napoleonic Wars, for example, British and neutral traders used Gothenburg and other Swedish ports to transport goods into French-dominated territory across the Baltic. When the wars ended, some Gothenburg merchants got caught with goods that were no longer hard to come by, but within a few years, the city overall was thriving again. The Trollhätte Canal, which was completed in 1800 and enlarged between 1838 and 1844, provided Gothenburg easier access across Lake Vänern to the ironworks and sawmills, which further enhanced its status as a seaport. According to one account, more than 40 millionaires lived in Gothenburg in the 1840s and 1850s.

Gothenburg developed its own bourgeois culture of intermarrying Swedes and foreigners. The daughters of Swedish East India Company founder Niclas Sahlgren, for example, married the sons of inventor Jonas Alströmer. One of the men who went to work for Sahlgren and Alströmer was John Hall (1735-1802), whose family came from Hull in England. Hall made a fortune exporting iron and timber to England and became Gothenburg's, and perhaps Sweden's, richest man. A few miles outside the city, Hall built a fabulous summer residence, Gunnebo. Francisco de Miranda, the Venezuelan liberator, visited the home, seeking financial support for his cause, and supposedly was so enchanted with Hall's wife, Christina, that he later said that he made the Venezuelan flag "yellow as Christina Hall's golden hair, blue as her eyes, red as her lips." The Halls' good fortune didn't last, however. Their son John, known as Skägg-Hallen (the Bearded Hall), was found frozen to death in a Stockholm bar in 1830.

In the early 19th century, David Otto (D.O.) Francke (1825-92) became the most famous—or infamous—business magnate in the Gothenburg area. Apparently of British Jewish ancestry (historian Gustavson reported that Francke's father, Johan, changed his name from Fränkel when he was baptized in 1816), D.O. Francke at age 23 took over the Rosendahl textile mill in nearby Mölndal. In 1856, he purchased the Korndal paper mill near Gothenburg and, facing a scarcity of rags and scrap paper for raw materials, he created the wood pulp industry in Sweden. Known as the "King of Mölndal," Francke was reviled by journalists and pastors for the low wages he paid and the accidents that occurred in his factories. Francke may have achieved a more permanent prominence or notoriety than any other Swedish businessman of his era when he became the model for a novel, *The Mölndal Girl*, in which he was portrayed as a lecher always on the lookout for new prey. Francke died at the breakfast table after returning from a business trip in 1892. (In 1895, Korndal was renamed Papyrus and in 1987 became part of Stora.)

In the late 19th century, shipping and shipbuilding became the most important industries in Gothenburg. Swedes so loved sailing ships that they were late to come to the steamship era, but the opening of the Suez Canal in 1869 forced them to modernize their fleets. Most Swedish emigrants to the United States left through Gothenburg, traveling not on Swedish ships, but on British vessels to Hull and from there took a four-hour train trip to Liverpool, where they boarded other British ships to cross the Atlantic. The British Wilson Line, founded by Thomas Wilson in Hull in 1835, provided regular steamship service between Gothenburg and Hull, and Wilson's son John West Wilson moved to Gothenburg to manage that end of the business. The first regular steamship service between Gothenburg and Hamburg was provided by the Svenska Lloyd Line, founded in Gothenburg in 1869.

Gothenburg would eventually become home to many shipping companies, but three were dominant. Axel Broström (1838-1905) began a shipping and shipbuilding empire by buying old ships to transport iron and timber between the Lake Vänern area and Gothenburg. His son Dan (1870-1925) developed Sweden's leading shipping and shipbuilding group. In 1915, Dan Broström bought the Eriksberg shipyard, which had been started by a Norwegian in 1853 as an iron and steel galvanizing shop. Broström founded the Swedish-America-Mexico Line and the Swedish Levant (later Swedish Orient) Co. in 1911. In 1914, he founded what would become known as the Swedish-American Line, which began trans-Atlantic passenger service to New York in 1915. In 1916, he gained majority control of Götaverken, Gothenburg's first engineering works, which had been started in 1841 by Alexander Keiller, a Scottish merchant from Dundee, who had come to Gothenburg in 1826. Dan Broström was killed in an automobile accident in 1925, but the family business continued to grow, with banking and investment advice from the Wallenbergs. In 1965, the Broström family owned 90 ships as well as Eriksberg and had ordered its first container ship. International competition had already gotten tough, however, and despite government assistance in the 1970s, the business came to an end in the 1980s.

Axel Johnson (1844-1910), a saddler's son who went to work at the age of 13, founded a company that imported coal and exported iron and timber. In 1890, he acquired the Nordstjernan shipping company, which evolved into the Johnson Line. His son Axel Ax:son Johnson

(1876-1958) expanded the company and also established the Lindholmen shipyards, among other investments. The founder of the third big Gothenburg shipping company was Wilhlem Lundgren (1854-1914). Lundgren was known as the "poor cousin" in comparison with the Broströms and the Johnsons, but the Nike Line that he started traveled all the way to South Africa and Australia.

Another group of industrial and shipping families emerged in Malmö, the small city at the tip of Sweden and only 16 miles across the Öresund from Copenhagen. Founded by the Danes in the 12th century and annexed to Sweden along with the rest of the province of Skåne in 1658, Malmö grew in population from only 4,000 in 1800 to 10,000 in 1840.

Long a naval base and seaport that maintained strong ties to Denmark and Germany, Malmö turned into an industrial city with sugar refineries, textile mills and machine shops in the early 19th century, but achieved its full economic importance after the Swedish government decided in the 1850s to make it the southern terminal of the country's railroad system. Malmö's most important shipping concern was the Kockum yard started by Frans Henrik Kockum (1802-75), whose mother's family had started out by founding a tobacco spinnery in 1726.

Stockholm remained Sweden's largest and most prominent city. Its role as the nation's capital meant that its economy was a mixture of government and business, with the royal family at the top of the social ladder. Stockholm had developed its own business community, focused toward Germany and the Baltic, and its own bourgeoisie, dominated, at least initially, by a group called the *Skeppsbroadel*—some 20 rich families who lived in the Skeppsbro harbor area facing the Baltic Sea and derived their wealth from commerce, shipping and finance.

Stockholm quadrupled in population from 75,000 in 1800 to 300,000 in 1900, and the nouveau riche put a permanent stamp on the city, improving building standards, sanitation and electricity, and—in contrast with the old noble families who entertained at their manor houses and castles— establishing fine restaurants and public theaters. Stockholm society was provincial and puritanical by the standards of London or Paris, but for those elites who could travel, there were always escapes. In winter, the king and wealthy Swedes traveled to Italy and the south of France. In the 1880s, K.A. Wallenberg put his brother Gustaf in charge of building a railroad from Stockholm east to the island of Saltsjöbaden and establishing a seaside resort like the one in Monaco.

Some wealthy Swedes who objected to the strictness of Swedish society simply took their money and moved abroad, returning only in the summer months. One was Rolf de Maré, the grandson of a Swiss nobleman who had married a wealthy Swedish woman of middle-class origins. In the 1920s, de Maré raided the conservative Royal Opera, taking away some of its finest ballet dancers, who went with him to Paris, where he founded the avant-garde Ballet Suédois. Led by de Maré's lover, Jean

Börlin, a mariner's son who had been born near the Arctic Circle, the Ballet Suédois used Swedish themes for inspiration but blended African, American and even Turkish rhythms with classical technique. The ballets were heralded by the critics in Paris, Latin America and the United States—but denounced in the Stockholm newspapers by the Swedish critics who traveled to Paris to review them.

The Magic of Djurgården

The purest expression of this new bourgeois society was the development of Djurgården near Stockholm. On this island, royalty, nobles and the new bourgeoisie, including Jews, met, partied, married, built houses and occasionally caused scandals. Only a short distance across the water from the Royal Palace, Djurgården had been a royal hunting ground since Gustaf Vasa's time and was later used as a military training ground. In 1809, the state had taken over ownership of the land, and in 1823, King Karl XIV Johan built Rosendals Slott, a small palace for summer entertaining, on a portion of the property.

Swedish and foreign tourists know Djurgården mostly for Skansen, an open-air museum established in 1891 to showcase Sweden's old rural culture. But from its opening in 1853, the social center of Djurgården was Hasselbacken, a restaurant and café close to the bridges and ferries to Stockholm. The owner of Hasselbacken was Wilhelm Davidson, a young Jew from Norrköping. After finishing his schooling in 1834, Davidson had traveled to Berlin and Vienna, where he trained as a baker. At that time, Swedish law did not permit a Jew to be an ordinary baker, so Davidson specialized in making the more intricate "Swiss" pastries. At Hasselbacken, a band played outdoors, and common people would come and drink coffee or the Swedish liqueur Punsch in the outdoor café, while wealthier people went indoors to eat oysters, lobster and exotic fruits. When Davidson died in 1883, his sons, Manne and Ernst, took over the restaurant. They kept up their father's innovations, introducing gaslights and electricity, and they even had a telegraph in the lobby in case their customers needed to send a quick message.

Djurgården was already home to military officers and court officials, but in the middle of the 19th century, the Swedish state began to allow the construction of private homes on the island, and it became the most fashionable place for the new elite to live. Because the state maintained ownership of the land on Djurgården and the Royal Palace had to give permission for construction to proceed, these homes became symbols of social acceptance and the decisions about who was and who was not allowed to build there became the subject of controversy. In the 1860s, for example, F. Cederlund, a celebrated maker of Punsch, the Swedish liquor, was allowed to build a house that came to be known as Täcka Udden. K.A. Wallenberg bought the house in 1889, and it remained the family residence until his widow, Alice, died in 1956. (Marcus Wallenberg Jr. lived in the house the year before his death in 1982, and the Skandinaviska Enskilda Bank still maintains the cream-colored turreted mansion as a site for entertaining guests.)

Just up the street from Täcka Udden lived the controversial Thiel. Thiel was born in Norrköping in 1859, his father a freethinking Walloon who became a textile technician, his mother a devout German Jew. Thiel left school at 15 to go to Hamburg to work in a bank and returned to Sweden in 1877 and was hired by the Stockholms Enskilda Bank, where he rose rapidly. In 1891, he set up his own credit and discount business called Stockholms Kredit- och Diskontförening (Diskont Bank). Thiel's reputation was rather like that of the junk-bond dealers of the 1980s in the United States. He claimed that he "lent a hand in numerous industrial innovations," while more-conservative bankers and business leaders shook their heads at the risky ventures he backed. By the mid-1890s, however, he was one of the wealthiest men in Sweden.

Thiel had married Anna Josephson, a daughter of one of the most prominent Jewish families in Sweden, in 1884. The marriage also made him a brother-in-law of publisher Karl Otto Bonnier. At Bonnier's home, Thiel met leading artists and writers, but later, he wrote that "I felt suffocated" in this bourgeois society. His new relatives reportedly found him arrogant and morose. In 1896, Thiel fell in love with his wife's companion, Signe Hansen, a beautiful young widow. He divorced his wife and married Signe, of whom he later wrote: "She taught me the nature of love. The crisis in my life cost me everything I had. Firstly, my place in society. The Wallenberg and Bonnier wives turned up their noses! My own brother took exception to me. I lost touch with my four oldest children and never came really close to them again. Last but not least, I became a nervous wreck, sneaking about the streets for fear of meeting an acquaintance."

In 1897, Thiel and Signe moved into a large apartment on Strandvägen, one of Stockholm's most fashionable streets. Cut off from high society, Thiel associated with his new wife and her artistic friends, many of them members of an independent artists' union that had been formed in 1886. On his wife's advice, he began reading Nietzsche (whose Swedish publisher was, ironically enough, Bonnier). Thiel became a staunch advocate of Nietzsche's view that morality is imposed by "the all-too-many" and that people do good not for its own sake but to please their peers and satisfy a herd instinct. His acceptance of Nietzsche's views, it is said, allowed Thiel to feel free from pain when he was called a merchant Jew, an upstart and an adulterer.

Thiel became an art collector, buying the works of Gauguin, Munch and van Gogh, but more important, the Swedish artists of the era. After obtaining the permission of the court to build a house on Djurgården, Thiel hired the prominent avant-garde architect Ferdinand Boberg to design him "a home decorated with paintings on every wall." The house, which had no ornamentation but contains what today are considered extraordinary spaces for the display of art, so thumbed its nose at contemporary bourgeois taste that even the architect pointed out to friends that his "patron" had conceived much of the interior himself. Prince Eugén, the acclaimed artist brother of the king, whose own estate Waldemarsudde was near Thiel's house, conferred respectability on both Thiel and the artists he supported by giving Thiel one of his best paintings, "Night Cloud."

Proper Swedish society would ultimately claim it was right about Thiel. In 1910, Signe Thiel declared to a friend, "Times have changed, we are no longer rich." She left her husband for another man and committed suicide in 1915. Thiel lost most of his fortune during World War I (partly, it's said, because he had made so many enemies among other Swedish financiers), sold most of his valuable foreign paintings and, in 1924, sold the entire property on Djurgården, including the Swedish art, to the state for 1.4 million kronor. Thiel, who lived until 1947, described himself late in life as "a genius at failing." But, as a guide to the now-public gallery says, "he managed to create an unrivaled monument to his epoch."

Anders Zorn and the Rise of The Ordinary Swedes

The story of Anders Zorn, one of the painters whose work Thiel collected, illustrates the gulf between this tiny privileged world of wealthy Swedes and the lives of most of their countrymen. Zorn was born in 1860 in the village of Utmeland in Mora. His mother was Grudd Anna Andersdotter, who had taken a seasonal job in a brewery in Uppsala and become pregnant by Leonhard Zorn, a German brewer. As Zorn's biographer, Birgitta Sandström, notes, "There is no evidence to indicate that there was any discussion of marriage between the two families when

Grudd Anna realized she was pregnant." Leonhard Zorn never saw his son, but when he died in Helsinki in 1872, Grudd Anna managed, with the help of Zorn's colleagues, to get Anders a small inheritance from his father's estate. The boy went to Enköping to school, registering first as Anders Leonhardsson and later changing his name to Leonhard Zorn. At school, Zorn's artistic talent became obvious, and the wives of his father's colleagues raised the money to send him to the Royal Academy of Fine Arts in London. Zorn's success as a painter of portraits of the children of Stockholm society led to his meeting in 1881 his future wife, Emma Lamm, a member of an affluent Jewish textile family that was very active in the arts. Zorn did not depend on Lamm's wealth for his living, and in fact, he did not marry her until 1885, when he felt able to support her. But Lamm did introduce him to Sir Ernest Cassel, the wealthy British-based industrialist and banker who had many Swedish interests. Cassel became one of Zorn's greatest patrons and urged his friends to hire him to paint their portraits. Zorn's portrait subjects eventually included Chicago socialite Mrs. Potter Palmer, Boston arts patron Isabella Stewart Gardner, U.S. Presidents Grover Cleveland and William Howard Taft and members of the Swedish royal family. Zorn's reputation was not limited to portraits of wealthy patrons. Before his death in 1920, he had achieved even greater renown in artistic circles for his paintings of the inhabitants and environments of his native Mora and of sturdy peasant women like his mother.

For every Anders Zorn, whose talent, luck and marriage propelled him to the very top of Swedish society, there must have been hundreds of thousands of young Swedes who felt that their country had little to offer them. Around 1900, investigators calculated that about one-third of the families in Stockholm consisted of mothers alone with children. Sociologists note that if the investigators had focused exclusively on lower-income people, the figure would have been higher. Another set of studies showed that children raised by their mothers alone suffered from poor nutrition.

In the first half of the 19th century, Sweden's population grew so fast that the lot of the poor seemed to get worse. But by the middle of the century, stimulated by social movements in other parts of Europe and the United States, as well as their own historic unwillingness to accept oppression, the Swedish masses began to improve their own lives by organizing themselves into cooperatives, discouraging the alcohol consumption that had become a major health problem, immigrating to America and, a little later, forming the labor unions and political parties that would bring them full suffrage.

Co-ops, Temperance and the Religious Awakening

Co-ops: The concept of co-ops as organizations in which people could work together to achieve economic goals they could not achieve alone or within the prevailing economic system was brought to Sweden in 1825 by Erik Gustaf Geijer, the Värmland historian and poet, who had been studying the miserable social conditions in the industrial areas of England. "Cooperation is a new social order, provoked by necessity in the present wilderness of civilization," Geijer wrote. Geijer's interest in co-ops came nearly 20 years before the English weavers of Rochdale formed a nonprofit association in 1844 to relieve the miserable conditions under which they lived. The Rochdale experiment inspired the Danes, and by 1865, Swedish university professors, lawyers and journalists were promulgating the theory that cooperatives could be a means whereby the masses might improve their economic situation.

In the 1880s, a wealthy industrialist named L.O. Smith promoted the idea that workers could reduce their cost of living by establishing "workers' rings," which would receive discounts from private merchants and wholesalers. Merchants didn't honor the arrangement, however, and the workers' rings dissolved. In 1899, the *Kooperativa Förbundet* (Peasants' Cooperative Association, or Union) was established as a central organization. Martin Sundell, a co-op association employee said to have been blessed with brains, a splendid voice and charm, traveled around the country signing up members. In 1904, the union rented a warehouse in Malmö, purchased commodities wholesale and sold them to members cheaper than retail grocers did. The National Union of Retailers tried to get the Riksdag to pass legislation making it illegal for banks to make loans to co-ops, but the movement continued to gain strength. A cartel controlled Swedish margarine, and in 1909, when the cartel refused to sell margarine to the co-op union, the union bought a small margarine factory. Over the next decades, the co-op union gradually brought down the prices of products by threatening to go into the manufacturing business if wholesalers would not sell to them. In the 20th century, farmers would also join together in producer co-ops that would become a major element in the Swedish economy.

Temperance: Physicians, psychologists and sociologists still debate whether Swedes as well as Finns and Russians were always attracted more than other people to strong alcohol and, if so, whether the cold weather or some genetic trait led them there. But all agree that drinking increased dramatically early in the 19th century, when people learned that it was easier to distill *brännvin* (aquavit) from potatoes than from grain. The government abandoned its failed attempts to monopolize aquavit production, and it became commonplace for farms to have their own distilling machines. As private distillers began to make liquor for urban consumers, their demand for grains and potatoes sometimes caused food shortages. King Karl IV Johan, who was abstemious despite his French origins, said he was afraid himself that alcohol would ruin the Swedish people.

Temperance societies were organized in 1830 in Gothenburg and Stockholm, and Per Wieselgren, a Lutheran pastor, led a movement against drinking. Wieselgren's work was aided by the visit to Sweden of Robert Baird, an American Presbyterian Sunday school worker and temperance advocate. The king endorsed Baird's work and the temperance movement, and by the 1840s, alcohol consumption in Sweden had declined dramatically. In 1853, the Riksdag passed an act restricting distilling. In the 1870s, a second anti-alcohol campaign began, this one encouraging total abstinence and organized mostly by the International Order of Good Templars, a lodge that originated in the United States. Prohibition was advocated and even tried for a brief period in 1910, but in 1917, Sweden "solved" the problem by making the distribution of liquor a state-controlled monopoly, allowing localities to decide whether to license restaurants and bars and providing each Swede who wanted one a liquor ration book *(motbok)* allowing the purchase of a certain amount each month. Liquor rationing remained in effect until 1955.

Free churches: Sweden's Conventicle Decree of 1726 forbade private religious gatherings, but as early as the mid-18th century, Swedes began meeting in their homes to read the Bible and Martin Luther's writings. Inspired by the Pietistic Movement in Germany, these Readers *(Läsare)* began to express dissatisfaction with the formal services of the state Church and also to question the control that the state Church and its clergy had over their lives.

Many of the Readers initially emphasized the importance of raising moral standards and saving souls by doing missionary work among the Lapps (Sami) in the north of Sweden. But in the 19th century, they increasingly emphasized personal salvation by declaration of faith and questioned the Lutheran service itself, demanding freedom from the Church handbook so that they could conduct services as they saw fit. When their requests were refused, they formed their own "free" churches (although most did not formally renounce membership in the state Lutheran Church, into which they were born and had to pay taxes). In 1830, George Scott, a Methodist preacher from Edinburgh, arrived in Sweden, and Baptists, Mormons and other Protestant evangelists soon followed.

Lutheran Church officials made some concessions to these folk movements, but used all their powers to stop the loss of authority. Swedes who participated in these movements were sometimes put on trial and sentenced to diets of bread and water and required to acknowledge in public their commitment to the "true faith." Sweden lagged behind the other Scandinavian countries in establishing freedom of religion, and the most radical of the religious rebels left for America. Among them were the followers of Erik Jansson, who went on trial for heresy in 1845 and escaped to found, in 1846, a Christian communitarian colony in Bishop Hill, Illinois. Norway passed a religious freedom law in 1845 and Denmark in 1849, but it was not until 1851 that a Society for the Advancement of Religious Freedom was organized in Sweden and 1873 that the first law guaranteeing freedom of religion was passed.

Letters from America

Mixed into all these movements and others was the impact of the great Swedish emigration to the United States. As historian Jörgen Weibull has noted, average Swedes in 1900 rarely traveled farther afield than a day's journey by cart or horseback, but they were removed from their isolation by letters from America, which brought them into contact with the powerful social changes that were occurring there.

Swedes had never really lost contact with the New World after the Swedish colonization of Delaware. The American Revolution aroused widespread enthusiasm in Sweden, especially after the French Revolution turned violent. The idea of America as Europe's last, best hope received its classic expression in the words of Esaias Tegnér, Sweden's most celebrated poet of the day, at the 300th anniversary of the Reformation at Lund University in 1817: "If it be true, as many aver, that dusk is descending over old Europe, far to the west, beyond the sea, where the sun sets for us, it rises for a more fortunate world. Thither has Europe already sent many of its fondest hopes, there mankind will save its household gods, as Aeneas rescued his from the fall of Ilium."

While Tegnér philosophized about the meaning of America and its settlement by Europeans, many of his fellow Swedes saw it as the land of religious freedom and real economic opportunity. Between 1820 and 1920, 1.25 million Swedes made their way to America, hoping to better themselves economically or to practice their religion in freedom. The emigrants had their own joys and sorrows in America, but they also inadvertently provided a critique of Swedish life in the 19th century and forced official Sweden to confront the reasons that so many people were leaving their homeland.

Both upper-class and ordinary Swedes who traveled to the United States in the 1800s wrote newspaper accounts that were positive about the egalitarianism and opportunity in the New World, even if they disdained some of the customs. Many Swedish farmers and laborers wrote their relatives back home that they were more productive in the United States because the economic and political system treated them better. Young Scandinavian women who became house maids in America wrote that, in contrast with life back home, they were not required to do heavy outdoor work, had rooms of their own and regular days off, and were paid weekly. They could also dress as fashionably as their mistresses without fear of criticism. In contrast with Sweden, where the law bound farm laborers, including household servants, to year-long contracts, America allowed workers to quit at any time and they seldom had any difficulty finding new positions. They also reported they were treated like "ladies" by American men, who showed them a courtesy and consideration to which they were quite unaccustomed at home. (Swedish male emigrants often grumbled that the women took on airs and were more demanding than the young women back home.)

Perhaps the most wounding letter to America was one from an emigrant who had gone back to Sweden for a visit and viewed the ceremonial opening of the Riksdag. "With all respect for old Swedish customs and manners," he wrote, "I cannot but compare this pageant to a great American circus—minus the menagerie, of course. I would like to describe this seriocomical demonstration for the benefit of my American readers; but I am sorry to say that I can no longer remember the titles of the different officers, heralds, guards, lackeys, pages, etc.—all of them dressed in the most gorgeous costumes, some of them preceding, others following the king and the royal princes, who were adorned with all the medieval claptrap insignia of royalty, and wrapped in huge mantles of gay colors, and with long trains borne by courtiers or pages. We can comprehend the importance of a display of this kind a couple of centuries ago, but it seems to me that the common sense of our times demands its abolishment."

Traditional upper-class Swedes and Romantic writers defended the old order and found the new industrial world, America and the emigrants soullessly materialistic and horrifying. In 1821, the literary critic Vilhelm Fredrik Palmblad wrote that liberalism "promises us no fruits but those the North America tree of liberty has already borne: commerce, wealth, the highest production of grain, wool, livestock, children; but where feeling is impoverished, genius is tolerated as a luxury or at most is valued for the mercantile value of its products, weighed upon the scale of commerce."

Upper-class Swedes and the government initially disdained the emigrants as a poor, even criminal, unpatriotic element that would soon miss their homeland, but by 1900, they became worried that the country was being drained of its best, brightest and most vigorous people. In 1907, a National Society Against Emigration was founded, and the Riksdag appointed a commission to investigate the causes of emigration. The society's attempt to discourage emigration is interesting in light of what was happening in the economy. The society started an "Own-Home" movement, supporting loan agencies to help poor Swedes buy homes and farms. The project had some justification because many farmers' sons and daughters said they would rather move to America than work for someone else or become industrial workers. Swedish industry was expanding rapidly at the time, but there is no record that the National Society Against Emigration attempted to find jobs for Swedes in Swedish industry or to improve the working conditions in Swedish industry so that ordinary Swedes would want to stay in the country of their birth. Jonsered, a textile complex near Gothenburg, did provide land and small detached houses for workers to discourage its employees from emigrating, but such acts were so rare that the village is now a museum.

Swedish businessmen rarely criticized the old order or defended America in public, and some Swedes viewed the National Society Against Emigration as a front group to keep labor plentiful and hold down the wages of Swedish workers. But Gustaf Wallenberg, the son of A.O. Wallenberg and grandfather of Raoul Wallenberg, who would became famous for saving Hungarian Jews from death during World War II, revealed his admiration for America in a letter he wrote to Raoul in 1929, after he decided to send the young man to the United States to study architecture at the University of Michigan. Gustaf Wallenberg, who had been in charge of building the railroad to Saltsjöbaden before becoming a diplomat and retiring in Istanbul, wrote to his grandson that "the common prejudice is that only criminals and losers went to America." But, he added, "I am firmly convinced that Father's [A.O. had gone with two Navy friends to the United States in 1838 and served in the U.S. merchant marine] financial acumen developed during the time he spent in America, and I am also persuaded that my own ambition grew out of my having spent rather long periods working in America 42 years ago." In a gibe against his brothers, Gustaf continued, "My brothers teased me plenty for what they saw as my perverse inclinations. None of them went there until 20 or 30 years later. But one thing is certain, and that is that neither Saltsjöbaden nor any undertaking requiring initiative other than the usual homegrown variety would have seen the light of day had it not been for my stay in America. . . . It put me ahead of my time and contributed to the feeling—which must not be taken as smug self-sufficiency but rather as a firm sense of purpose—that I could accomplish whatever I had undertaken. Do you think that anyone taught to keep 'in step' could have carried off as enormous a project as Saltsjöbaden at the age of 30, and practically single-handedly? . . . It is because of what both my father and I found in America that makes me so eager for you to get your *direction in life* there. No one has ever understood as well as I have, because I saw it in my youth, how decisive his time there was for my father. I use the expression *direction in life* and not "education" on purpose. . . . The curriculum offered by an American school is in no way superior or even equal to that offered in Sweden. No, what I am trying to give you is completely different: insight into the American frame of mind, the kind of upbringing aimed at teaching men to be self-reliant, even to feel that they are better than others, which may just be the basis and the source of America's position of leadership today. This is something very different from 'keeping in step' here at home. The frame of mind struck me so forcefully when I first went to America that I never even talked about it with my brothers when I came home: I listened, smiling secretly and silently, from an American point of view, to all the naive viewpoints prevalent at that time, because I knew they came from a different perspective. Maybe now you can begin to see that what I want you to get there is not schooling but life, contact with young Americans, so that you can learn how to develop into a well-organized fighter ready to make his way in the world. Allow me to point out a few Swedes who have made more of a mark in life than others: Edström, head of Asea; Lundhqvist, head of Stora Kopparbergs Bergslag; Prytz, SKF; and Ivar Kreuger, who has done better than the whole pack of them, including the Wallenbergs. Where did they get their direction? Where did they learn how to run an organization? In America!" (Gustaf Wallenberg wrote his letter three years before Kreuger's empire fell apart and Kreuger committed suicide.)

It would take several generations for Swedes to come to terms with the fact that, while most Swedish Americans were content to lead middle class lives, a few actually got as rich as the richest Swedes and became benefactors of Swedish causes. The most prominent of these was Curtis L. Carlson, the creator of Gold Bond Stamps and later the driving force behind Carlson Companies Inc., whose holdings include the Radisson hotels. Carlson was born in 1914, in Minneapolis, Minn., a son of a father from Småland and a mother from Värmland. When Carlson died in 1999 at the age of 84, he had been honored by the Swedish government and was ranked by Forbes magazine as the richest Minnesotan, with a net worth of $1.7 billion. He was described by *Vestkusten*, the California Swedish newspaper, as "the ultimate Swedish-American self-made man."

The Rise of Socialism, the Unions and The Swedish Employer's Confederation

Co-ops, the temperance lodges and free churches all encouraged the Swedes to organize themselves and run their organizations on democratic principles imported from the United States. But the Swedes eventually turned to the Social Democratic Party and labor unions that took a much tougher line than American-style reform groups in confrontations with the capitalist elite.

Swedish workers' organizations began to appear at the local level in the 1860s, and the first formal union, that of tobacco workers in Malmö, appeared in 1874. Its inspiration was not indigenous, however; it was organized by Danes who feared that Swedes would move to Denmark and depress wages in that country, where unions had already made headway. As more and more Swedes went to work in industry, strikes broke out. In 1879, workers at a sawmill in Sundsvall went on strike when the owners announced that they would reduce their 2.5 kronor per 12-hour-day wages by 15 to 20 percent. The governor of the province appealed to King Oskar II, who had taken power in 1872, for help, and Oskar replied, "Calm all the right-minded and warn all the disturbers, for patience must have a limit. Cannon boats and soldiers are on the way." The governor could not force the workers back to their jobs, because there was no law against strikes, but he did force them to leave and managed to imprison their leaders. The result of his actions and King Oskar's cable was public sympathy for the workers.

In 1881, a tailor named August Palm, who had come in contact with socialism while he was working in Germany and Denmark, gave the first public address on the doctrine in Sweden. The same year, building workers struck in Stockholm and turned to Dr. Anton Nyström, a socially conscious physician, who urged them to organize unions complete with strike funds. Nyström's agenda was not a challenge to the capitalist system, but a broad liberal agenda including the establishment of an employment office, an increase in state stipends for workers to study abroad, the use of committees in arbitration, universal suffrage, a 10-hour workday, a progressive income tax and religious freedom. Europe was engulfed in revolutionary thinking, however, and in 1886, a convention of Scandinavian trade unionists held in Gothenburg declared that "the private capitalistic method of production is a permanent hindrance for bringing about prosperity and happiness in the community." The same year, the first Swedish trade union in the modern sense, that of typesetters, was founded. In 1889, the Social Democratic Party—Sweden's first political party—was founded, inextricably linking the union movement and the party. In 1896, Hjalmar Branting, an Uppsala University astronomy student and schoolmate of Crown Prince Gustaf who had converted to the Social Democratic cause, was elected to the Riksdag. That year, the number of unions had grown to 21, with a total of about 25,000 members, about one-tenth of all workers. The largest was the Iron and Metal Workers' Union, with about 5,000 members. In 1898, a general labor federation for the entire country, the *Landsorganisationen* (Swedish Trades Union Congress), or LO, as it is called, was formed.

Aware of the violent strikes that had broken out in other countries, neither the Swedish business establishment nor the general public approved of the union effort. In 1899, the Riksdag passed the Åkarp Law, which pledged government protection for strikebreakers and created two government commissions to study employment-contract legislation and arbitration. As early as 1896, employers of metalworkers in Gothenburg had created their own organization, the Metal Trades Employers' Association *(Verkstadsföreningen)*, or VF; and two other employer associations had been founded in the south of Sweden, one in 1899 and one in 1902. Danish employers formed their own national association in 1899, and the same year, Harald Hjärne, a Swedish historian began to argue that employers should establish their own national groups so that individual employers would not have to fight the unions on their own.

While Swedish citizens may have been skeptical about labor unions, the vast majority wanted the right to vote expanded beyond men of property, and the issues of universal suffrage and workers' rights became entangled. In 1901, concerned by the wars in the Balkans, Russia's attempts to "Russify" Finland and tensions between Germany and Russia, the Swedish government instituted a military draft requiring each young man to serve 240 days. The draft, in turn, produced a rallying cry of "One man, one vote, one gun." In 1902, the Social Democratic Party declared a three-day suffrage strike, and 120,000 employees stopped working. In response, the government granted enough electoral reform that three more Social Democrats joined Branting in the Riskdag, but this bold action by the labor unions caused the employers to form, on September 17, 1902, at the Grand Hotel in Stockholm, the Swedish Employers' Confederation *(Svenska Arbetsgivareföreningen)*, or SAF. The meeting was initiated by Gustaf Fredrik (Dick) Östberg, a farmer who had become head of a firm that sold milk in Stockholm and who was a member of Parliament; Robert Almström, head of a porcelain factory; and Oscar Carlson, founder and head of a super phosphate plant.

In addition to representing its members in discussions with unions and the government, SAF set up a kind of reverse strike fund. SAF charged its members annual dues based on the number of their employees and put the bulk of the money into an insurance fund, from which a predetermined sum was to be paid to the employers in case of strikes. As the unions grew, so did SAF. In 1903, SAF had 101 member companies employing 24,000 workers. By 1907, the number of workers who were members of LO unions had risen to 240,000; and the number of companies that were members of SAF had multiplied by 10, to 997 companies employing 127,126 workers.

As de Geer has noted, the formation of both strong unions and a strong Employers' Confederation reflected the Swedish history of preferring negotiation rather than confrontation, and a political tradition in which the peasants always had a role. "It was through negotiation rather than by insurrection or the exercise of power that people promoted their interests," de Geer has written. "This can be interpreted as a peaceableness, a diffidence, or an anti-aggressiveness in the Swedish national character. What counted was cooperation. To take no part in discussing the concerns of a village or the country was a cause for anxiety. Conformity has always been more important than originality—for better or worse."

Neither the workers nor the employers found it easy to create organizations that worked well. After getting over the initial issue of whether they should be loyal to their employers or their fellow workers, with whom they often competed for jobs, Swedish unionists reflected the divisions within the union movement worldwide and were split between the reformers (who favored improving working conditions within industry and striking against individual companies and industries) and the radicals (who wanted to destroy the capitalist system and favored general strikes that would paralyze society). Swedish employers, meanwhile, were split between the liberals (who favored free trade) and the conservatives (who favored protection from imports). The liberals feared that the creation and growth of the employers' organizations would help the protectionists gain more political power, especially because Östberg, who was elected chairman of the SAF board in 1903, was a convinced protectionist.

The pattern of national union-employer relations was established not by SAF, but by the Metal Trades Employers' Association in an agreement it signed with the Iron and Metal Workers' Union in 1905. The metal trades employers wanted to be able to fire strike-prone workers, and the union wanted guarantees that if the union adopted a hard line in negotiations, members would not be subject to discrimination. The union tried to establish a closed shop, and the industry locked out the workers in the summer. In November, the two parties agreed that employers would have the right to hire, fire and distribute work, but that the workers would have the right to join unions without fear of retribution and if a dismissed union member believed his dismissal was related to his union membership, he had the right to call for an investigation.

SAF's board, meanwhile, adopted a statement that all collective agreements should contain a provision confirming the employers' right to "freely appoint and dismiss employees, and to assign jobs and manage production." The provision, which came to be known in labor negotiators' shorthand as "Paragraph 23," (later, in some documents known as "Paragraph 32") initially raised the ire of SAF members because it implied acceptance of collective agreements, but aroused even greater indignation among workers. In 1906, after more labor strife, SAF's board and the LO leaders came to an agreement similar to the one between the metal factory owners and their workers. It recognized the employers' right to hire, fire and assign work and also the workers' "right of association," their right to negotiate and the acceptance of collective agreements as the appropriate method for resolving disputes. A side agreement said that union members' refusal to work with strikebreakers should not be regarded as a breach of the basic document. De Geer notes that the 1906 agreement "involved no radical new thinking," but that Swedish employers "had shown a quite remarkable collective liberalism in their attitude towards the trade union movement" in comparison with their counterparts in France, Germany and the United States.

Union members grudgingly accepted the agreement, but some SAF members balked, charging that Östberg had missed an opportunity to confront the unions and was more loyal to the Conservative government, which did not want a labor conflict, than he was to the members. In 1906, the Riksdag had overcome industry opposition to pass a law on mediation that set up a national government conciliation office and divided the country into districts with appointed conciliators ready to mediate whenever a conflict arose. When a strike broke out at the Kosta glassworks in Småland, Östberg, after consultation with the state conciliator and the LO chairman, tried to get Kosta to reinstate some workers, but the SAF board refused to endorse his action. With this lack of support, Östberg declined to run for reelection and was succeeded by Hjalmar von Sydow, a deputy district court judge, who would run SAF until 1931.

Between 1907 and 1909, the Swedish economy was in recession, and the labor movement turned radical. In 1908, SAF and the Shipowners Association tried to create stevedoring companies that would be independent of the trade unions, and they brought in stevedores from England. Young socialists blew up one of their ships, the *Amalthea*, in Malmö harbor. The government appointed a mediation commission, the first of its kind under the 1906 law, to deal with the labor dispute; the employers compromised, but only after they had held out as long as possible. In 1909, after a scattered series of labor disputes, SAF ordered a general lockout and LO responded with a general strike. The public sympathized with the strikers, but when the public transport and print workers joined them, transportation and communications were disrupted, public support plunged and the government declined to intervene. LO was forced to call off the then-five-week-old strike, but it refused a SAF proposal for a uniform central agreement that would have specified the employer's right to hire, fire and distribute work; the right to impose sympathetic lockouts; and the principle that foremen are managers and should be prohibited from becoming part of the trade unions.

SAF's lockout tactic had succeeded, and employers felt more loyalty to the organization. The defeat left LO weak and divided, its 1907 membership of 240,000 reduced to 118,000 by 1911, a decline of about 57 percent. The period also brought a break between the reformers and the union radicals, who opposed collective agreements as restrictions on workers' freedom of action and viewed the sudden general strike without warning as the essential method of social and political struggle. An anarchist faction was expelled from the Social Democratic Party in 1908, and after open confrontation at the LO congress in November 1909, the radicals founded the Central Organization of Swedish Workers (SAC) in 1910. For the next few years, until the beginning of World War I, the employers had the upper hand. But the political left was growing steadily stronger and becoming more radical, and in 1914, the Social Democrats became the largest party in the Lower Chamber.

Suffrage and Political Parties

While employers and unions struggled to achieve a balance, the issue of universal suffrage had gone unresolved. The two-chamber Riksdag established in 1867 had disappointed many social reformers. Industrialists and high officials dominated the indirectly elected Upper Chamber, while farmers dominated the Lower Chamber. The two chambers were often at loggerheads, but both found it difficult to acknowledge that the franchise should be broadened to include average citizens, who were demanding a say in issues of defense, industrial protectionism and Sweden's union with Norway.

The suffrage movement had its spokesmen in the Riksdag, such as Adolf Hedin, a journalist who was a member from 1870-1905. The movement got a great boost in 1882, when a group of Uppsala University students formed a liberal-radical society called Verdandi. Inspired by Strindberg and the Norwegian dramatist Henrik Ibsen, members of

Verdandi shocked conservative university officials by insisting on free discussion of all public problems, including suffrage, religious freedom, temperance and union politics. Verdandi's leader was Karl Staaf, who would later serve two nonconsecutive terms as prime minister. Branting, the first Social Democrat in the Riksdag—and later a prime minister—was an honorary member of Verdandi and, in 1886, declared that "universal suffrage is the price with which the bourgeoisie can buy a settlement through administration in place of liquidation ordered by the court of revolution."

Suffragists kept up the pressure. In 1893 and 1894, "folkriksdag" were organized to prove that common people could discuss important issues. After the Norwegians established suffrage for all men in 1898, reformers pointed out that the world had not come to an end in that adjoining country, which, after all, was in a union with Sweden. That year, suffrage petitioners in Sweden gathered 364,000 signatures, including 63,000 from women.

At the same time, there was a somewhat separate fight to reduce the power of the monarch in favor of parliamentary government. Historians say that the exiling of Gustaf IV Adolf and the recruitment of Karl XIV Johan from France freed the Swedish people from thinking that their king had a divine right or the kind of ancient dynastic authority that emanated from Gustaf Vasa. Karl XIV Johan's descendants did not want to give up their royal authority, however. In 1866, when King Karl XV had approved changing the Riksdag from four estates to two chambers, it was with the understanding that his authority to appoint his ministers—almost always nobles and senior bureaucrats—would not change. In the course of day-to-day policy making, the ministers had to work with the Riksdag, and the king had to appoint ministers who were cooperative. Despite the history of the Hats and the Caps in the 18th century, Louis Gerhard De Geer, the father of the two-chamber Riksdag, had hated political parties and intended to put in place a system that would discourage their creation. But groups emerged naturally within the Riksdag for purposes of building support for legislation and outside for purposes of debate and election. The Social Democrats created a formal party in 1889, even before they were represented; but the farmers were already organized, and the first liberal group in the Riksdag, the *Folkpartiet*, was formed in 1895. Farmers, social reformers, teetotalers and intellectuals who were united by their belief in the extension of suffrage formed a Liberal Coalition Party, which merged with *Folkpartiet* in 1900. In 1904, conservatives in both chambers of the Riksdag formed the Voters' General Association as an umbrella organization.

Staaf, meanwhile, had become the first lawyer appointed to the king's council, and in 1905, after he won plaudits for his role in the delicate negotiations that dissolved the union between Sweden and Norway, King Oskar II made him prime minister. Staaf and his Liberals made a suffrage proposal, but it failed and he resigned. He was replaced by Conservative Arvid Lindman, an industrialist and former naval officer. After the 1908 elections showed the Conservatives and the Liberals in roughly equal numbers and the Social Democrats growing, the Conservative government headed by Lindman wrote a law that allowed all tax-paying men over 24 to vote for members of the Lower Chamber and reduced the wealth requirements for members of the Upper Chamber. The measure doubled the size of the electorate from 9.5 to 19 percent of the population. In the 1911 elections, the Liberals and the Social Democrats increased their ranks at the expense of the Conservatives and Staaf became prime minister again. Staaf and Branting worked closely together, and the Riksdag passed key social legislation such as that which established a social welfare board and a pension system to be financed by the state tobacco monopoly.

Staaf and Branting were more progressive than the Conservatives, but the entire period from 1900 until the beginning of World War I was marked by the passage of progressive legislation, whether Conservatives or Liberals led the government. In the 1990s, conservative scholar Emil Uddhammar pointed out that although Swedish Conservatives later criticized the Social Democrats for increasing the role of government, Conservative governments initiated progressive income and property taxes in 1902 and 1910; the nationalization of the minefields in Lappland and the passage of city planning laws, both in 1907; and the reform of the universal old-age pension in 1913. The initiation of these laws by Conservative governments and their passage "without significant opposition from any of the four major parties" signaled "an unopposed emergence of the big state in Sweden," Uddhammar concluded.

Staaf wanted to make suffrage universal, but he got into political trouble. Even though World War I was looming, Staaf, his party and his allies among the Social Democrats disliked shifting money from social welfare to rearmament. He resisted a military buildup, but after a massive public outcry, announced that he would support rearmament but not extension of military service. That wasn't enough for King Gustaf V, who had been crowned in 1907. With Gustaf V's and the Conservatives' encouragement, some 31,000 farmers marched on Stockholm on February 6, 1914, to show their support for the king's position. Staaf resigned, and a Conservative government headed by Hjalmar Hammarskjöld was appointed. It was the king's—indeed the Swedish monarchy's— last hurrah, however. Two days after the farmers' march, 50,000 workers organized by Branting marched to pledge support for Staaf and protest Gustaf's attempt at "personal monarchy." With the

Social Democrats on the rise once more, Gustaf did not again attempt to rally "his" people.

The Impact of World War I and the Russian Revolution

When World War I broke out, the political parties made a truce not to push for further political reform until after the war, and the employers and the unions joined the truce to assure that industrial production would be maintained. Sweden continued the neutrality it had practiced since the end of the Napoleonic Wars, although a number of well-placed Swedes favored the German side, including Sven Hedin, a noted explorer who had the distinction, in 1902, of being the last Swede to be ennobled, and Gustaf V's wife, Queen Viktoria, who was a granddaughter of Kaiser Wilhelm I.

World War I forced changes in Sweden's trade relations. Before the war, Britain had been Sweden's main trading partner; during the war, however, Germany blocked Swedish trade with Britain. But it was geographically difficult for Britain to block Swedish trade with Germany across the Baltic. Germany became such a good customer for Swedish iron ore and agricultural goods that Sweden was able to pay off most of its foreign debt with profits from its German trade. This situation deteriorated in 1917 after Germany began a submarine campaign and the Allies became more diligent in stopping the ships of neutral countries. Sweden could no longer import coal or food.

When the war led to high profits and inflation without an increase in wages, workers once again started joining labor unions. Prices rose 30 percent between 1914 and 1916 and another 20 percent between 1916 and 1917. SAF opposed wage increases because it feared they would be permanent; employers instead paid gratuities or gave Christmas presents to employees. Industrialists were distressed when angry workers began joining unions again, but they soon learned that the unions could be helpful in controlling workers. When food shortages caused riots, syndicalists and other radicals tried to exploit them only to find their efforts countered by LO. At a SAF board meeting in June 1917, von Sydow declared that the authority of LO had saved the industrial peace.

Swedes had become so impressed with German technology and efficiency that even Prime Minister Hammarskjöld was sure that Germany would win the war. In March 1917, when it became clear that

Germany would lose and Sweden had to develop better relations with the Allies, Hammarskjöld was forced to resign.

The impact of the war's end was complicated by the revolution in nearby Russia, which raised hopes among radicals and sent shudders down the spines of upper-class Swedes. A Social Democratic Youth League was formed, which later become the Social Democratic Party of the Left and officially became the Swedish Communist Party in 1921.

In the 1917 elections, the Conservatives did poorly because of economic discontent and revelations that neutral Sweden had allowed Germany to use Swedish channels for diplomatic cables. In October, Nils Edén, an Uppsala University history professor who was the head of the Liberal Party, became prime minister in the first Liberal-Social Democratic coalition. With the war ending and the Russian Revolution under way, the Swedish establishment could no longer resist the pressure for political reform. In November 1918, the Riksdag ended property requirements for candidates for the Upper Chamber (though it maintained the system of indirect election) and established almost universal suffrage for both men and women.

In 1920, the Liberal-Social Democratic coalition government also established the eight-hour workday. Once universal suffrage was achieved, the divisions between the Liberals and the Social Democrats grew because the Social Democrats proposed an increasingly radical program of inheritance taxes, unemployment insurance, abolition of the monarchy, more regulation of business and expropriation of large estates. In March 1920, Edén resigned and Branting became the first Social Democratic prime minister in any country to reach power by peaceful means. Branting's first prime ministership lasted only until November, when Conservatives won more seats in the Lower Chamber, but he set up commissions to investigate industrial democracy and state control of natural resources.

During Branting's eight months in office, De Geer has written, the employers learned that "the government's neutrality in labor market disputes could by no means be taken for granted." After the eight-hour workday went into effect, builders and their unions got into a dispute over changes in compensation, and the Association of Building Contractors subsequently declared a lockout. Because the building contractors were part of SAF, the material suppliers' association refused to provide them with cement. But the government was encouraging the construction of housing and bought up a large quantity of cement and placed it at the disposal of nonorganized builders. Without assurances of the government's neutrality, SAF leader von Sydow decided he could not extend the lockout to other suppliers.

One reason SAF members tried to avoid a confrontation with the unions was that Sweden was in a postwar boom and its members did not want to shut down when they had the opportunity to make a lot of money. But in the autumn of 1920, when Sweden's economic situation deteriorated and prices fell, SAF got the unions to agree to silence when wages were reduced 20 percent.

The 1922 parliamentary elections were the first in which universal suffrage was in effect, and the Social Democrats became the largest single party in the Lower Chamber. The Social Democrats did not have a majority of votes, but Branting again became prime minister. Unemployment continued to be high, the Communists were agitating and Branting resigned in April 1923. A Conservative government ruled until October 1924, when Branting returned for a third term. Branting died in 1925, and there were expressions of profound grief for the king's onetime schoolmate who had taken the Social Democratic Party down a moderate path. The Social Democrats remained in power, led by Rickard Sandler, who served as prime minister until 1926, when the Riksdag directed that miners who had been striking at the Stripa mine in central Sweden should receive no unemployment benefits. At that point, the Liberals, led by C.G. Ekman, took over.

Sweden had been engaged for some years in a debate over government regulation of the labor market, with both the unions and the employers distrusting the government but also expressing some hope that the state could play a mediating role. In the '20s, syndicalist agitators had become increasingly active, particularly in the forestry and building sectors, and employers began to fear their avowed unwillingness to follow labor contracts for the duration of time specified. In 1928, the Riksdag passed the Collective Agreements Act and the Labor Court Act, which declared collective agreements binding on the individual even if he or she joined or left a union during the period of an agreement. It also forbade strikes and slowdowns over interpretation of the agreement; disputes were instead to be referred to a court of seven members, three trained in the law and appointed by the government and two each appointed by SAF and LO. LO opposed the law and told 400,000 workers to put down their tools for two hours in protest against it. In retrospect, De Geer has written, it is clear that LO's decision was intended to deflect criticism from its Communist competitors rather than to keep the law from being enacted.

The 1928 campaign turned bitter. The Social Democrats proposed equalizing wealth and said that "poverty is accepted with equanimity when it is shared by all," a tenet that made business leaders afraid that if the Social Democrats remained in power, they would not care whether the country was being productive and increasing its wealth. According to former Swedish Trade Federation research director Clas-Erik Odhner, the Social Democrats still call the '28 elections the "Cossack elections" because the Conservative Party won by combining "the old fear of Russians with the new fear of Communists" and charging that if the Social Democrats won, they would allow Russian Cossacks to ravage the land and rape the women.

The '28 elections brought Lindman back as prime minister, but his administration turned out to be the Conservatives' swan song. The Great Depression began in 1929, and the first indication that it had reached Sweden was a drop in sugar and grain prices. Ekman and the Liberals came back into power in 1930, but the times were helping the Social Democrats. In May 1931, workers were on strike at Ådalen, a sawmill region in northern Sweden; the military was called in to protect strikebreakers, stones were thrown, the military answered with shots and five people died. All over Sweden there were demonstrations in support of the strikers and against the armed forces, with Social Democrats and Communists marching side by side. Arthur Engberg, one of the leading Social Democrats in the Riksdag, called the soldiers "murderers" and the strikebreakers "vermin." As Swedish political scientist Stig Hadenius has noted, "The armed forces were regarded as the long arm of the old ruling class. For some people, the fatal shootings in the Ådalen valley served to confirm that this idea was correct."

Meanwhile, in 1926, Nils Karleby, who had studied with the classic conservative economists Eli Heckscher and Gösta Bagge but had become a charismatic leader among radical young intellectuals, wrote *Socialism Faces Reality,* in which he reemphasized Swedish socialism's roots in the Enlightenment of the 18th century, rejected Karl Marx and called for a socialist doctrine based on democracy with a goal of improving the lives of all citizens. Per Albin Hansson, the Social Democratic leader, had begun to search for a political line with broader appeal and adopted Karleby's thinking. In 1929, Hansson wrote that the key words in the Social Democratic movement should not be "class" and "struggle," but "people" and "cooperation." Hansson's ideal was that Sweden should become a *folkhemmet* ("people's home") in which the state would take care of all its citizens. In November 1931, Ernst Wigforss, another Social Democratic leader, said that "up to now, we Social Democrats have said no to all help to farmers which would involve any considerable costs. This policy can no longer be justified." Wigforss was one of the first Social Democrats to recognize the problems in rural Sweden. Not only were Sweden's small farmers having a difficult time coping with the Depression, but the law still allowed the lowest class of farm laborers to be paid wages in kind. Unionization of farm workers had made some progress in the 20th century and the farmworkers' union had joined LO in 1930.

Continuing unemployment, low farm prices, the dissolution of Match King Ivar Kreuger's empire and his suicide in Paris all helped make the Social Democratic Party the biggest winner in the 1932 elections and Hansson the prime minister. The Social Democrats have held the prime ministership almost continuously ever since, but in 1932, they held only 104 seats in the Lower Chamber, 12 short of a majority, and had to search for support among the other parties. Their ideological differences with the Liberals were now too great to allow the formation of another coalition. But the Agrarians had been taken over by younger members, and they were desperately seeking aid for farmers. In a political deal that became known in Sweden as the *kohandel* ("cow trade"), the Social Democrats formed an alliance with the Agrarian Party. After the election, the Social Democrats agreed that the government would assume responsibility for the incomes of small farmers through subsidies, price regulations and protection from imports. The Agrarian Party agreed to the Social Democrats' plan to create jobs for the unemployed at standard wages and to do it with the deficit financing schemes suggested by British economist John Maynard Keynes—the same approach that would soon be tried in the United States under President Franklin D. Roosevelt.

Between 1933 and 1936, the Agrarians were not part of the Social Democratic Cabinet, but the two parties voted together in 1934 to pass housing construction subsidies and unemployment insurance, in 1935 to raise basic pensions and in 1936 to regulate the working hours of rural laborers.

Under the Social Democratic government, the consumer co-op movement continued to strengthen. Farmers also began forming co-ops to process their commodities and to sell their products themselves. A farmers' co-operative for the purchase of seeds, fertilizers and cattle feed had been formed in 1905, but Swedish farmers didn't take much of an interest in producer co-operatives until the crisis of the '30s. In 1932, the National Federation of Creameries, the Swedish Slaughterhouse Association and the Swedish Egg Cooperative Federation were all formed, and in 1934, a National Fruit Union of fruit growers. Farmers of all social classes and all sizes of property joined the co-ops, and they brought much greater stability to Swedish agriculture. By 1936, Sweden was coming out of the Depression, and it was the stories of these government economic initiatives and co-ops that American writer Marquis Childs told the world in *Sweden: The Middle Way*.

The Social Democrats were still in such internal disagreement on national defense that they could not come up with a viable policy. In 1936, after the League of Nations failed to address the Italian invasion of Ethiopia and Germany was rearming, Swedes became worried about their own defenses, and the Riksdag passed a bill sponsored by the nonsocialists to strengthen the nation's armed forces. The Social Democratic Cabinet resigned, and Agrarians ruled the country for the summer of 1936. After elections in September, the Social Democrats and the Agrarians created a formal coalition. The Riksdag continued advancement of the social agenda, approving in 1937 aid to mothers and state loans for young couples and in 1938 mandatory two-week vacations for all workers.

The Population "Crisis", the Myrdals and the Socialization of Swedish Housing

The rise of the Social Democrats coincided with a growing national concern, almost obsession, about Sweden's low birthrate. The birthrate issue, which interested every class and political party, provided an opening for the young, dynamic and ambitious social scientists Gunnar and Alva Myrdal to popularize their ideas on how society should be organized. Their work would indirectly socialize the production of housing and influences Sweden's economic structure to this day.

Swedes had been debating the issues of population growth and birth control since the early 19th century when Thomas Malthus, a British parson, began arguing that population would outstrip the food supply. In 1876, the issue of birth control had gained a wider audience when Knut Wicksell, a young student of economics at Uppsala University, told a temperance meeting that the cause of alcoholism was not immorality but poverty and that poverty could be solved by couples' voluntarily limiting the number of children they had. Knowledge of birth control spread widely during the late 19th and early 20th centuries. In 1910, out of concern for both the dropping birthrate and the moral implications of sexual relations without reproduction, the Swedish government forbade the exhibition and advertising of birth control devices. The ban had no impact. In 1913, Hinke Berggren, leader of the syndicalist Social Democratic Youth League began Sweden's sexual liberation with a lecture that advocated female sexual freedom, premarital sex and birth control. By the mid-1920s, statistics showed that the Swedish birthrate had fallen below replacement level. Intellectuals of every ideology and leaders of all parties argued over why Swedes were not bearing children, with the conservatives charging a decline in morality and the leftists arguing that poorer Swedes were making a logical economic decision.

Into this heated battle came the Myrdals: Gunnar, a construction worker's son whose brilliance had won him a place at the University of Stockholm, and his wife, Alva, a master builder's daughter who was unusually well educated for the time and also a University of Stockholm graduate. Gunnar Myrdal earned his law degree in 1923, but found that

157

he did not like practicing law. He returned to the university to study under Gustav Cassel, Sweden's most prominent economist. The Myrdals spent the 1929-30 academic year on Rockefeller grants in the United States, where Gunnar concentrated on population movement as societies changed from agriculture to industry and Alva on child psychology with an emphasis on how families changed as societies industrialized.

In 1933, Gunnar Myrdal succeeded Cassel in a University of Stockholm professorship in political economy and financial science named after newspaperman Lars Johan Hierta, but his ideas soon diverged dramatically from those of the free-market oriented Hierta and Cassel. The Myrdals' intellectual social set included the young Swedish architects who believed that design should serve the masses. In 1932, Gunnar Myrdal and one of the architects, Uno Åhrén, who was chief city planner in Gothenburg, met with the new Social Democratic social minister, Gustav Möller, and declared to him that housing was a serious social problem that should be addressed as part of the planned economy the Social Democrats were trying to develop. Möller, a trade unionist of modest origins, proved distrustful of the two young intellectuals. But Ernst Wigforss, who had become minister of finance and was in charge of housing statistics, liked the idea and commissioned Myrdal and Åhrén to conduct a housing study. Their results showed that large families lived in poor housing partly because they chose to spend their money on other things. Myrdal and Åhrén concluded that the Swedish people needed "housing enlightenment" and that the state should subsidize housing production so that children would not grow up in unhealthy conditions.

Alva Myrdal, meanwhile, had continued to work on children's welfare, and in 1934, the Myrdals decided to co-write a book on the population question. Gunnar came to believe an increase in the birthrate was necessary for the welfare of the country, while Alva held to a feminist position that the decision to bear a child should be up to a woman and that women should not be subjected to social pressure to bear more children. The couple agreed, however, on the idea that Sweden needed a stable population base, which could be achieved with a 40 percent increase in the birthrate, and on a range of social policies to encourage Swedes to have children. The editor of a publishing house specializing in works to advance "people's movements" rejected the book, fearing it would offend working-class sensibilities, but Bonnier's, Sweden's largest commercial publisher, accepted it and gave it the sensational (for that time) title *Crisis in the Population Question*.

In the book, the Myrdals broke with the international socialist tradition, which held that the workers had no stake in any nation's birthrate because workers really had no home state. The Swedish birthrate, the Myrdals said, had "fallen catastrophically" and needed to rise if Sweden were to continue to exist as a nation and a culture. With the Nazis and their theories of the Aryan super-race on the rise in Germany, that statement sounded right-wing, but the Myrdals deflected criticism by adding that women should not have to bear children as a duty to the state. Instead, the Myrdals argued in favor of voluntary parenthood, sex education in the schools, legalization of birth control and a woman's right to work. If a socialist redistribution of wealth were geared toward couples of childbearing age, the Myrdals argued, couples would choose to bear more children. The Myrdals rejected the simple solutions of higher wages or tax reductions because, they said, the state could not be sure the money would be spent on children. Instead, they proposed rent subsidies for families with children, free school lunches, free medical care, free kindergartens and other services. They also advocated direct intervention in housing, which they believed had to be socialized because overcrowding led to both physical and psychological illnesses.

Cassel, Heckscher, and Bagge, another Cassel protégé, who was then the Rockefeller Foundation's principal coordinator in Sweden and later became the leader of the Conservative Party, all denounced parts of Myrdal's argument publicly. Cassel noted that humanity's "incomparable advance" in the 19th century had been based on free-market economics and questioned Myrdal's plan to throw out the free-market system in favor of a socialist economy. The conservatives' critiques were to no avail, however. The book became a national best-seller, and a Conservative Party motion led to the appointment in 1935 of a royal commission to study the population issue. Nonsocialist and far leftist members of the commission objected to some of the ideas of Gunnar Myrdal, who directed much of the commission's work; but he proved such a deft publicist that the commission adopted his basic argument that the cost of children was the cause of the decline in the birthrate and recommended socialist policy changes to counteract it.

In 1936, the Social Democrats ran on a platform that "a good home and a secure existence are prerequisites for the healthy formation of families and the maintenance of the population stock." After the election, the Social Democrats continued their building program. In 1937, the Riksdag began passing the commission's recommendations, and in 1938, repealed the anti-birth-control laws. In 1938, the need for Sweden to rearm its military stopped the passage of more-costly recommendations. That same year, the Myrdals left for the United States, where under a Carnegie Foundation grant, Gunnar began the research for *An American Dilemma—The Negro Problem and Modern Democracy,* which was published in 1944.

The Swedish government's decision to intervene in the housing market was the only direct impact of the Myrdals' work on the structure of the Swedish economy, but their writings and advocacy affected nearly every aspect of Swedish society. Over the coming decades, subsidizing construction of multifamily, cooperatively owned housing became a key method for the Swedish government to reduce unemployment and indirectly bring about a rise in wages by competing with private industry for labor.

In *The Swedish Experiment in Family Politics: The Myrdals and the Interwar Population Crisis*, American scholar Allan Carlson has said that the Myrdals "abused" social science by manipulating their findings to engineer a new social order that was a violation of Sweden's rural Christian and bourgeois traditions. In 1997, the Social Democrats' policies encountered deeper revisionist criticism when a series in *Dagens Nyheter* revealed that Sweden sterilized more than 60,000 "feeble-minded" and other "weak" persons, mostly women, between the 1930s and the 1970s. The report also said that the Myrdals had been among the few Swedes to speak out against the sterilization policy.

The Myrdals' impact on Swedish society is mixed. Sweden has never achieved high birthrates, but today demographers recognize a lower birthrate as a natural phenomenon of a rich, industrial society. Later generations of Swedish architects and planners have questioned and occasionally denounced the sterile high-rise buildings in which most Swedes now live. The Myrdals' recommendations can ultimately be faulted for not paying attention to the production of wealth, and Swedish historian Ann Katrin Hatje has charged that the Myrdals were publicists who compiled existing policy ideas and were reactionaries on the abortion issue because they did not advocate completely a woman's right to choose. In political terms, the Myrdals' success in transforming Swedish social policy revealed that Swedish conservative leaders of the 1930s were still old-fashioned and rural-oriented and offered no solutions to social problems in an urban, industrial society in which women both needed to earn money and were no longer content to stay at home.

The Road to Saltsjöbaden

In the years immediately following the Social Democrats' takeover of the Swedish government in 1932, Swedish employers and labor unions ended their strident attacks on one another and began to restore the model of cooperation that had marked Swedish society since its beginnings. The reasons for the renewed willingness to cooperate were several. First, the economic crisis of the early 1930s was so severe that it inspired Swedes of all classes to work together. Second, after the Agrarians formed a coalition with the Social Democrats, the likelihood that the Conservatives or the Liberals would control the government seemed remote. Third, the Social Democrats had softened their rhetoric and their actions. By 1933, De Geer has written, industrialists recognized that "it was obvious that no sudden socialist upheaval was in the offing. The economic crisis had to be tackled; the government was looking for collaboration, not confrontation. Nor were the old ideas of socialization or industrial democracy revived even when the crisis was over. The creation of the 'People's Home' was the new political dream, and attention to the needs of industry was essential to the social reforms topping the agenda. . . . The [Swedish] corporate world accepted and even approved of the Social Democratic government. Its most important benefit was the political stability which it provided."

The basis for cooperation between employers and labor had been established years earlier. It was already apparent in the late '20s that SAF was not as strong as it had once been. Industrial production was becoming more complicated, and it was getting harder for employers to replace competent employees with strikebreakers off the street. LO had grown in the public sector and could get money from its public employee members even if private-sector workers had gone on strike—a factor that would become even more important in the '30s as white-collar workers in both government and private business joined unions.

Sven Lübeck, the minister for social affairs in the Conservative government that came to power in 1928, was an engineer who sought consensus on industrial relations. Inspired by a conference held in England on the initiative of industrialist Alfred Mond, Lübeck encouraged industrialists, union leaders and politicians to sit down together. Some of the sessions were held under the auspices of the Lutheran Church, which had wisely decided, under the leadership of Archbishop Nathan Söderblom, not to take sides between the capitalists and the labor unions. At one of these joint conferences, Lübeck said that to reduce confrontation, the workers would have to distance themselves from Communism, and he told the employers that they would have to trust the workers with more information about their jobs and companies. An industrial peace conference had failed in 1926, but another one was set up, and it led to SAF and the Swedish Confederation of Industries creating a new institute for the training of foremen. The meeting also led to the creation of a permanent joint committee to act as a contact group between business and labor. The committee's work was suspended when the workers were killed at Ådalen in 1931, but the contacts continued.

In a lecture delivered at a Social Democratic training center in the summer of 1935, Gustaf Söderlund, the director-general of SAF, invited LO to talks on issues of mutual interest. LO responded, and deliberations continued from the summer of 1936 until December 1938, when business, labor and political leaders met to sign a general agreement. The signing ceremony took place at Saltsjöbaden, the island the Wallenbergs had developed so many years earlier.

The Saltsjöbaden Accord, as it has come to be called, contained five sections regulating the Labor Market Council, a national negotiating body that would attempt to resolve disputes between LO and SAF without referring them to the Labor Court; negotiation procedures for disputes during the period covered by a union contract; rules for dismissals and layoffs; and two sections dealing with the rights of third parties and the protection of functions vital to the life of the community in the case of strikes. When LO proposed changes in the principles of Paragraph 23 as a condition of its signature, the employers almost balked, but Söderlund and J. Sigfrid Edström, Asea's managing director and the chairman of SAF, succeeded in persuading the employers to accept the changes. The accord also stated that it was the responsibility of SAF and LO to enforce the rules of the labor market. The signators assumed that SAF would no longer support strikebreakers and that LO would combat Communists and syndicalists in the trade unions. The strength of the accord became clear in 1942, when the Labor Court forced LO agreements upon syndicalist unions.

The impact of the Saltsjöbaden Accord on Sweden and the rest of the world cannot be overestimated. Because the Social Democrats have controlled the Swedish government almost continuously since 1932, many historians have written that the "bourgeois" period in Swedish history ended when the Social Democrats took power. That is more than an overstatement. It is an error that results in both foreigners and Swedes misunderstanding the structure of Swedish society. Just as the Swedish people did not destroy the monarchy, the nobility, the state Church or the military in their period of greatest socialist zeal, they did not destroy private business.

Saltsjöbaden established what become known as the Swedish Model, the concept that business and labor can work together peaceably for the mutual benefit of society. Its "spirit" set up a relationship between management and labor that worked well as long as Swedish exports were competitively priced and the employers and labor unions could divide up an ever-expanding pie of profits.

The "spirit" of Saltsjöbaden had its defects. Its presumption that workers would join unions and companies would join SAF encouraged rigidities that have made it difficult for Swedish industry to grow. It left no room for the entrepreneur and the small, growing business that cannot afford to pay high wages or benefits but yet is the lifeblood needed to keep renewing the capitalist system. There is, however, no question that Saltsjöbaden certified that Sweden would remain a capitalistic country.

Sir Ernest Cassel, a London-based banker with interests of Sweden, had his portrait painted by Anders Zorn, a Swede of modest roots who became famous for his portraits and landscapes of an agrarian Sweden that was disappearing as industrialization occurred.

Louis Fränkel, a German-born Jew, became head of Stockholms Handelsbank in 1893 and provided a high level of advice to early industrialists until his death in 1911.

Theodor Mannheimer, a Danish Jew who immigrated to Sweden, helped found the Skandinaviska Kreditaktiebolaget, later known as Skandinaviska Banken, in 1864.

165

The Swedish mining industry grows at the turn of the century, but the working conditions are hard.

The first series of Volvo cars.

A classic ad for a milk and cream separator.

In 1885 L. M. Ericsson and his wife display some instruments made by him in his home at Thulegatan 5 in Stockholm.

The first Electrolux vacuum cleaner. *One of the latest Electrolux cleaners.*

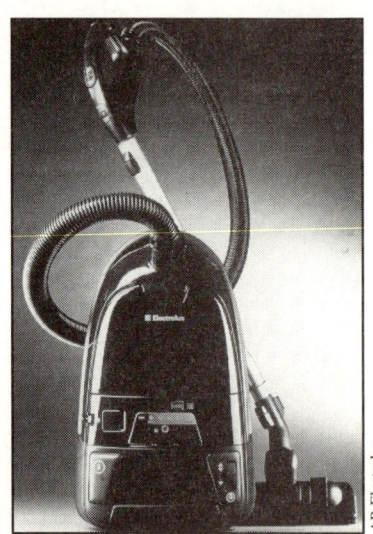

168

Swedish industrialists and labor leaders gather in 1938 on the island of Saltsjöbaden to sign the famous agreement between business and labor. In the front from the left are Wiking Johnsson, August Lindberg, S. Edström and Gunnar Andersson. In the back from left are Arnold Sölven, G. Söderlund, Oscar Karlen, H. Nilsson, Axel Bergengren, Nils Holmström, Ivar Larson and Hilding Molander.

On his 60th birthday, in 1945, Prime Minister Per Albin Hansson is interviewed by Sven Jerring, the most important radio personality of the day.

169

A rare undated photo shows Swedish industrialist and inventor Ivar Kreuger, whose 1932 suicide in Paris set off a reorganization of Swedish industry.

Ruben Rausing of Tetra Pak and a doctor's wife who was the chairwomen of the Malmö Housewives Association in 1957 the day Tetra Pak launches a new milk product coming from Rausing's experimental farm.

Dr. Gad Rausing, founder of Tetra Pak.

170

Prime Minister Olof Palme appears at a 1968 anti-Vietnam war demonstration that was one element in disturbing Swedish relations with the United States. At his side is the North Vietnamese ambassador to the Soviet Union.

Industrialist Curt Nicolin makes the victory sign after the march against union-controlled pension funds in 1985.

Anders Wall, chairman of Beijer Invest,. announces the merger between Volvo and Beijer in 1980.

Volvo Chief Pehr Gyllenhammar, 43, gets into a Volvo in 1977 at the time of discussions of a merger between Volvo and Saab.

IKEA founder Ingvar Kamprad poses for a rare photo in 1995 while visiting one of his stores.

Berit Svärd, owner of Gafs Kartong, a box company.

173

Magnus Petterson, owner of Hestra, a company with the Gnosjö spirit.

Laurent Leksell, runs Elekta AB, the company which makes the Gamma Knife and other medical devices.

In 1974, Marcus Wallenberg, 75, resigns as chairman of the board of Atlas Copco at a shareholders meeting. With him is his son Peter, 48.

Peter Wallenberg, Sweden's most important financier and investor, poses with his key executives on his 70th birthday in 1996. From left to right are Claes Dahlbäck, then managing director of Investor, Peter Wallenberg, his son Jacob Wallenberg and his nephew Marcus Wallenberg.

175

6

Swedish Modern - the Golden Years, 1933-1973

FOR 40 YEARS after the Social Democrats took power in 1932, Sweden seemed to work better than any other country in the world. Sweden ended the Great Depression faster than most other countries; managed to stay neutral during World War II; and in the postwar era established one of the world's highest standards of living by selling its wood, iron ore, engineering skills, Volvos and other finished products to a rebuilding Europe in the late 1940s and '50s and to the world in the 1960s and '70s.

Both Swedes and foreigners began to regard Sweden as a paradise on earth. Sweden's "Third Way" between communism and capitalism—as American writer Marquis Childs called it—could do no wrong. Hopeful people around the world began to think of the Swedish Model not as just the smooth labor-management relations established by the 1938 Saltsjöbaden agreement, but as a way of life being led by an entire country. And who could argue against it? Products were excellent, profits were high, labor-management relations were generally smooth. After World War II, unemployment was zero. Immigrants from Finland and Southern Europe were invited to take the jobs Swedes didn't want and were absorbed into the society without major incident. The welfare state kept expanding, providing every service that Sweden's planners and social tinkerers could conceive.

U.S. President Dwight Eisenhower in 1960 claimed that the Swedish welfare state had increased suicide and promiscuity, and American conservatives criticized Sweden for stifling individual initiative. But the productivity of Sweden's economy and its low unemployment rate discouraged both Swedes and foreigners from paying attention to that line of thinking—and after Eisenhower left office he visited Sweden and announced he had softened his views. Swedish business leaders often grumbled about taxes, but they were also comforted by the fact that political and social commentators around world came to look upon them as great humanitarians, one of the few groups of wealthy people who had accepted the idea that it was more important for lower-income people to get every social service than it was for them to have bigger houses or yachts.

On the surface, the story of Swedish business in these years is a rather dull one of high profit making by the companies that had been established in the late 19th and early 20th centuries and of markedly lower entrepreneurship compared with previous decades. A book published by the Wallenbergs in 1991 about the history of Investor, the holding company for their industrial interests, said that "the first quarter-century after the Second World War is hardly among the most dramatic periods in Investor's history." Only decades later has it become clear that the Swedish business story from the '30s through the early '70s is not so uneventful. In these decades, Sweden established an international business image that was in line with its socialist politics, the Wallenbergs solidified their empire, Swedish companies made morally questionable profits on sales to Nazi Germany even while one Wallenberg, Raoul, was saving Jews in Hungary, and the country mortgaged its future by not encouraging entrepreneurship or paying attention to growing world competition.

The story of Swedish politics in these years seems equally dull. The Social Democrats held the prime ministership from 1936 until 1976, an extraordinary record for any political party, and the Swedish government presented the world an image of such unity and solidarity that people in other countries began to assume that all segments of Swedish society were always in agreement. Behind this show of unity, there was often turmoil. The Social Democrats never had to relinquish the prime minister's office, but most of the time they did not have a clear majority in the Riksdag. During the war, a coalition government of all major parties led by a Social Democratic prime minister ruled. After the war, the Social Democrats governed in coalition with the Agrarian (later Center) Party, or depended on the Communists not to vote against them.

Skyrocketing world energy prices in the early 1970s brought an end to the golden age. But only after both Sweden's business and political worlds ended in crisis did Swedes realize that the weaknesses in their economy went beyond a dependence on imported oil and had their roots in the management of the country over the previous 40 years.

Glass and Home Furnishings Symbol of the New Sweden

As long as Swedish exports remained iron ore, lumber and ball bearings, which were hidden in consumer goods, or paper, whose place of origin is rarely noticed, Swedish industry had no image. In the '20s, however, that began to change with the design and production of Swedish home furnishings for the masses, especially glass.

Glassmaking was an old industry in Sweden, but one that focused on the domestic market until the late 19th century. Monks belonging to the order founded by St. Birgitta, a 14th-century Swedish nun, had brought glassmaking techniques to Sweden in the 15th or 16th century. But the monks made glass only for the Church. Gustaf Vasa brought Venetian glassblowers to Stockholm in the 16th century to reduce the cost of glass used for his palaces and other government buildings. By 1700, noblemen and senior civil servants had established about 20 glassworks to make windows and table objects. In 1742, Anders Koskull and Bogislaus Staël von Holstein, two army generals and county governors, established in Småland a glassworks they called Kosta, a word made up of the first syllables of their surnames. The skilled craftsmen at Kosta and other glassworks came mostly from Germany and Italy, and they used designs imported from the continent.

In the second half of the 19th century, as the Swedish population expanded, Swedish glassmakers could supply only 75 percent of the domestic demand, and rural shopkeepers and peasants began to start glassworks. Between 1850 and 1900, 77 glassworks were started in Sweden, 45 of them in Småland, which became known as the "Kingdom of Glass." Glass had been sold first by door-to-door peddlers, but Kosta established a Stockholm store in 1866. Design ideas and technological innovations came from Germany, England, France, Belgium and Bohemia, and the range of items expanded greatly. In the 1890s, Kosta and Reijmyre, then another prominent glass producer, followed Swedish painters' fascination with France and began making art glass in the style of French glass designer Emile Gallé. As trade barriers fell in Europe, the larger Swedish glassworks began to sell abroad, particularly after the 1897 Stockholm Art and Industrial Exhibition showed foreigners that Swedish glass was of a high technical quality.

Like their counterparts on the continent, the Swedish glassmakers saw the market for quality glass among the nobles and the bourgeoisie and paid little attention to the average consumer. In the late 19th century, however, their elitism began to be challenged by social reformers, writers and artists who came from privileged backgrounds but devoted themselves to promoting a better life for ordinary people. As early as 1870, Lorentz Dietrichson, a Norwegian professor of art history at the University of Stockholm, started a "beauty in the home" movement. Compared with those who would follow him, Dietrichson was old-fashioned in that he viewed aristocratic homes, with their dark walls, heavy curtains and large pieces of furniture, as ideal. But Dietrichson equated beauty with morality and truth. His argument that a beautiful home (or "private sphere") was necessary for a beautiful, healthy and moral society ("public sphere") appealed to Ellen Key, a Swedish politician's daughter who became a writer, activist and educational reformer. Key, who was born in 1849, socialized with painters Anders Zorn, Carl Larsson, Prince Eugén and publishing magnate Karl Bonnier in the Junta Society, a group whose members considered themselves "enlightened" radicals. Also influenced by trends in Germany, Austria and Britain, Key in 1899 wrote a book, *Beauty for All*, which argued that people of all economic classes needed beauty in their homes and could have it if industry and handicrafts cooperated.

"Above all one must not believe that beauty is a good fortune which only a few can obtain," Key wrote. "And the only possibility to obtain anything of beauty which is mass-produced for a reasonable price is that the factories, especially of furniture, wallpapers, glass, textiles, porcelain and metals unite with the practices of *konstslöjd* (art handicrafts) , in order that everything, from the simplest and smallest object (e.g., the matchbox) to the largest, yield beautiful forms and appropriate directions."

Swedish intellectuals and artists were romanticizing the disappearing rural life at that time, but Key broke with many of her contemporaries by stating her belief that Swedes moving to the cities could also achieve a good and decent life. Key praised the interiors of the rural peasantry for their simplicity and functionalism, but she also wrote that urban dwellers could achieve beauty by embellishing rooms with books and art, including reproductions of masterpieces found in big-city museums. To demonstrate how people of modest income could create simple and cozy rooms, Key and several artists designed rooms that were exhibited at the Workers' Institute in Stockholm in 1899. Her ideas were backed up by the design reforms advocated by German architect Hermann Muthesius and the Deutscher Werkbund, a group founded in Munich in 1907 to unite architects, artists and craftsmen with industry to improve the quality of mass-produced items. Key made deep impressions on Gregor Paulsson, a budding art historian who was also influenced by the Deutscher Werkbund, the Social Democratic movement, and Erik Wettergren, secretary of *Svenska Slöjdföreningen* (the Swedish Society of Craft and Industrial Design), the Swedish counterpart of the Werkbund.

In 1914, a Baltic Exhibition was held in Malmö to encourage trade between the countries that bordered the Baltic Sea. Paulsson and Wettergren bitterly criticized the Swedish exhibitors for showing objects in the 18th-century and art nouveau styles while the Danes and the Germans exhibited more-modern items. To encourage industry to hire modern artists, the Swedish Society of Craft and Industrial Design established an employment agency. Some of the manufacturers reacted angrily to the criticism and pointed out that they had often employed artists. But Orrefors, a glassworks that had been established in 1898 as a way for the owners of a *bruk* on the Orrenäs estate to use waste from its sawmill, hired master-blower Knut Bergqvist from Kosta in 1914 and made Simon Gate, a Royal Institute of Technology and Royal Academy of Art graduate, its art director in 1916. In 1917, Orrefors hired Edward Hald, who had a rare combination of business, architecture and art training, to design glass for the company. The same year Kosta hired Edvin Ollers, a drawing instructor and painter, to compete with Orrefors in creating art glass.

Sweden faced a severe urban housing crisis in the 1920s, and the Society of Craft and Industrial Design decided to organize an exhibition showing small apartments furnished with high-quality goods at low prices. The Home Exhibition, which opened in the fall of 1917 at the Liljevalchs Konsthall, an art gallery in the Djurgården section of Stockholm, featured "Turbine," a table service designed by Hald to show that a machine aesthetic could be compatible with good design; glassware designed by Ollers to show that blisters and bubbles caused by impurities in glass could have their own design impact; and architecture, textiles, furniture and ceramics by modern designers. The products were really too expensive for low-income people to buy, but they were noticed by the outside world. In 1919, Paulsson published a manifesto, *More Beautiful Things for Everyday Use,* arguing that artists could help industry develop.

The impact of Paulsson's manifesto was not immediate. The 1923 Gothenburg Jubilee Exhibition, which celebrated the 300th anniversary of the city's birth, featured conservative designs, but once again showed the quality of Swedish glass. Years later, Paulsson would express his disappointment that more artists did not go to work for industry during this period. Artists, Paulsson said, did not see themselves as serving society but rather as serving beauty. In 1945, Hald said, "We [who went to work in industry] were regarded with a certain disdain. The work was viewed as a lesser form of artistic activity that was suitable for those with less ability. There was seldom any recognition of an intellectual or social agenda." Hald obviously ignored his fellow artists, because he became managing director of Orrefors from 1933-44 and remained a designer at the company into the 1970s.

The 1925 Exposition des Arts Décoratifs et Industriels Modernes in Paris was "the ultimate test of the Swedish glass industry," art critic Elsebeth Welander-Berggren has written. The Swedes exhibited both luxury goods, such as a lady's salon meant for a modern-day Madame Récamier and Orrefors' most progressive art glass and won 31 grand prizes. "Orrefors glass in Paris came, was seen and conquered," said one headline. Paulsson noted that in eight years Orrefors had created "from nothing the world's finest glassworks." The prizes in Paris also made Americans aware of the high quality of modern Swedish glass. The Art Institute of Chicago bought an engraved decanter by Gate, which it put on display in 1925, and Paulsson's group, the Swedish Society of Craft and Industrial Design, organized a smaller version of the Paris exhibition that was shown at the Metropolitan Museum of Art in New York City in 1927.

Hald and J.H. Danius, the director of Orrefors, knew when to make the most of a commercial opportunity and in 1928 traveled throughout the United States to promote modern Swedish glass. Scholars preparing the 1996 exhibition "The Brilliance of Swedish Glass, 1918-1939: An Alliance of Art and Industry" at the Bard Graduate Center for Studies in the Decorative Arts in New York City could not determine exactly how Swedish glass was wholesaled in the United States in the 1920s, but it soon became available in major U.S. department stores and smaller specialty shops. Also in 1928, Hald modified an Orrefors chandelier as a prototype for 20 light fixtures in the dining hall of the Cranbook Academy of Art in Michigan. The same year, the Swedish American Line's trans-Atlantic passenger ship, the *M/S Kungsholm,* was decorated in the best of modern Swedish design.

In 1927, the Deutscher Werkbund had held an exhibition in Stuttgart on "The Dwelling." Paulsson proposed that the Swedish Society of Craft and Industrial Design mount an exhibition in Stockholm in 1930 to demonstrate the Swedish contribution to modern industrial design and low-cost housing. Gunnar Asplund, a well-known Swedish architect, served as chief architect of the exhibition and broke with tradition by creating an area away from the handicrafts display for the presentation of mass-produced items. He also used horizontal rather than vertical displays to emphasize the democratic nature of modern Swedish society. The ideological foundation of the Swedish Exhibition of 1930 was captured by Wilhelm Kåge's dinnerware—"Praktika"—which had covers that doubled as serving dishes and was designed to stack compactly in small kitchens.

Carl Malmsten, one of Sweden's premier furniture designers at the time, condemned the Stockholm exhibition as "mechanization and cold intellectualism." But in 1931, Paulsson and a group of architects including Asplund published the manifesto *Acceptera* (*Accept*), in which they argued that "there exists a necessary connection between [artistic forms] and the political and social character of the period during which they originated." In the 1930s, Swedish furniture designers who challenged tradition also began to gain prominence. One of the best known was Bruno Mathsson, who made an armchair of bent, laminated wood and cotton webbing. Mathsson was concerned with durability and comfort and later used leather and steel as his materials. In 1937, *Nordiska Kompaniet,* Sweden's leading department store hired Astrid Sampe to design textiles. Sampe's first designs were made on handlooms, but were soon transferred to industrial production. Sampe's relationship with the department store and manufacturers, art critic Anne-Marie Ericsson has written, "represents the peak period in modern Swedish design, a period that would reach fruition after the Second World War. . . . Instead of the artist as autocrat, dictating design and production, however, it was a far more equitable relationship. Artists and manufacturers had come to know each other and their mutual needs, and there was increasing cooperation between producers."

All the best in modern Swedish design came together at the Swedish pavilion at the 1937 Paris *Exposition Internationale des Arts et Techniques dans la Vie Moderne* (International Exposition of Arts and Techniques in Modern Life). The pavilion was designed by Sven-Ivar Lind, who had studied with Asplund; the furniture, by a young Swedish designer, Elias Svedberg; and the textiles, by Sampe. There was also an installation featuring work by Estrid Ericson and Josef Frank, a Viennese architect who had fled the Nazi regime's crackdown on modern design. Ericson, who worked in pewter, had started *Svenskt Tenn* (Swedish Pewter), a small shop with a workshop in Stockholm in 1924, and after the Stockholm Exhibition of 1930, opened a department store and invited Frank to work with her. The installation in Paris featured Frank's geometric patterns and a kidney-shaped desk and low sofa.

Swedish art critics found the design too severe, but foreigners found the spaciousness and "Nordic gravity," as English journalist P. Morton Shand had called it, intriguing. In 1930, Shand used the term "Swedish Grace" to describe Swedish designs that were modern but still had surface decoration. At the 1937 Paris Exposition, the English-speaking press began using the term "Swedish Modern" to describe designs that were more concerned with overall form than with surface decoration such as color. At the entrance to the Swedish pavilion in Paris, there was also "Technology and the Future," a monumental window designed and made by Orrefors artist Vicke Lindstrand. It was praised as a masterpiece of modern glass, its luxury proving that Sweden remained in top form in the elitist tradition.

The journalists' title inspired the Swedish government to call its exhibition at the 1939 New York World's Fair "Swedish Modern: A Movement Toward Sanity in Design." Modern Swedish decorative arts had won plaudits at the Century of Progress Fair in Chicago in 1933, but full American recognition of Sweden's place in the forefront of the international design world really came at the New York fair. In addition to rooms designed by Svedberg and Sampe, the pavilion featured an installation by Ericson and Frank. The Swedish pavilion was one of the most popular at the fair, Anne-Marie Ericsson has written, because "it offered a more humanistic approach to modern design than the streamlined machine-age objects shown in other World's Fair pavilions."

Swedish Modern design was brought to the West Coast of the United States at the Golden Gate International Exhibition, honoring the completion of the Golden Gate Bridge and the San Francisco-Oakland Bay Bridge, in 1939 and 1940. By the time the United States entered World War II in 1941, Swedish Modern design had become fashionable in the homes of progressive Americans, especially President Roosevelt's New Dealers who were trying to turn the United States into a welfare state. The war years were a loss for Swedish home furnishings exports, but they were an artistic triumph. With the Bauhaus school closed down and German design reduced to what art critic Alf Bøe called a "cult of banalized tradition," Sweden and other Nordic countries remained almost alone in Europe in the movement to make glass and other home furnishings on the principles of functionalism and altruism touched by socialism. Despite the isolation and deprivations of war and the shortages of materials, Swedish, Danish, Finnish and Norwegian artists continued to be creative and to exchange ideas whenever possible.

The end of the war coincided with the centenary of the Swedish Society of Craft and Industrial Design, and Scandinavian design companies used the anniversary to launch a series of international promotions that have never really stopped. In the 1950s and '60s, especially between 1953 and 1961 when Dag Hammarskjöld was secretary-general of the United Nations, Swedish Modern furniture and glassware became popular throughout the world for their innate design elements and as symbols of the success of the Swedish Model and Swedish 20th-century ideals. Both at home and abroad, the Swedish "movement" toward "beauty for all" failed in a way because Swedish home furnishings—even those that were mass-produced—never became cheap enough for the average person to afford. But the movement made functionalism and simplicity, rather than ornamentation, the world standard. And it turned Orrefors and Kosta (which in 1971 bought Boda, another glassworks, and in 1990 merged with Orrefors to form Orrefors Kosta Boda) and other Swedish manufacturers of home furnishings into major international exporters.

The Kreuger Crisis, the Banks and the Wallenbergs

The collapse of Ivar Kreuger's Swedish Match empire in 1932 set the stage for a reorganization of the ownership of Swedish industry. The Swedish Bank Inspection Board had been right to be concerned about Swedish banks holding stock in companies to which they also made loans. Skandinaviska Banken, Stockholms Handelsbank and the Wallenbergs' Stockholms Enskilda Bank had all established separate investment companies in the early 1900s. But in the series of economic crises between 1908 and 1927, so many banks had gotten into trouble and merged that the number of active banks declined from 83 to 28. In the various economic crises, frozen claims were converted to shares, banks participated in reconstructions and the Bank Inspection Board's campaign to divorce the banks from the companies was reversed.

After Kreuger's suicide, it became apparent that Skandinaviska Banken had put almost 40 percent of its loans in Kreuger companies. Oscar Rydbeck, Skandinaviska Banken's well-regarded head, was forced to retire, and the government had to provide support loans to save the institution. Handelsbanken, which had acquired several northern banks in the 1920s and inherited their loans to forestry and steel companies, made more loans to them and had to accept stock in the companies when they got into trouble. Handelsbanken also had to assume control of Svenska Cellulosa Aktiebolaget, the Kreuger forestry conglomerate it had helped create.

Neither the Wallenbergs nor their Stockholms Enskilda Bank was as threatened as Skandinaviska and Handelsbanken, and the Kreuger crisis provided the Wallenberg family an opportunity to increase their holdings. At the time of the Kreuger collapse in 1932, Kreuger had 8.6 percent of voting rights in Stora and the Wallenbergs had increased their share to 11.7 percent. The venerable Swedish company had become the second-largest in the portfolio of Investor, the family holding company. In the wake of the Kreuger collapse, the Wallenbergs increased their stakes in the ball bearing company SKF, Ericsson and Swedish Match. Between 1924 and 1944, the Wallenbergs increased their voting rights in Atlas Diesel from 20 to 54 percent and in Stora from 3 percent to 12 percent; they bought 5 percent of Asea, 7 percent of Separator, 9 percent of Ericsson, 25 percent of Swedish Match and 29 percent of Saab. The family continued to control 100 percent of Scania-Vabis, but its percentage of voting stock in SKF declined from 14 to 11 percent and in Astra from 50 to 33 percent. It also held substantial interests in lesser known Swedish companies.

The '30s were not all easy times for the Wallenbergs, however. In 1933, the German government prohibited currency transfers and froze the German assets of Instor, the Wallenberg company with international investments. The Wallenbergs managed, however, to transfer some of Instor's assets out of the country. In the 1930s, Investor also made money by selling a large share of Aug Stenman AB to a British screw manufacturer and by acting as an intermediary between a Swedish firm and the Romanian government in a deal in which the Romanian government paid gold worth 70 million Swedish kronor to have 750 kilometers (465 miles) of road built. In 1940, after the Swedish Parliament had prohibited the use of foreign currency for acquisition of securities outside Sweden, the Wallenbergs dissolved Instor and turned its assets over to AB Duba, another Investor subsidiary.

To avoid a repeat of the economic crises of the 1920s, the government decided in 1934 to forbid banks from purchasing shares and debentures without security. The Bank Inspection Board allowed the banks four years to transfer their assets to wholly owned subsidiaries still controlled by bank management through shares with disproportionate voting rights. In 1937, the Skandinaviska Banken became the first to transfer holdings from its own portfolio, mostly in steel mills and foundries in central Sweden and in Swedish Match. It formed a new company, AB Custos, which was traded on the stock exchange. Skandinaviska Banken board members were still able to maintain control even though the stock was publicly sold because they were able to buy 1,200 preferred shares, which carried 100 votes per share, while the public was offered 122,800 ordinary shares which had one vote each. A Bank Inspection Board investigation later showed that shareholders and bank officials had agreed that the preferred shares would not pass outside control of the board. In 1943, Handelsbanken, following the AB Custos model, cleared out its shares, many in companies involved in the development of Norrland, by forming a holding company, AB Industrivärden. In 1944, in a further attempt to discourage concentrated economic power, the Riksdag passed a law stating that after 1948, on new share issues, no share could exceed the value of other shares by a factor of more than 10.

The 1944 law established a set of banking and business ownership arrangements that lasted for a quarter of a century.

Jacob Wallenberg had revived the old Providentia as an investment company, and in 1945, the Wallenbergs, complying with the government's directive to dissolve Providentia, transferred the greater part of the portfolios of both the bank and Providentia to a new holding company, Förvaltnings AB Providentia. Each share carried the same weight, but the Wallenbergs gave shareholders of Stockholms Enskilda Bank the first chance to buy the new shares, to ensure that their family would be dominant in controlling the company.

As the Wallenbergs' 1945 machinations prove, the relationship between banking and industry was still closer in Sweden than in Great Britain or the United States. But Swedish banking historian Håkan Lindgren called the 1944 act "a first step towards the principle that equal risks should carry equal rights." As Lindgren noted, the law requiring transference was an important step toward improving depositors' security, because exchange-listed companies, with some outside distribution of shares, are subject to more press and shareholder scrutiny than wholly owned subsidiaries.

The Recovery of Business and Labor

The Swedish Social Democrats have claimed—and gotten—so much credit for intervening in the economy in the 1930s to pull their country out of the Depression, but more modern historians and economists say that Swedish industry's competitiveness vis-à-vis other countries at that time has not gotten full credit for Sweden's turnaround. While the United States and some European countries were booming in the 1920s, Sweden went through a major depression with high unemployment and was forced to adjust wages downward.

Swedish business bitterly opposed the introduction of the eight-hour workday in 1920, but the need to adjust to a higher cost of labor encouraged Swedish industrialists to use the latest labor-saving devices. Swedish labor productivity increased by 4 percent per year during the 1920s and 3 percent per year during the 1930s. The world still needed Sweden's iron ore and timber, and by 1937, in the middle of the Great Depression, the volume of Swedish exports was 20 percent higher than in the previous record year of 1929.

Sweden's competitiveness in this period is all the more surprising because unionization was growing rapidly. By the end of the 1930s almost one million Swedes were members of some 60 unions, making Sweden, along with the other Scandinavian countries part of the most unionized region in the capitalist world. Unions no longer had to struggle to get management to listen to them, because the size of their memberships gave them power that no one denied. Swedish labor union leaders acquired a reputation as the most rational-thinking in the world. While the union leaders demanded that for an eight-hour day the workers be paid the same as (or more than) they had been paid for longer days, they also acknowledged that keeping Swedish industry profitable and competitive was key to improving their workers' standard of living. At an international trade union congress in Stockholm in 1930, the Swedish unions had agreed to a policy program that called for promotion of the planned development of industry, structural rationalization into larger units, financial reorganization, and the substitution of new plants and innovations for old machinery. While these policies showed that Swedish unions had a better understanding of international economics than did unions in most countries, the Swedish union movement exhibited other tendencies that would make it difficult for Swedish industry to remain cost-competitive. More and more unions joined LO, the general labor federation, which believed in centralized bargaining and a "solidaristic" wage strategy, under which higher-paid workers called for improvement in the wages of the lower-paid.

Hitler's Rise and His Impact on Sweden

Adolf Hitler's assumption of the German chancellorship on January 30, 1933, produced a psychological—though not political, economic or diplomatic—crisis in Sweden. Swedes of all political stripes had so long relied on Germany as a source of inspiration that it was hard for either Swedish conservatives or socialists to believe that a country whose science and development they so respected had become so aggressive, violent and anti-Semitic. In the Swedish mind, U.S. historian Steven Koblik has written, "what Germany represented in a broad and simplified sense was a combination of order, achievement, symmetrical forms, respect for the past, and Christian (Lutheran) tradition. It stood in contrast to either Western culture or the Bolshevik menace. Bolshevism was not only the latest version of the traditional Russian threat to

Sweden, but it was godless, dictatorial, totalitarian and lacking in humanism. England and especially France in a cultural sense stood for experimentation, democracy, and chaos." The Swedes' reverence bordering on obsession with German culture is perhaps best expressed by economic historian Eli Heckscher. Heckscher was an assimilated Jew who still practiced his religion. In 1938, Heckscher reacted to the worsening plight of the Jews in Germany by writing that "it is not so much a question of German Jewish appeals for help as of the total devastation of what one regarded as an inalienable heritage of Western Man, perhaps of Mankind in general."

The rebuilding of Germany after its defeat in World War I represented economic opportunity for the Swedes through the 1920s and '30s. In the '20s, German companies and the German government had used Sweden to avoid some of the military limitations of the 1919 Treaty of Versailles. The German Krupp munitions concern had a very close relationship with Bofors, and German capital controlled AB Flygindustri, an aviation company, in Malmö. The German military buildup under Hitler was, in fact, a problem to which the Swedes contributed, because the half-government-owned LKAB iron ore company and SKF made sales to Germany. "Germany's very existence depended upon the import of iron ore from Sweden," William L. Shirer wrote in *The Rise and Fall of the Third Reich*, noting that Germany obtained from Sweden as much as 11 million of the 15 million tons of iron it was using per year. U.S. Secretary of State Cordell Hull wrote in his *Memoirs*, published in 1948, that "the traffic of iron ore is the most important single contribution, in terms of raw material, made to Germany by any nation outside its prewar borders."

Hitler said in 1934 that Sweden should eventually become a part of greater Germany. But while the Swedes respected Germany, they were determined to remain independent and neutral, and few were interested in becoming Nazis. A National Socialist Party was formed in Sweden, and some Conservatives, Agrarians and a few Liberals and Social Democrats joined, but the party never elected anyone to the Riksdag and even Swedish Nazis and their sympathizers wanted their country to remain independent. The Germans expressed continual frustration with the Swedes' unwillingness to join the cause of creating a world dominated by Aryans, and one German official called the Swedes "swine in dinner jackets."

Sweden's first diplomatic crisis after the rise of Hitler was the collapse of the League of Nations. World War I had taught Sweden that it could not stay out of world affairs, and in 1920, it had decided that its policy would not be violated by joining the League of Nations. Sweden became one of the league's most ardent members, and its officials were disappointed by the decision of the United States not to join and the league's members' inability to address Italy's invasion of Ethiopia in 1935. In another display of political liberalism, some 600 Swedes volunteered to fight against the fascists in the 1936 Spanish Civil War, which was regarded as the rehearsal for World War II.

Sweden had also reduced its defenses in the 1920s, but after a lengthy political debate, the country began rebuilding its military in 1936. Germany's remilitarization was a factor in that decision, but Swedes were also troubled by the situation in the Soviet Union. On the one hand, they still regarded that country as the traditional Swedish enemy of Russia now run by a new and more ruthless gang. On the other, changes in the Soviet military command made it unlikely that the Soviets would prove strong enough to be a counterbalance to Hitler.

Hitler's discrimination against Jews became almost immediately apparent after he took power, and it bothered some Swedes in high level positions. In May 1933, only five months after Hitler came to power, King Gustav V traveled to Germany to tell President Hindenburg that Hitler's anti-Semitic policies were damaging the country's reputation abroad. The Lutheran archbishop Erling Eidem and a few intellectuals also made pilgrimages to Germany for the same purpose. Prime Minister Per Albin Hansson also deplored the Nazis' violence the same year. The newspaper *Göteborgs Handels —och Sjöfartstidning,* edited by Torgny Segerstedt, became Sweden's most consistent and outspoken critic of Hitler. Writings published after the war give an indication of the ignorance and prejudice that Segerstedt faced, however. Tage Erlander, prime minister from 1946-68, wrote in the mid-1970s that Segerstedt had little support among the Swedish people. K.G. Westman, the Agrarian Party leader who was minister of justice during the war, wrote in his wartime diary, which was published in 1981, that Segerstedt's "Jewish mistress has removed his soul and replaced it with a Jewish one."

As Hitler tried to rid Germany of Jews through forced emigration, Sweden faced both domestic and diplomatic conflicts. Despite the protests of King Gustav V and a few other Swedes over Germany's policies toward the Jews, Sweden's attitude toward the German Jews in the late 1930s has been accurately characterized as indifferent. Swedes who wished to avoid involvement in the "Jewish problem," as it was called, included many of Sweden's 7,000 highly assimilated Jews, who feared that increased immigration would jeopardize their position. By the '30s, Jews had intermarried with the Swedish bourgeoisie and the nobility and held high positions in government, academic and business, but there was no question that anti-Semitism lurked beneath the surface. Koblik has written that the Bonnier family's ownership of *Dagens Nyheter,* a major Stockholm newspaper, was cited "by anti-Semites in Germany and Sweden alike as the example of 'Jewish control' of the Swedish media," even though Bonniers had married non-Jews and Jews alike. No Bonnier played a role in the Stockholm synagogue at that time, and many family members had converted to Lutheranism. The general secretary of the Swedish Foreign Office was Erik Boheman, who had one Jewish grandparent. When Westman was dissatisfied with Swedish foreign policy, he ascribed it to Boheman's "Jewishness."

A Swedish committee to save Jews from Hitler was established, however, headed by Gunnar Josephson, who owned one of the best bookstores in Sweden and was, incidentally, married to Boheman's sister. But the committee was reluctant to be outspoken, and its existence did not prevent the Swedish government from encouraging the German government to develop the "J" passport. Germans (and Austrians after Germany occupied Austria in 1938) could enter Sweden without a passport, but the Germans would not allow Jews to return to their homes. Switzerland, which was also neutral, faced the same problem. Individually but simultaneously, Switzerland and Sweden warned Germany that if it did not somehow distinguish the passports of German Jews, they would establish visa requirements for all Germans. The Germans created passports with the letter "J" stamped across them for those holders who were legally classified as Jews.

Some of the pressure to keep Jews from entering Sweden came from working-class Swedes. But the level of anti-Semitism among upper-class, highly educated people may be gauged by the protests by Swedish doctors against allowing German Jewish doctors into Sweden and by the 1939 demonstrations at three major universities against easing restrictions on Jewish immigration.

Sweden did allow immigration for political asylum and, before the war, accepted some 3,000 Jewish refugees, including Czech labor officials who were Jewish. But the number of Jewish refugees who settled in Sweden was proportionally lower than the number who found asylum in Holland, Belgium, France and Great Britain. Sweden's reluctance to allow Jews to immigrate did not go without comment. In 1939, the Social Democratic economist and social scientist Gunnar Myrdal and the internationally recognized economics professor and Liberal politician Bertil Ohlin pointed out in parliamentary debate that Sweden could afford to accept more refugees.

The War Years - Neutrality, Profits and, Finally, Help for the Jews

Sweden was able to hold out hope that war would not break out until the August 1939 pact between Hitler and Stalin under which the Germans agreed that the Baltic states (Estonia, Latvia and Lithuania) and Finland would fall within the Soviet sphere of influence. On November 30, 1939, the Soviets bombed the Finnish capital of Helsinki. Horrified at the invasion of a country that had once been part of their own and fearing that Sweden would be next, thousands of Swedes volunteered for service in the Finnish army in the Winter War that lasted from December 1939 to March 1940. Sweden sent arms to Finland, but officially remained neutral in the conflict. When Great Britain and France asked permission to send troops through Sweden to help Finland, Sweden refused. On March 12, 1940, Finland surrendered to the Soviets. Four weeks later, Germany invaded Denmark and Norway, and after April 9, 1940, Sweden was the only Scandinavian country completely in control of its own territory.

Sweden managed to remain neutral throughout the war, avoiding invasion and the severity of deprivation that its neighbors suffered. It did, however, live under the constant fear of German invasion, experienced shortages, and eventually opened its doors to thousands of refugees. But Sweden's sales of goods to Germany during the early war years and its continued economic advancement even as its neighbors were subject to aggression make its wartime behavior controversial to this day.

To ensure a solid front, Hansson in December 1939 expanded the Social Democratic-Agrarian coalition to include all the parties represented in the Riksdag. In the 1940 election, the Social Democrats won a solid majority of 53.8 percent in the Lower Chamber, but Hansson continued to include members of Conservative, Agrarian and Liberal parties in the coalition cabinet. Swedish scholars Alf W. Johansson and Torbjörn Norman have described Hansson's attitude toward foreign affairs as a *lillsvensk* ("small Swedish") policy and said that Hansson viewed the war as "a temporary disturbance in the building of the welfare state; therefore it had to be waited out." Johansson and Norman compared the Social Democratic Hansson's view with the *storsvensk* ("big Swedish") policy of Conservative leader Gösta Bagge, who favored more assistance to Finland. Johansson and Norman note, however, that when it came to the war between Germany and the Allies, the Swedish Social Democrats and Conservatives did not clash.

During the war years, both the Swedish economy and the social welfare state continued to grow, if more slowly than they might have in peacetime. When the war broke out in Europe in September 1939, stock prices around the world dropped but the stock market in neutral Sweden was quiet. During the war years, stock prices in Sweden rose 25 percent while general prices rose at double that rate. The imperative of short-term practical cooperation between many groups—including SAF, the Swedish Employers' Confederation; LO; and the public authorities—created a new spirit of collaboration whose benefits and costs would not be realized until after the war. SAF agreed to LO's demand that workers be compensated for increases in the cost of living by comparable increases in wage scales. The result was that workers did better than investors during the war.

Sweden managed to maintain some international commerce with the United States and South America; but it lost 11 ships and submarines and 100 lives to bombings, and its imports in 1945 were a third of what they had been in 1939. The impossibility of obtaining imported goods such as fertilizers led to the development of new industries for the home market and the establishment of some new businesses such as Victor Hasselblad AB, which made cameras Swedes could no longer import. The increased military spending—from $50 million in 1938 to $400 million in 1939 and $600 million per year by the end of the war—resulted in the development of new armaments and innovations in the engineering field that put Swedish business ahead of its competitors after the war.

The mining of the Skagerak waters in 1940 had made Sweden entirely dependent on Germany for coal. From Germany Sweden was able to get only half of what it was used to importing, mostly from Great Britain, before the war. The deficiency in fuel supplies was made up by the collection of wood from forests, and the percentage of the annual wood cut used for fuel rose from 9 percent in 1937 to 40 percent during the war years. The use of wood for fuel had another socioeconomic impact because the government put the farmers' producer co-ops rather than the government itself or a corporate entity in charge of the collection of the wood. After the war, the producer co-ops became major players in the forestry industry.

While Sweden's neutrality infuriated the Germans, the Allies became angrier and angrier that Sweden continued exporting iron ore and ball bearings to Germany. Germany's invasion of Norway and subsequent occupation caused a diplomatic crisis over the shipment of the ore. During the warm-weather months, the ore was transported from northern Sweden down the Gulf of Bothnia and across the Baltic, which was not patrolled by British submarines. But in the winter months, the Swedish ore had to be shipped by rail to the nearby Norwegian port of Narvik and brought down the Norwegian coast to be shipped in Norway's neutral territorial waters. After the Nazis occupied Norway, the Norwegian government-in-exile contended its waters were not German. But Germany insisted that Norway was conquered territory and told Sweden that continuing the shipments did not violate any Swedish policies.

The day-to-day exports may have aided both the German cause and the Swedish economy at the expense of the Allied cause, but they are not the most controversial Swedish acts during the war. In 1940, the Swedes allowed German soldiers on leave from their duties in Norway to travel through Sweden. On June 22, 1941, the day Germany began its attack on the Soviet Union, the Germans demanded that an entire division of German soldiers be allowed to pass through Sweden on the way to the Finnish battleground. Hansson hinted that King Gustav V, Sweden's symbol of unity, said he would abdicate if the government did not agree to let the German soldiers pass, the government agreed to the demand, and the troops passed from June 25 to July 12 without incident. The Swedes also allowed the Germans to use Swedish water and air to reach Finland.

There will always remain the question of why the Germans did not invade Sweden. On a number of occasions, the Swedes told the Germans that troops or goods could not travel through their country because the railbeds were undergoing repair. Johansson and Norman maintain that the Germans were so intent upon preserving their access to Swedish iron ore that they did not want to risk conflict with the Swedes.

The Swedes were supposed to have access to Allied oil supplies under a 1939 Anglo-Swedish agreement, but by 1942, the Allies had almost stopped sending oil to Sweden, partly out of fear that the Swedes might be forced to send it on to Germany. In 1943, after the battle of Stalingrad turned in the Allies' favor, Sweden and the United States signed an agreement under which the Allies were to send oil and other "basic rations" to Sweden, and Sweden was to refuse further credits to Germany, prohibit the export of arms to Germany, reduce other exports to Germany and end all German troop traffic through Sweden.

Boheman, the secretary general of the Swedish Foreign Ministry, who negotiated with the Americans, later complained bitterly that American officials did not understand the difficulty of the Swedish situation. In turn, U.S. Secretary of State Dean Acheson, who negotiated the agreement with the Swedes, wrote in his memoirs that "the Swedes failed to live up to it. . . . By interpretations more ingenious than ingenuous, the Swedish Foreign Office attempted to explain away iron ore exports to Germany not only above those for 1942 but above the limits set in 1939." Even more exasperating to the Allies, the Swedish company SKF increased exports of all ball bearings and their parts far beyond the 1942 level, despite governmental promises to the contrary and very considerable British preclusive buying. This Swedish action, counteracting as it did the risks and losses incurred in bombing the ball bearing plants at Schweinfurt, enraged American opinion. An investigation disclosed that to accommodate British buying intended to limit German purchases, SKF had to build a new factory. In 1944, the United States threatened what Acheson called "a direct assault" on SKF's assets in the United States by threatening to blacklist the company and seize its assets. In December 1944, Sweden broke off commercial relations with Germany, hastening the end of the war.

When Swedish newspapers informed the Swedish people in 1942 that Hitler's policy on Jews had switched in 1941 from forced emigration to extermination, Swedish public opinion about helping Jews began to change. In July 1942, the Polish government in exile in London released information on the systematic campaign to kill the Jews. That information, it turned out, had Swedish sources and had passed through Stockholm, where authorities, in an attempt to avoid German government anger, had confiscated Swedish language copies. German officials in Poland arrested five Swedish businessmen who had been serving as couriers for the Polish groups in Stockholm ever since the occupation.

In the summer of 1942, Swedish newspapers reported on the roundup of Dutch and French Jews, but it was Germany's decision in November 1942 to apply the Final Solution to Norway's Jews that changed public opinion to the point that the government had to respond. The Norwegian bishops risked death to issue a joint protest, and Olle Nystedt, chief Lutheran pastor in Stockholm said in his sermon, "If we remain silent, the stones will cry out." In early December, the Swedish government reversed its policy and began to help Norwegian Jews get Swedish passports and, when possible, passage out of the country. Danish Jews had been thought safe because Germany considered Denmark a "model protectorate," but in October 1943, when German officials made plans to round up Danish Jews, Sweden opened its doors and nearly 95 percent of the 7,000 Danish Jews found a safe haven in Sweden. Count Folke Bernadotte, the head of the Swedish Red Cross, arranged the release of 19,000 Danish and Norwegian prisoners.

By January 1944, the one million Jews in Hungary were the only large Jewish population in Europe, and the Germans began making plans for their elimination. Valdemar Langlet, a Swedish academic who was residing in Budapest and who had already begun helping Hungarian Jews; Carl Ivan Danielsson, the Swedish minister; and Per Anger, a diplomatic attaché with the complete backing of the Foreign Office in Stockholm, began a valiant effort to help any Jews they could. It was into this atmosphere that Raoul Wallenberg arrived.

After the war, Sweden came under much criticism for putting its neutrality ahead of the mass murder taking place the short distance across the Baltic. Historian Steven Koblik titled a 1998 book *The Stones Cry Out* and wrote that Sweden's response to the Holocaust was too little and too late. Another U.S. scholar, Paul Levine, has taken a softer approach than Koblik. Tracing the development of Sweden's policy through the end of the war, Levine in a 1996 dissertation for a Ph.D. in history from Uppsala University contended that the Swedes moved from "indifference to activism." Levine acknowledged that the Swedish government did not respond to the plight of the Jews until the Swedish people protested the German deportation of Norwegian Jews and also that the Swedish government sometimes cynically used its efforts on behalf of Jews to improve its standing in the United States while still exporting iron ore and ball bearings to Germany. But Levine concluded that "Sweden ceased to be a bystander" and its diplomats used bureaucratic resistance to obstruct the Germans' policies and save Jews earlier than the other democracies, including the United States.

Raoul and the Other Wallenbergs in Wartime

More than 50 years after World War II, the story of the Wallenbergs during those years remains divided between Raoul and members of the family who were engaged in trade with both the Germans and the Allies. Some Swedes today say that writers swept up in the drama of Raoul Wallenberg have overestimated the role he played in helping Hungarian Jews, particularly in light of the efforts in which Swedish diplomats were already engaged. But he remains a genuine hero, and his story is interesting as much for what it tells about the Wallenberg family and Swedish life as for what it reveals about his activities. Most accounts describe Raoul Wallenberg as a diplomat, but he got that status only when he started his war work. Raoul Wallenberg initially went to Hungary as a businessman and his business background probably determined the vigor with which he went about his task.

Raoul Wallenberg was a great-grandson of A.O. Wallenberg, the son of a nephew of Marcus Sr. and Jacob Wallenberg and a typical offspring of the Swedish bourgeoisie. His father, also named Raoul, was the son of Gustaf Wallenberg, who had supervised the day-to-day construction of the railroad to Saltsjöbaden and later been sent by King Oskar II to London to explain that Sweden's acquiescence in dissolving its political union with Norway was not defeatist. Gustaf's success in that endeavor began a career in diplomacy that took him to Japan and China as ambassador and finally to Turkey in 1920. Gustaf's son, Raoul Sr., who was born in 1888, was a second lieutenant in the Swedish Navy in 1911 when he married Mai Wising, the daughter of Sweden's first professor of neurology and the great-granddaughter of Michael Benedicks, the German Jew who had emigrated to Sweden in 1780, become a jeweler and later a financier in Stockholm. Raoul was raised a Christian, but friends have recalled that he was proud of his one-sixteenth Jewish ancestry.

Raoul Wallenberg Sr. had died in 1912 only 11 months after his marriage and shortly before his son and namesake was born. His widow, six years later, married Fredrik von Dardel and had two more children. Raoul's early life and education were supervised by his grandfather Gustaf, who eventually retired in Istanbul. After Raoul completed high school and military service in Sweden, Gustaf sent him to France for a year and then to the United States to the University of Michigan at Ann Arbor to study architecture and learn the international outlook the grandfather felt was lacking in Sweden. After Raoul's graduation from Michigan in 1935, Gustaf Wallenberg pushed the young man into business, arranging jobs for him in South Africa and at a Jewish-run bank in Haifa, Palestine, where Raoul first heard tales of Jews fleeing Hitler's Germany. Raoul's work in Haifa did not excite him, and in 1936, he returned to Sweden. He would have preferred to work as an architect, but because his degree came from an American university, he was prevented from practicing in his home country. Gustaf Wallenberg died in 1937, and for Raoul, life without his grandfather's influence was hard. K.A. and Marcus Sr., who were running the family bank and businesses, did not deem him enthusiastic enough for big business, but through Jacob, Raoul was introduced to Káláman Lauer, a Hungarian Jew who was a director of an import business called the Central European Trading Co. Inc. Raoul became his junior partner. As a Jew, Lauer was no longer allowed to travel freely to Hungary. In 1941, Raoul traveled to France, Germany, Romania, and Switzerland on business and, in 1942 and 1943, to Budapest, where he learned that the plight of the Jews was worsening.

On March 19, 1944, the Germans seized control of Hungary, and Lauer's apprehension about his Hungarian relatives and friends grew. The same year, U.S. President Franklin Roosevelt, who had been criticized for ignoring the stories of what was happening to European Jewry, also set up the U.S. War Refugee Board, an institution whose purpose was to save Jews and other potential victims of Nazi persecution. The U.S. government asked several neutral countries to increase the size of their diplomatic staffs in Hungary and to use their influence to stop the slaughter, but Sweden and Switzerland were the only ones to reply in the affirmative. John Bierman, a biographer of Raoul Wallenberg, has written that the Swedes were more cooperative because "they may have felt guilty" that they had allowed German troops to transit the country and because "they were also conscious that they had a high reputation in humanitarian matters to be upheld."

At the urging of U.S. Treasury Secretary Henry Morgenthau, President Roosevelt had designated Ivar C. Olsen, the financial attaché at the American legation in Stockholm, as the War Refugee Board's representative in Sweden. Olsen organized a committee of prominent Swedish Jews to advise him on the best way to help Hungarian Jews. The group included Lauer and Norbert Masur, a businessman and the representative of the World Jewish Congress, who had suggested to the chief rabbi of Stockholm that the Swedish government send someone, preferably a non-Jew, to try to rescue the Hungarian Jews. Olsen approved the idea.

Lauer suggested Wallenberg for the job, but at just this moment, Wallenberg was called up for army duty. A 24-hour leave was arranged, and Olsen met Wallenberg and approved him. At Bellmansro, one of Stockholm's finest restaurants, at a dinner that lasted from 7 P.M. on June 8, 1944, until 5 A.M. the next morning, Lauer, Olsen, Herschel Johnson, the U.S. minister, and Wallenberg developed a plan in which Wallenberg would be sent to Hungary as a Swedish attaché with backing from the War Refugee Board.

The Swedish government had already agreed to send a special envoy to Budapest with diplomatic cover, but was unprepared for the idea of sending someone without diplomatic experience. As Bierman describes the situation, when Wallenberg expressed his businessman's disdain for bureaucracy and demanded authority to bribe Hungarian officials, "the Foreign Office mandarins to whom he made his feelings known were shocked; 130 years of neutrality had bred a particularly cautious and protocol-bound outlook among them." Fourteen days of negotiations ensued before the Foreign Office agreed to make him secretary of the legation with full powers to issue passports and grant asylum. The U.S. War Refugee Board agreed to make $50,000 available to him to be used for bribes if necessary.

Raoul arrived in Budapest on July 9, 1944, bringing, as Levine has noted, "his tremendous energy, creativity and sense of humanity" to the ongoing effort. Wallenberg distributed as many Swedish passports as he could and otherwise assisted Hungarian Jews before the Soviet army liberated Budapest on December 8, 1944. The Soviets took Raoul Wallenberg into "protective custody" and sent him to Lubyanka Prison in Moscow in 1947. There is evidence they believed he was an American spy. In 1957, Soviet Foreign Minister Andrei Gromyko said that Wallenberg had died of a heart attack in 1947. Efforts to confirm Gromyko's account or to determine whether Wallenberg met another fate have continued to the present day.

Raoul's powerful relatives spent the war years tending to business that had become more than usual. K.A. Wallenberg remained chairman of the bank until he died in 1938 and Marcus Sr. took over as chairman. When Marcus Sr. died in 1943, Johannes Hellner, a justice of the Supreme Court and foreign minister, was appointed chairman of the bank and Investor, positions he held until the end of the war.

Marcus's sons Jacob, born in 1892, and Marcus Jr., born in 1899 and known by the nickname "Dodde," had joined the bank in the 1920s. Jacob Wallenberg graduated from the naval college at the head of his class, then received a degree from the Stockholm School of Economics in two years and worked at banks in other countries before starting at Stockholms Enskilda Bank as an assistant manager in 1920. Marcus Jr. also graduated from the Stockholm School of Economics. He became Sweden's national tennis champion in 1920 and the first Swede to play on center court at Wimbledon, in 1925, the same year he began working as an assistant manager at the bank.

As a neutral country, Sweden was by international law free to do business with any country during World War II. The Wallenbergs had business dealings with both sides, with Marcus Jr. handling relations with the Allies, particularly Great Britain, and Jacob with the Germans. SKF sold ball bearings to both countries, for example.

After the Allies won the war and the full extent of German atrocities became known, the Wallenbergs—and Sweden—were criticized for making money by doing business with the Germans. But what got them into formal, legal trouble after the war was a 1939 decision to assist the German Bosch corporation, a manufacturer of electronic products, in "cloaking" its ownership of its U.S. operations. Bosch had started business in 1886, invented a spark plug and was based in Stuttgart. In the early 1900s it opened a plant in the United States, which was seized by the U.S. government's Alien Property Custodian during World War I. In 1918, the U.S. government sold the American Bosch subsidiary, including its patents and trademarks, to American owners with the stipulation that it could not be resold to the Germans. German Bosch, however, started to build up a new foreign network and in 1931 the U.S. company and a U.S. subsidiary of German Bosch merged as the American Bosch Corporation. The U.S.-owned company appeared to be dominant, but German Bosch secretly increased its role.

In 1936, as the Nazis were gaining power, Bosch placed control of its foreign subsidiaries in the hands of a Dutch bank. The Dutch bank collapsed in 1939. According to an account of the case in *The Art of Cloaking: The Secret Collaboration and Protection of the German War Industry by the Neutrals* by Gerard Aalders and Cees Wiebes, two Dutch scholars, Bosch turned to the Wallenberg bank to play the same role the Dutch had played. The Wallenbergs agreed that for a commission they would purchase and cloak the Bosch shares and reached a secret, gentlemen's agreement to hold all dividends for Bosch until after the war and then sell the firm back to the Germans. Thus, the German owners were able to make money selling armaments to both sides in the war and expected to get their company back within two years after the war ended. In November 1940, Marcus Wallenberg traveled to the United States and, with the assistance of John Foster Dulles, a senior partner in the New York law firm of Sullivan & Cromwell and a future U.S. secretary of state, established a voting trust.

On Dec. 15, 1941, only four days after Germany declared war on the United States, a suspicious U.S. Treasury Department took charge of the American Bosch shares. The Wallenbergs apparently kept their arrangement with Bosch from the Swedish authorities, and on Jan. 17, 1942, the Swedish government informed the U.S. government that the Swedish ownership of American Bosch was bona fide as Swedish. The U.S. Treasury was not satisfied and suspected American Bosch officials of espionage on behalf of the Nazis. In May, 1942, the Alien Property Office confiscated American Bosch and on Dec. 29, 1942 forced American Bosch to issue licenses under all Bosch patents to American firms, but with no royalties.

The Wallenbergs destroyed the secret Bosch contracts, but after the war the Allies found the contracts with the Wallenbergs in the Bosch archives in Stuttgart. On Aug. 12, 1945, the U.S. placed the bank and the Wallenberg brothers on a list of special blocked nationals, which meant that no U.S. firm could engage in financial transactions with them without the permission of the Treasury. The United States granted Marcus Wallenberg a visa so that he could try to refute the charges, and he arrived in Washington on Aug. 14, 1945. Later that month, Jacob Wallenberg and Rolf Calissendorff, a Wallenberg executive, were granted visas and arrived in New York. The Wallenbergs were interrogated by an agent of the U.S. Army Counter-Intelligence Group and on Oct. 2, 1945 the two brothers and Calissendorf told Treasury that the transactions with Bosch had been essentially a banking matter and that the deal was structured as a purchase to protect them as lenders. The Americans were also upset that the Wallenberg bank had given a large credit to Norsk Hydro so that the Germans could place orders with Swedish firms to reconstruct it.

The British, however, remained appreciative that SKF had sold them ball bearings during the war and in early 1946, Great Britain announced it would not blacklist Enskilda or the Wallenbergs. Sir Charles Hambro, a British investor and diplomat, wrote John Foster Dulles that "the Enskilda bank and the Wallenbergs are treated by the U.S. government as war criminals on documentary evidence from Germany, after all they have done for us, and when so many bankers and businesses in Finland especially and in Scandinavia in general have been whitewashed, makes one doubt whether any justice remains on your great continent."

The Wallenbergs' lawyers used Hambro's letter to try to convince U.S. authorities to take the Wallenbergs off the blacklist. The Allies did end the blacklist, but Jacob paid a price, which some historians say was at American insistence. In 1946, Hellner had been replaced by Robert Ljunglöf, a vice chairman of Investor, as chairman of the bank and by Jacob as president. But Jacob had signed the Bosch documents and on March 12, 1946, Enskilda officially announced Jacob's resignation as president of the bank and said that Marcus would head the bank. Jacob became chairman of the less visible Investor and of Providentia until it was dissolved. The Wallenbergs did get some vindication, however. With the help of Sullivan & Cromwell, they sued the Alien Property Office for $8 million compensation for the confiscation of the Bosch shares. The case dragged on until 1950 when the U.S. government agreed to pay the Wallenberg bank $2.6 million, about the same amount as their original investment.

The profitable wartime dealings of Wallenberg-controlled companies with the Germans became controversial again in 1996, during the investigation of Nazi gold in Swiss banks. The Riksbank released documents showing that it had warned the government that Swedish trade with Germany might be bankrolled with stolen bullion, but that Herman Eriksson, the Swedish trade minister, had replied that the government wanted to maintain the trade and had said that the Riksbank should not ask the Germans to account for the gold's provenance. After an investigation in the late 1940s, Sweden did return most of the gold of questionable origin that was in the form of money. But in the 1990s—after the role that Swiss banks played in the transfer of gold Nazis stole from the Jews became an international issue—a special government commission was appointed to probe allegations that Jacob Wallenberg had urged the Riksbank to accept gold from Germany even if it had been stolen from Jews.

For many years after the war, the Swedish people and Swedish government officials found the Holocaust an uncomfortable subject. But in 1998, in an attempt to teach the Swedish people more about the Holocaust, the Swedish government commissioned a book, *Tell Ye Your Children*, by Stéphane Bruchfeld and Paul A. Levine, which has been used worldwide to teach children about the Holocaust.

IKEA, 1943 and Tetra Pak, 1951
Gambro, 1964 and SAS, 1950

The combination of the Depression, the war and the Social Democrats' negative attitude toward entrepreneurship discouraged the formation and growth of Swedish companies after 1932. But two new companies, Tetra Pak and IKEA, did emerge from the '30s and '40s to become multinational businesses.

In 1930, Ruben Rausing and Erik Åkerlund bought a bag and cardboard factory in Malmö. Åkerlund soon left the company, but Rausing and Holger Crafoord, an industrial innovator, continued to develop the enterprise, making a flour bag that transformed the packaging industry. After the city of Lund offered the company a free site, it moved there in 1937. The Rausing family's goal was—and remains—to produce packages that use a minimum of resources and energy, and are as thin, light and tight as possible, and yet allow for the design and printing that are so important to commercial products.

In 1951, figuring that Europe would follow the lead of the United States and build supermarkets, Rausing formed a subsidiary, Tetra Pak, to develop a milk container. At a May 18, 1951, press conference, he announced his "tetrahedron" packaging system. Its name, derived from the Greek words tetra (four) and hedra (base, face), mean a polyhedron with four faces. At the same press conference, Rausing coined the phrase, "A package must save more than it costs." Swedish dairies began using Tetra Pak's new containers for cream in 1952 and for milk in 1955. In succeeding years, Tetra Pak moved beyond "Tetra Classic" to introduce other food packaging such as brick-shaped "Tetra Brik," which is used for international shipping; "Tetra Rex," a ridge-top container used for milk, juices and other pasteurized products; "Tetra Top," a resealable round or rectangular package; and "Tetra King," which is made from expanded polystyrene and used for milk and yogurt. Tetra Pak has also developed an aseptic packaging system used for foods that have to be refrigerated during long periods of distribution and storage. In 1989, the American Food Technology Institute declared Tetra Pak's aseptic packing to be the greatest innovation in food technology since 1939. Rausing's sons, Gad and Hans, continue to operate the company. Tetra Pak's headquarters eventually moved to Switzerland, and it bought Alfa Laval, becoming Tetra Laval. Gad Rausing, who lives in England and Switzerland, has become one of Sweden's tax refugees. To the great woe of the Swedish tax collectors, the Rausings have replaced Queen Elizabeth as the wealthiest people in Great Britain.

In 1964, Holger Crafoord, a Tetra Pak executive, left to found Gambro AB, a medical devices company. With Professor Nils Alwall of Lund University as scientific adviser, the firm produced the kidney dialysis machines developed by Dutch physician Willem Kolff. Gambro's dialysis machines are used all over the world and are the most frequently used in some countries, in part because Gambro emphasizes that patients should receive factual and psychological information about their treatment. In the mid 1990s, the Wallenberg family announced that it would make a major investment in Gambro as a way of diversifying its holdings beyond cyclical industries.

Meanwhile, Ivar Kamprad, a resident of Elmtaryd, a small town near Agunnaryd in the county of Småland, was building upon the Social Democratic ideal of offering good quality at low prices to the average person. In 1943, in the middle of World War II, Kamprad started a mail order business that he called IKEA, a name that combined his own initials with an "E" for Elmtaryd and an "A" for Agunnaryd. Kamprad's mail order business started out with small items such as teat ointment and ballpoint pens, but in 1950, he published a catalogue that included furniture. Because furniture companies did not like selling to a mail order house, he opened a showroom in the town of Älmhult. In 1953, he opened a department store in Älmhult, convincing newlyweds to come to the out-of-the-way location. In 1965, he opened a department store in the Stockholm suburb of Skärholmen, where homes and other buildings had not yet been built. The location was far out of the city and might have been unfamiliar to most Swedes but for the fact that King Gustav V's car had gone off the road there. Indeed, the spot where the accident occurred had been named Kungens Kurva, or the King's Bend, and was famous throughout Sweden. In the 1970s, Kamprad's greatest success came when he introduced the idea of selling furniture that the customers would assemble.

Famed for bringing a sandwich to work and refusing to allow his executives to fly first class, Kamprad emerged as one of the great characters on the world business scene, maintaining his popularity even after revelations that he had been friends with Nazis. Kamprad brought his three sons—Peter, Jonas and Mathias—into the company, but decided that he did not want any of them to inherit it because he was worried that they might fight over the future of the company. In 1984, he transferred 100 percent of his equity in Ikea to a Dutch-based foundation. In 1986, he made Anders Moberg, a Swede, who had dropped out of college to join Ikea's mail order department, president of the company. By 1997, Ikea had 129 outlets in 28 countries and was expanding into central Europe and China, countries which Kamprad realized had few retail facilities for their growing economies. Ikea had a few false starts in the United Stats when Kamprad met strong competition from Wal-Mart and Target stores and learned that he could not, for example, sell European-size curtains to American homeowners. Ikea's U.S. slogan "It's a big country. Someone's got to furnish it" was popular but in 1997 Kamprad decided the idea was too arrogant and abandoned it.

Regularly scheduled air service began in Sweden in 1924 after a group of individual investors formed AB Aerotransport (ABA). In 1936, the Swedish government took over AB Aerotransport, which was then providing air service between Sweden and other European cities. In 1943, partly at Marcus Wallenberg's urging, investors formed Svensk Interkontinental Lufttrafik Aktiebolaget—SILA—to provide intercontinental air and cargo service. After the war, Sweden, Denmark and Norway agreed to cooperate on air service between Scandinavia and North and South America and Europe and in 1950 set up Scandinavian Airlines System (SAS). SAS's ownership structure was set up with Denmark's and Norway's aviation authorities each owning two-sevenths of SAS's shares and the Swedish three-sevenths of the shares and the Swedish three-sevenths held by ABA, which was owned half by SILA and half by the Swedish government. The Wallenberg sphere controls 50 percent of the shares in SILA, but the shares are split among a number of Wallenberg companies.

Harvest Time

After the war, Sweden boomed in every way. Its companies marketed inventions of the '30s and '40s that had been prevented from full commercialization by the Depression and World War II while Social Democratic politicians declared it was "harvest time" for workers who had been deprived of social advances.

Swedish industry had continued to adapt to new technology and to develop its own. In the early 1930s, for example, Swedish engineer Arne Asplund had invented the Defilbrator method for pulp making, which has found wide application in the production of fiberboard. The method makes pulp out of wood by heating wood chips and grinding them between disks.

Asea began to commercialize the inventions of Uno Lamm, who graduated from the Royal Institute of Technology in 1927 and joined Asea a year later. Known for his cigars and bow ties, Lamm had more than 150 inventions to his credit, including a system for transmitting high-voltage direct current over long distances with a mercury-arc iconic valve. The device enabled high-voltage electrical energy to be converted from alternating current to direct current and back again. Lamm started his project in 1929, but it did not become a commercial endeavor until 1954, when the Swedish State Power Board commissioned a 60-mile undersea cable for transmitting power from the Swedish mainland to the island of Gotland. The success of the Gotland cable led English and French officials to choose the same system for a cable under the English Channel and to ask Asea to supply the methodology and the conversion equipment for the project. The English Channel project made sense for England and France, Lamm wrote, because the two countries' peak power use occurred at different times of the day. If each country imported power at its own times of peak usage, it could make more efficient use of its power stations. In 1964, the U.S. Congress approved the use of the Asea system to transmit electric power from the Columbia River in Oregon to Los Angeles, Calif.

In 1952, Asea also built the world's longest high-voltage line, a 400,000-volt system covering more than 600 miles from Harsprånget in the far north of Sweden to cities in the south. In 1965, Asea completed a 735,000-volt system in Canada. By 1965, the Asea group had 22 factories in Sweden, employed 33,500 people worldwide and was represented in 70 countries. It also made drive equipment for locomotives, mine hoists and cranes, elevators and synthetic diamonds. It was the main contractor for Sweden's first nuclear power plant at Lake Ågesta, south of Stockholm, and also won contracts for nuclear projects at Marviken and Oskarshamn.

Swedish firms also continued a pattern of opening plants abroad that had been established by such pioneers as Alfa-Laval (which had established its first U.S. factory in Poughkeepsie, N.Y., in 1899), Alfred Nobel, Ericsson and SKF. As Sweden's labor costs rose, conservatives charged that Swedish companies were being forced to invest abroad, but industrialists readily acknowledged to scholar Ulf Olsson that locating plants abroad had more to do with avoiding tariffs and pleasing foreign officials who demanded local production than it did with Swedish wage demands.

While most of Europe was still embroiled in war, the Swedish Social Democrats were already preparing to finish the job of transforming Sweden into a more equal, just and efficient society. In 1939, the government initiated discussions with the unions, industry and government officials on the possibility of planning the national economy over the long term. The war interrupted that process, but in 1944, the Swedish government set up a planning commission representing every sector of society from business and labor to women and agriculture.

Economists in Sweden, like those in the United States and Western Europe, assumed that if the postwar economy were left to uncontrolled market forces, the same kind of prolonged recession that had followed World War I would result. The commission began its work with that assumption, but also incorporated Social Democratic ideology which still expressed reservations about the capitalist system. The 1938 Saltsjöbaden agreement between management and labor had indirectly negated the clause in the 1920 Social Democratic platform that stated that capitalism "exploited" workers, but the clause remained official party rhetoric until the 1944 party platform statement replaced the exploitation clause and the call for nationalization of industry with a statement stressing the importance of full employment. To achieve that goal, the party proposed a state-owned commercial bank; nationalization of some insurance companies; and the creation of state-owned enterprises in industries in which strong monopolies could exploit their market power, decrease production and cause low growth and high unemployment.

The rhetoric of the Swedish labor unions and the Social Democrats turned more leftist in this period partly because the Nazi atrocities and the Soviet Union's membership in the winning Allied cause helped the Swedish Communists get 10.3 percent of the vote in the 1944 parliamentary elections, nearly double the 5.9 percent they had gotten in the 1942 municipal elections. The Communists won at the expense of the Social Democrats, whose vote went down from 53.8 percent in the 1940 parliamentary elections to 50.3 percent in the 1942 municipal elections to 46.7 percent in the 1944 elections.

As the war came to an end, Swedish workers began to express frustration with what they saw as inequalities between workers in different industries. Between February and June of 1945, Sweden was hit by the longest wave of strikes since the general strike of 1909. The Communists had become influential in the metal workers' union, and the most violent of the strikes were in the engineering industry. Both the employers and the middle of the road union leaders saw these battles as an ideological confrontation between the Swedish system and communism and fought back. The workers gained very little through these strikes, however, and the Communists were discredited. The business community, meanwhile, launched a campaign that Prime Minister Per Albin Hansson derisively called *planhushållningsmotståndet (PHM)*, opposition to a planned economy.

In July 1945, Hansson dissolved the wartime coalition government and Social Democrats assumed all Cabinet posts. In late 1946, Hansson died, and there was an important ideological and personal struggle for succession within the Social Democratic Party. Old-time Social Democrats thought that Minister of Social Affairs Gustav Möller should become prime minister, but Minister of Finance Ernst Wigforss and younger Social Democrats refused to accept Möller, and the party turned to Erlander, a University of Lund graduate who had served in Parliament since 1932 and was Möller's undersecretary for social affairs.

The postwar government's economic policy proceeded from the fear that a decrease in demand would be responsible for a recession. The government reduced interest rates, repealed the wartime sales tax, increased old-age pensions and established a number of measures designed to support families with children. Payments began going to families, in part as a straightforward attempt to encourage consumption. Swedes also hoped the payments would encourage more couples to have children; the persistent decline in the birthrate during the '30s—between the years 1933 and 1935, the birthrate dropped below 14 per 1,000—had reached such a level that there were real fears that the population would fall.

Sweden also went back to free trade. The free-trade policy included agreements with Poland in 1945 and the Soviet Union in 1946 negotiated by social scientist Gunnar Myrdal, who was trade minister at the end of the war. Myrdal also offered the Soviets credits to make Swedish purchases. The agreements with the Soviet Union came under criticism both from those who feared that an export of Swedish capital would cause balance-of-payments problems and from anti-Communists. The Social Democrats pointed out that the coalition government had started the negotiations with the Soviet Union in part because the Western powers, including the United States, were slow to develop a postwar policy and because Swedish officials were worried that the powerful Soviets were still offended by Sweden's support for Finland in the early part of World War II. The criticism continued, however, and Myrdal resigned partly over the trade issue. (Myrdal went on to work for the United Nations and in 1974 was awarded the Nobel prize for economics. Frederik von Hayek, who was Myrdal's ideological opposite and the inspiration for Swedish conservatives, was also awarded the Nobel economics prize that year.)

Sweden did have real foreign exchange and balance-of-payments fears. With Europe in a shambles, Sweden got most of its imports from the United States while selling goods on the European markets. The European currencies were largely nonconvertible and could not be used to pay debts in dollars. In 1947, however, the United States started the Marshall Plan. Because Sweden had not been at war, the United States did not give it any money; but it did grant loans, and Swedish businesses got many contracts for the rebuilding of Western Europe's infrastructure. Sweden's greatest advantage from the Marshall Plan, however, was its access to the dollar as currency.

In 1947, Sweden also began a new agricultural policy that was halfway between protection of the old rural life and modern international competition. The end of the wartime blockade could have subjected Swedish agriculture to international competition, but Sweden was grateful to its farmers for feeding the nation in wartime. The new agricultural policy favored larger units and modern farming methods but guaranteed farmers the same standard of living as urban workers by establishing farm prices through government negotiations.

Sweden's increased social spending was justified partly on the basis that defense spending would go down. But as the Soviet Union showed itself to be an aggressor, that didn't happen. As a result of all this stimulus, the Swedish economy did not go into recession, but into a boom that resulted in rampant inflation and a shortage of workers. Finns and refugees from the Soviet-occupied Baltic states were welcomed as workers, while companies recruited workers from southern Europe. Immigration kept wages down to a degree, but according to the Swedish Board of Social Welfare, hourly wages in industry rose by around 14 percent from 1946 to 1947. To keep wages from rising even higher, the government tried moderating prices. There was such a demand for Swedish goods in war-torn Europe, however, that despite the increases in the cost of production, Swedish business—and Swedish workers—still prospered.

Postwar Politics - the Price for Small Business

Swedish politics in the immediate postwar period was much more contentious than the election results showed. Business leaders and nonsocialist politicians challenged the Social Democratic view of the world with their opposition to a planned economy, but they never came up with a message that had appeal beyond their own narrow constituencies. Each party represented a very separate segment of Swedish society—the Conservatives: the old nobility, Lutheran clergy, the military and some business executives; the Agrarians: the lower-income farmers; the Liberals: "free thinkers" united by their belief in free-market economics and freedom from the state church. The campaigns succeeded only in getting nonsocialists to switch from one nonsocialist party to another. At the same time, another small group of voters went back and forth between the Social Democrats and the Communists.

The Conservatives (today's Moderates) remained an important nonsocialist party, but the Liberals elected Ohlin as their leader and became the largest nonsocialist party. Ohlin stepped away from the old Liberal doctrine of free markets, which he called "freedom for business executives," and joined the Social Democrats in advocating the elimination of poverty through government intervention and industrialization. But Ohlin also led the other nonsocialists in charging that the Social Democratic government wanted to "socialize Sweden by subterfuge." The Liberals began improving their position in the 1946 local elections, winning 15.6 percent of the vote. In the 1948 elections, the increased socialization of Sweden and the Communist seizure of power in Czechoslovakia were both big issues, giving the nonsocialists their best chance in years. But the election results showed why the nonsocialists would find it almost impossible to gain control over the government. The Liberals won 22.8 percent of the vote (7.2 percent more than in 1946), but most of their support came from the Conservatives, whose vote share went down from 14.9 percent in 1946 to 12.3 percent in 1948, and the Agrarians, whose vote went from 13.6 percent in 1946 to 12.4 percent in 1948. The Communist vote dropped dramatically, from 11.2 percent in 1946 to 6.3 percent in 1948, while the Social Democrats' vote went up from 44.4 percent to 46.1 percent. The Social Democrats did not have a clear national majority, but they maintained control of the government because they kept their majority of seats in the Upper Chamber and got support from the Communists in the Lower Chamber.

The Agrarian Party had begun losing members because of a decline in the number of farmers, and the Social Democrats feared that the transformation of Sweden into a white-collar society would cause voters to leave their party also. By 1951, Prime Minister Erlander and Gunnar Hedlund, the leader of the Agrarians, were worried by the narrowing gap in the number of seats in the Riksdag between their two parties and the other parties and entered their parties into a formal coalition. The other nonsocialist party leaders denounced the Agrarians, charging that they had become hostage to the Social Democrats so that they could "get an extra penny for milk." The coalition was strong enough, however, that in 1956, Erlander and Hedlund went together on a visit to the Soviet Union. In the 1952 and 1956 elections, the Liberals and Conservatives both increased their percentages in Parliament while the Agrarians' declined to less than 10 percent, but the Social Democratic-Agrarian coalition survived.

In 1957, Sweden became immersed in a debate over establishing a supplementary pension system. The Social Democrats wanted to make the system mandatory while the Agrarians favored a voluntary plan, and the coalition fell apart. The entire Cabinet resigned, and King Gustav VI

Adolf asked the nonsocialist parties to try to form a government. But the Agrarians were unwilling to join a coalition with the Liberals and the Conservatives, and the king had to turn back to Erlander to form another government. A national advisory referendum on the issue only showed that Swedes were split into three groups, depending on which plan would be the best for them personally. When public opinion turned in their favor on the pension issue in 1958, the Social Democrats called a snap election. The Liberals, who had been dithering about their position, and the Communists lost seats, while the Social Democrats, the Conservatives and the Agrarians—who had renamed themselves the Center Party and attracted urbanites concerned about the environment—gained seats.

The pension issue was settled in what might be considered a classic case of Swedish consensus politics. The Social Democrats and the Communists together held 116 seats in the Lower Chamber, and the three nonsocialist parties 115 seats. Because the speaker was a Social Democrat and had no vote, the two sides were dead even when the time came to vote on the pension issue. A Liberal parliamentarian who was a shipyard worker declared he would abstain because he could not vote against a pension bill that helped workers so much. Thus, supposedly solidly Social Democratic Sweden voted by only one vote to transform its pension system.

Swedish business had opposed the mandatory pension system, but in reality its leaders were prospering—at least for the short term—under a system of centralized negotiation. When a period of wage negotiations began in 1955, both the employers and the unions decided that the best way to restrain inflationary wage demands and not endanger the prosperity of both business and workers would be to coordinate the negotiations. The employers called a roundtable conference that included not only the LO leaders of the blue-collar unions but also representatives of the white-collar Central Organization of Salaried Employees (TCO) A central agreement was reached, and others were concluded in 1957 and 1959. While there were disagreements, both labor and management relied on the same wage and economic statistics. "The whole process was reasonably smooth and rational," Hans De Geer has written. "A decision procedure had evolved whereby the central bodies accepted their economic responsibility for setting wage norms. This satisfied the interests of the government. The employers were happy with the efficiency of the model, which pacified the whole labor market with the help of a single decision."

The employers also agreed to the unions' solidaristic wage policy—one that sought to increase the wages of lower-income workers. Leftists in the labor movement who had come to criticize the close relations between labor and management charged that they colluded when they met together at a government-owned rural estate called Harpsund.

But the solidaristic wage policy, De Geer has noted, carried a very powerful ideological charge and provided legitimacy for cooperating "across class divisions."

The Social Democratic government, meanwhile, had evolved a new role for itself in retraining workers and finding them jobs. Immediately after the war, the Social Democratic dream of industrial planning had become deadlocked because the party platform held that the state would intervene only if the structure of an industry proved ineffective. With Swedish industry so fantastically successful in this period, little intervention occurred except in agriculture.

In the '50s, however, the Social Democrats developed a program that justified more government intervention. According to this theory, the solidaristic wage policy would increase efficiency in the economy because it would encourage inefficient businesses that could not afford to pay the high wages negotiated in centralized agreements to fail faster. Neither the businesses nor the workers would have to worry about the fate of the workers because the government would maintain an "active" labor policy, meaning that the government would take responsibility for unemployment and retraining. Workers who lost their jobs because of the elimination of low-productivity businesses would be retrained and found new jobs. The retraining was financed by taxes on "excess profits." The tax increase was also justified as a way of preventing inflation.

Thus government retraining was added to the Swedish Model, making it even more respected around the world. As De Geer concludes: "This negotiating model absorbed a good deal of social unrest and uncertainty. There was something sincere, something of responsibility and sportsmanship about the Swedish labor market during this period. Like many Swedish quality products, it was exported to other parts of the world. And the image often dazzled people, even at home."

The model was not dazzling for small business, however. From the 1930s onward, stories circulated about Social Democratic politicians who publicly made positive comments about small business but privately said that they favored big business over small, because they did not want a petit bourgeoisie to compete with them for the political hearts, minds and votes of people in every small town in the country. Whether the criticism was true or not, the Social Democratic policy of favoring the most-profitable businesses, encouraging weak firms to go out of business and retraining the workers had its effect. According to a study by the Industrial Institute for Economic and Social Research in Stockholm, there was substantial entrepreneurial activity through the 1940s, but the creation of new firms slowed in the 1950s and fell further from 1965-75. According to the study, "regulatory credit markets characterized by rationing" favored large firms that used some of the money to acquire smaller ones. The Institute's Clas Wihlborg wrote in 1992 that "the major problem" for Gunnar Sträng, the Social Democratic minister of finance in the 1950s, was "to channel domestic savings into residential construction without reducing industrial investments and without directly subsidizing construction." Throughout Sträng's administration, the public sector gained control over an increasing share of the nation's financial resources, particularly after the pension reform of 1958. With it came the public sector's influence on credit allocation.

In 1959, the possibility that the Swedish Model might not work perfectly became apparent when Sträng introduced Sweden's first budget with a deficit. The Conservatives proposed cutting child allowances, school lunches and textbooks, but the Social Democrats and the Liberals won the day with reintroduction of the wartime sales tax, which was later transformed into a value-added tax (VAT).

Danger Signs

Just as it became clear that the competitors of Swedish export industries had overcome their war-induced disadvantages, Sweden solidified its image at home and abroad as a rich world power and one with a vision that it could pursue no matter what other, larger powers did. After World War II, Sweden had maintained its neutrality but avoided isolationism. It joined the United Nations, and in 1953, Dag Hammarskjöld, a son of former Prime Minister Hjalmar Hammarskjöld, had been elected secretary general of the young world body. Dag Hammarskjöld believed in sticking up for small nations, especially Third World countries, and his death on a peace keeping mission in the Congo in 1961 heightened the Swedish commitment to solidarity with poor, countries, especially small ones, in opposition to domination by the Western and Soviet Blocs. In 1962, Sweden set up its own international development agency (known after 1965 by the acronym SIDA) to work both through international organizations, such as the United Nations, and directly with poor countries. In 1968, Sweden set a standard for other countries by committing 1 percent of its gross national product to foreign aid. Equally symbolic of Sweden's economic strength and independence was its decision not to join the North Atlantic Treaty Organization, or the European Economic Community, which had been established by the 1957 Treaty of Rome. Membership in the European Community was under discussion in 1961, but Prime

Minister Erlander successfully urged Sweden to stay out on the grounds that the European Community had goals of political unity, particularly on foreign policy, that would interfere with Swedish neutrality. Business executives expressed fears that Sweden would lose the ability to export to European countries, but that issue remained purely academic for many years because France refused to accept Great Britain's application for membership in the Community. Sweden joined the European Free Trade Association (EFTA) of nonmember European countries, which were allowed to trade with the Community.

In the early-to-mid-'60s Sweden, like much of the Western world, was moving gradually toward the left. The idea of planning economies, long advocated by Swedish Social Democrats, had gained strength. The Soviet Union and its client states were advancing economically; institutions such as the World Bank and the Inter-American Development Bank and the U.S. government's Agency for International Development were encouraging planning in poor countries with few capitalists; and as De Geer has noted, "a plan, and not the market forces, . . . put Neil Armstrong on the Moon before the end of the decade."

In both government and business, big was beautiful. Sweden had rejected nuclear arms in the '50s—in large part because Swedish women organized a movement against them—but in 1964, it began building nuclear power plants. Swedish companies, ASEA in particular, formed joint ventures with the government to build the plants. There were still housing shortages in the cities, and the government began sponsoring enormous new towns and fortress-like apartment complexes that towered in dramatic contrast with the small houses typical of rural Sweden. Companies were practicing economies of scale, and the wage agreements between the unions and SAF, the Swedish Employers' Confederation, began to encompass more and more details. In 1967, SAF and LO, the Swedish Trades Union Congress, agreed to a new negotiating system. Expert economists and accountants hired together by SAF and LO were to determine the size of a national "wage kitty" and figure out, in a series of phased negotiations, how to allocate it.

The Social Democrats, meanwhile, remained in power, winning about 45 percent of the vote and governing in an informal coalition with the Communists. In 1964, the position of the nonsocialist parties became even more fragmented when the free-church and teetotaler factions of the Liberal Party broke away to form the Christian Democratic Party. The Conservative, Center and Liberal Parties, frustrated by the inability of nonsocialists to win control of the government, tried running as a coalition in the southern part of the country, but as political scientist Stig Hadenius has written, "a large number of Center and Liberal Party members could not accept the thought of close cooperation with the Conservatives." The

Swedish Communist Party, which had lost members after the 1956 Soviet invasion of Hungary, got new life in the early '60s by changing its name to the Left Party Communists *(Vänsterpartiet Kommunisterna, VPK)*, declaring its independence from Moscow and abandoning the commitment to achieving power by violent means in favor of an endorsement of the Swedish electoral and parliamentary system.

After the "new" Communist Party won 6.4 percent of the vote in the 1966 local elections—its highest percentage since 1948—the Social Democrats pushed the government toward greater involvement in the economy. In 1967, the government set up an investment bank to supply risk capital to companies that were unable to obtain it through normal banking channels. The government had reason to be concerned about shortages of capital. After the war, the Social Democrats announced that they wanted to "wind down" the fortunes of capitalists and said that they were worried that individuals would save too much. The Social Democrats preferred "collective" forms of saving. Government tax breaks from 1938 onward encouraged companies to retain earnings, deposit them in the Riksbank and take them out as needed and sometimes follow government advice to invest them in certain parts of the country to encourage employment. The industrialists objected mildly but appreciated the tax breaks.

In its economic reform of 1967, the government also created the position of Minister of Industry; established a national Board for Technical Development to distribute state grants for technological research; and set up a holding company, *Statsföretag AB*, to bring together state-owned companies. The Social Democrats argued both that it was aiding business and that it was fulfilling the socialist goal of control of the means of production. But the unions were not enthusiastic about these state-owned enterprises. In the '50s, LO had strongly criticized government committee reports urging price regulation and tariffs. LO argued that tariffs would decrease productivity growth because they would protect stagnating and less competitive industries. The politicians didn't like to see constituents lose their jobs, however, and in the late '60s the state tried buying up shipyards, ironworks, and paper and pulp plants whose products couldn't compete in the international market.

In 1968, students at the University of Stockholm, like those in other countries, protested the Vietnam war, challenging the old-fashioned formal relationships between faculty and students and demanding more resources for higher education. The 1968 Swedish elections followed the Soviet invasion of Czechoslovakia, however, and the Communist vote fell by more than half, to only 3 percent. The big beneficiary was the Social Democratic Party, which won more than 50 percent of the vote for the first time since 1962. Political analysts said that part of the reason for the high Social Democratic vote was to say "thank you" to Erlander, who was near retirement. In 1969, Erlander stepped down as prime minister in favor of his longtime close associate, Olof Palme. The party's selection of Palme marked a distinct change in leadership because Palme came from a background so different from that of the working-class Erlander and his predecessor Per Albin Hansson. A lesser noble whose wife, Lisbeth, came from the high nobility, Palme had studied in the United States at the private Kenyon College in Ohio and had been dramatically affected by the divisions between wealth and poverty that he had seen in the United States. As early as 1965, he had expressed his bitter opposition to the Vietnam war. Palme vigorously pursued Sweden's postwar policy of "active neutrality" in foreign affairs. "For us, neutrality does not and cannot signify isolation, silence," he told the French newspaper Le Monde. "We remain neutral vis-à-vis the military blocks, but we cannot be indifferent to the problems of the world."

Palme was beloved by youth worldwide for opposing the Vietnam war so vigorously that he offended U.S. politicians, including President Nixon. But it was during his years as prime minister (he was assassinated in 1986), that the Swedish Model collapsed. With the Vietnam war perceived in Sweden as an imperialist project of the U.S. government and anti-capitalist rhetoric seemingly encouraged by Palme, dockworkers in Gothenburg staged wildcat strikes—a violation of the spirit of Saltsjöbaden. In December 1969, 5,000 mineworkers also struck against LKAB, the state-owned company 600 miles north of Stockholm. The workers declared that LKAB was sucking them and northern Sweden dry and that they had lost faith in the Social Democratic-led labor movement. As Hadenius has noted, Swedes were not impressed when university students occupied their own student union, but took this strike far more seriously. "This time," Hadenius said, "the criticism was coming not from predominantly middle-class students who had occupied a building of which they themselves were part-owners, but from blue-collar workers who performed one of the toughest jobs in the country."

Meanwhile, Sweden attempted to modernize its society and government by implementing a new constitution. The document had been in the works since after World War II when Swedish Liberals, in particular, began campaigning for a modernization of the 1809 Constitution. In 1954, a government commission had been appointed to review election procedures, the two-chamber system and parliamentary rule. The new Constitution, whose implementation began in 1969, got rid of the indirectly elected Upper Chamber in favor of a one-house Parliament of 350 (later 349) members elected through a system of proportional representation, scheduled parliamentary and local elections for the same day and reduced the king's role to ceremonial duties. (King Gustav VI Adolf, who had ascended the throne in 1950, died in 1973 and was succeeded by his grandson, Carl XVI Gustaf, who became the first Swedish king to reign, but not rule.)

In the 1970 elections, the Social Democrats' support declined to 45 percent of the vote, while the vote for the Center Party, which was gaining the allegiance of the growing environmental movement, rose 4 percent, to reach 19.9 percent, and support for the Communists rose to 4.8 percent. The Moderate Party fell slightly to 11.5 percent and the Liberals rose to 16.2 percent. With 163 of the 350 seats, the Social Democrats kept a governing majority by once again forming an alliance with the Communists.

Between 1970 and 1973, the economic problems got worse. Well aware that Swedish prosperity depended on exports, Swedish unions had agreed with business that Swedish wages could not endanger the sale of exported products and had also agreed that wages in other sectors would be kept in line with those in the export sector. But the policy that favored efficient businesses over inefficient ones, combined with the policy of creating government jobs for those who could not find them in the private sector, eventually led to inflation. In 1971-72, a balance of payments deficit of about 2 percent of gross domestic product emerged. To their credit, the Social Democrats increased the rate of unemployment they found acceptable from 1.5 percent to 2.7 percent, and the balance of payments was brought into equilibrium.

The Social Democrats' other major achievement was to make it compulsory for husbands and wives to file separate tax returns. Filing individually reduced people's taxable incomes and gave women a greater incentive to work. But those advantages were somewhat offset by the Social Democrats' subsequent decision to raise tax rates once again. During this period, the government also established a pension fund that could invest in companies, which nonsocialists said would lead to indirect nationalization of industry.

By the 1973 campaign, the gulf between left and right had widened. Palme had denounced the American bombings of Hanoi in 1972, and in 1973, relations between the United States and Sweden became so acrimonious that President Nixon refused to accept the Swedish ambassador and withdrew the U.S. ambassador to Sweden. Nonsocialist leaders declared that Sweden should not be the conscience of the world, but their statements on any subject had little impact and Sweden's drift to the left continued. In 1971, LO had asked the government and Parliament to intervene in order to limit the power of employers at work, and the government appointed a commission to figure out how this could be done. Meanwhile, wildcat strikes continued, and leftists, including many journalists, regularly denounced the Social Democrats as "bourgeois."

The 1973 election results showed dramatic changes in party support. The Center Party got 25 percent of the vote, and the Moderate Party, reenergized by new leadership, got 14.3 percent, while the Liberal Party declined to 9.4 percent—their worst showing to date—and the Christian Democrats received 1.8 percent. The Social Democrats got only 43.2 percent, and the Communists 5.1 percent, but between them, they had exactly the same number of seats (175) as the nonsocialists. A new election might have been called, but the Liberals joined the Social Democrats in opposing a second election because they feared greater losses. Olof Palme's Social Democratic government stayed in power. A short time later, Palme had further reason not to call another election. The outbreak of war in the Middle East had created the oil crisis, which wreaked havoc on every economy in the world. Sweden needed all the stability it could muster.

7

Paradise on a Roller Coaster
1971-1999

ON NOVEMBER 18, 1971, Marc Wallenberg, the 47-year-old president of Stockholms Enskilda Bank and heir apparent to Sweden's largest industrial empire, committed suicide. His death, though a personal and family tragedy, had no direct impact on the Swedish economy or the profitability of the Wallenberg enterprises; but along with the oil shock two years later, it signaled that Swedish business's long run of stable management and prosperity had ended. Over the next quarter-century, Sweden's business and political worlds would prove chaotic. From the '70s to the '90s, Sweden experienced a series of events that other countries would have considered par for the course but that shocked Stockholm and Gothenburg and others that would shock any nation: the rise of Volvo and the challenge of its president Pehr Gyllenhammar to the Wallenbergs' power; the end of foreign exchange and investment controls; a seemingly irresolvable debate over nuclear power; the assassination of Prime Minister Olof Palme and the election of two nonsocialist governments; a banking crisis; and a series of mergers culminating in the sale of Volvo to the U.S.-based Ford Motor Co. During these same years, IKEA rose to become as a major home furnishings retailer in Europe and the United States. Perhaps oddest of all, government-owned Absolut vodka became a spectacular success in the United States.

Modernization of the Wallenberg Sphere

Since the end of World War II, the Wallenbergs' dominance over important Swedish companies had increased dramatically; but the sphere's internal structure, which tied together Stockholms Enskilda Bank with Investor and other industrial holding companies, had changed only as much as was legally required.

A 1944 law had intensified the pressure on Investor and other bank holding companies to distance themselves from their banker founders, and in 1948, Investor finally moved out of the Stockholms Enskilda Bank at Kungsträdgårdsgatan 8 up the street to Kungsträdgårdsgatan 10. In 1949, also to comply with Swedish law, Investor named its first president, Frans Liljenroth, a longtime industrial specialist. In 1950, Liljenroth was succeeded by Rolf Calissendorff, a longtime Stockholms Enskilda Bank employee who had worked closely with Marcus Jr. and Jacob Wallenberg and served as president of Emissionsinstitutet, another Wallenberg portfolio management firm. In 1957, Calissendorff was succeeded by Walter Wehtje, formerly a manager at Atlas Copco, who held the job until Carl de Geer took over in 1970.

These presidents did not really have much authority, according to Count Peder Bonde, a son of Jacob and Marcus Jr.'s sister Ebba Wallenberg Bonde and a longtime executive with Stockholms Enskilda Bank and later Investor. "It was common that the positions as heads of Investor and Providentia were given to competent though aging executives to help them round off their careers," Bonde has said in an interview for a history of Investor. "Their role was to watch over the development of the sphere's companies by participating on their boards. Investor and Providentia were not expected to carry out any research of their own."

In 1958, the power structure within the family did change when Marcus Wallenberg Jr. stepped down as president of Stockholms Enskilda Bank and was succeeded by his eldest son, Marc, born in 1924, nicknamed "Boy Boy" and educated at Harvard. Jacob Wallenberg remained chairman of the bank, and Marcus Jr. returned to the board of Investor, to which he had first been elected in 1927, and to the board of Providentia.

A few years after joining Providentia's board, Marcus Jr. was named president of the company.

In the 1950s, the Wallenbergs had increased their voting rights in some companies, sold a few other companies and saw their control diminish in some that grew much bigger in the years that followed. In 1954, the Wallenbergs acquired 9,000 more shares in Astra and, in 1956, 45 percent of the capital stock in Svenska Dataregister AB (Swedish Cash Register, formerly a division of L.M. Ericsson), which they sold to the U.S.-based Litton Industries. In 1956, Axel Wenner-Gren sold the Wallenbergs his controlling interest in Electrolux, and in 1960, the Wallenbergs formed a consortium to purchase International Telephone & Telegraph's shares in Ericsson. In 1963, Marcus Jr. also established Incentive, as a company to buy the Swedish family businesses that, because of Swedish tax laws, were not finding it worthwhile to expand or that had been inherited by relatives who didn't want to run them. Investor's official history shows that between 1944 and 1963, the Wallenberg sphere's control over the companies' voting rights grew from 7 percent of Separator AB to 11 percent of Alfa-Laval (as Separator was renamed in 1963), from 5 percent of Asea to 8 percent, from 9 percent of L.M. Ericsson to 30 percent, from 12 percent of Stora to 14 percent, from 26 percent of Stockholms Enskilda Bank to 28 percent, from 25 percent of Swedish Match to 32 percent. Investor also increased its control of Electrolux and its holdings in several other, less famous Swedish companies. But also between '44 and '63, the Wallenbergs' voting rights in Atlas Diesel (or Atlas Copco as the company was renamed) dropped from 54 to 30 percent, in Saab-Scania from 100 percent to 27 percent, in Saab from 29 percent to 16 percent, from 11 percent of SKF to 10 percent and in Astra from 33 percent to 27 percent.

Over time, it became apparent that the brothers Jacob and Marcus Jr. increasingly disagreed. During the 1962 Cuban missile crisis, Investor's history notes, Jacob ordered Investor's U.S. affiliate to buy as much stock as possible at the same time that Marcus was ordering them to sell. Stockholm School of Economics professor Ulf Olsson has written that, while Jacob's meticulousness made him a fine board member, Marcus dominated the sphere in the later years. Marcus's view of industry, Olsson wrote, was based on technical developments, a view that engineering companies had to be international and that international competition was vital for a company to prove itself. Marcus Jr. also kept close track of his managers, Olsson wrote, and was prepared to replace them quickly if he became displeased with them.

The differences between the approaches of the two men had become apparent in 1969 when the Wallenbergs arranged the merger of Scania-Vabis, the bus and truck company, with Saab, the airplane and automobile manufacturer. Jacob opposed the merger on the grounds that it was impossible to make money manufacturing cars in Sweden, but Marcus favored it and prevailed.

The clash between Marcus Jr. and Jacob Wallenberg over Saab and Scania-Vabis was a small matter, however, in comparison with other events that occurred in 1969. Marcus decided that the growth of Sweden's industrial corporations meant that Sweden needed a bigger bank, and he proposed a merger of Stockholms Enskilda Bank with Skandinaviska Banken. Again Jacob, in his role as chairman of Stockholms Enskilda Bank, resisted. Marcus Jr. threatened to resign, arguing that Jacob was not thinking about the next generation. Jacob realized that the trends were against him, and he resigned instead. Marcus Jr. was quickly elected chairman.

Jacob and Marcus Jr. continued to feud openly, but intense negotiations took place with Skandinaviska Banken in 1970 and 1971. Marc Wallenberg was a key figure in the negotiations, and when he took his own life a few weeks before the banks were scheduled to merge, there was speculation that Marcus Jr. had put intense pressure on Marc and that Marc had agreed with Jacob that the merger was a bad idea. After Marc's death, his friends said that he had been severely stressed and had become physically ill, and that he had been depressed and improperly medicated. Even the Investor history acknowledges that Marcus Wallenberg Jr. was a "dominating" figure.

Marcus Jr. continued to chair the bank and Jacob to chair Investor, but Marc's suicide catapulted Marc's younger brother Peter to heir apparent. The question of whether Peter could hold the Wallenberg empire together would be the talk of Swedish and international business and political circles for the next two decades.

Peter Wallenberg, who was born in 1926 and nicknamed "Pirre," received a bachelor of laws degree from the University of Stockholm in 1953 and then seemed to have been banished to the far reaches of the Wallenberg businesses. He went to work for Atlas Copco, spending the years 1956-59 in the United States, 1959-62 in Rhodesia, 1960-62 in the Congo and 1962-67 in Great Britain as executive vice chairman of Atlas Copco. He finally returned to Sweden in 1968 as managing director of Atlas Copco MCT AB, the product company for mining and construction. He was named a director of Investor in 1969 and deputy managing director of Atlas Copco in 1970, but was still relatively little known to the Swedish public.

The Wallenberg holding companies, Investor and Providentia, came under professional management after the merger of Stockholms Enskilda Bank and Skandinaviska Banken, Count Bonde has said. In 1973, de Geer hired Claes Dahlbäck, a 25-year-old investment analyst and sent him to New York City to work at Investor's office there. In 1977, de Geer became seriously ill, and in 1978, Marcus Wallenberg Jr. summoned the young Dahlbäck to Täcka Udden and said: "I wonder if we shouldn't let you have a shot at president of Investor. We'll try it, but remember I'm the one who makes the decisions." The appointment of Dahlbäck as president of Investor and Per Lundberg as president of Providentia were signals that the two holding companies would really be operated independent of the bank, according to Bonde.

Despite the professionalization of management at Investor and Providentia, the intense speculation about Peter Wallenberg's future continued as Jacob and Marcus Jr. got older. In 1974, Peter had been named as an industrial adviser to Skandinaviska Enskilda Banken, and he became chairman of the board of Atlas Copco the same year. At the 1978 Investor annual meeting, Jacob stepped down as chairman and was succeeded by Marcus as chairman and Peter as vice chairman. But there were constant rumors that Marcus did not have faith in his second son's skills and was considering someone else, namely Pehr G. Gyllenhammar, head of Volvo, the only major Swedish industry that the Wallenbergs did not control, to take over the Wallenberg empire.

Volvo on a Roll

By the 1970s, Volvo had come a long way from the early 1930s, when it was blatantly copying the design of American cars and was forced into the taxi, truck, bus and military markets to make a profit. By 1935, Volvo had made a profit for five years in succession, and SKF, still its dominant owner, listed it on the Stockholm Stock Exchange. Volvo quickly became a popular stock and was known in Sweden as "the people's share."

In 1937, Volvo expanded its involvement with the Swedish military by building large, off-road vehicles for the country's armed forces. In 1941, it further added to its military capability, this time by buying Svenska Flygmotor, a Trollhättan-based aircraft engine company that had been formed with government support in 1930 as a subsidiary of Nydqvist & Holm AB (NOAB). The Swedish state actually offered Svenska Flygmotor to Volvo because NOAB was dominated by the Wallenbergs, who also dominated Saab, the other major supplier of aircraft, and the government wanted to create competition in the field. During the war, the government prohibited the manufacture of private cars, but encouraged Volvo to produce agricultural tractors and military

223

equipment, including airplanes. The Swedish defense forces became a big customer for vehicles and spare parts, and the official Volvo history says "the entire period of the war (1939-45) was a golden time for Volvo."

As the war came to a close, Volvo began to prepare for peacetime sales and, in September 1944, booked the Royal Tennis Hall in Stockholm for two weeks. Volvo showed off its entire product line, but it showcased its new, smaller, more fuel efficient car, the PV444, which it hoped would appeal to consumer demand pent up by the war. At the show, Volvo also introduced its four-door PV600, a car that the Volvo history admits was obviously copied from a 1939 Pontiac. The Volvo history also acknowledges that many of the finished body parts were purchased in the United States.

After the war, Volvo continued to manufacture agricultural tractors. It became an important exporter of agricultural equipment to continental Europe and to other parts of the world and continued to supply aircraft to the Royal Swedish Air Force. But the surprise was its extraordinary success in marketing and selling its cars both at home and abroad. At Christmas 1952, all Swedish children born in 1945 received an illustrated book of family tales from Volvo, describing the adventures of Ville (Willie) Volvo, a courageous little PV444.

One market Volvo had ignored, however, was the United States. Assar Gabrielsson, who with Gustaf Larsson had founded Volvo in 1926, was still running the company in the 1950s. While Gabrielsson encouraged exports to continental Europe, Latin America and the Middle East, he was hesitant to face the competition in the United States, where there were so many domestic car companies. In 1947, a PV444 was sent to Pittsburgh, Pennsylvania, where it won an award for its safe performance in traffic. In 1955, two entrepreneurs, one Swedish, one American, acting separately, brought Volvos to the U.S. market.

Nils Sefeldt, a Volvo aeronautical engineer who had a dream of selling a Swedish car in the southern United States, sailed for New York City with his family and a Volvo and drove to Fort Worth, Texas, where he set up an agency. Volvo's gas consumption, low by U.S. standards, became a selling point. But Sefeldt found sales sluggish, though they improved after he moved to Houston in 1956. In 1955, Leo Hirsch, a Los Angeles businessman visiting Sweden to buy nails got into a Volvo taxi, was impressed and convinced Volvo to sign a contract granting him rights to import Volvos to 11 western states.

In 1956, Gunnar Engellau, who had been president of Svenska Flygmotor for 13 years, succeeded Gabrielsson as president of Volvo. Engellau threw himself into the U.S. promotion, and Volvo exports to the United States rose to 5,000 cars in 1956, doubled to 10,300 in 1957 and went up from there. Over the 15 years that Engellau ran Volvo, business increased tenfold and the number of cars produced per year rose from 31,000 to 205,000. In 1964, at a speech laying the foundation for a new plant near Gothenburg, Engellau noted, "It took Volvo 23 years to produce its first 100,000 vehicles, which is less than we now make in a single year."

In the 1950s, Volvo also began promoting its cars in ways that were flashy by Swedish standards. Volvo entered auto races in the United States and, in the early '60s, got a boost when Roger Moore, as the lead character in *The Saint* TV series, drove a Volvo. In the '60s, Volvo went upscale, concentrating on the production of comfortable medium-size cars rather than small models. While other carmakers emphasized style, Volvo stressed safety. The reason, according to TV commercials shown on U.S. television in the 1980s, was because a founder's wife, a nurse, was horrified by what happened to people in car accidents.

In 1962, Volvo received the first of its many awards for safety, from the Danish Road Safety Board. The award commended Volvo for pursuing development of the seat belt, even though Volvo executives believed it would be more difficult to sell cars fitted with them. The Volvo 144, with its all-welded monocoque body and its dual, triangular braking system, introduced in 1966, confirmed the Volvo as the world's safest car. For 115 kronor extra, buyers could add a revolutionary rearward-facing seat designed for children between 1 and 7 years old.

In 1963, Volvo opened a production plant in Dartmouth, Nova Scotia, Canada, and became the first European manufacturer to set up car production in North America. The Canadian operation was only the beginning of a worldwide expansion. Volvo's main production plant was still located in Lundby, Gothenburg, on premises that had been discarded by its onetime parent, SKF. In 1964, Volvo opened its Torslanda plant on Hisingen Island farther outside Gothenburg and in 1965 proceeded to build "Volvo City" so that employees could shop and go the bank, the post office and the doctor near work. The new head office, the first in Sweden to be designed as an open plan office, became known as "My Square Lady" after the popular Broadway musical of nearly the same name.

To ensure its market in the European Economic Community (the forerunner of the European Union), Volvo in 1964 also opened a truck assembly plant at Alsemberg, Belgium, near Brussels. In 1966, the company opened a truck assembly plant in Lima, Peru, and, in 1968, a truck assembly plant in Australia and an assembly plant in Malaysia.

In 1971, Engellau chose his son-in-law, Pehr Gyllenhammar, a 36-year-old insurance executive, as his successor. Engellau's decision was criticized as nepotism, but in an interview for this book, Gyllenhammar said his father-in-law had overcome his view that "it's absurd for members of the family to come into the same business" and told his son-in-law that he would encourage the board to appoint him, even though he was his son-in-law, because he was the best man for the job. Gyllenhammar did come to the position with sterling credentials. Born in 1935 in Gothenburg, the son of an insurance executive, Gyllenhammar broke with the expectation that he would attend Uppsala University to go to Lund University, where, he said, he acquired an appreciation of different ways of thinking that would one day help him in his global business career. Though Gothenburg and Lund may look close on a map, Gyllenhammar pointed out that because they did not have good road connections in centuries past and because they were in separate countries, the two cities had populations with quite different mentalities. Gyllenhammar graduated from Lund in 1959, studied international law in Great Britain and worked on Wall Street for a year before returning to Sweden to join the Amphion Insurance Co. in 1961.

In 1966, at age 31, he got a call from Jacob Wallenberg asking him to audit Stora. Gyllenhammar said that he asked Wallenberg whether he was qualified for the job, and Wallenberg replied, "I don't make mistakes." In reality, Gyllenhammar recalled, the auditing job was a typical Wallenberg method of assessing a potential employee's "judgment and energy" with a short tryout. Skandia, an insurance company in which the Wallenbergs had a major investment, offered Gyllenhammar a job, and he became Skandia's chief executive in 1970 at age 35. When his father-in-law chose him to head Volvo only one year later, Gyllenhammar obviously had no experience in the car industry, but said in the interview that he "always had an appetite for industry" and wanted to run "the flagship or potential flagship of Sweden."

Gyllenhammar turned out to be a charismatic dealmaker, the sort of high-flyer who makes other Swedes jealous. Gyllenhammar's deal making began less than a year after he assumed his post with the acquisition of a third of DAF, a Dutch carmaker. In 1973, Gyllenhammar announced that Volvo would open a car manufacturing plant in the U.S. state of Virginia. The plant never produced cars, but to this day, it produces Volvo Penta marine engines.

In 1974, Gyllenhammar opened in Kalmar a futuristic assembly plant that became a symbol of the more "human" factory because it replaced assembly lines with manually controlled trolleys and its employees were organized into self-managing groups. In 1985, Gyllenhammar announced plans to build another state-of-the-art car plant, in the municipality of Uddevalla, which had been hit hard by the downturn in shipyard operations and was willing to provide Volvo with a grant to help build the plant even though Volvo at the time was enjoying high profits.

Gyllenhammar and the Wallenbergs

The first signal that Gyllenhammar and his onetime mentors, the Wallenbergs, might develop a closer relationship, came in May 1977, when the boards of Volvo and the Wallenberg-controlled Saab-Scania proposed a merger of the two companies. Only four months later, after Saab-Scania said it needed more time for internal discussions, the Volvo board announced the deal was off. It was Gyllenhammar's first public failure, a taste of the ups and downs to come.

In 1978, Gyllenhammar reached an agreement with the Norwegian government to create a joint Swedish-Norwegian company in which Volvo shareholders would hold 60 percent of the stock and the Norwegian government, which was rich with North Sea oil money, would hold 40 percent and invest in the development of a new car, which would be produced in Norway. The reaction to Gyllenhammar's Norway deal provoked the first sign that the number of players in the Swedish business world was increasing. Small investors in Sweden had long been organized into the National Shareholders Association, but the organization had only 1,700 members and was not very effective in exerting shareholders' rights in the early 1970s. Then Håkan Gergils, a Gothenburg University-educated retailer's son, assumed the group's top leadership position and began setting up chapters all over the country. Sweden did not yet have mutual funds, Gergils noted in an interview, and "the mission was to get people involved by their own pocket interest." Gergils pointed out that Swedish stock values were low in comparison with the assets of the companies. To get stockholders interested in the fact that their shares were undervalued, he began to pressure management by agitating in favor of scheduling annual stockholders meetings on Saturdays, when small investors could attend them, and even opening up the meetings of publicly held companies to the press.

Although Gyllenhammar ran Volvo, he did not control the stock. There was no single large stockholder, and small investors held 40 percent of the stock. The National Shareholders Association opposed the Norway deal on the ground that forming a partnership with a government would lead to decisions that would not necessarily be good for Volvo. In addition, Marcus Wallenberg Jr. granted *Dagens Nyheter*, a Stockholm newspaper, a rare interview, in which he said that he didn't like the deal because "it's too much of a mix of politics and business." Because two-thirds of shareholders had to approve the deal, the Volvo board canceled the agreement four days before a planned stockholder vote on the issue

In 1980, Gyllenhammar announced that Volvo would take over Beijer Invest, a company with oil, food and pharmaceutical investments run by Anders Wall, an investor and former Volvo vice president. The merger made Volvo a diversified company, creating many new complications for its management. In January 1982, Beijer Invest began buying up stock in SILA, the Wallenberg company that holds the family's investment in Scandinavian Airlines System (SAS), the Scandinavian worldwide airline whose other owners are the Swedish, Danish and Norwegian governments. Marcus Wallenberg Jr., who was in Mexico, was informed that someone was buying shares in SILA, flew home, discovered that it was Beijer Invest and asked Gyllenhammar to stop the purchases, which he did.

Despite Marcus Wallenberg Jr.'s seemingly frequent and harsh criticism of Gyllenhammar's deals, there were constant rumors that Marcus considered Gyllenhammar a greater business talent than his own son Peter and that he intended to merge the Wallenberg sphere with Volvo. Later in 1982, Marcus offered Volvo an opportunity to become a part owner of Atlas Copco, whose stock had fallen. According to Investor's history, Marcus wanted "to avoid a future conflict between the Wallenberg sphere and Volvo, which [was] growing in financial strength." Volvo bought a 25 percent share in Atlas Copco.

The time for generational transition had come. Jacob had died in 1980 at 87, and Marcus died on September 13, 1982, at 83. Gyllenhammar was elected to the Atlas Copco board that fall, but he also challenged the Wallenberg sphere by announcing that Volvo had purchased 9.1 percent of Stora and that before Marcus died he had made an agreement that Volvo could buy 25 percent of Stora. Peter Wallenberg, who had become chairman of Investor after his father's death, agreed to the sale of Stora stock, but also began buying up Volvo stock.

Sweden was soon treated to a world-class public relations war between two big business titans. Gyllenhammar tried to appoint his own man as a link between himself and Stora's president and said he wanted to reorganize the company's management. He also proposed that Volvo buy out the Wallenbergs' share of Stora and sell its shares in Atlas Copco back to the Wallenbergs and that the Wallenbergs sell their shares in Volvo to buyers selected by Volvo. Peter Wallenberg was willing to sell Volvo, but not Stora, in which the family had had an investment for generations. Gyllenhammar's negotiator, Ulf G. Lindén, replied that under those circumstances Volvo would sell back both the Atlas Copco and Stora stock but not at a bargain price. In 1984, the Wallenbergs bought Volvo's shares in Atlas Copco and Stora for 3 billion kronor. The family formed Patricia, yet another investment company, to hold the shares. In what was the largest offering of private bonds in Swedish history, the deal was financed by selling the same amount in bonds to stockholders of Investor and Providentia.

The deal confirmed that Peter Wallenberg did intend to hold the Wallenberg sphere together and to run it himself. Asked later by *The New York Times* "whether his father's doubts had anything to do with his success in countering Gyllenhammar," Peter Wallenberg said, "Let's put it this way: I rather like a fight, and he gave me an opening."

Mercurial Politics

The battles between the Wallenbergs and Gyllenhammar took place against a backdrop of political and economic turmoil that would have been disturbing in any country. Even though the 1973 elections had split the seats in Parliament evenly between the Social Democrats and the Communists on one side and the nonsocialist parties on the other—and the world was in an economic crisis caused by skyrocketing oil prices—Social Democratic Prime Minister Palme and his deputies were unwilling to accept the idea that the days when Sweden was so rich it could do whatever it wanted were over.

Rather than cut spending, the Palme government encouraged private consumption on the theory that Sweden could "bridge over" the recession. The government did fear inflation and a reduction in the international competitiveness of Swedish products and to that end cut taxes and increased social insurance contributions in hopes of avoiding wage negotiations.

The Social Democrats' inclination toward increasing workers' control over their lives—and curbing employers' freedom to make decisions about their factories and other workplaces—continued. In 1974, the Riksdag passed the Security of Employment Act, which gave employees legal protection against arbitrary dismissal. Under this law, a fired employee could take an employer to court and the employer would have to prove there were "objective grounds" for the firing. Isolated cases of misconduct were not considered sufficient cause for dismissal. In the case of production cutbacks, employers were required to adhere strictly to a policy of "last hired, first fired." In 1974, the Riksdag also passed laws designed to encourage employers to hire people with disabilities, and it protected shop stewards who became union activists from discrimination.

Meanwhile, the Social Democrats' hold on the hearts and minds of the Swedish people was threatened by the rise of anti-nuclear activism. Sweden had rejected nuclear weapons, but all the Swedish parties had endorsed the development of nuclear power plants for peaceful purposes.

In the 1970s, as the Center Party's membership base of farmers declined, the party began attracting urban and suburban Swedes who disliked the "bigness" of everything the Social Democrats and Sweden had promoted: destruction of historic buildings in favor of public housing; big companies and big unions; and, most of all, nuclear power, whose safety the activists questioned. In 1973, the Center Party took a formal position against expansion of nuclear power plants. As the 1976 election approached, Center Party leader Thorbjörn Fälldin, a sheep farmer from northern Sweden, announced his opposition to loading any more fuel into reactors and proposed dismantling all nuclear power plants in Sweden by 1985. Furthermore, Fälldin announced that he would be a candidate for prime minister and that if he were elected, he would follow through on his anti-nuclear commitments.

Swedes also began to see evidence that the Social Democrats had grown arrogant from controlling the government continuously since 1933 (except for the summer of 1936). In their quest to achieve equality, Social Democratic ideology seemed to hold that all people with money had gotten it dishonestly. The authorities arrested famed film director Ingmar Bergman on charges of tax evasion, and he went into exile in Germany. After world-renowned children's author Astrid Lindgren was required to pay more in taxes one year than she had earned, she wrote a fairy tale about the unfairness of the tax system for the self-employed. If those events were not enough to convince Swedes that the Social Democrats had been in power too long, a trade union leader was caught vacationing in the Canary islands at a time the *Landsorganisationen* (Trades Union Congress) was boycotting Spain because of Francisco Franco's repression and a Social Democratic politician was caught conspiring to influence an election in Finland.

All these factors added up to the extraordinary results of the 1976 general elections. Support for the Center Party, whose rhetoric had played such a large role in the debate over nuclear power, actually went down 1 percent compared with the 1973 vote. The Moderates gained 1.3 percent, and the Liberals 1.7 percent. But the Social Democrats lost 0.8 percent, and the Communists 0.5 percent—just enough of a decrease for the nonsocialists to win a majority in Parliament, forcing Palme to be the first Social Democratic prime minister to step down in 40 years and allowing Fälldin to take over.

The nonsocialist government was chaotic from the beginning. A new reactor at a nuclear power plant on the southwestern coast of Sweden had been completed, and to win allies to form a nonsocialist coalition government, Fälldin had to back down from his campaign promise and allow the reactor to be filled with fuel. Any hopes or fears that the nonsocialists would lower taxes, reduce the bureaucracy and dismantle the welfare state were quickly set aside. Hans Zetterberg, a sociologist who has taught in both Sweden and the United States, has described the government between 1976 and 1982 as "a different group of people administering Social Democratic government." Political scientist Stig Hadenius has written "the government was eager to show that the Social Democrats were wrong when they claimed that the welfare state would be wrecked by the nonsocialists."

In fact, noted Hadenius, "during the six years of nonsocialist government starting in 1976, a larger proportion of Swedish industry was nationalized than under all the previous Social Democratic Cabinets" combined. The reason was the continuing economic crisis. Swedish shipyards, steel mills and mines were subjected to increased energy costs and competition from countries where labor and other costs of production were lower. To avoid job losses (as opposed to following any ideological commitment to the socialization of industry), the nonsocialist government created separate holding companies for the shipyards, the steel mills and the textile companies. Business executives were split over the subsidies, but Erik Dahmén, the dean of Sweden's conservative economists, said in an interview that despite Austrian economist Joseph Schumpeter's view that it would be wrong to interfere in the "creative destruction" phase of capitalism, he was "not so sure [the subsidies were] completely wrong," because the subsidies allowed Sweden to restructure faster than France and Belgium, which were also faced with aging industries. The subsidies, Dahmén noted, discouraged social tensions and reduced "objections from the union side" because the process "took longer and it was possible to get people employed in expanding sectors." Later, when Sweden faced another economic crisis in the early '80s, Dahmén said, "we had fewer structural problems in Swedish industry; it was mainly a new cost crisis."

Fälldin could not resolve the nuclear power issue, and in 1978, the Center Party left the Cabinet and Liberal Party chairman Ola Ullsten took over as minority prime minister. The accident at the Three Mile Island nuclear energy plant near Harrisburg, Pennsylvania, in the United States on March 28, 1979, brought the nuclear issue back to front and center. In April, with parliamentary elections scheduled for later that year, all the parties agreed to put off dealing with the nuclear issue by scheduling a national referendum on nuclear power in March 1980. In the 1979 campaign, the newly energized Moderate Party proposed a plan to reduce taxes on increases in personal income. The Moderates were the big winners (their support was 4.7 percent higher than it was in 1976) and became the largest nonsocialist party; the Liberals and the Center Party lost votes. The Social Democrats saw a 0.5 percent increase in support compared with 1976, but it was not enough to recapture the prime ministership. A new, triparty nonsocialist government was formed comprising the Liberal, Center and Moderate Parties with Fälldin as prime minister because, as Hadenius has noted, "neither of the middle parties could consider letting the post of prime minister go to the real winner of the election—the Moderate Party."

After the accident at Three Mile Island, there was no question that Sweden was going to phase out nuclear power in the 1980 referendum. The issue was how long the phase out should be. The referendum consisted of three choices—Line 1: a plan supported by the Moderates, business organizations and people who still favored a slow cutback on nuclear power; Line 2: a phase out plan similar to Line 1's, but backed by the Social Democratic and Liberal Parties and LO because they could not face being on the same side as the Moderates; and Line 3: a rapid phase out favored by the Center Party, the Communists and a citizens' movement called the Popular Campaign Against Atomic Power.

The vote showed that Swedes were clearly opposed to nuclear power, although it was by less than 1 percent that they voted for the slow phase out rather than the rapid one. The vote was 39.3 percent for Line 2, 38.6 percent for Line 3 and only 18.7 percent for Line 1. The referendum was necessary because the Social Democrats were split on the nuclear issue, but it settled nothing and the controversies over the speed of the phase out continue to this day. Swedish industry remains dependent on nuclear power. Neither the Swedish government nor private industry has come up with a clear alternative to replace it.

Time did not make life easier for Fälldin. In May 1981, the Moderates, disappointed by the government, left the coalition. Fälldin's Center Party formed a new Cabinet with the Liberals, but it was an extremely weak government because the Center and Liberal Parties had won only 18.1 and 10.6 percent of the vote, respectively, in the 1979 elections, less than what they had gotten in 1976. The economic problems persisted. In the fall of 1981, the government devalued the krona by 10 percent and, in 1982, introduced an austerity program to counter the mounting government budget deficit, negative balance of payments and growing unemployment. Swedes were also troubled when a Soviet submarine ran aground in a restricted military area in the Karlskrona archipelago, although the sharp note of protest Fälldin sent to the Soviets was one action on which all Swedish political leaders agreed.

By 1982, Swedes no longer believed the nonsocialist promise that their political parties would bring better times. In addition, interest in environmental issues had broadened, and a new Green Party had arisen. In the 1982 campaign, the Social Democrats told the voters that Sweden could "save and work its way out of the economic crisis." In the election, both parties that were running the government were the big losers, with the Liberal vote declining almost by half, to 5.9 percent, and the Center vote declining to 15.5 percent. The Moderates' support rose from 20.3 percent to 23.6 percent, and the Green Party got 2 percent. The Social Democrats gained only 2.4 percent, receiving 45.6 percent of the vote. With the support of the Communists, who got 5.4 percent, they returned to power, and Olof Palme resumed the prime ministership.

Because it was the first time he had become party leader by election, Palme was freer to put his mark on the government than he had been when he took over the post from Tage Erlander in 1969. Palme pursued his international agenda, encouraging thousands of political refugees who were fleeing repressive regimes in Latin America and Africa to settle in Sweden. But the Vietnam war, which he had so eloquently opposed, was over and he found himself dealing with the Soviet Union over the pesky submarine issue and with a changing world economy.

Palme's most important appointment was the young technocrat Kjell-Olof Feldt, rather than a party ideologue, to be finance minister. Feldt became the architect of Sweden's economic reforms of the 1980s. In 1982, he rejected both Keynesian reflation to create jobs and Thatcher-style tactics of fighting inflation with unemployment, choosing what the press called a "third way" to reduce inflation and unemployment simultaneously by devaluing the currency and turning the budget deficit into a surplus.

Under Felt's guidance, Palme's very first action was to devalue the krona by 16 percent. Palme also reduced or ended the subsidies to declining industries and told LO not to try to seek a wage agreement that would keep up with inflation.

Exports boomed and unemployment and inflation fell, but between 1985 and 1990 Swedish GDP grew only 2.3 percent, well below the OECD average of 3.5 percent. Business leaders sometimes criticized Feldt's economic thinking, but it is important to remember that Feldt oversaw much of the deregulation of domestic financial markets and scrapped the foreign exchange controls which had isolated Sweden from international markets for half a century. Feldt served until 1990 when he resigned over the government's unwillingness to make tough spending cuts. Feldt left government the longest serving finance minister in the OECD at that time and later served as head of the Riksbank until 1998 when the Riksdag separated the central bank from the government to bring it into conformity with other member countries of the European Union.

While Palme allowed Feldt to pursue many of his ideas to open up the economy, he also agreed to push forward LO's long-standing proposal for a union-controlled system of mandatory profit sharing. LO had commissioned its economist Rudolf Meidner to come up with such a proposal in 1971, and it was published in 1975. After the Social Democrats came back to power in 1982, they agreed to consider an LO proposal under which part of the profits of all companies over a certain size would be transferred to "wage-earner" investment funds, which would be used to buy shares in companies. The end result could mean that the funds, whose boards' majorities would consist of union representatives, would become the owners of the companies. The workers' acquisition of the means of production would be complete. In that debate, however, Palme and LO would meet a newly reenergized Swedish Employers' Confederation.

Curt Nicolin and the Revitalization of The Swedish Employer's Confederation

By the late 1960s, many SAF members, especially the heads of smaller companies, had lost faith that the organization could make the case for business in the public policy arena. The radicalization of the Swedish Trades Union Congress, rising wages, inflation, student protests and the anti-nuclear campaign forced Swedish business leaders into public involvement in politics. In 1968, the SAF division that conducted wage negotiations approached the Moderate Party students association about working together to oppose the left-wing tendency in Swedish society. Among the Moderate student leaders at that time was Carl Bildt, who would later become Moderate Party leader and prime minister. In 1970, Marcus Wallenberg gathered together for the first time the executives of the companies he controlled to discuss how both the Wallenbergs and SAF could become more engaged in the political debate.

These initial forays into politics did not stop the wages negotiated in central agreements from rising. In fact, the tendency was toward higher and higher wages because, as the 1969 wildcat strike at the LKAB iron ore mine proved, LO had lost the ability to convince its membership to abide by negotiated agreements. That strike caused one employer to claim that "the Swedish Model lost its innocence, and the LO lost its honor." After a two-year agreement negotiated in 1975 called for a 40 percent wage increase over the next two years, SAF's member companies began to lose confidence in the organization.

In 1976, SAF got a burst of new energy when Curt Nicolin, then president of Asea, the Wallenberg-controlled engineering firm, was elected chairman and in effect its chief executive officer. With the economic might of the Wallenbergs behind him, Nicolin became Swedish business's first leader in at least a generation to engage in public debate. The nonsocialist victory in the 1976 elections, two weeks after Nicolin's election, quickened the employers' hopes for a future in which their views would be considered more seriously. But Nicolin soon found that the nonsocialists were more interested in keeping the public peace than in making pro-business changes in government policy or praising what he was trying to accomplish. "I expected their support, but was criticized by them the very same day," Nicolin said in an interview.

Unlike many previous Swedish business leaders, who shrank from politics at the first hint of criticism, Nicolin persevered. The descendant of a Walloon engineer who came to Sweden in 1860, Nicolin was born in 1921 to a forester and his wife and was raised at Lycksele in northern Sweden. Nicolin spent his teenage summers working as a lumberjack and did not expect to receive any advanced schooling until a teacher found him and his brother so gifted that he managed to get them scholarships to Sigtuna, a boarding school that has survived the Social Democratic takeover of the educational system by catering to the children of Swedish diplomats and executives posted abroad. After receiving his university education as an aerospace engineer, Nicolin went to work for Stal, a company in Finspång originally controlled by Emanuel Nobel and since the 1940s by Asea. In 1954, Nicolin became president of Stal and, in 1960, president of Asea. Nicolin first rose to prominence in 1961, when SAS was in a crisis and Marcus Wallenberg arranged for him to take a leave of absence from Asea to become president of the airline. In nine months at SAS, Nicolin managed to make the company's operations more efficient by forcing 2,600 employees to leave. That Nicolin was able to fire employees yet still hold on to support from those who remained was extraordinary in Sweden, but he managed it by being publicly critical of the former management and telling employees that the hard times were not their fault but the fault of their former bosses. Back at Asea, Nicolin led the company into nuclear power plant development, a segment of business filled with political controversy.

Nicolin's activism did not mean that the tendency for worker control stopped. In 1977, the Co-Determination Act began to require employers to give employees regular information on their company's economic performance and also helped employees play a bigger role in administration and financial management of companies. In the employers' minds, the Co-Determination Act violated the spirit of Saltsjöbaden, under which the employers were responsible for industrial modernization and the government was supposed to make up for any negative financial consequences of it. Owners of small firms viewed the regulation requiring them to inform employees about their company's finances and to allow employees to participate in administration as interference in their personal business, and they also detested an LO campaign for a regulation to require them to seat laborers on their boards of directors.

Nicolin and other business leaders were determined to stop the wage hikes and the shifting of costs onto their backs. When wage negotiations came up in 1980, Nicolin declared that the employers would counter every demand by the union and insist that every wage hike be "financed" by productivity increases or by payroll tax reductions. The talks finally reached the breaking point. In the biggest labor conflict in Sweden since 1909, 750,000 workers went on strike. Nicolin declared a lockout of the workers and caused a sensation by calling his move an "investment for the future." When the nonsocialist Cabinet asked him to accept LO's offer, he acquiesced. The public interpreted the government's demand and Nicolin's acceptance as a loss for SAF even though the final offer was lower in cost than earlier ones. In 1980, Nicolin, the Moderates and major business organizations all campaigned for the line in the nuclear power referendum that would have deactivated nuclear power plants on the slowest schedule. They lost that particular battle, but the wage conflict had energized SAF and paved the way for an end to all-controlling central agreements.

Since the 1960s, interpretation of the central agreements had shifted. They were construed not as representing a ceiling on wages, but as setting a starting point for further wage increases at the local level. The central agreements then became particularly annoying to those employers who believed that they would be paying lower wages if they didn't have to start negotiating from the level of the central agreement. This conflict led to a split between two major employer groups, the engineering industry, which found that its highly skilled workers used the central agreement as a starting point for negotiations, and the forestry industry, which found the central agreement easier than company-by-company negotiations, because its lesser-skilled workers were usually willing to accept the centrally negotiated wages.

In 1982, employers concluded that the Social Democrats would win that year's elections. To make matters worse from the employers' perspective, LO and the Social Democrats had begun seriously proposing the establishment of the wage-earner funds and a bill forbidding use of the lockout.

The Metal Trades Employers' Association, which represents the engineering companies and is the largest and most powerful group within SAF, declared, as Hans De Geer has written, that it wanted to "escape from the encircling forces of the left" by negotiating on its own. In May 1982, SAF declared that associations had the authority to negotiate with unions themselves and that a three-quarters majority of SAF's board would be required before SAF could enjoin associations to cancel agreements likely to conflict with the employers' common interests. If an association proposed a lockout, SAF could prevent it only if two-thirds of the board voted to stop it. Some SAF members objected to the changes, but as De Geer said, the changes were "the only way of holding the confederation together. The engineering industry is so strong in SAF that it cannot be ignored."

The Swedish Model of labor-management relations—at least in its most comprehensive, centralized, nationwide form—was dead. While the political conflict between left and right played a role in the model's demise, however, it would be a mistake to view politics as the only factor. The conditions of production and work had changed since the turn of the century, when Swedish employers depended on muscular male workers to produce steel and lumber. By the 1980s, unions found it harder to recruit members, and employers found it more expensive to shut down production in labor conflicts. And perhaps most important, Sweden was now subject to international competition.

The prospect of wage-earner investments and worker-owned companies mobilized SAF and the Moderate Party as never before. Nicolin led the debate against the proposal and finally, in the summer of 1983, decided to fight the Social Democrats with their own weapon: a public demonstration against the funds. The event, on October 4, 1983, the first day of the autumn Riksdag, amazed even the organizers. More than 100,000 Swedes turned out to protest against creation of the funds. The crowd was so large that all attempts to count it failed, although Swedes agree that it was the largest demonstration since the farmers and the workers marched over Sweden's role in World War I.

The legislation creating the wage-earner funds still went through the Riksdag in December 1983, but in a much weakened form that disappointed LO economist Meidner. The government said the funds were supposed to increase employee influence on companies, but it softened the ideological reasoning under which the funds had been proposed by saying that the funds were also being established to maintain employment and ensure the value of public pensions.

The government also put severe restrictions on the funds by establishing five regional funds and by advising the funds' managers that each fund was expected to show a 3 percent profit after inflation and that no single fund could own more than 8 percent of a company.

The "Great Muddle" of Deregulation and the Boom/Bust Cycle of the '80s

As countries around the world deregulated their economies, Sweden found it harder and harder to resist the pressures to reduce its strict controls on currency, banks and investments. In 1975, the Riksbank decided to grant permission for foreign portfolio investments if they were sold abroad in the form of convertible bonds, warrants or targeted share issues that were deemed "long-term investments." In 1983, the 1916 law restricting foreigners' ability to buy Swedish real estate was liberalized.

The combination of the '81 and '82 devaluations and the liberalization of banking and investment laws produced an economic boom that seemed wonderful in the short run but led to chaos within just a few years. Odd Engström, a Finance Ministry civil servant and Social Democratic deputy prime minister who would later head a commission to clean up a banking crisis, recalled in an interview that the economy boomed for 30 months after the 1982 devaluation, but that by 1984 Palme began to give in to party and union demands for new government services. "It was too much to ask that the Social Democratic Party which had built up its image for 50 years as a reform-making party could stay with that program of no reforms" for 10 years, Engström said. The inflation that resulted encouraged Swedes to borrow money to buy consumer goods. Swedes paid up to 85 percent of their incomes in taxes, but could deduct interest. "If you borrowed 100,000 kronor, after one year you owed the bank only 88,000 kronor," Engström explained.

The relaxation of investment controls revitalized the Stockholm Stock Exchange, which had been relatively quiet since the '30s because Swedish tax laws had made it advantageous for companies to finance their expansions by retaining earnings or by borrowing from special government-run accounts rather than by issuing new shares through the market. In 1979, the exchange's annual volume was only 5 billion Swedish kronor. By 1981, the volume was 10 billion kronor—about the same amount of business the exchange saw in a single week in the 1990s.

With the internationalization of the credit markets, private finance companies had become legal in Sweden, and in 1985, the banks demanded and won the freedom to increase their volume of loans. "[The bankers] had been driving a small Volkswagen with some capacity of making 50 to 60 kilometers an hour on a highway on which no other traffic was allowed," noted Engström. "Suddenly someone made it possible for other traffic to drive onto the highway and gave everyone freedom to speed. Into that Volkswagen someone put a Maserati motor—the international capital market."

The value of commercial real estate had skyrocketed in the United States and Europe during this period, and Swedish investors and banks became involved in the property market game, both at home and abroad. Between 1986 and 1989, property values in Stockholm doubled in value, and over the 10-year period of the '80s, the value of the stock market appreciated 1,200 percent, noted Jacob Palmstierna, an executive with Skandinaviska Enskilda Banken who became head of the government-originated Nordbanken. The government's 1989 decision to end currency controls, which had prohibited wealthy Swedes from investing abroad, was the beginning of the end. International investment analysts and Swedes who could now invest anywhere began looking at the Swedish situation more closely. By 1990, the entire bubble collapsed and the government had to appoint a banking commission headed by Engström to clean up the mess. Engström noted that other countries that deregulated their capital systems also experienced boom and bust, but that the process was faster in Sweden because it had managed to "live outside" the international economy for several decades. Deregulation, Engström said, made the Swedish economy explode in a "great muddle."

The events of the '80s proved that Swedes could be attracted to business ventures, but as Bengt Rydén, president of the Stockholm Stock Exchange noted, "very few industries were created out of the profits of the character in the '80s. The [investors and speculators] had no ambition to run companies." For those who advocated capitalism and free markets, the '80s were a negative. For the average Swede, the collapse, like the Kreuger crash in the '30s, contributed to the view that capitalism is a questionable way to organize a country's economy. Engström said that blaming the directors and boards of the banks amounted to "scapegoating." All Swedes, from the bankers who loaned the money to the politicians who maintained the deductibility of interest to the individuals who borrowed the money—"we all have a finger or two [in the crisis]," Engström, said. "Who is without guilt?"

But making that case to the Swedish people was difficult, he added. "I have never seen such anger, almost hate toward certain institutions, in all social categories," Engström said. "The most simple person and the most elegant old lady in her fur coat stop me on the street [and say], 'If you don't take them hard, we'll kill you. The bankers are trying to trick you, don't give them a krona more than necessary.' "

The Volvo-Renault Merger - Gyllenhammar's and the Wallenbergs' Final Round

As Sweden boomed, Pehr Gyllenhammar's deal making continued. Volvo already owned Provendor, a food group, and in a 1985 effort to bring Volvo further into the field of biotechnology, Gyllenhammar tried putting together a deal in which Volvo would become a 20 percent owner of Fermenta, a company run by Egyptian immigrant Refaat el-Sayed, who was considered a rising star in Swedish business. Just before the deal was to be completed in January 1986, an environmental activist revealed that el-Sayed did not have the doctoral degree he claimed. Further investigations ensued, the deal was canceled, el-Sayed was convicted of economic crimes and eventually sent to prison. Gyllenhammar's reputation was, of course, damaged.

Subsequently, Volvo faced difficulties raising capital for the development of new vehicles, and in 1990, Gyllenhammar announced at a press conference in Amsterdam that Volvo and Renault, the largely state-owned French automaker, had entered into an "alliance." It was not the first time Volvo and Renault had gone into business together. In 1979, when Gyllenhammar also had a hard time raising capital to develop new car lines, he had sold 10 percent of Volvo to Renault. Renault received an option to increase its holdings, but Volvo bought back those shares during the '80s boom.

The 1990 "alliance" was on a much larger scale than the earlier arrangement. Gyllenhammar handed over the job of managing director of AB Volvo to Christer Zetterberg, a former forestry and bank executive, so that he could concentrate on the alliance. For the next three years, Volvo and Renault "cooperation" intensified, and in 1993, the two companies announced that they would merge. Because Renault was bigger and was performing better than Volvo at the time, Swedes assumed that Renault would swallow Volvo. The National Shareholders Association's membership had risen to 100,000, and the organization took a dim view of merging Volvo with government-controlled Renault. An enormous public debate ensued, with two highly respected former Volvo executives, Lars Malmros and Håkan Frisinger, opposing the merger.

On December 2, 1993, Sören Gyll, a former forestry and steel executive, who had replaced Zetterberg as managing director, came to a Volvo board meeting with a letter signed by a majority of Volvo's top managers expressing their opposition to the merger. With journalists from all over the world in attendance, Gyllenhammar resigned. The Swedish press was only too happy to follow the "Jante law"—"Do not think that you are someone"—to point out that the man who had once insisted, during the Renault period, that he deserved to walk alongside French President François Mitterrand, had been brought down.

Analyzing Gyllenhammar, his legacy and his relationship with the Wallenbergs is still a frequent topic in the boardrooms and hunting lodges where Swedish business executives gather. Gyllenhammar, who became an adviser to the Lazard Freres investment-banking house in London, denounced his forced resignation as a power play by Peter Wallenberg, who controlled a pension fund that was a key stockholder in Volvo. Wallenberg has said that he had nothing to do with the failure of the Renault-Volvo merger and that the French "put out the word that the Wallenberg group torpedoed the deal," because they could not understand why the deal didn't go through. There is evidence that the French did not realize that Swedish business really is privately held and that Swedish stockholders would have found it unacceptable if the deal had gone through and Volvo had come under French government influence, if not control. Nina Ersman, a former Swedish business journalist who was press counselor at the Swedish Embassy in Paris during the Volvo-Renault negotiations, said in an interview that when the deal was falling apart, French journalists kept saying that the Swedish prime minister or Parliament should be able to intervene because Volvo was such a big company. "The French could not understand that Volvo was privately owned, with a large number of small, but actively interested stockholders," Ersman said.

Gyllenhammar's suspicions about Peter Wallenberg acquired a certain credibility when Bert-Olof Svanholm, chairman of ABB Sweden, a Wallenberg-controlled company, was named chairman of Volvo. But others said that Svanholm had such a strong reputation on his own that he would have been appointed even if he had had no connection to the Wallenbergs. In an interview, Gyllenhammar repeated his charge that the Wallenbergs wanted to get rid of him because he was a threat to their position in the Swedish business world. "In my job, I was the only real countervailing force," Gyllenhammar said. "Now there is no countervailing force." Gyllenhammar maintained that the Wallenbergs "are extremely capable," but that "pluralism" with a larger range of business players would be better for Sweden. The Wallenbergs, he said, want to maintain a dynasty, and "a dynasty has different priorities" from modern business. Gyllenhammar said he is opposed to the continuation of the Swedish system of A and B shares, which the Wallenbergs use to control Swedish companies, because the A shares have 10 times the voting power of the B shares. Gyllenhammar said he always prided himself on the "wide ownership" of Volvo.

Gyllenhammar's critics point out, however, that it was he, not the Wallenbergs, who tried to do emotion-laden deals with the Norwegian government, French government-owned Renault and other entities not based on free-market principles; that his management style was so autocratic he was known in his company as "The Emperor"; that he made speeches and wrote articles in which he maintained that Volvo was "more" than a profit-maximizing company, it was the "soul" of western Sweden. They also noted that he had become an adviser to Jacques Delors, the European Commission president whose socialist vision of Europe was opposed by most European business leaders as economically unfeasible.

There was no denying, however, that during Gyllenhammar's 22 years as head of Volvo, the company's volume of business had risen from 6,000 million kronor to 100,000 million kronor and that the number of employees had risen from 40,000 to 75,000. While his competitors, journalists and intellectuals may jeer, he remains a hero to the average Swede and is warmly greeted on the street when he visits Stockholm and Gothenburg.

Volvo executives decidedly sadly that Volvo's independence could not last in an increasingly globalized economy and one in which the cost of introducing new car models has increased dramatically. In late January, 1999, Ford Motor Co. announced that it had agreed to acquire Volvo's car operations at a cost of $6.5 billion. Volvo executives put the best face on the decision to sell, saying that selling out to Ford would give Volvo the financial muscle to sell more cars in Eastern Europe, Latin America and other developing countries. Stockholders did not put up the same battle against the Ford that they had against the merger with Renault because Ford is a private business and Swedes feel more comfortable doing business with the Americans than with the French. Ford said Volvo would remain Swedish based, but Swedes worried that Volvo manufacturing would leave the country. The psychological blow was tremendous even to those Swedes who agreed with the economic underpinnings of the deal. "What is Sweden without Volvo?" asked a member of one pension board with a stake in Volvo.

The Wallenbergs' Fall, Rise and Generational Shift

The Wallenbergs' dealings with Gyllenhammar came in the midst of both a management and generational transition. After Peter Wallenberg took over, Count Bonde has said, Investor, Providentia and Export-Invest, another investment company, became more independent than in the past. "The transition to more active ownership of publicly traded companies and a large volume of successful short-term trading—in part through well-balanced funding—created the need for a larger back office," Bonde said. "With the exception of in-house attorneys, which Investor does not have, it now has taken over all of the research and specialist positions previously maintained by the old Stockholms Enskilda Bank," he continued. "Today, the presidents of Investor and Providentia take initiatives on their own and present their own proposals and solutions, which are then implemented."

The first of Peter Wallenberg's big deals—the 1987 merger of Swedish Asea with the Swiss company Brown Boveri—has been by all standards an enormous success. Formed in 1883 to electrify Sweden, Asea's business of building electric transmission systems and offering other engineering services grew more and more international in the 20th century. In 1950, exports made up 20 percent of its revenues, but by 1970, exports were 50 percent of Asea's business. Asea had signed a cooperative agreement with Brown Boveri, the fourth-largest company in the European power transmission industry, toward the end of the 1960s. In April 1987, Curt Nicolin, then chairman of Asea, shared breakfast with Fritz Leutwiler, chairman of Brown Boveri, in Heidelberg to discuss a closer form of cooperation. Peter Wallenberg, who maintained close ties to Stephen Schmidheiny, the majority owner of Brown Boveri, and Asea president Percy Barnevik, also got involved. On August 10, 1987, the merger of Asea and Brown Boveri into Asea Brown Boveri (ABB) was announced at joint press conferences in Stockholm and Zurich. Olof Ehrenkrona, Nicolin's biographer, wrote that the merger provided Asea "a welcome foothold in the [European Community]," today's European Union. Brown Boveri, half of whose business was in West Germany, got access to Asea's technology and worldwide business. The deal resulted in the breakup of Asea into two parts. One company, which kept the name Asea was formed to hold the Swedish share in ABB. Asea included the Broström shipping businesses, which it had acquired from Investor in the 1980s and which, by the time of the ABB deal, had been losing money for 14 years. The second was Incentive, the smaller Wallenberg holding company, which had been formed in the 1960s.

In 1989, the Wallenbergs decided to address the continuing unprofitability of the passenger car division of Saab-Scania, in which they controlled 20 percent of the voting shares, by forming a new company, Saab Automobil AB, with General Motors Corp. of the United States. In 1990, however, Sven Olof Johansson—one of the Swedish property developers who had made a fortune in the '80s—built up a 22 percent share in Saab-Scania, the company that makes commuter aircraft and trucks. In 1991, the Wallenbergs decided to pay Johansson whatever he wanted to buy him out through Investor. The acquisition of Saab-Scania transformed Investor from a financial holding company into an industrial company, a legal distinction that made it easier for Investor to sell stock to a wider group of buyers, particularly in the United States. But Saab-Scania was also supposed to be a cash cow that would enable Investor to diversify by redirecting its investments out of Sweden's heavy, cyclical industries and into more-modern technology, medical and information businesses. In the European recession of the early '90s, however, a severe downturn occurred in the truck and auto markets, and Saab-Scania ended up draining the Wallenbergs' resources rather than making money.

By the early 1990s, the Wallenbergs controlled investments valued at $33 billion. In 1991, Investor sold its 15 percent stake in Alfa Laval to Tetra Pak. Dahlbäck, Investor's president, noted that Alfa Laval and Tetra Pak were already cooperating on some ventures and that it made sense for Alfa Laval, a producer of food-processing equipment, and Tetra Pak, the packager, to merge. Because the Rausing family, who founded Tetra Pak, had relocated their company's headquarters to Switzerland, the merged company, which was called Tetra Laval, was located in Zurich. Production facilities, however, stayed in Sweden.

Peter Wallenberg's victory over Gyllenhammar came at a price. *Business Week* reported in 1993 that Wallenberg "ran up debt in the turbulent 1980s by expanding while fighting off takeover threats" from Gyllenhammar. In the process, he violated a key family dictum: stay liquid. "Peter's father always used to say you need to have ammunition to mobilize money quickly," said economics professor Olsson, the semiofficial family historian. According to *Business Week*, the Wallenbergs were still considered "overextended as profits weaken, debts increase, markets change and competition strengthens." In February 1993, SE- Banken's nonoperating loans rose to 7.9 percent of total lending and the bank had to inform the Swedish government that it might need assistance in maintaining its capital adequacy ratios; but by August of '93, falling interest rates had relieved the bank's burden so that it could announce it would not need state help. That same August, the Wallenbergs' vulnerability in once-safe Sweden became apparent when three Russians and a Pole attempted to kidnap Peter Wallenberg and take him to a deserted island and demand a $10 million ransom. The kidnappers fought among themselves, and they failed to nab him.

Peter had a hard time getting Swedes to accept him as the head of the family. When he used a racist term to refer to South Africans in a rare television interview, Swedes of all classes seemed to take pleasure in recounting his mistake. It's true he did not look the part of a captain of industry or dynastic chief. Invariably described as rumpled, with a big stomach, Peter often harked back to his Atlas Copco days, saying, "I am an old-fashioned peddler, knocking on doors, selling what I have to sell."

Peter Wallenberg's unpretentious style may play better in the United States than in Europe, where the fact that he is not the family's first-born son is still frequently noted. But over time, even Europeans have begun to give Peter Wallenberg credit for holding the sphere together. In 1994, *The Economist* wrote that, "with Italy's Agnelli and Ferruzzi families in the doldrums, Sweden's Wallenberg family stands out more clearly than ever as Europe's preeminent industrial dynasty." In 1994, *Euromoney* also awarded Peter Wallenberg a modicum of respect. "Peter has gradually rewarded [investors'] confidence and won the respect of the business community," *Euromoney* said. Peter's role, *Euromoney* continued, "is somewhat vague. He has little day-to-day management responsibility in either the bank, where his office is, or in Investor, but talks frequently to Dahlbäck on the telephone rather than sending memos." The exact way in which Peter Wallenberg, Dahlbäck and his other deputies maintained control over their companies remained a bit of a mystery. In 1995, Peter Wallenberg told *Europe* magazine "basically we're not so very unique, except that we have holdings that give us a leading position among the owners of the companies that we are involved in. Then we follow that by assuming the responsibility of the running of the company in the wider sense of the word, meaning we will put people on the board; and we will become more or less active owners; and, basically, we will meet the rest of the stockholders at the annual meeting. But what we try to do is to apply the economic basics that we believe in to all these companies. It has to do with, for instance, margins of profit; it has to do with growth in the market areas. And we will discuss these things with them. You might describe us as active owners, and that is not altogether common here, although much more common here than it is in the United States until recent years."

In his book *Owning Large Corporations*, Dahlbäck explained "communication is informal and continuous, with Peter Wallenberg discreetly at the center. Countless contacts between the 16 directors on Investor's and Providentia's boards at meetings, conferences, trips, lunches, dinners and all types of leisure activities (sailing, hunting and so on) give ample opportunities to bring up questions, pass along information or make decisions. In fact, even the most private of dinners is used to gain something 'nutritious' in a business sense as well." The decision-making process, Dahlbäck wrote, "is an informal one, in which Peter Wallenberg has the last say. And it is not unusual that he uses his veto." The process, Dahlbäck said, "lacks formalism, you could call it a form of systematic brainstorming."

In the 1990s, the Wallenbergs tried to address their frustration that the stock price of Investor continually traded at less than the underlying value of the shares it holds because the company has been so diversified. In 1994, the Incentive division of Asea sold Esab, the world's leading welding equipment producer, and purchased Gambro, a Swedish medical supplies company. In 1996, Incentive also sold off Hasselblad, a distinguished Swedish camera company that had come into being in the 1940s when Swedes could not get cameras from other countries.

As Peter Wallenberg's 70th birthday approached in 1996, the curiosity about whether he could hold the empire together shifted to a focus on the Wallenbergs who would be expected to maintain the sphere into the fifth generation: Peter's son Jacob and his nephew Marcus, the son of the late Marc Wallenberg. Both were born in 1956 and educated at Sigtuna, the boarding school north of Stockholm. Then both went to college in the United States.

Jacob got a bachelor's degree from the University of Pennsylvania and a master's in business administration from Penn's Wharton School of Business before working for Morgan Stanley in the United States. He also worked in Britain and Asia.

Marcus graduated from the Georgetown University School of Foreign Service in Washington, D.C., and later went to a summer program for executives at Stanford University in Palo Alto, California.

Marcus worked for Citicorp S.G. Warburg and SE-Banken and spent three years marketing newsprint for Stora's Dusseldorf-based Stora Feldmühle before becoming executive vice president of Investor.

In 1995, Peter told the *The European* that "I would hate to see them fail. I am prepared to let these boys take over provided they come out right." The same article quoted a Wallenberg executive describing young Jacob as a "terrier" with a go-getting style and young Marcus as a "poodle" with a more reflective nature.

By 1997, Peter Wallenberg apparently decided that they were ready, because he appointed Jacob at age 41 president of the bank. The same year, Asea president Percy Barnevik became chairman of Investor. Jacob's cousin, Marcus, later replaced Dahlbäck as CEO of Investor.

The emergence of the fifth generation coincided with the Wallenbergs' decision to broaden the shareholder base in Investor and to raise capital outside Sweden. To that end, Wallenberg executives have made statements that would have been unthinkable only a few years earlier. In 1995, Dahlbäck told *The New York Times* that attracting foreign investors may be "deeper water than we're used to, and uncharted. But we have to move into it because, what is Sweden? In a few years, just another province of Europe."

The same year, Erik Belfrage, a former Swedish diplomat who is the Wallenbergs' gatekeeper, told *The European* that "today, we are identified as Swedish. In 30 years' time, I hope we are identified as European. That is the big challenge."

Such statements have led some Swedes to fear that the Wallenbergs will abandon their commitment to Sweden. Even if their investments become more international, however, the Wallenbergs have reason to keep Sweden as their base. Although they live well and dominate Swedish business, the Wallenbergs appear not to be as personally wealthy as industrial leaders in other countries. While U.S. law makes it difficult or impossible for wealthy individuals and families to put stock in charitable foundations and still control it, Swedish law does not, and most of the stock the Wallenbergs control is actually owned by foundations that contribute to medical research and other causes. Peter Wallenberg was paid $1.1 million in 1995, a sum that caused Swedish pension fund managers and the public to kick up a stir, but that was a pittance compared with what executives and owners in other countries earn. The Wallenbergs have a place in Sweden that would be hard to establish elsewhere. Gyllenhammar has said that the Wallenberg aura is part of their power. "It isn't control so much as the aura of control," Gyllenhammar told *The New York Times* in 1995. The Wallenbergs share control of Ericsson with Handelsbanken, Gyllenhammar said, "but you'd never know it. Everyone regards Ericsson as a Wallenberg company—and in many ways it is—simply because of that perception." So the question will remain: Do the Wallenbergs want to be the No. 1 business dynasty in Sweden or a personally richer family with their investments scattered?

Politics 1986 to 1998

The 1985 elections took place in the midst of the economic boom. The Social Democrats got 44.7 percent of the vote and, with support from the Communists, maintained the prime ministership. But in February 1986, Palme was assassinated on Sveavägen, a downtown

Stockholm street, after attending a movie, an event from which Swedish society in some ways has yet to recover. Many Swedes said the country "lost its innocence," its feeling that Sweden was separate from the world, that the assassinations that have plagued other societies could not happen in its peaceful, egalitarian, homogenous society. In the investigation to apprehend the assassin, Swedish authorities interviewed international arms dealers, and some Swedes were shocked to find that Sweden's arms industry was such an integral part of the economy that even Palme had, as one cynical observer put it, "preached peace in the mornings and sold arms in the afternoon." Swedes' deep confidence in their government as the finest in the world was further damaged by the authorities' inability to solve the crime (the case remains open to this day) and by revelations in 1988 that a government minister and a former editor of a Social Democratic newspaper had carried out private investigations to try to find the assassin. Ingvar Carlson, a colorless Palme deputy, took over, and in the 1988 elections, the Social Democrats again stayed in power.

Shortly thereafter, Swedes became swept up in the fall of Communism in the Soviet Union and the rest of Eastern Europe. Although Sweden had always avoided becoming a totalitarian society, the yearnings of their Eastern European neighbors to throw off the Communist yoke made Swedes question their own acquiescence to governmental power. Carl Bildt, one of the Conservative student activists with whom the Employers' Confederation had made common cause in the late '60s, took over the Moderate Party leadership after the 1985 elections at age 37. Although Bildt came from a noble family, under his leadership the Moderates seemed to lose some of the upper-class taint that had caused the Liberal and Center Parties to deny Moderate Party politicians their rightful place of leadership during the nonsocialist era of 1970-76. Before the 1991 election, however, another party, New Democracy, was formed, the result of a chance airport meeting between Ian Wachtmeister, a count, businessman and humorous social commentator, and Bert Karlsson, the owner of an amusement park. Other Scandinavian countries had had populist political parties for years, but New Democracy was Sweden's first. Wachtmeister, a natural showman, took great pleasure in flaunting his disdain for the close relationship between Sweden's politicians, industrialists and union members, which he said produced a culture of high taxes and insider dealing that discouraged entrepreneurship. "They're all in it together. We need a revolution," he declared.

Wachtmeister was an unprecedented phenomenon in Swedish politics. A journalist from Norway, where people still point out that average Norwegians got voting rights 100 years before Swedes, said, "How Swedish! They finally have a populist party and it's led by a count." One Swedish executive's wife said in an interview that her friends had voted for Wachtmeister because "he acts like we wish our husbands would." New Democracy Party's positions ranged from less taxation and less regulation for small business to restrictions on immigration, which the other political parties treated as a racist stance against the thousands of political refugees who had been brought into the country.

In 1991, the nonsocialists won control of the government only because New Democracy got enough votes to make it into Parliament. But the Moderate, Liberal, Center and Christian Democratic Party leaders considered Wachtmeister too vulgar and Karlsson too unspeakable to make New Democracy part of their coalition. Some of Wachtmeister's and Karlsson's statements about immigrants sounded racist, and New Democracy was too new and unstable an organization to be a reliable party. But the traditional nonsocialists' snobbish manner with Wachtmeister and Karlsson personally and their lack of interest in dealing with New Democracy and the issues the party raised demonstrated their lack of seriousness in forming a solid nonsocialist majority.

After the 1991 elections, there was no longer any question that the Moderate Party was the largest and most important nonsocialist party and that their leader, Carl Bildt, would be prime minister. The Moderates got 21.9 percent of the vote, the Liberals 9.1 percent, the Center Party 8.5 percent, the Christian Democrats 7.1 percent and New Democracy 6.7 percent. The Social Democrats remained the single largest party, but their percentage fell from 43.2 percent in 1988 to 37.6 percent this time around, and the Left Party, on which they depended for support, saw its support fall from 5.8 to 4.5 percent. The Greens' percentage fell from 5.5 percent to 3.4 percent, and they lost their seats in the Riksdag.

Unlike the nonsocialist leaders from 1976-82, who wanted to prove that they too could run the welfare state, Bildt promised a "New Start for Sweden." Over the next three years, Bildt fulfilled campaign promises to get rid of the wage-earner investment funds, cut some taxes, deregulated the telecommunications sector, liberalized labor laws to allow the hiring of temporary employees, eased conditions for private day care and private schools and helped turn state-owned forest enterprises into the public-private company Assi Domän. Bildt also had accomplishments in setting the stage for the vote on joining the European Union and re-establishing Swedish influence in the Soviet-dominated Baltic countries of Estonia, Lithuania and Latvia.

But his pro-market advances were quickly overwhelmed by deteriorating economic conditions. In 1992, all the political leaders and the Riksbank agreed to try to avoid devaluation of the krona by paying up to 500 percent per year in interest, but the effort failed. Unemployment soared, and in the 1994 elections, the Social Democrats again took control of the government. Another reason for the lack of support for the nonsocialists in 1994 was fear in the business community that Swedes would not vote to join the European Union if nonsocialists were in control of the Swedish government.

Ingvar Carlsson, who had assumed the prime ministership after Palme was killed, held the job again until 1996, when he retired and Finance Minister Göran Persson took over. Bildt remained Moderate Party chairman but, following his interest in foreign affairs, took the job of U.N. commissioner in Bosnia.

In February 1997, after the Social Democrats had declared that they would follow the 1980 plan to shut down nuclear power, the Moderates surged 9 percent ahead of the Social Democrats for the first time in Swedish public opinion polling history. A *Svenska Dagbladet* poll showed that 34.5 percent of Swedes favored the Moderates, compared with 25.9 percent for the Social Democrats. The Moderates' improved standing led political scientists to say that Sweden might be slowly moving toward a two-party system of the Social Democrats and the Moderates. Bildt returned to Sweden to prepare for the 1998 parliamentary elections, but the Moderates' popularity soon faded. When industrialists criticized Persson for continuing the phase out of nuclear power plants, raising taxes and extending welfare benefits, Persson accused the industrialists of meddling in party politics and responded with classic Swedish Social Democratic rhetoric: "The Swedish people have in practice paid for industry's good years through tough economic policies."

In the September 1998 elections, the Moderates got only 22.9 percent of the vote, half a percentage point less than they had gotten in 1994. The Liberal Party fell from 7.2 to 4.7 percent and the Center Party from 7.7 to 5.1 percent. The Christian Democratic Party surged from 4.1 to 11.8 percent. The Social Democrats got 36.6 percent while the Left (formerly Communist) Party nearly doubled its percentage from 6.2 to 12 percent. The Green Party fell from 5 to 4.5 percent. The election confirmed Swedish public opinion polls showing that, when the Social Democrats cut social spending, they lost ground to the Leftists. The Social Democrats held on to the prime ministership, but were forced to forge a closer alliance with the Leftists to govern. In the long run, the Social Democrats' willingness to cut spending and increase taxes to satisfy investors appears to show that they were intent upon maintaining their image as a practical party that could work with big business even when it offended their own members.

Absolut Success

In the midst of all the political and economic turmoil of the '70s, '80s and '90s, Absolut vodka, which is produced by a state-owned company, rose from nothing to being the No. 1 imported vodka in the United States. Absolut's success shows that, even after 40 years of Social Democratic government, entrepreneurial skills still lurk deep in the Swedish soul.

As Richard Lewis, the advertising executive in charge of the Absolut account since 1987, wrote in his best-selling *Absolut Book: The Absolut Vodka Advertising Story*, Sweden already had a "bustling" vodka distilling industry in the 15th century, with hundreds of entrepreneurs turning "pure Swedish water and rich Swedish wheat" into vodka to help their family and friends "get through the long, tough Swedish winters."

In 1879, Lars Olsson Smith, a Swedish inventor and industrialist, created a distillation method called rectification, which used a series of distillation columns to remove almost all the impurities produced during the process of making aquavit, a vodka-like product. Smith called his product *Absolut rent brännvin* (Absolute pure aquavit) and became known as the aquavit king. In 1917, at the height of the temperance movement, the Swedish government took over all of Sweden's alcohol producers and distributors and set up Vin & Spritcentralen. For 54 years, Vin & Spritcentralen did as much to discourage liquor sales as to promote them. In 1974, Lars Lindmark, director-general of the Swedish National Audit Bureau, became managing director, with the job of transforming the government-owned company into a modern commercial enterprise. In 1976, with an eye toward increasing exports, Lindmark began studying the alcohol trade in different countries, and his research showed that in the United States, where people already used vodka as the base for mixed drinks (the Swedes drink aquavit and vodka straight) and the market for colorless spirits was growing, well-educated, high-income Americans might be willing to buy a premium, imported vodka. Lindmark was undeterred by the fact that market studies showed that most Americans thought "all vodkas are alike" or by the fact that the tiny imported-vodka market in the U.S.—1 percent of vodka sales—was controlled by Stolichnaya, which Pepsi Cola imported from Russia as payment for Pepsi sold in the Soviet Union, and by Finlandia.

In 1978, Lindmark and Curt Nycander, export director of Vin & Sprit (V&S), as the company has been renamed, went to the United States with six different vodkas. The big liquor distributors rejected all their products, but Al Singer, head of Carillon Importers, a small New York firm that imported Grand Marnier and Bombay gin, took an interest.

Singer and Martin Landey of the advertising firm Martin Landey Arlow traveled to Sweden to figure out how to promote this vodka in the United States. There, they put together a Swedish-American design team that included Lars-Börje Carlsson and Gunnar Broman of the Stockholm advertising agency Carlsson & Broman. The group developed the clear, medicine-flask-type glass bottle that is instantly recognized around the world today. They marked it with a medallion bearing a likeness of the 19th-century industrialist L.O. Smith and settled on a name: "Absolut Vodka." In a rich, dark blue, those words were stamped on the glass, followed by "Country of Sweden" and below that a full description of the product's fine qualities. Production was located in Åhus, a picturesque port town on the Baltic Sea in southern Sweden, in a distillery that had been in danger of being shut down.

Singer and Michael Roux, the head of sales at Carillon and later its president, made plans to launch Absolut in Boston in 1980, but just as they were about to proceed, the Martin Landey Arlow ad agency was sold to a British firm that already had a even-larger liquor client. Ninety-four agencies competed for Carillon's business (probably because they wanted the Grand Marnier account) before October 1980, when Singer chose the New York office TBWA, an internationally oriented agency that had been formed by Bill Tragos, a St. Louis-born Greek-American, and a French strategist, a Swiss copywriter and an Italian account manger. The grand prize of the deal was the $3 million Grand Marnier account; the Absolut account was worth only $800,000. Tragos put Geoff Hayes, a South African, and Graham Turner, an Englishman from Yorkshire, in charge of the account. As Lewis has written, "Hayes and Turner understood that the concept of 'Sweden' often draws a blank. When there *is* some recognition, it's usually dominated by tall blondes, fields of snow and maybe a Volvo. Otherwise, it's simply confused with the other 'Sw' country, Switzerland." One November evening in 1980, Hayes was relaxing, watching *The Honeymooners* on TV and sketching. He drew a picture of the Absolut bottle, and then he casually added a halo, like an angel's, above it and jotted down the line: "Absolut. It's the perfect vodka." The next day, when Turner saw the sketch, he suggested shortening the line to "Absolut Perfection," and the Absolut ad campaign was born.

Absolut wasn't a hit immediately. Lewis notes that photographers at first had trouble lighting the clear bottle, and the budget was so small in the early years that ads were purchased in *The New York Times* on a standby basis, meaning that the ad could run on any date in any section. *The Times* ad staff, thinking it was doing Absolut a favor, ran a ad with angel wings and titled "Absolut Heaven" next to the obituaries. Sales began to climb, and the copywriters and photographers built on their theme that Absolut was superlative by using imaginative art to tie it to golf courses (Absolut 19th), ski hills (Absolut Peak) and cities (Absolut D.C. featured a bottle wrapped in red tape). When those ideas ran out, they hired Andy Warhol, Keith Haring and other artists to paint the bottle, and the Absolut ads themselves became the talk of cocktail parties around the country. More concerned about developing new markets than afraid of middle-class reaction, Absolut's ad team was also one of the first to recognize the buying power of gay Americans and advertised in gay publications long before most mainstream products did.

In the mid-1980s, Absolut also launched a series of highly successful flavored vodkas, such as *peppar, citron* and *kurant*, based on recipes that Swedes had been making for centuries. Absolut's ads have won hundreds of awards, but their designers are particularly proud that Absolut was one of three brands (the others are Coca Cola and Nike) to become charter members in the American Marketing Association Marketing Hall of Fame in 1992. Absolut, Lewis notes, "accomplished this feat without the benefit of another, much more powerful advertising medium: television."

When the flashiness of '80s society went out of fashion, Absolut's owners were pleased to discover that it is one icon of the indulgent '80s to remain popular in the less flashy '90s (Lewis points out that it is an *affordable* luxury). In 1992, Vin & Sprit launched Absolut in Europe, using ads produced by TBWA's Paris office that salute European landmarks. In 1994, to launch Absolut worldwide, Vin & Sprit left Carillon for Joseph E. Seagram & Sons, but kept TBWA, which merged with Chiat Day in 1995. Some Swedes still question the propriety of a Swedish government-owned company encouraging people all over the world to drink an alcoholic product. Appropriate or not, the export of Absolut proves how a Swedish product can sell when it's marketed and advertised. The total annual sales of Absolut, including some three million cases purchased in the United States, exceed the yearly sales of all alcoholic beverages combined in Sweden.

8

The Empire and the Cottage - Sweden's Business Future

ON OCT. 8, 1999, a front-page *New York Times* story declared "Sweden, the Welfare State, Basks in New Prosperity." The story reported that the annual growth rate was projected at 3.8 percent, far more rapid than that of Europe as a whole and close to the rate in the United States, and that the official unemployment rate had fallen from 8.2 percent in 1993 to 6.1 percent.

The news came as something of a shock to Swedes who were in mourning over the recent sales of Volvo, Astra and smaller companies to foreign owners and the merger of Stora with a Finnish firm. Most of the new business development was in "information technology," a field barely understood by Swedes, who were used to an economy based the car, steel and forestry industries. Ericsson, the longtime Swedish producer of telephones and telephone systems, led the way into "IT" by becoming a world leader in making mobile telephones. But much of the new growth was in new businesses started by a generation of 20-something Swedes who absorbed the lesson from the innovation and wealth that Internet-startups had brought to Americans.

As the 21st century began, there seemed to be no end to the kudos for Sweden. The international edition of *Newsweek* featured Stockholm on its cover, declaring the Swedish capital to be "Europe's Internet capital" filled with "hot IPOs [initial public offerings] and cool clubs." *Stockholm New,* a magazine, told the English-speaking world of new Swedish design and cuisine. *Red Herring,* the San Francisco-based high technology magazine, said Stockholm is "arguably the most important city in the wireless world."

Sweden's new wave of entrepreneurship and prosperity provided a challenge to Swedish conservatives and free-market intellectuals who had portrayed Sweden as a country in decline. It was certainly true that capitalism and business were more secure in Sweden now than at any other time since the Social Democrats took power in 1932. The fall of Communism in the Soviet Union and Eastern Europe and the popularity of capitalism throughout the world had ended any serious thought that some alternative economic system would be better for Sweden.

Longer-term thinkers warned, however, that Swedish business and the Swedish people still must cope with a set of challenges that is peculiar to Sweden: high unemployment; plans to decommission nuclear power plants, which provide 50 percent of the country's energy supply; a national preference for big government, big labor and big business; political parties that are indifferent to business issues; and a national mentality that creates difficulties for international management and is less than enthusiastic about entrepreneurship. They also noted that Sweden's ranking in gross domestic product per capita among the wealthy Organization for Economic Cooperation and Development countries had fallen from third in the 1970s to the upper teens today. At the same time, Sweden's taxes as a percentage of gross domestic product, its government outlays as a percentage of GDP and its taxes on wealth had risen to the top of the OECD charts.

Sweden's close economic ties to the European continent and the worldwide relaxation of trade and investment rules have created new opportunities for Swedes and dangers for Sweden. Since joining the European Union, Sweden has achieved new status as, for example, the number one European producer of gold, silver, lead and iron ore and the number two producer of copper and zinc. Sweden's (and Finland's) forests are gargantuan compared with those on the continent and in the British Isles, and after entering the European Union, the two countries gained a new sobriquet: the "wood yard of Europe."

A visitor to Sweden can sense new opportunities throughout the country. Both Swedish government officials and Stockholm executives believe that Stockholm's location makes it the logical economic capital of a new Baltic region, which Swedish business brochures claim has a population of 100 million people. In an almost eerie recollection of the period when large parts of the countries across the Baltic belonged to the Swedish empire and Swedes talked of making the Baltic "a Swedish lake," one brochure claims that the formerly Communist Baltic states are emerging from a "50-year standstill in the 1,000-year" process of integrating the economies of Northeastern Europe.

In Gothenburg, where civic leaders have been troubled that the seaport city once dominated by shipbuilders and shipping companies has become "Volvoland," there's hope that the city will diversify to become the center of a business community enveloping western Sweden, Norway, Denmark and Great Britain. Malmö is hoping that the Öresund bridge and tunnel linking Sweden to Denmark and the rest of the European continent will bring a new level of economic dynamism to its region, including the high-tech university city of Lund.

In the 1990s, Sweden's big businesses proved that they can and will do whatever is necessary to stay at the top of their fields in the highly competitive global economy: make production at home more efficient, even if that means laying off employees, establishing plants overseas or merging with other companies, Swedish or foreign.

The Swedish companies have been rewarded with one of the highest levels of foreign investment in the world. The fact that the prices of Swedish stocks now rise and fall with markets in New York, London and Tokyo rather than depending on events in Stockholm shows how global and competitive these companies have become.

The sale of a number of Sweden's biggest, oldest firms to foreigners in the 1990s raised questions about whether Sweden can compete in world business in the future. Fortunately, the new era of entrepreneurship revealed Sweden has a hardy, unheralded band of entrepreneurs, including some pioneering women, who ignore every cultural and governmental obstacle to go into business.

The Swedes' willingness to overcome those obstacles may indeed make them some of the most dedicated entrepreneurs in the world and proves the depth of the entrepreneurial spirit within the Swedish people. But their numbers and success will be limited if Sweden doesn't have the tax, regulatory and educational public policies that will encourage the formation of more businesses and jobs. The single most important question facing Sweden is whether the country can develop and sustain the political and business leadership to forge the policies that will allow it to create jobs and prosper in the years ahead.

The Gnosjö Spirit and Other Entrepreneurial Adventures - In Småland...

No place in Sweden, not even the forests and minefields of Norrland, seems as remote from Stockholm and its Lutheran churches, governmental palaces, boardrooms and labor union headquarters as Jönköping in the province of Småland. Located at the southern base of Lake Vättern, Jönköping is known as the Jerusalem of Sweden because it was here that the 19th-century evangelical fervor took hold and it is here that the Filadelfia Pentecostal Church and others that have been "free" from state connection since the 19th-century are headquartered.

Småland is also known as the home of the Gnosjö spirit, a term derived from a village deep in the heart of the province and meaning an unusual inclination toward entrepreneurship and success in small business. Government officials, corporate executives and unionized laborers in Stockholm and other cities have long given lip service to the idea that the Gnosjö spirit was admirable, but during Sweden's years of postwar abundance, all of them somehow managed to convey their view that the world of big business, big labor and big government was superior to a puritanical petit bourgeoisie running its little factories in small towns. Then came the economic crisis of the 1990s. Government statistics showed that Småland and the surrounding territory had the lowest unemployment rate in the country and the Gnosjö spirit became a matter of serious scholarship.

The connection between the Smålanders' attraction to both free churches and free enterprise lies in the fact that Småland was so poor that its people began to question the entire structure of the medieval world, from the landed estates to the state church and the centralized government. The soil was rocky, and the people of Småland learned that they wouldn't survive by working the land. They would have to find another way to make a living. Småland contributed a higher percentage of its population to the immigration to America than any other province in Sweden. It was in Småland that Vilhelm Moberg set *The Emigrants,* the first of his series of novels about the Swedes who went to America. The Smålanders who stayed at home also broke with the Swedish social structure, joining the evangelical churches and, more often than their countrymen, going into business making small items with wood, stone, wire or glass.

Even Smålanders have a hard time describing the exact nature of the Gnosjö spirit and how it developed. "It was more that people were searching for something to do. It was very poor people, a very poor area with no possibilities," said the grandson of a company founder. In the 17th century, he said, many young men from Småland went to work in arms factories and came home and set up small ironworks. But he acknowledged that, as sociologists have found, the 19th-century free churches' strict moral codes forbidding drinking, dancing, card playing and gambling probably played a role in encouraging people to accumulate some money to invest and to develop a strong work ethic. Unlike the state church, into which people were born, he noted, the free churches were voluntary associations, and there was great social pressure among their members to follow the churches' strict teachings about how people should live.

The church was "a meeting point, and people went there every weekend," he noted. "The church," he said, "was controlling the system. When you were in church, you had to think about your relationships. The religion had a message—live up to what you were professing on Sunday."

Many young Smålanders walked away from their religion in the 1960s, never to return. "I was born in the period of drugs, sex, rock 'n' roll," said one business owner. "I had my belief. I was in the church, playing in the orchestra," he said, but he left when he decided to play rock 'n' roll music and his parents and the pastor objected.

Today's Småland business owners may not be as religious as their grandparents were (though many do send their children to Sunday school), but the Gnosjö spirit and the local culture thrive as their businesses grow and expand. It's considered very wise to marry the daughter of an entrepreneur, because she will understand the demands of the business, noted a business owner. In the current generation, some of those women are starting their own businesses. There are also local customs about how to compete and how to cooperate in these small communities. It's not proper for a firm to offer jobs directly to employees of a competitor, for example, but if a worker sees a job advertised and applies for it, the first employer is not supposed to become angry.

Småland businesses are still small compared with Sweden's international giants, but they have shown a remarkable ability to expand and take advantage of Sweden's ever-closer ties with the continent. "My grandfather's business was pulling iron into wire. He was a hired hand, but that wasn't what he wanted to be. He started a small factory and took the name of the town, Hageberg. This was in 1850, when it was hard to make a living and many people were emigrating," said Thorleif Hageberg, managing director of Sigarth, a firm in the village of Hillerstorp.

Ironically, Hageberg noted, his grandfather became so involved in the free church he had joined that the business didn't really thrive until "my father and uncle also started with wires, but welded wire together and made displays for the shops." Thorleif Hageberg joined the family business in 1971, eight years after his brother Sten. In 1963, a radiator company asked the Sigarth firm to make radiator covers, then to make small machines and small parts.

Sigarth had 12 or 13 employees when Thorleif joined the business. "I was very interested in automation," Thorleif said, and in 1977, the company got a contract for a very large order from a company supplying the Swedish army with vehicles that go into all kinds of terrain. The army, he recalled, "wanted to know our quality [control] system, and we had to create one." Now, he said, the company is certified by the Swedish National Standards Board, which is being adapted to a European Union standards system based in Geneva. Swedish army contracts make up less than 5 percent of the company's business, but it's important because the army insists on "top quality." In 1986, the company decided to try exporting brackets for radiators to Germany. Thorleif Hageberg traveled back and forth to Germany for four years and in 1990 decided to employ a German to open a sales office.

"It's a very simple product, Hageberg explained, "a small-niche market," but the products now include end covers and wheels for radiators, grills, side panels and accessories, and the number of employees has expanded to 90. In total, Sigarth's business doubled from 60 million kronor in 1990 to 110 million in 1995, with 80 percent of the business in exports. "The radiator covers fit on non-Swedish radiators," he said. "The German market is the most important market because the Germans need central heating north of the Alps. But he added that he expects Eastern Europe to be a good market as well.

A few miles down the road, Magnus Petersson recalled that his grandfather, a farmer and free-church member, started a carpentry business in 1900 to make doors and kitchens for farmers and later for churches and offices. During World War II, the firm did some work for the Swedish government and after the war began making the fittings for hardware stores and later for reception desks at hotels and schools. Magnus followed his older brother into the business in 1975 when he was 25. Today Hestra, as the family firm is known, uses Italian designs to make the interior fittings for Levi's stores throughout Europe.

Small businesses in Småland are not removed from the regulations of Swedish life. Most firms are, for example, unionized. Hageberg described his relations with the unions as "very good." Both Hageberg and Petersson said that they have more confidence than in the past that Swedish politics will treat entrepreneurs decently in the future. "The Conservatives 20 years ago were left of where the Social Democrats are today," said Petersson. Both men described the volatility of the krona as one of the biggest problems in their businesses. Hageberg called his firm's location on the highway that goes to Stockholm and Malmö and across the bridge to Denmark one of his greatest advantages.

The only drawback for the entrepreneurs with the Gnosjö spirit is that they rarely have university-level training in either engineering or business. Many of the items they produce are relatively low-tech, made under contract to the larger Swedish companies, and the owners often lack sophistication as they enter markets in other countries. In 1995, Jönköping University established the Jönköping International Business School to add book learning to the entrepreneurial skills that seem to thrive naturally in the region. It's too early to tell whether Småland's business owners and their employees will gain new skills from the school or whether students from outside the region will pick up the Gnosjö spirit, but school officials say they are determined to develop a niche of helping smaller businesses move into the international field.

...with Berit Svärd in Värnamo...

When Swedes are asked about women in business, they inevitably point out Antonia Ax:son Mörner, the head of Johnson Koncernen, a conglomerate that started out as a shipping line. Ax:son Mörner, who inherited her company, is a rarity in Swedish business circles. Swedes are very proud of the equality they have promoted between the sexes and achieved in some ways. That equality does not extend to the business world, however. Most Swedish feminist leaders have been middle-class leftists who have questioned, if not opposed, the capitalist system, and they have pushed for the advancement of women in government, academia and the factory more than in business. There has never existed in Sweden a counterpart to the U.S. movement of women of upper- and middle-class backgrounds who wanted to break through the "glass ceiling" to follow their fathers as high-ranking executives and partners in law firms. Swedish upper-class women have not, for example, marched outside all-male private clubs, demanding that they be allowed to dine at the same tables where men are making business deals.

The result is that the sight of a woman in a Swedish executive suite or on a corporate board is still unusual. Maria Leissner, the former leader of the Liberal Party, explained in an interview that the Swedish system of day care has also made it difficult for women to advance in Sweden's big export-oriented companies. Government day care centers are plentiful and well run, but they close in the late afternoon, Leissner noted, and women are expected to pick up their children and take them home. Thus, Leissner explained, a woman working for Volvo or Ericsson on a big deal in another time zone, would find it very difficult to return to the office in the evening or to travel. Hiring help at home is almost prohibitively expensive, she added, because employers of household help are required to pay the same taxes and benefits that are paid to employees in other fields. Asked whether this difficulty in day care was keeping women from advancing in business, a Social Democratic Party Labor Ministry official was unapologetic. "We are not interested in the problems of women like that," he said.

The Social Democrats, who have taken great pride in creating an economy in which people can get jobs other than as servants, have traditionally opposed any measures that would encourage the reintroduction of household servants. Feminists have argued that fathers' taking care of their children should solve any such problems. Such arguments ignore the fact that ambitious women are likely to be married to ambitious men, who also work late and at odd hours, or to be single mothers. In recent years, there have been proposals to make it easier and cheaper to hire child care workers in the home, and some women have taken the matter into their own hands by hiring immigrants on the black market at cheap, illegal wages. But the combination of low regard for the capitalist tradition among women in Sweden and the day care problem make women one of Swedish business's most underestimated and underused resources.

Berit Svärd, however, the owner of GAFS Kartong, a packaging business in Värnamo, near Jönköping, has proved that the Gnosjö spirit applies to women as well as men. Svärd often jokes that she was "born in a cardboard box." Her father, a carpenter, her mother and Gunnar Andersson, a family friend, started GAFS Kartong, making mostly small brown and white boxes, in 1947, the same year that Berit was born. Berit helped out at the company while she was growing up, but did not initially want to take over. She married, had her own children, born in 1967, 1970 and 1978, but worked in the company through those years. In 1978, she went to school to become an interior designer, but in 1980, just as she was about to take the exam for certification as an interior designer, her parents told her it was time to decide whether or not she would take over the company. She decided she would, and the employees supported her decision; but because she didn't want her parents to give her the company, she bought it from them. Her parents still worked there for another four or five years.

Svärd, in fact, gives more credit to her workers than to her mother and father for her success. "The staff pushed me to take it over," she said. "Both Mother and Father thought I was too immature. Today my parents are proud and support me every day. They say, 'We didn't know you were so smart.' "

In the early '80s, Svärd began to increase the business's investment, buying offset presses. By 1980, she had 20 employees, and turnover was about four million kronor. In 1983, she was divorced. In 1984, her parents pulled back from their involvement in the company, but that year, Svärd invested about 6.2 million kronor in a multicolor offset press. Lacking customers for her company's new printing capability, she went to a business fair in Gothenburg, where she found Trelleborg, a rubber and mining company, and other firms interested in obtaining packaging from her small company.

By 1987, turnover was 12 million kronor and she decided to become a specialist in printing on thick paper. She also married an employee who had come to her looking for a job. "We live together day and night," she said in an interview. Formerly a manager of parks in the public sector, he is GAFS's production manager."

GAFS Kartong has become the third-largest paper-packaging company in Sweden, making boxes for Marabou and Freia chocolates, the Bonnier publishing companies' book clubs and SCA, the forestry giant. It also packages fireworks and salmon.

On May 10, 1995, Svärd's tale of the sexism she had experienced at the hands of Swedish banks and the way she turned it to her own advantage ended up on the front page of *Dagens Industri*, the daily business newspaper. In 1993, Svärd's biggest customer had gone bankrupt. "I went down to my bank, Götabanken, which I had banked with all my life, and told my bank manager the entire story in an endeavor to increase my overdraft limit," recalled Svärd. "But if I had problems when I went into the bank, I certainly had even greater problems when I left."

The bank came to the company and examined the accounts in detail. "I had no idea what they were doing. We had a loan in German marks, which they would perhaps rescind. At the time I was not nervous, I was just frightened." The bank refused point-blank to give her bridge financing to survive the crisis and required her to report the company's financial position to the bank each month. Just as business was turning up, a Götabanken officer said, "Berit, why don't you liquidate your company? If you do that, we can tidy up all your present problems and you can start afresh."

Svärd said she asked, " 'Should I liquidate the family business? The company my parents had started almost 50 years ago and which I had inherited from them to look after?' I was so indignant, angry and unhappy that I immediately went to my accountant and asked him if GAFS was really in such a bad state that we were forced to go into liquidation."

The accountant confirmed that the company was not on the edge of ruin. "That day I decided to change my bank just as soon as I could afford it," Svärd said, adding that she told the Götabanken officer that "I'll work all day and night if I have to, to save the business, and you won't make a decision for me. You're just a bank officer." (The officer has since left the bank.)

When Svärd decided to expand once again, she asked Götabanken for help, but was encouraged to repay her existing loans first. Angry, she contacted Svenska Handelsbanken and could hardly believe her eyes when Handelsbanken quoted her an interest rate 3 percent lower than what she had been paying at Götabanken. The Götabanken employee, of course, begged her to stay and then quoted a rate a half-percent lower than Handelsbanken's. Handelsbanken responded with another half-percent lower to get her business.

Svärd's latest venture is printing on micro-corrugated paper, a technique she developed herself. Printing on corrugated paper had proved difficult. When the printing image was applied to corrugated cardboard, the corrugated layer of paper moved slightly, causing the color printing to smudge. SCA had been searching for a way to use the corrugated paper in consumer marketing, and after Svärd sat next to an SCA salesman at a conference, she offered to try to figure out a method. Svärd won't reveal the technique, but it involves controlling the movement of the corrugated cardboard sheet during the printing process. She says GAFS Kartong is "overwhelmed" with orders from SCA Packaging, which markets corrugated cardboard under the trade name "Currulite."

"This lightweight and strong packaging material, with good offset-printing capability, means that the customer can dispense with the extra outer packaging and instead stack the sales-display packaging directly onto the loading pallet," said Pierre Bruce of SCA Packaging. "In the shop, it is then simple to roll in the pallet, and the protective transport packaging becomes the sales packaging with its in-built display function."

Svärd is true to Swedish management traditions in her appreciation of employees. "It would never have been possible without my competent printing workers," she said of her success. She also noted that she is not "a boss up here," who believes she has the answers to every question. "All personnel have the right to say something," she added. Like many women entrepreneurs in other countries, Svärd has gotten used to being the only woman in the room, and says she has little time for business groups; but she is a member of the Swedish Packaging Association, which is composed of 24 men and her, and notes that she has made "a number of interesting observations" about being a woman in business, particularly the packaging business. As she looks back, Svärd said, she realizes that Götabanken "looked upon me as a little girl, and the [bankers] were going to tell me what the world was like." At the first meeting during her business crisis, she said, "there were six men and me." Sometimes, she added, "I have simply signed letters as 'Managing Director B. Svärd,' and everyone naturally thinks that 'B' stands for Bert, Bob, Brian or some other male name. This even happens if I write my full name, for people think it must be misspelled. I have to prove all the time that I'm as good as a man can be. When letters come written, they are addressed " 'Bertil,' not 'Berit.' " Svärd also laments that she has only one woman customer, a woman doctor who works for a plastics company. "Women want to go into service businesses," she said, and shop owners don't come to her, because her business is too big.

One of Svärd's daughters is a teacher, the other a university economist whom Svärd is trying to make into a saleswoman. Her teenage son may become a truck driver. Whether her children go into the business or not, Svärd is enjoying herself, saying "It's great fun, the expansion is so overwhelming. You feel every day how much you are increasing."

...in Stockholm...

The background of Laurent Leksell, president of Stockholm-based Elekta, is about as far from Jönköping and the Gnosjö spirit as a Swede can get. Born the son of Lars Leksell, a professor and the chief neurosurgeon at Karolinska Medical Institute in Stockholm, Laurent Leksell seemed destined for a career in the government-run and -subsidized Swedish medical system. His two older brothers followed in their father's footsteps to become doctors, and his sister became a researcher.

But Laurent Leksell defied both family tradition and the leftist era of his youth by entering the Stockholm School of Economics in the late '60s. He graduated in 1971 and then went to Harvard Business School where he earned a doctorate, and stayed in the United States to teach and work in business consulting. He later returned to Sweden to start a company manufacturing surgical devices his father invented.

In an interview, Leksell explained the origins of his company. "In the late 1940s," Leksell recalled, "it became clear to my father that neurosurgical techniques with much blood, sweat and tears had their limitations because of the damage [they could cause] to the surrounding areas of the brain. He proposed a new kind of neurosurgery: leading electrodes into the inner part of the brain; guiding them mechanically; and by means of the brain's own electrical activity, burning off the pain connections or making other deep interventions. He believed that he could exchange the knife for electrodes or a narrow beam of some kind—an X ray or ultrasound."

The senior Leksell traveled to Philadelphia, Pennsylvania, to consult with Henry Wycis, a prominent American doctor who was performing surgery by fastening a semicircular arch to the head of the patient and using X rays to localize the point of treatment for tumors and other problems.

In 1952, Lars Leksell constructed his own instrument and became convinced that radiation could be used to create therapeutic brain lesions. Working for years with a team of doctors at Karolinska and with funding from the Swedish government, Lars Leksell in the late 1960s built the first prototype of his surgical instrument that delivers a massive dose of ionizing radiation to a very small and confined part of the brain to kill cancer without opening the skull and risking complications from bleeding and infection. Lars Leksell called his invention the Gamma Knife because its beam functions as a scalpel.

As his son recalls, Lars Leksell "was not at all commercially interested. He could not care less if capital existed or did not exist. Money or no money, he was scientifically driven." Like many other Swedish scientists, rather than manufacturing his inventions, the senior Leksell decided to form a company to license their production, marketing and sales. Laurent Leksell was involved in the formation of Elekta Instrument AB as a licensing firm in 1971.

Neither Lars nor Laurent Leksell was happy with the licensing arrangements. "About 10 years after the formation of the company, we started to integrate backwards," Laurent Leksell said. "What triggered the change was a realization that it was dangerous not to control your own investment—not only the research and development but production, commercialization and marketing. Sales and profits had stayed low. In certain countries, our licensees had problems, so we started to help them in the marketing and sales efforts."

In 1983, Elekta began a U.S. operation in Atlanta, Georgia, a daring move because the company had only 200,000 kronor in capital. "We had the advantage that the people in Atlanta knew one thing: There was no use to call Sweden for new money because there wasn't any money. They had to cope with a preset sum." In 1985, the business had gotten large enough that Laurent Leksell decided to quit his consulting business, become CEO and put the business on a growth track. In the early years, while the Gamma Knife was still in the trial stage, the company's first commercial product was the Leksell planning system for stereotaxically guided microsurgery, which allows doctors to guide surgery more precisely so that surrounding tissue is not inadvertently damaged. Compared with traditional procedures, the Leksell planning system also saves time and money because it creates fewer complications for the patient.

In 1986, after 25 years of trials, the company began to commercialize the Gamma Knife, and within 10 years, it accounted for 70 percent of Elekta's sales. Elekta, meanwhile, grew from five or six employees in the mid-'80s to 200 by 1997. The Gamma Knife costs $3 million. Leksell noted that even though all countries are becoming concerned about health care costs, he expects Elekta to do well because so much money has been spent on diagnosing patients but less on improving the quality and efficiency of care. Parkinson's disease and epilepsy, for example, account for such high health care costs, Leksell noted, that there will be pressure to cure them.

Elekta services its customers worldwide, but avoids manufacturing as much as possible and instead has built what Leksell calls a "network of long-term alliances with good and solid manufacturing companies." It attempts to keep up with technological change as rapidly as possible. "It's been very important," Leksell said, "not to tie up capital in the part of the business that has the lowest returns. The biggest returns, he said, come from research and development and distribution, not manufacturing.

The only exception is that Elekta owns Motala Verkstad, the famed Swedish company that started out as a shipyard and is mentioned in Jules Verne's novel *Twenty Thousand Leagues Under the Sea* as the builder of the submarine *Nautilus*. "Motala was one of our licensees, and when the shipbuilding industry got into trouble in the '70s, they got into trouble," said Leksell, noting that Elekta took it over so that the company would not lose a supplier.

Sixty percent of Elekta's manufacturing is done in Sweden, and most of that in the central area around Linköping. Leksell said it's most important to find the best manufacturer, but that he prefers Swedish manufacture because sourcing outside Sweden requires complicated management. Elekta has also bought Ruggles Instrument of Boston and has a minority holding in another U.S. firm.

For Leksell, like all other high-tech entrepreneurs, the biggest challenge is to maintain control of the company while raising capital. "We want management to be in control of the company, but at the same time, we want to broaden the shareholder base to ensure that our company is financially stable," Leksell said. One-third of Elekta's ownership is Swedish investors, one-third foreign and one-third the managers. As for management style, Leksell's philosophy is to be "flexible, [keep] an open-door policy, more like a young service company than an industrial company."

As a Swede who has come home, Leksell said that foreigners' observations of Sweden as an anti-entrepreneurial society have not been overestimated. "The cultural barriers between academia and business are substantial in Sweden," Leksell said. "In Sweden, you run a civil service career or you run a business."

In addition, he noted, "Swedish tax laws didn't breed a type of entrepreneurs that were financially driven. It's difficult to get rich. In

Sweden, making money doing business was not appropriate or accepted in the '60s and '70s. In the '70s, the wealth tax combined with the inheritance tax forced many entrepreneurs and family-owned companies to exit. Personal dividends were highly taxed. People spent a lot of money on unproductive tax planning, and people sold companies to investment companies, where you lost the entrepreneurial spirit."

Swedish entrepreneurship still faces challenges, Leksell warned. "People have left Sweden to go to work in other, non-Swedish companies, or Swedes have been working for Swedish companies outside Sweden. A lot of managers prefer not to be in their own countries, to get away from the bureaucracies of their headquarters."

Well-educated Swedes, he added, are still more inclined toward big business than starting and running their own firms. "I would say what we're lacking is initiative, training, background," he said. "People are not being trained to run their own show. At the Stockholm School of Economics, my students were trained to go into big business. Teaching at Harvard [University in the United States] was quite different."

Leksell is confident that entrepreneurs in Sweden will fare better in the future than they did in the past quarter-century. "Business has gained in relative social value, and other occupations have lost in relative value," he said. "To be an entrepreneur in Sweden is 'in.' " But, he continued, only certain ways of making money are socially acceptable. "If you are making money in industry, it's starting to be OK. If you make your money on stocks, houses, cars, art, it's not OK. There's another trend culturally. Swedes are so egalitarian. We don't want anyone to stick out. You never talk about it, you never show it. You won't see many Donald Trumps in Sweden."

... and in Kista and Other Science Parks

In the late 1970s, when the Swedish military left a training ground north of Stockholm near the small suburb of Kista, the city decided to locate industry there. Kista lacked restaurants and recreation facilities, but Ericsson and IBM set up facilities there, followed by Microsoft, Intel, Siemens, Oracle and Hewlett Packard. The Royal Institute of Technology located some of its studies and facilities in Kista in 1988. By 2000, some 3,100 science students were based in the park studying electronics, telecommunications, systems and programming and the Royal Institute of Technology set up a university dedicated to information technology. In 2000, 28,000 people were working at approximately 650 companies in Kista, and the city of Stockholm said optimum employment in Kista would be 40,000 workers.

Ericsson, which had moved beyond its expertise in fixed location phones to be the world's largest supplier of mobile network infrastructure and one of the largest suppliers of mobile phones, emerged as the most important company in Kista and seemed destined to remain so with the development of its wireless application protocol (WAP). The future, Ericsson and other Swedish companies said, is marrying the Internet and mobile phones to create the wireless world.

While big companies, both Swedish and foreign, have prospered in Kista, Harvard Business School Professor of Business Administration Michael Porter and his associates have said the breakups and spin-off companies from Ericsson and other large companies have been crucial to Sweden's new business development. Porter noted that Swedish entrepreneur Jan Stenbeck had acquired a radio operation in 1981 and turned it into Comvik (later Comviq), which opened up an early mobile telephone system. The Stenbeck sphere, Porter noted in an analysis for Invest in Sweden, a government-sponsored agency, "played a crucial role in breaking up monopolies and creating new business concepts and firms, which later supplied entrepreneurial talent for a host of new media and Internet-related startups. The process in this respect resembles Samuel Owen's establishment of a steam engine workshop in Sweden in 1809, a completely new technology, which later spawned a large number of mechanical engineering firms throughout the country."

By 2000, the most famous of the new generation of Swedish entrepreneurs in cellular phones, computer software and Internet consulting was Jonas Birgersson, the founder of Framfab, an Internet consulting firm. Obsessed with military history as a child, Birgersson was analyzing the international arms trade at 14 and turned a small group of fanatics of the Dungeons and Dragons game into a computer network of 25,000 players. In 1995, at age 23, he founded Framfab—or "future factory" to create Websites. In 1999, Framfab grew from 270 to 1,500 employees and acquired 11 companies in Sweden, the United Kingdom, the United States, Germany and France. Birgersson also started a company to bring high-speed Internet service to homes.

Like any other good Swede, Birgersson enjoyed being known for living in a small apartment, owning no car and sleeping in the office. He also enjoyed shocking older businessmen by saying he despised the luxury lifestyle of chief executives and supporting high taxes and the welfare state. . "If I pay a lot of taxes and I get good value for the money I spend, then there's no big problem.," he told the *Financial Times*. Birgersson may not be in business to develop a luxurious lifestyle (at least not yet) but he has also shown he has plenty of entrepreneurial eccentricity. He liked to appear in a fleecy jump suit, combat boots and a 5 o'clock shadow for business meetings at McDonald's. And there was no question that his nature is competitive. In 2000, Birgersson launched a new software, Brikks, with a press conference at an old Stockholm movie theater in which a brick was thrown through a window. "Bricks smashes Windows," Birgersson said in a reference to his plans to compete with the software of the U.S. giant Microsoft. "Here we are in old, cold Sweden, fighting against the very best brains of the American market," he said. But, as he launched his European expansion, he said his favorite quotation is from Napoleon: "In war nothing compensates for lost time, nothing."

Kista and Stockholm are not the only centers for new business. The old naval and shipyard center of Karlskrona and nearby Ronneby, which have a college of technology, have become home to companies involved in program development and telecommunications. Prosolvia, founded in 1988 by two Chalmers Institute of Technology classmates, develops software programs for interactive simulation. Not all the companies are in Sweden's populous south. Daydream Software in Umeå has targeted the game market for personal computers. Some of the largest corporations in the world have located their European telemarketing call centers in Sweden, and more than 80,000 people are employed in the Swedish call center industry. They provide technical support in many different languages—English, Estonian, Finnish, French, German, Italian, Russian. The Swedish Medical Products Agency (Läkemedelsverket), located in Uppsala, has established a reputation as one of the fastest government agencies in Europe that review new medical products.

In addition, the Swedish government is trying to promote entrepreneurship by establishing institutions such as Ideon Vision, which was set up in Lund in 1983. Established to protect Lund University's investments in research, Ideon is now a vehicle for Lund University professors and students to commercialize their ideas and inventions. Kai Varman, a former big-business executive who founded his own firm, Probi AB, to make ProViva, a drink of fermented oatmeal, and serves on Ideon's board, said that foundations such as Ideon were needed in Sweden because Swedish businesses had a hard time raising capital for the long cycle of developing "knowledge-based" products before the venture capital business got started in Sweden in the late '90s.

"We have to take care of young geniuses, and we know it," said Sven-Thore Holm, Ideon's managing director. Labor union leaders, Holm said, have shown more interest in Ideon than have the Ministry of Industry or Sweden's big businesses, which may mechanize or move production overseas to reduce costs. "I have a very close relationship with the labor union leaders," he said. "They are listening to [the idea] of spin-off companies. I negotiated with the labor unions for seed money. They have realized that the major Swedish companies won't provide new jobs." (Many Swedish business leaders disagree, of course, with this view on the unions.)

The Need for Leadership

Kjell Nordström, a professor known as Doctor Spray, who is also a member of the board of Spray, the noted Swedish Internet company that has become a part of U.S.-based Razorfish, and the author of a book on the Internet age entitled *Funky Business* says Sweden's Internet success is due to the freedom of thought nurtured by the social experiments in the 1930s and the country's sensitivity to local issues. Massachusetts Institute of Technology economics professor Paul Krugman declared in a late 1999 *Fortune* magazine column that "the Swedish model is working." These observations are undoubtedly true, but Sweden nevertheless lacks balanced political leadership.

In 1995, Carl Bildt, the Swedish prime minister from 1991 until the Social Democrats won back control in 1994, announced that he would take the position of the European Union's High Representative in war-torn Bosnia, but would keep his chairmanship of the Moderate Party and his seat in Parliament. In most countries of the world, it would have been considered odd at any time for the leader of the principal opposition party to take a job outside the country and keep his party post, and absolutely unthinkable when the nation's unemployment stood at its highest level since the Great Depression and the country was trying to adapt to the globalization of the economy. But Swedes accepted Bildt's decision with little debate, and Swedish public opinion polls showed that in his absence Bildt's approval ratings rose, making him by far the most popular politician in the country. When Bildt returned home in 1997 to lead the nonsocialist parties into the 1998 parliamentary elections, Mats Johansson, a columnist for the conservative newspaper *Svenska Dagbladet,* wrote that if Bildt did not get a second chance to form a government, "Europe will be calling again; there is so much to do, you see, to finish building the European house instead of carving the corners of the little red cottage."

Johansson turned out to be right. The nonsocialists lost the 1998 elections and in 1999 Bildt accepted an offer from the United Nations to be an envoy in the troubled Balkans. Bildt's earlier decision to spend close to two years in Bosnia managing the civilian peace effort rather than fight with the Social Democrats on economic issues, the Swedish people's acceptance of it and Bildt's decision to leave again rather than remain a minority political leader in Sweden, symbolize the questions of political and business leadership Sweden faces in the future.

Individual Swedes have long shown they have the talent to succeed in political, business and intellectual venues much bigger than their own small country. In accepting the positions out of the country, Bildt followed in the tradition of Dag Hammarskjöld, who headed the United Nations; Gunnar and Alva Myrdal, who did important research in the United States and worked for international organizations; and Olof Palme, who established an international commission on Third World countries. But Bildt was the first party leader and parliamentarian to leave while in office, and he raised the specter that other Swedish politicians will also be attracted to Brussels as the European Union assumes more and more power. Swedish civil servants are already clamoring to find jobs at the headquarters of the European Union in Brussels, where the pay is better than in Stockholm and the potential exists to have power over the affairs of all of Europe rather than just Sweden.

Sweden's talented, young business executives and entrepreneurs have even more reasons than Bildt and civil servants to focus their attentions abroad. Sweden's big businesses constitute a modern-day worldwide empire without borders. An argument can be made that, for all of Sweden's pride in the performance of its politicians and civil servants at the United Nations, Swedish executives have achieved proportionately greater power in their realm. Swedes may be the world's biggest donors of foreign aid on a per capita basis, and its officials some of the most important players within the United Nations and other international bodies, but there are limits to the amount of money a country of fewer than nine million people can give and to the power its civil servants can achieve in comparison with their counterparts in more-populous countries. SKF, on the other hand, is the world's largest maker of ball bearings, and Ericsson a worthy competitor with the biggest telephone manufacturers based in the biggest countries.

The managers of Sweden's multinational companies have always found it necessary to focus their attention on international business conditions and the countries where they sell their products. Swedish economic policymaking has paid a price for Swedish business's need to monitor and affect events worldwide. In an interview for this book, Lars Ramquist, then the president of Ericsson, acknowledged that was often difficult for him to pay attention to Swedish business and political affairs when he had to worry about currency trading in Singapore and other matters in the huge markets where Ericsson sells its phones and services. As sales extend to farther-flung countries and production moves abroad, the executives' focus is becoming even more international. In addition, they frequently receive tempting offers from multinationals based in countries where executive compensation is higher.

Today's liberal investment and employment rules make it possible for young entrepreneurial Swedes to start their enterprises in whatever country they think their businesses will prosper most. Sweden endured the loss of nearly one-quarter of its population, mostly to the United States, before World War I. Since World War II, there has been a slow, but steady trickle of scientists and entrepreneurs leaving the country, as well as what economics professor Magnus Blomström, who divides his time between Stockholm and New York, calls an "internal brain drain" of talented people who went into fields such as sociology and planning rather than the more economically productive science and business. Jan O. Berg, president of SIFO, a Stockholm public opinion polling firm, warned in an interview, that young Swedes today have traveled so much and are so exposed to U.S. and European culture that they feel much more comfortable living in other countries than did previous generations.

A generation ago, Curt Nicolin became the first Swedish executive in modern times to engage openly in public debate. "I found it's not so dangerous to tell your honest view," said Nicolin, who has encouraged others to follow in his footsteps. Nicolin so far has, sadly, found few followers. If the next generation of Swedish business managers spend their time managing their worldwide empire of businesses, and Swedish entrepreneurs build their own empires outside the country, the question is who, if anyone, will "carve the corners" of the cottage of entrepreneurship that's vital to the creation of new products, wealth and jobs in Sweden.

The System Intact - Big Business, Big Labor, Big Government

In the early 1990s, after the fall of Communism and during the worst depression that Sweden had faced since the 1930s, it was fashionable to speculate that the days of "bigness" in Sweden were over, that the old companies would fail and that the Swedish people would turn against big government and big labor. Within a few years, all the principal institutions of Swedish society proved that they would survive, and the Swedish people indicated, with their votes and opinions, that they were not willing to give up on a society that they loved and that had brought them stability and high living standards for the past century.

Sweden's greatest comparative advantage in the future may be where Swedish industry started—in forest products. Even in this age of

Volvos, Saabs and Ericsson cellular phones, the Swedish forest products industry has remained Sweden's biggest net earner of foreign exchange, for the simple reason that it doesn't have to import any components. With mergers and consolidations, the forest products industry has become concentrated in four firms: SCA; Stora; MoDo; and Assi Domän, a half-government company formed in 1994 by combining Assi, a government-owned forest products company that had been set up in the 1970s to operate failed mills, and Domän Verket, a government agency that held forest land. Together, the four companies account for about 80 percent of forest product sales, but they pursue quite different business strategies. SCA, for example, specializes in processed products, such as diapers, and Assi Domän in sawed products and brown paper bags. A fifth key player is SODRA, a cooperatively owned company that has become the world's largest producer of chlorine-free pulp.

After nuclear power, Sweden's large forest products sector poses the country's most difficult environmental problems. As one forest products industry executive put it, "When people think of paper, they think of pollution." But Swedish forestry companies have pursued cleanup strategies to the point that their environmental reports are often as long as their annual reports on corporate earnings. As a group, Swedish forestry executives say that their advanced position in environmental protection is one of their greatest market advantages.

Sweden's large forest holdings make Europe self-sufficient, at least statistically, in pulp and paper for the first time. Swedish forestry executives say, however, that the European Union is having difficulty adapting to and regulating this globally competitive industry. The Swedish executives say that French and German forestry companies, which are smaller, fear the giants of the north and may encourage regulations that make it difficult for the Swedish companies to compete with those in North America and other parts of the world. Sweden never subsidized forestry in the same way it subsidized agriculture; but the European Union subsidizes forestry research, and the Swedes are determined to get their fair share of the money. Membership in the European Union has also raised issues of European versus Swedish views of forestry management. Countries on the continent seem to have separated the management of private and government-owned lands much more than Sweden has.

Globalization and double-digit unemployment have not reduced the power of Sweden's unions as much as some analysts predicted they would. Economists have been troubled that Sweden's union-negotiated wages rose 1 percent faster per year than the average European wage rose in 1995 and 1996. In 1997, a strike by newspaper distributors blocked newspaper delivery to hundreds of thousands of subscribers. As corporate profits rose, union members began demanding higher wages. Swedish executives and union leaders still want to maintain the consensus between business and labor that has produced generally harmonious relations and few strikes since the 1930s. In 1997, companies and unions representing 800,000 manufacturing workers, including the metalworkers, reached an agreement that, in the future, pay would reflect "existing economic conditions." The two sides also agreed to appoint an industrial committee to oversee labor market stability and mediate in conflicts. The committee was also given the authority to impose a two-week cooling-off period in the event of a threatened strike. The agreement gave rise to hopes that the main blue-collar trade union federation, LO, which has two million members, could reach a new trade accord with the Swedish Employers' Confederation. In late 1997, when new collective wage bargaining began, LO demanded a 3.7 percent increase in wages, with most of the gains going to low-skilled workers, who, by international standards, were already highly paid. The Social Democratic government had warned earlier that it would intervene to prevent wage hikes of more than 3.5 percent but had little reaction despite warnings that high wage hikes would reduce economic growth and government revenues, start another cycle of inflation and raise government borrowing costs.

But perhaps the greatest sign that Sweden will evolve rather than change quickly is the political scene since 1994, when Sweden returned to the "normalcy" of Social Democratic rule after a three-year experiment in nonsocialist government. The nonsocialist period had coincided with the worst depression since the 1930s, and the government's debt skyrocketed as Sweden paid unemployment benefits to hundreds of thousands of workers who lost their jobs. In 1993, Sweden's budget deficit was 12.3 percent of gross domestic product (GDP), the highest among the Organization of Economic Cooperation and Development (OECD) countries. Interest rates had soared, and business investments had fallen to levels some analysts said were below those of the 1930s.

The Social Democrats promised to restore Sweden's reputation as a fiscally responsible country and specifically to reduce the government deficit to less than 3 percent of GDP by 1997 so that Sweden could meet the rules for entry into the European Monetary Union and make its own decision about joining the EMU, rather than having one imposed by Brussels. Over the next three years, in an informal coalition with the Center Party, the Social Democrats ignored the pleas of their left-leaning members and turned in a remarkable performance of reducing the annual deficit by cutting government spending and raising personal taxes. They reintroduced double taxation of dividends, hiked property taxes (conservatives said the intent was to destroy family-owned companies) and imposed a special tax to maintain the welfare state that heads of high-tech companies say makes it difficult for them to keep talented young people who are tempted to move abroad.

The job of explaining Sweden's financial plans to the investment community fell to Prime Minister Göran Persson, who served as finance minister before he became prime minister in 1996. Persson frequently noted his distaste for being grilled by "grinning 25-year-old finance yuppies" on Wall Street, but his performances convinced international investors to buy both Swedish stocks and government bonds. In late 1997, Persson had the twofold pleasure of returning to New York City to explain that Sweden expected its government surpluses to begin occurring in 1999 and to run 2 percent of GDP by 2001—and of winning praise from the same analysts who had viewed him so skeptically before. Under Persson's leadership, the Swedish government decided to use tax breaks to put a computer in every Swedish home and made plans to provide high-speed Internet service to rural as well as urban Sweden. In 2000, Persson received an invitation that would have made the founders of the Swedish social welfare state proud: to explain to the U.S. National Governors Association how Sweden was using the powers of government to lead the world in connecting its people to the information society.

The 1998 general elections in which the Social Democrats held on to the prime ministership proved Swedes are unlikely to reject their traditional politics anytime soon. Sweden's improved economic performance under Persson proved both his personal skill and the Social Democrats' ability to adapt to changing times. But there were limits to the Social Democrats' pragmatism. Business analysts complained that the Social Democrats were unwilling to reduce personal taxes or taxes on stock options to encourage either entrepreneurs or corporate executives to stay in the country. Sweden simply doesn't have a political party for which business is as high a priority as it is for either the U.S. Republican Party under President Ronald Reagan or the Democratic Party under President Bill Clinton. Under Carl Bildt's successor as party leader, deputy Finance Minister Bo Lundgren, the Moderates have emphasized the free market mantra, but the party originated as a preindustrial upper-class conservative organization and remains more interested in military matters and foreign policy than in economics. It was the Liberal Party whose leadership put free-market institutions into law in Sweden in the late 19th and early 20th centuries, and it is now clear that when the Liberals gradually made free-market economics secondary to providing social benefits and maintaining civil liberties, Sweden lost an important voice in economic debate.

The defining political issues of the coming years appear to be nuclear power, entry into the European monetary union and deciding whether the country is willing to reduce levels of personal taxation to keep engineering and executive talent. Although Swedes agreed in the 1980 referendum to close down nuclear power plants, achieving that goal without severe economic repercussions is proving very difficult, if not impossible. Business and labor both oppose closing the nuclear power plants, while the Center and Green Parties and the environmental movement favor the shutdown. The only way the Moderate Party appears able to gain the prime ministership is by attracting the farmer- and environmentalist-oriented Center Party to a nonsocialist coalition government. But the Center Party's vigorous opposition to maintaining nuclear power makes the prospect of forming a successful nonsocialist governing coalition difficult at best. The question of joining the European monetary union has also split Sweden, with open disagreements within most political parties. Swedish business leaders have favored integration with Europe as soon as possible. But some nonbusiness conservative Swedish political theorists say that the business leaders' attitude is risky because socialists could easily gain control over the European Union and its currency. The business leaders' view, said one conservative, is an indication of how "helpless" Swedish business feels. "They see the European Union as a crowbar for opening up Sweden and finally breaking the Social Democratic power," he said.

Swedish Mentality and the Swedish "Way" of Management

In an analysis published in 1953, economic historian Eli F. Heckscher and E.F. Söderlund, then head of the Swedish Employers' Confederation, wrote that business visitors often reported that "industrially" Sweden more resembled the United States than any other European country. At the time, the remark was a rare comparison of Swedish industry with that of other countries. In those days, Swedish business was Swedish, except for the overseas production plants, which specialized in practical industrial products such as vacuum cleaners and telephones, and the sales forces, which had no trouble selling Sweden's technically superior products.

Today there are many reasons to be interested in the character of Swedish business. It's doubtful that any other country Sweden's size has had its companies featured on the front page of *The Wall Street Journal* as examples of the best (ABB) and worst (Pharmacia & Upjohn) in international management. *The Journal* and other publications have continually cited ABB as one of the best-managed global companies in the world, and its longtime chief executive officer Percy Barnevik, who had been Asea's president, won many awards from business groups as manager of the year. The merger between Sweden's Pharmacia and the U.S. company Upjohn has often been cited for the problems in communication between its Swedish and U.S. managers.

The Hecksher-Söderlund analysis that Swedish industry was most similar to the United States was also logical. Swedes had been traveling back and forth to the United States for more than a century, studying American technology and production methods. After World War II, while France, Germany, Great Britain and Italy were rebuilding and often experimenting with state-owned enterprises, Sweden kept almost all its enterprises private (at least until the economic troubles of the late '60s) and sent its students and executives to American universities and technical centers for advanced training. Swedes also shared with Americans an unpretentious, straightforward business style, which involved almost none of the behind-the-scenes favoritism and bribery that characterized business in many Third World countries and even some in Europe.

Since the 1970s, however, when Swedish business began to face unprecedented competition from Western Europe and cheaper Third World producers, and Swedish products no longer sold themselves, business owners have had to face the question of whether their executives and sales force were really as modern as they once assumed. In particular, the owners of Swedish business have become painfully aware that Swedish executives and sales representatives (who are mostly men) have reputations for being brutally honest, emotionally distant, neurotically punctual and averse to engaging in small talk, the very balm of international business relationships. The realization that many Swedish executives and sales reps do not act like their counterparts from other countries has led to introspection and the discovery that Sweden's historical experience has produced distinctly Swedish attitudes toward salesmanship, capitalism, management and entrepreneurship.

The self-examination appears to have begun in the 1970s, when some Swedish export firms hired Jean Phillips-Martinson, an English consultant who lived in Sweden and became a pioneer of cross-cultural communication, to study their employees and conduct seminars for them on how to get along with foreigners. In her 1981 book, *Swedes as Others See Them*, Phillips-Martinson noted that Swedish exporters told her that they prided themselves on "sticking to the facts, not talking rubbish"—an attitude salespersons in many countries would find preposterous. Phillips-Martinson also reported on the impression that the Swedish delegation to the Organization for Economic Cooperation and Development in Paris made on the representatives of other countries. "We had nicknames for all delegations, Phillips-Martinson wrote, and the Swedish delegation was nicknamed 'The Quiet Men'—they arrived punctually, were always very polite and well-dressed, but stuck together and rarely opened their mouths!"

The Swedes' inclination to draw such a strict line between public and private life, Phillips-Martinson concluded, made it difficult for them to engage in negotiations with foreigners, who were used to small talk about children, family, sports, art and maybe even politics to get to know the stranger with whom they were doing business. Other studies showed that some of the characteristics that Swedes viewed as unquestionable virtues were not viewed the same way in other countries. Swedes' strict punctuality, one study showed, can be seen as "an unsympathetic and impractical rigidity when it comes to human relations." Foreigners lauded Swedes for their honesty, but one commentator wrote that their attitudes are "naive, blue-eyed, principle-bound, wooden and remote from the conditions of real life."

Phillips-Martinson's work and a growing stream of inquiries by foreigners about the Swedish national character led Åke Daun, head of the Institute of Ethnology at Stockholm University and the Nordic Museum, to undertake academic work on the subject. In his landmark 1989 study, *Swedish Mentality,* Daun wrote that Swedes initially regarded such national character studies as anathema for three reasons: a) Hitler had emphasized national traits in his despicable racial theories, b) Swedes thought of themselves as so homogeneous that they had little reason to think in terms of cultural differences and c) Swedes thought of their country as modern, just, rational and without a national culture. In fact, Daun wrote, Swedes associate the concept of national culture with lesser-developed countries "entrenched in their sundry picturesque customs and irrational religious beliefs."

Daun nevertheless persevered, focusing on the Swedes' reputation for being dense, slow and shy, which they've acquired because they talk so little. This unwillingness to talk is not necessarily communication anxiety, Daun wrote, but a behavior pattern that developed early in the country's history. Using theories ranging from the Baron de Montesquieu's 1748 *On the Spirit of the Laws,* which stressed the impact of climate and geography on national psyche, to the many sociological studies of the United States published in the 1970s, Daun concluded that Sweden's remote, northern location; centuries of isolation from international conflict; lack of immigration; and long Social Democratic rule had produced some behaviors that may well be logical, but seem strange to people from other countries.

Most peasant societies rewarded cooperation and did little to praise individual initiative that threatened the solidarity of the group. But Daun pointed out that the Swedish people have always had to deal with the hardship of a three-month growing season, one of the shortest in the world. The harshness of life in early Sweden, Daun said, led Swedish society to reward development of practical "engineering" solutions to problems and to respect facts rather than revere the religious, artistic or speculative side of life—an explanation for why Sweden has invented so many practical items and produces them so well. But this hard life also gave preindustrial Swedes a greater incentive than most peoples to work together and "do" rather than "talk" in order to raise and harvest the food to survive the winter. Swedes, Daun noted, call small talk *kallprata*, literally "cold talk," and have other pejorative terms for people who talk a lot. Even in preindustrial times, historians say, Swedes spent little time in village squares, cafés or taverns, preferring to drink both coffee and spirits in their cottages. Social gatherings were primarily religious, Daun noted, until the 19th century, when they gave way to meetings of labor, temperance and evangelical groups.

Daun's studies also provided another possible reason Swedes don't enjoy small talk and business negotiations the way executives from other countries might. Because Swedes speak so little, when they do speak, their words assume great power, Daun said. And the fact that Sweden has had so few invasions and is so homogeneous means that it's very easy for a Swede to detect the deeper meaning behind another Swede's statement, which makes speaking dangerously revealing, something not to be done without careful consideration. Ethnologist Annick Sjögren, who was raised in France, told Daun that in France words "weigh lightly," while in Sweden they are heavy with symbolism. Swedes hold consensus and amiability in such high regard Daun wrote, that "in contrast to many other cultures, the typical Swede feels no joy or elation at opportunities to use his or her crushing arguments. Instead, the Swede feels some discomfort and prefers to wait and see rather than start an argument."

Swedish life, Daun continued, is governed by *duktighet*—a peculiarly Swedish concept that "being capable" involves both achievement and inherent qualities. Daun agreed with early-20th-century Danish-Norwegian author Aksel Sandemose that a Scandinavian is raised under village law not to think of himself or herself as "anything special" and that personal worth comes from being industrious in both one's work and personal life. Even if Swedes achieve success, they are taught it should not be enjoyed too much, because "Pride goeth before a fall." Swedes are ambivalent about "stars" in any field, Daun noted, admiring them, but also envying them and taking great pleasure if those in high positions fall. Eccentrics are not regarded with the same positive interest as they are in most other countries, he added.

Daun also noted that Swedes' aversion to violence is another expression of conflict avoidance. Sweden is a "low-anxiety" society, Daun wrote, and Swedes do not become aroused to strong emotion, either positive or negative, very easily. Daun noted that some Swedes have considered their countrymen cowardly because they do not easily stand up to bullies—a view that other Scandinavians came to share when Sweden declined to come to their defense against Nazi Germany. Some observers have speculated that Sweden's tolerance of Hitler meant that Sweden was like Germany, but Daun noted that Umeå University linguist Astrid Stejdie has written that the popular Swedish feeling that "one should not stick one's nose into other people's business" proves that the Swedes' attitude is the opposite of that of Germans, whose inclination, she wrote, has been to regulate human behavior.

Daun made few observations on the direct impact of these attitudes on Swedish business behavior. He did note that the ability to cooperate is highly valued in the recruitment of upper-level staff. But as Swedish companies have acquired more overseas subsidiaries and entered into joint ventures in which Swedes manage people of other nationalities or vice versa, explaining Swedish management practices to the outside world has become something of a cottage industry. In 1993, Bengt Anderson, a Swedish multinational-executive-turned-consultant wrote that the stereotype of Swedish managers is that they are "practical and technically capable but not very imaginative. Philosophy and abstract thinking baffle them. They have no humor and take everything you say literally. They often spend more time telling you what's wrong with their products than what's good about them." Swedish managers, he continued, have the reputation that they "shun conflicts and put off decisions until they reach consensus (in a manner that appears wishy-washy even to the Japanese). Organizations are flat, with responsibility delegated way down. It's never clear who's in charge of what, and why. Swedes dress in sports shirts, slacks and sandals for business meetings. Being neurotic about punctuality, they begin and end meetings exactly on schedule. They go straight to the point, without preliminaries. Their answers are short, and they remain silent if they have nothing to say (although Finns think Swedes talk too much)."

Anderson added that while such "stereotypes stink" because individual executives do not all conform to them, the caricature had some validity. When a Swedish corporation bought an American company, Anderson wrote, it put a top Swedish design engineer in charge of an important product development project. A few months later, work had come to a standstill and a management consultant was brought in. The Swedish head of design complained that the American engineers did no work except when directed, and the Americans complained that the Swede exhibited so little interest in their work they thought he didn't care about it and was perhaps planning to fire them.

The Swedish word for supervisor, *övervakare,* Anderson noted, is the same as for probation officer. "In most countries," Anderson wrote, "if given an assignment, you naturally assume you'll be supervised while completing it. In Sweden, you naturally assume you are on your own. If you need guidance or help, you ask for it. Swedish management begins from the idea that the individual is both willing and able to do a good job and the recognition that the person who does the work knows more about it than anybody else. As the Swedes see it, management in some countries assumes that the individual worker is a lazy, incompetent, untrustworthy malingerer who has to be watched constantly. A Swedish manager thinks of himself more as a coach than a commander."

Swedish management is similar to Japanese management, Anderson continued, but he refuted those who have written that the Swedes are "obedient" like the Japanese. Both are seeking consensus and harmony, he wrote, but "the art of managing Swedes is the art of managing people who don't comply. Managers never manage out of a position of fear or formal power. A good manager is a good listener, with the ability to reach consensus among his fellow workers and encourage them to do their best."

"Employees of Swedish companies are never afraid of their bosses and normally don't feel inferior to them," Anderson added. "They see the head of the company as a specialist among other specialists. Specializing in management doesn't make an individual more valuable as a human being than specializing in, for instance, machine design, accounting, secretarial or janitorial work. Everyone has a job to do and feels respected for doing it well."

Anderson also offered an extraordinary insight into Swedish entrepreneurship. A study he cited showed that while entrepreneurs in other countries start businesses to make money, in Sweden they start businesses because they want to make their own decisions. Because larger businesses require more personnel and decrease the owner's independence, Swedish entrepreneurs have less incentive to grow larger.

The analyses of the Swedish mentality have undoubtedly helped foreigners understand Swedes, and Swedes to understand themselves, but it's still interesting to note those behaviors that are so sensitive that Swedish analysts barely describe them. Daun and Swedish anthropologist and ethnologist Gillis Herlitz, who wrote his own book on Swedish behavior, devoted about a paragraph each to how much Swedes enjoy drinking. "Alcohol helps many Swedes to relax," Daun noted. "Alcohol permits a different identity, even without being very intoxicated. Liberating its user from the norms prescribing emotional control and from the pressures of everyday problems, alcohol acquires a pivotal value. Nevertheless, the next day, many Swedes may suffer from a bad conscience. Despite being temporary, the altered identity brought about through alcohol is after all a breach of norms, and the attitude toward alcohol has long been ambiguous."

Herlitz wrote: "Some Swedes use alcohol on festive occasions to loosen their inhibitions. Everything that one has previously not said, but wanted to, can be expressed now that alcohol is involved. Swedes dance more, sing more, talk more, quarrel more, and discuss more when they have drunk alcohol. Even if the amount of alcohol they've consumed hasn't really made them drunk, it's as if just being in the vicinity of alcohol and a tiny glass can relieve their tensions and make them more personal—for better and worse."

Those commentaries could describe the use of alcohol in any country, but in Sweden the level of alcohol consumption has long been a public concern (although Swedes do note that statistics show they do consume less alcohol than the French and some other Europeans). The temperance movement has been a major player in politics since the 19th century, and the question of whether the European Union will force Sweden to allow the sale of alcoholic beverages at competitive prices is a major social issue. Daun noted that "in the public debates on alcohol, it would be as unthinkable to mention that alcohol also gives pleasure, as it would be in Norway to claim that the population drinks itself into the intimacy that Norwegian mentality does not naturally contain." But neither Daun nor other analysts describe what Swedes actually do and say when they drink, or speculate on whether they would drink less and communicate more easily if society were not so inhibiting.

While pointing out Sweden's homogeneity and aversion to violence as cultural characteristics, none of the analyses of Swedish mentality, business or otherwise, made any reference to what impact the history of violence may have on the character of modern Sweden. Daun left the discussion of Swedish violence and anti-violence to quotations from American writer Susan Sontag. After a visit to Sweden in 1969, Sontag wrote that Swedish repression of anger "greatly exceeds the demands of justice and rational self-control; I find it little short of pathological. The demand for repression seems to arise from some naive misunderstanding or simplification of what goes on between human beings; it's simply not true that strong feelings escalate so inevitably into violence." Swedish avoidance of confrontation, Sontag continued, "shades, rather often, into passivity and indifferentism. For instance, I'm sure that it isn't only because of the chronic shortage of labor that people rarely get fired here, no matter how they bungle their jobs. It's also true that most Swedes would prefer to continue operating some activity with incompetent personnel than face the unpleasantness of speaking severely to someone, hurting their feelings and incurring their hostility."

Swedes rarely mention the subject today, but their history is filled with violence. Sweden was an aggressor for about one thousand years, from the time of the Vikings until 1809, and ruled large swaths of foreign territory by force for many years. Swedish domestic history has its own share of violence—from the Viking times to the assassination of Gustav III in 1792—and the coup d'etat that sent King Gustav IV Adolf into exile in 1809 could have turned violent if the king had not stepped down peaceably. Questions about Swedish attitudes toward violence beg to be answered. Is there no legacy from this history? Or is the reason Swedes defend their censorship of movies for violent scenes (but not sexual ones), even when they are intended for adult audiences, that they fear a violent streak lurking beneath their placid present? Does a fear of violence have an impact on Swedes' attitudes toward competition in life and business?

Daun and the other analysts also appear to be as determined as the general Swedish population to think of all Swedes as being the same. None of these studies mention Swedish nobles, Jews, free-church members, Swedes who emigrated or young Swedes who have immigrant parents. While Swedish studies show that the country's educated elite is more self-perpetuating than the Social Democrats would like, government statistics also show that today's Swedish business executives are likelier than their predecessors to have working-class origins. The trend raises two questions: whether the upbringing of this generation of executives was different from that of the previous generations of executives who came from upper-class families and whether the executives of working-class origin were raised with different and probably poorer communication skills. In private conversations, Swedes of average background will say they believe the nobility, *brukspatroner* and Jewish families raise their children differently from the majority of the Swedish people and may still teach them to be freer about expressing themselves. In an interview, Daun was asked if he had done any studies on whether Swedish nobles raise their children differently, because records show at least 40 percent of the nobles have some ancestors who were not Swedish, but he said Swedes are not interested in this sort of study because they regard that ancestry as "ancient history."

As business becomes more global and more competitive, the question of which Swedes can be successful executives may be paramount in the big Swedish companies' continued success. "An ordinary reserved and thoughtful Swede can't change his personality and suddenly become spirited, talkative and full of wit," Anderson wrote. "But to communicate effectively with people from other countries, he has to break the cultural pattern engraved on his mind from childhood. Many Swedish business people do so with great mastery. Others never succeed—because they fail to discern their own culture and understand how it differs from others." Anderson warned his readers that one of the worst mistakes Swedes can make is to state, "In Sweden, we do it this way." But he does not say how Swedish business owners might identify who would become the successful executives, what backgrounds they might have or how Swedish society might encourage more of its youth to develop the skills and attitudes they need for more successful business careers.

The Swedish mentality makes the success of Swedish international business all the more remarkable. Swedes can seem so silent that it's easy to forget how successful they have been. Foreigners invariably praise Swedes for being factual, correct and honest—characteristics of the highest order in any business environment. Two of the reasons Swedes are successful, Anderson noted, are that the "low-anxiety" society makes Swedish executives unafraid that experiments that fail could lead to punishment from above and that while Swedish managers may be criticized for not leading, they "seek to liberate people to express the natural energy that's within them." Some Swedes resist the idea that Swedish executives will have to change their behavior. "These square types with a low charm factor have a 100-year history of success" in producing and selling goods all over the world, noted one Swedish business writer. Still, as more and more foreigners work for Swedes, their executives' ability to manage a diverse work force may determine whether there's black ink or red on the bottom line.

The Necessity of Sticking Out

To spend time with the new generation of Swedish entrepreneurs is to visit an exciting and forward-looking Sweden—one far removed from the rigidities of social democracy of the 1970s and '80s or of people mourning the loss of old companies and despairing about the country's future. There are limits to the value of the pride many of these entrepreneurs take in remaining low key, however. Alfred Nobel, L.M. Ericsson and A.O. Wallenberg were too big to be invisible, and if Swedes are going to encourage a new generation of entrepreneurs who will create new products and new jobs, they will have to tolerate and maybe even revel in people who stick out and believe, as Axel Sandemose might have said, "they are something."

Sweden's attempt at classlessness and lack of support for entrepreneurs since World War II have encouraged so much emigration that around the world, but especially in the United States, London and a few other world capitals there is a new class of overseas Swedes. Like the overseas Chinese, the overseas Swedes have found that their talents are more appreciated in foreign countries than at home. The exact number of overseas Swedes is unknown, but there is reason to believe they are increasing. In 1998, 24,600 Swedes emigrated, double the number in

1992, mostly to Norway, Great Britain and the United States. The Swedish Federation of Industries still worries about the emigration of Swedish engineers. The new immigration has led to the formation of organizations such as the Silicon Vikings in San Francisco, a kind of social club and business network for Scandinavians in high tech. Kjell Olson, head of the Silicon Vikings, says many Swedes in the United States plan to return to Sweden, but an indication of the growing strength of their overseas ties has been the formation of an organization to urge the Swedish government to change the law which forbids dual citizenship. These overseas Swedes represent a substantial loss for Sweden. As Henry Hanson, a U.S. scholar of Scandinavian-American history, has noted, the postwar overseas Swedes differ from the Swedish emigrants of the late 19th and early 20th centuries because they are better educated than the average Swede and because they prefer to hang on to their Swedish citizenship. Swedes like to think of them as living overseas temporarily.

Sweden is too rich and important to disappear from the economic map. Sweden's new wave of entrepreneurship also demonstrates that Swedes don't have to leave the country. The real question about Sweden's economic future is whether it will live up to its potential and allow the Swedish people to maintain or improve their standard of living. The success of young Swedes in finding jobs and starting companies abroad is only proof that the world still values Swedes for their inventiveness, efficiency and honesty. The future for Swedish business appears secure—even great. The only question is whether Swedish business will be in Sweden.

Acknowledgements

Researching and writing this book has been both a professional and personal joy, an opportunity to learn about a professional world I did not know and also to understand the land of my ancestors in a new way. Many Swedes and Americans provided both wise counsel and enthusiasm for this project.

Lars Romert, the press counselor at the Swedish Embassy in Washington, D.C., in the 1980s, deserves credit for my association with modern Sweden and for this book's existence. In 1989, Lars Romert invited me to speak on American politics to a group of Swedish members of Parliament at a luncheon given by Ambassador Anders Thunborg. One speech led to many others. In 1991, to thank me for my efforts, the Swedish Embassy in Washington sent me on a trip to Sweden to observe the elections. When I found Swedish business to be fascinating, Mats Johansson, then president of Timbro, a Stockholm think tank, invited me to return to Sweden to conduct more research. Janerik Larsson, then senior vice president of the Swedish Employers Confederation, initiated the book project and never flagged in his interest. After Janerik Larsson left the Employers Confederation, H.G. Wessberg of the Federation of Swedish Industries assumed responsibility for completing it.

Lennart Lundh, president of SkanAtlantic, a Washington media firm, arranged publication through the George Washington University School of Business and Public Management, and he also provided wise counsel on the intellectual content of the book. Dr. Robert F. Dyer, associate dean of the school, shepherded the book through the university's publications process.

The staff of the Swedish Embassy in Washington has been unfailingly helpful and encouraging. Ambassador Thunborg and his wife, Lilianne, and Ambassador Henrik Liljegren and his wife, Nil, invited me to their homes many times to meet Swedes who became sources for the book. I owe a particular debt of gratitude to the Liljegrens, who were so generous with their invitations. Ambassador Rolf Ekéus and his wife, Kim, and Ambassador Jan Eliasson and his wife, Kerstin, also opened their homes to me.

Ingmar Björkstén, the cultural counselor at the embassy in the early 1990s, was unsparingly generous in taking time to discuss many of the ideas in the book. Later, after Nina Ersman came from the Swedish Embassy in Paris to the embassy in Washington as press counselor, she proved to be a Swedish national treasure, both as a personal friend and as a final reader of the manuscript.

I also wish to thank Marianne Norrby, the Ministry of Foreign Affairs press officer who arranged appointments on my first visit to Stockholm, and Jacqueline Stare, the Jewish Museum curator who found answers to some of my most difficult questions.

I am particularly indebted to the work of two historians of Swedish business, Carl Gustavson and Hans De Geer.

I cannot think of words to express enough appreciation to Johan Hakélius, a Swedish writer, who started out as a researcher and arranger of interviews in Stockholm and who evolved into the book's editor, and to Jo Anne Moncrief, who was hired as a copy editor in Washington but who functioned as an editor on a much higher scale. Both of them improved the book immensely.

Finally, I must thank my mother, Marion Hagstrom of Bismarck, N.D., and my many friends for enduring the absences that a long project such as his necessitates.

Biography of Jerry Hagstrom

Jerry Hagstrom is a journalist, book author, and commentator on American government and political life. Mr. Hagstrom pioneered the coverage of the polling and media consulting industries for National Journal, and he has lectured on modern U.S. political campaigns in 25 countries as the guest of the U.S. Information Agency, now the public diplomacy section of the State Department.

Mr. Hagstrom has been a contributing editor of National Journal, the Washington weekly on government and national politics, since 1976. He is the co-author with Neal R. Peirce of *The Book of America: Inside Fifty States Today*, an exploration of the politics and character of each of the 50 states, and the author of *Beyond Reagan: The New Landscape of American Politics*. From 1976 until 1988, Mr. Hagstrom was Mr. Peirce's associate on his newspaper column, which is syndicated nationally in the United States. Since 1995, Mr. Hagstrom has covered agricultural policy for National Journal and other publications.

Mr. Hagstrom was born in North Dakota, where he grew up on a farm homesteaded by his Swedish immigrant grandparents. He is a graduate of the University of Denver and has been a Loeb Fellow at Harvard University and a research fellow at the Freedom Forum Media Studies Center at Columbia University.

Interviews and Conversations

All affiliations are of the time of the interview. Interviewees are located in Stockholm unless otherwise noted.

Almqvist, Per, assistant under-secretary, Ministry of Labor.
Andersson, Håkan, head of section, Secretariat for Labor Market Research, Ministry of Labor.
Andersson, Monica, international secretary, Social Democratic Party.
Arwidson, Marie Schrewelius, director, international relations, Skogsindustrierna (Swedish Forest Industries Association).
Bandling, Lars, vice president, Volvo Aero Corporation, Vienna, Va.
Beijbom, Karl, CARTA Corporate Advisors AB, Gothenburg.
Belfrage, Erik, Skandinaviska Enskilda Banken.
Berg, Jan, managing director, SIFO.
Bildt, Carl, Prime Minister.
Björkstén, Ingmar, critic and cultural counselor, Swedish Embassy, Washington D.C.
Blomström, Magnus, National Bureau of Economic Research, New York, N.Y.
Bonde, Peder, chairman Investor International, Washington.
Boström, Jan-Erik, director, Swedish Employers Confederation, Jönköping.
Brifalk, Anette, head of information, Liberal Party.
Broström, Jacob, chairman, Jacob Broström & Partners, AB, Gothenburg.
Bringéus, Krister, counselor, Swedish Embassy, Washington.
Carlsson, Bo, Grafiska Företagen, Jönköping.
Carlsson, May-Britt, ombudsman, Central Organization of Salaried Employees in Sweden.
Carlsson, Ingvar, Prime Minister.
Carlsson, Sten, marketing director Swedform AB, Skillingaryd.
Cars, Hadar, Member of Parliament, Liberal Party.
Christiansson, Lars, press secretary to the Prime Minister.
Dahlén, Ove, chairman, Saab Aircraft of America Inc., Sterling, Va.
Dahmén, Erik, professor of economic history, Stockholm School of Economics.
Danielsson, Håkan, president, HIAB Cranes & Loaders, Inc., New Castle, Del.
Daun, Åke, professor of ethnology, Stockholm University.
Daveby, Fredrik, Federation of Swedish Farmers.
De Geer, Hans, professor, Stockholm School of Economics.
Dimming, Janerik, editor-in-chief, SKF Public Affairs Group, Gothenburg.
Dinkelspiel, Ulf, Ambassador, Trade Department, Ministry for Foreign Affairs.
Douglas, Archibald and Walburga, Ekensholm, Malmköping.
Edenborg, Mats, director, press relations, AB Volvo, Gothenburg.
Ehrenkrona, Olof, chief of planning to Prime Minister Carl Bildt.
Engström, Odd, former Vice Prime Minister; chairman, Banking Support Council.
Ericsson, Dan, Member of Parliament, Christian Democrat.
Eriksson, Rolf, director, Federation of Swedish Farmers, Brussels.
Ersman, Nina, press counselor Swedish Embassy, Paris and Washington,
Ferm, Anders, former aide to Prime Minister Olof Palme, former ambassador of Sweden to the United Nations and former editor, *Arbetet*.
Folkesson, Marie, educational curator, Maritime Museum and Aquarium, Gothenburg.

Gergils, Håkan, former president, Swedish Shareholders Association; former chairman, World Federation of Investment Clubs, Ecofin.
Grönberg, Tomas, press and cultural staff, U.S. Embassy.
Hadénius, Stig, professor, Institute of Journalism, Media and Communication.
Hagard, John, assistant undersecretary, Ministry for Foreign Affairs.
Hageberg, Thorleif, managing director, Sigarth AB, Hillerstorp.
Hakélius, Olle, chairman, Svenska Lantmännens Riksförbund (Swedish Farmers' Supply & Crop Marketing Association).
Hammarskjöld, Michael, secretary general, House of Nobility.
Hedélius, Tom, chairman, Svenska Handelsbanken.
Heister, Per, communications director, Moderate Party.
Hellström, Bertil, director of information services, Ericsson Microwave Systems, Mölndal.
Hökmark, Gunnar, Member of Parliament, Secretary General, Moderate Party.
Hollner, Lars-Olof, Counselor, Ministry for Foreign Affairs.
Holm, Kjell, head of press center, Ministry for Foreign Affairs.
Holm, Sven-Tore, managing director, Idéon Vision AB, Lund.
Holmquist, Jörgen, budget chief, Finance Ministry.
Ihre, Torbjörn, president, Ericsson Corp., Washington, D.C.
Jannerfeldt, Eric, medical attache, Swedish Embassy, Washington D.C.
Johansson, Bo, marketing engineer, Swedform Metall AB, Skillingaryd.
Johansson, Mats, president, Timbro.
Jondélius, Per-Olof, curator, Volvo Museum, Gothenburg.
Karlsson, Charlie, president, Jönköping International Business School.
Kling, Dick, Federation of Swedish Industries.
Krogvig, Bo, director of information and political campaigns, Social Democratic Party.
Kuylenstierna, Jan, First Marshal of the Court of H.M. the King of Sweden.
Landerholm, Henrik, Member of Parliament, Moderate Party, political adviser to the Minister of Defense.
Larsson, Janerik, senior vice president, Swedish Employers Confederation.
Leissner, Maria, Member of Parliament and leader, Liberal Party.
Lewell, Christer, vice president, MoDo, Stockholm.
Lignell, Christer, kanslichef, Royal Palace.
Liljegren, Henrik, ambassador of Sweden to the United States, Washington, D.C.
Lindholm, Gabriella, deputy assistant undersecretary, Department of International Development and Co-operation (SIDA), Stockholm.
Lindholm, Sten, senior vice president, corporate communications, SCA.
Lindmark, Leif, professor, Umeå Business School, University of Umeå, Umcå.
Ljungberg, Carl-Johan, research coordinator, Timbro, Stockholm.
Ljungqvist, Rolf, HVDC Division, ABB Power Systems AB, Ludvika.
Leksell, Laurent, president, Elekta AB.
Lindbeck, Assar, Institute for International Economic Studies, Stockholm.
Lundgren, Bo, minister for fiscal and financial affairs.
Lundh, Lennart, president SkanAtlantic, Washington, D.C.; former foreign editor and U.S.-correspondent, *Swedish Television, Channel One,* and U.S.-correspondent, *TV 4 Sweden.*
Lundin, Sven, president, Munters Corporation, Fort Myers, Fla.
Malmros, Claes, senior vice president for corporate strategy and business development, Volvo, Gothenburg.
Mathlein, Lars, minister for economic and financial affairs, Swedish Embassy, Washington, D.C.

Mattsson, Britt Marie, journalist, Gothenburg.
Melin, Leif, professor of management, Jönköping International Business School, Jönköping.
Molin, Klas, first secretary, Ministry for Foreign Affairs.
Moliteus, Magnus, former chairman, Procordia USA Inc. and president, Invest in Sweden Agency, New York, N.Y.
Myrén, Gunnar, Cooperative Enterprise Division, Federation of Swedish Farmers.
Müchler, Stephen, vice president, marketing and public relations, Chamber of Commerce of Southern Sweden, Malmö.
Nicolin, Curt, honorary Chairman, ASEA, and former president, Swedish Employers Confederation.
Norrby, Marianne, press officer, Ministry for Foreign Affairs.
Nuder, Pär, member of Parliament, Social Democratic Party.
Olausson, Lennart, director of industrial policy, Trade and Industry Development Agency, Gothenburg.
Olsson, Ulf, professor of economic history, Stockholm School of Economics.
Ördell, Kristian, information officer, Jönköping International Business School, Jönköping.
Pagrotsky, Leif, Minister of Trade, Commerce and Industry.
Palmstierna, Jacob, chairman of the board, Nordbanken.
Petterson, Magnus, president, Hestra Inredningar AB, Hestra.
Petterson, Sven-Olof, Minister, Swedish Embassy, Washington.
Ramberg, Hans-Olof, director of strategic planning, Federation of Swedish Farmers.
Ramqvist, Lars, president, Ericsson.
Romert, Lars, press counselor, Swedish Embassy, Washington, D.C.
Rosander, Tomas, counselor, Ministry for Foreign Affairs.
Rydén, Bengt, president, Stockholm Stock Exchange.
Sandberg, Roland, executive manager, Svensk Musik.
Siebert, Thomas Leland, U.S. Ambassador to Sweden.
Sjöberg, Richard, campaign adviser, Moderate Party.
Södersten, Bo, professor of economics, Lund University.
Strömbom, Inger, information manager, Swedish Federation of Forest Owners.
Stare, Jacqueline, curator, Jewish Museum.
Svanholm, Bert-Olof, president ABB-Sweden; chairman, Volvo, Gothenburg; chairman, Federation of Swedish Engineering Industries.
Svärd, Berit, managing director, GAFS Kartong AB, Värnamo.
Tarschys, Daniel, Member of Parliament, Liberal Party, Stockholm.
Tejler, Peter, deputy chief of mission, Swedish Embassy, Washington.
Tengroth, Bengt, former labor leader and consultant.
Thunborg, Anders, Swedish ambassador to the United States.
Ulpe, Gunnar, Svensk Oljedistribution AB, Jönköping.
Vareman, Kaj, Probi AB, Lund.
Wachtmeister, Ian, industrialist and chairman, New Democracy Party.
Wahlbin, Clas, president Jönköping University, Jönköping.
Wallenberg, Peter, chairman, Investor.
Wallenberg, Jacob, Skandinaviska Enskilda Banken.
Weslien, Lars H., managing director, Springwire Sweden AB, Lesjöfors.
Wessberg, H.G., Federation of Swedish Industries.
Westholm, Carl-Johan, president, Confederation of Private Enterprises; secretary, Mont Pelerin Society.
Zetterberg, Hans, sociologist.

Bibliography

Aalders, Gerard, and Wiebes, Cees, *The Art of Cloaking Ownership: The Secret Collaboration and Protection of the German War Industry By the Neutrals.* Amsterdam: Amsterdam University Press, 1996.

Åberg, Alf, *A Concise History of Sweden.* Kristianstad: Krisitianstads Boktryckeri AB, 1991.

———, *The People of New Sweden.* Stockholm: Bokförlaget Natur Och Kultur, 1988.

Acheson, Dean, *Present at the Creation: My Years in the State Department.* New York: W.W. Norton & Co. Inc., 1969.

Ahtola-Moorhouse, Leena; Edam, Carl Thomas; and Schreiber, Birgitta, eds., *Dreams of a Summer Night: Scandinavian Painting at the Turn of the Century,* London: Arts Council of Great Britain, 1986.

Andersson, Bengt, *Swedishness.* Stockholm: Positiva Sverige, 1993 and 1995.

Baer, Nancy Van Norman, *Paris Modern: The Swedish Ballet 1920-1925.* San Francisco: Fine Arts Museum of San Francisco, 1995.

Bergman, Ingmar, *Images: My Life in Film.* New York: Arcade Publishing, 1990.

Bierman, John, *Righteous Gentile: The Story of Raoul Wallenberg, Missing Hero of the Holocaust* (revised edition). London: Penguin Books, 1981 and 1995.

Blomstedt, Magnus, and Book, Fredrik, eds., *Sweden of Today: a Survey of its Intellectual and Material Culture.* Stockholm: A.B. Hasse W. Tullbergs Förlag, 1930.

Blomström, Magnus, and Meller, Patricio, *Diverging Paths: Comparing a Century of Scandinavian and Latin American Economic Development.* Washington, D.C.: Inter-American Development Bank and Johns Hopkins University Press, 1991.

———; Lipsey, Robert E.; and Ohlsson, Lennart, *Economic Relations Between the United States and Sweden.* Stockholm: Federation of Swedish Industries/Svenska Handelsbanken, 1988.

Bosworth, Barry, and Rivlin, Alice, *The Swedish Economy.* Washington, D.C.: Brookings Institution, 1987.

Brantingson, Charlie, *Investor 1916-1991.* Stockholm: AB Investor, 1991.

Carlson, Allan, *The Swedish Experiment in Family Politics: The Myrdals and the Interwar Population Crisis.* New Brunswick, N.J.: Transaction Publishers, 1990.

Carlson, Sune, *Swedish Industry Goes Abroad: An Essay on Industrialization and Internationalization.* Lund: Studenlitteratur, 1979.

Childs, Marquis, *Sweden: The Middle Way* (updated edition). New Haven: Yale University Press, 1951.

Childs, Marquis, *Sweden: The Middle Way on Trial.* New Haven: Yale University Press, 1980.

Dahmén, Erik, *Entrepreneurial Activity and the Development of Swedish Industry, 1919-1939.* Translated by Axel Leijonhufvud. Homewood, Ill.: American Economic Association/Richard D. Irwin Inc., 1970.

Daun, Åke, *Swedish Mentality.* University Park, Pa.: Pennsylvania State University Press, 1989.

De Geer, Hans *The Rise and Fall of the Swedish Model: The Swedish Employers' Confederation, SAF, and Industrial Relations Over Ten Decades.* West Sussex, U.K.: Carden Publications, 1992

Derry, T.K., *A History of Scandinavia: Norway, Sweden, Denmark, Finland & Iceland.* Minneapolis, Minn.: University of Minnesota Press, 1979.

Edenheim, Ralph et al., *Skansen: Traditional Swedish Style.* London: Scala Books, 1995.

Ekman, Bo, ed., *Sweden Works—Industry in Transition.* Stockholm: Volvo Media/New Sweden 1988 Organization, 1987.

Eizenstat, Stuart E., coordinator, and Slany, William, historian, *U.S. and Allied Efforts to Recover and Restore Gold and Other Assets Stolen or Hidden by Germany during World War II.* Washington, D.C.: U.S. Department of State, 1997. *Facts About the Swedish Economy 1992.* Stockholm: Swedish Employers Confederation, 1992.

Fant, Kenne, *Alfred Nobel: A Biography.* New York: Arcade Publishing, 1991.
Frängsmyr, Tore, *Alfred Nobel.* Stockholm: Swedish Institute, 1996.
Frängsmyr, Tore, ed., *Science in Sweden: The Royal Swedish Academy of Sciences 1739-1989.* Canton, Mass.: Science History Publications, USA, 1989.
Freeman, Richard B.; Swedenborg, Birgitta; and Topel, Robert, *Economic Troubles in Sweden's Welfare State.* Stockholm: Center for Business and Policy Studies and National Bureau of Economic Research, 1995.
Grape-Lantz, Margareta; Karlsson, Ingvar; and Andersson, Sven O., *The Swedish Labour Movement.* Stockholm: International Center of the Swedish Labor Movement, 1989.
Gustavson, Carl, *The Small Giant.* Columbus: Ohio State University Press, 1986.
Gyllenpalm, Bo, *Ingmar Bergman and Creative Leadership: How To Create Self-Directed Peak Performing Teams.* Stockholm: Stabim, 1995.
Häger, Bengt et al., *Ballets Suedois (The Swedish Ballet).* New York: Harry N. Abrams Inc., Publishers, 1990.
Hadenius, Stig, *Swedish Politics During the 20th Century.* Stockholm: Swedish Institute, 1990. Hadenius, Stig, and Lindgren, Ann, *On Sweden.* Stockholm: Swedish Institute, 1992.
Hallvarsson, Mats, *Swedish Industry Faces the 80s.* Stockholm: Federation of Swedish Industries/Swedish Institute, 1981.
———, and Svensk, Rune, *De Första 100 Åren: Svenska Företagsbilder.* Stockholm: Timbro, 1986.
Heckscher, Eli F., *An Economic History of Sweden.* Cambridge, Mass.: Harvard University Press, 1954.
———, and Rasmusson, Nils Ludvig, *The Monetary History of Sweden.* Stockholm: Almqvist & Wiksell, 1964.
Hedin, Gunnar, *Quality Made in Sweden.* Stockholm: Informationsförlaget, 1991.
———, *The Swedish Oil Kings.* Stockholm: Ekerlids Förlag, 1994.
Henriksson, Fritz, *The Nobel Prizes and Their Founder Alfred Nobel.* Stockholm: Albert Bonniers Boktryckeri, 1938.
Herlitz, Gillis, *Swedes: What We Are Like and Why We Are As We Are.* Uppsala: Konsultförlaget i Uppsala AB, 1995.
Hildebrand, Karl-Gustaf, *Banking in a Growing Economy: Svenska Handelsbanken Since 1871.* Stockholm: Svenska Handelsbanken, undated.
Hult, Jan, and Nyström, Bengt, eds., *Technology & Industry: A Nordic Heritage.* Canton, Mass.: Science History Publications, USA, 1992.
Jenkins, David, *Sweden and the Price of Progress.* New York: Coward-McCann Inc., 1968.
Jörberg, Lennart, *Growth and Fluctuations of Swedish Industry 1869-1912.* Stockholm: Almqvist & Wiksell, 1961.
Jörberg, Lennart, and Krantz, Olle, "Scandinavia 1914-1970." In *The Fontana Economic History of Europe,* edited by Carlo M. Cipolla. London: Collins/Fontana Books, 1976.
Kastrup, Allen, *The Swedish Heritage in America.* Chicago: The Swedish Council of America, 1975.
Koblik, Steven, *The Stones Cry Out: Sweden's Response to the Persecution of the Jews 1933-45.* New York: Holocaust Library, 1988.
———, ed., *Sweden's Development From Poverty to Affluence, 1750-1970.* Minneapolis, Minn.: University of Minnesota Press, 1975.
Koskinen, Maaret, *Ingmar Bergman.* Stockholm: Swedish Institute, 1993.
Lagerlöf, Selma, *The Story of Gösta Berling.* Karlstad: Press Förlagstryckeri, 1982.
Levin, Britt, *Hasselbackskungen: Wilhelm Davidson 1812-1883.* Stockholm: privately published, 1992.
Levine, Paul A., *From Indifference to Activism: Swedish Diplomacy and the Holocaust, 1938-1944.* Stockholm: Almqvist & Wiksell International, 1996.
———and Bruchfeld, Stéphane, *Tell Ye Your Children...A Book about the Holocaust in Europe 1933-1945.* Stockholm: Regeringskansliet Levande Historia, 1998.
Lewis, Richard W., *Absolut Book: The Absolut Vodka Advertising Story.* Boston: Journey Editions, 1996.

Lindgren, Håkan, "Banking Group Investments in Swedish Industry," Uppsala Papers in Economic History, 1987.
Lodin, Sven-Olof, *The Swedish Tax Reform of 1991*. Stockholm: Federation of Swedish Industries, 1991.
Lundgren, Håkan, *Sacred Cows and the Future—On the Change of System in the Labour Market*. Stockholm: Swedish Employers' Confederation, 1994.
Lundström, Evert, *Come to Gothenburg*. Gothenburg: Tema Reklam Information AB, 1988.
Lutteman, Helena Dahlbäck, and Uggla, Marianne, *The Lunning Prize*. Stockholm: Nationalmuseum, 1986.
Marton, Kati, *Wallenberg: Missing Hero*. New York: Arcade Publishing, 1995.
Mathias, Peter, and Postan, M.M., *The Cambridge History of Europe, Volume VII: The Industrial Economies, Capital, Labour, and Enterprise, Part 1: Britain, France, Germany and Scandinavia*. Cambridge, England: Cambridge University Press, 1978.
Mattsson, Algot, *New Sweden: The Dream of an Empire*. Gothenburg: Tre Böcker Förlag AB, 1987.
Maze, Edward, *Creative Sweden*, Stockholm: Almqvist & Wiksell/Gebers Förlag AB, 1965.
Misgeld, Klaus; Molin, Karl; and Åmark, Klas, eds., *Creating Social Democracy: A Century of the Social Democratic Labor Party in Sweden*. University Park, Pa.: Pennsylvania State University Press, 1988.
Moberg, Vilhelm, *A History of the Swedish People From Pre-history to the Renaissance*. New York: Pantheon, 1972.
Montgomery, Arthur, *Scandinavia Past and Present*. Arkkrone, Denmark, 1959.
Nilzson, Göran B., *Banker i bystningstid: A.O. Wallenberg i svensk bankpolitik 1850-1856*. Stockholm: Institutet för Ekonomisk Historisk Forskning vid Handelshögskolan, undated.
Olson, Mancur, *How Bright Are the Northern Lights? Some Questions About Sweden*. Lund: Institute of Economic Research/Lund University Press, 1990.
Olsson, Christer, and Moberger, Henrik, *Volvo Gothenburg Sweden* (English edition). St. Gallen, Switzerland: Norden Publishing House Ltd., 1995.
Ostergard, Derek, and Stritzler-Levine, Nina, eds., *The Brilliance of Swedish Glass, 1918-39: An Alliance of Art and Industry*. New Haven, Conn.: Yale University Press, 1996.
Redau, Christiane, *Scandinavian Painters: Impressionism and Naturalism at the Turn of the Century*. Germany: Artbook International, 1992.
Roesdahl, Else, *The Vikings*. New York: Allen Lane/ Penguin Press, 1987.
Rosenfeld, Harvey, *Raoul Wallenberg*. New York: Holmes & Meier, 1995.
Rydberg, Sven, *The Great Copper Mountain: The Stora Story*. Hedemora: Stora Kopparbergs Bergslags AB and Gidlunds Publishers, 1988.
Sahlin, Mona, *Survey of Swedish Labor Market Policy*. Stockholm: Swedish Ministry of Labor, Labor Market Division, 1991.
Sandemose, Aksel, *A Fugitive Crosses His Tracks*. New York: Alfred A. Knopf, 1936.
Sandström, Birgitta, *Anders Zorn 1860-1920: An Introduction to His Life and Achievements*. Mora: Zornsamlingarna, 1996.
Scott, Franklin D., *Sweden: The Nation's History Enlarged Edition—With an Epilogue by Steven Koblik*. Carbondale: Southern Illinois University Press, 1988.
Shirer, William L., *The Challenge of Scandinavia*. Boston: Little, Brown and Co., 1955.
Shirer, William L., *The Rise and Fall of the Third Reich: A History of Nazi Germany*. New York: Simon & Schuster Inc., 1960.
Smith, Howard G., ed., *The Development and Present Scope of Industry in Sweden*. Stockholm: AB Svenska Industriförlaget, 1953.
Sohlman, Ragnar, *The Legacy of Alfred Nobel: The Story Behind the Nobel Prizes*. London: Bodley Head, 1983.
Stare, Jacqueline, ed., *Femtio år efter Förintelsen*. Stockholm: Judiska Museet i Stockholm, 1995.
———, ed., *Judiska Gårdfarihandlare i Sverige*. Stockholm: Judiska Museet i Stockholm, 1996.

———, ed., *Porträtt: Speglingar av svensk judisk kultur.* Stockholm: Judiska Museet i Stockholm, 1993.
Strode, Herman, *Sweden: Model for a World.* New York: Harcourt, Brace and Co., 1949.
Uddhammar, Emil, *Partierna och den stora staten.* Stockholm: City University Press, 1993.
Van Lede, Cees J.A., *Small Countries in a Borderless World: A Natural Partnership?* Arnhem, Netherlands: Azko Nobel Corporate Communications, 1995.
Verba, Sidney and Steven Kelman et al., *Elites and the Idea of Equality: A Comparison of Japan, Sweden and the United States.* Cambridge and London: Harvard University Press, 1987.
Wallenberg, Raoul, *Letters and Dispatches: 1924-44.* New York: Arcade Publishing, 1987.
Wästfelt, Berit; Gyllensvärd, Bo; and Weibull, Jörgen, *Porcelain From the East Indiaman Götheborg.* Copenhagen: Förlags AB Wiken, 1991.
Wedel, Kristian, *Guide to Göteborg.* Stockholm: Rabén Prisma, 1995.
Weibull, Jörgen, *Swedish History in Outline.* Stockholm: Swedish Institute, 1993.
Wihlborg, Clas, *The Scandinavian Models for Development and Welfare.* Stockholm: Industrial Institute for Economic and Social Research, 1992.
Yergin, Daniel, *The Prize: The Epic Quest for Oil, Money and Power.* New York: Simon & Schuster Inc., 1991.
Zetterberg, Hans, *Before and Beyond the Welfare State.* Stockholm: City University Press, 1995.
———, *The Crisis in the Welfare State: A Swedish Perspective.* Stockholm: Atlas/Timbro, 1993.

Periodicals

Various issues of *Asi Posten*, published by the American Swedish Institute, Minneapolis, Minn.; the *Bulletin of the American Scandinavian Foundation* and *Scandinavian Review*, both published by the ASF in New York; *Faxed from Sweden*, published bimonthly by the Swedish Institute, Stockholm; *Sweden & America*, published by the Swedish Council of America, Minneapolis; and *Vestkusten*, published in Mill Valley, Calif.

Andrews, Edmund L., "Sweden, the Welfare State, Basks in New Prosperity," *The New York Times*, Oct. 8, 1999.
Balch, Trudy, "A Little Bit of Sweden in Western Illinois," *The New York Times*, Oct. 23, 1994.
Bardach, Ann Louise, "Edgar's List," *Vanity Fair*, March 1997.
Belt, Don, "Sweden," *National Geographic*, August 1993.
Bergström, Hans, "Sweden's Politics and Party System at the Crossroads," *West European Politics*, London: Frank Cass & Co. Ltd., July 1991.
Branegan, Jay, "Model No More," *Time*, July 19, 1993.
Brown-Humes, Christopher, "Stuntman in a Fleecy Jumper," *Financial Times*, April 7, 2000.
Bruce-Martinsson, Madeleine, "She Forced the Bank to Cut Its Interest Rate," *Dagens Industri*, May 10, 1995.
Brunnberg, Kerstin, "Election Year '91: Undramatic Election Campaign Leads to Change of Government and Shift Toward the Right," *Current Sweden*, Swedish Institute, October 1991.
Carnegy, Hugh, "Exposed Empire Wraps Itself in High-Tech Stocks," *Financial Times*, October 1, 1996.
Dyer, Geoff, "The Wallenbergs' Narrow Escape," *Euromoney*, May 1994.
Eklund, Klas et al., *Sweden's Economic Crisis: Diagnosis and Cure.* Stockholm: Swedish Center for Business and Policy Studies, 1993.
Eliasson, Gunnar, *Is the Swedish Welfare State in Trouble? A New Policy Model.* Stockholm: Industrial Institute for Economic and Social Research, 1985.
Eronn, Robert, "The Sami, Indigenous People of the North," *Current Sweden*, Swedish Institute, March 1993.

"European Finance and Investment: Nordic Countries," *Financial Times,* March 23, 1992.
Flynn, Julia, "IKEA's New Game Plan," *Business Week*, Oct. 6, 1997.
"Fortune Directory," *Fortune,* August 1963.
Gowers, Andrew; Carnegy, Hugh; and Brown-Humes, Christopher, "Generation Game Winner," *Financial Times,* June 1993.
Guttman, Robert J., and Kasteng, Frida, "Something About *Amelia,*" *Europe,* March 1997.
Hanson, Henry Jr., "A Yankee From Småland: An Immigrant Saga," *Swedish American Historical Quarterly*, April 1985.
Huber, Evelyn, and Stephens, John D., "The Swedish Welfare State at the Crossroads," *Current Sweden,* January 1993.
Holmberg, Sören, *A Social Democratic Nosedive: Recent Trends in Swedish Public Opinion*, Swedish Election Studies, Department of Political Science, Gothenburg University, March 1991.
Iloneiemi, Ero, and Flythström, Christer, "The Glass Ceiling," *Nordicum*, April 1994.
Johansson, Mats, "The House That Carl Bildt," *Scandinavian Review,* Spring/Summer 1997.
Kronenberger, Louis, "A Man Looks Back on His Past," a review of *A Fugitive Crosses His Tracks* by Aksel Sandemose, *New York Times Book Review,* July 12, 1936.
Krugman, Paul, "Who Knew? The Swedish Model Is Working," *Fortune,* Oct. 25, 1999.
Lindmarker, Ingmar, "How Sweden's Political Parties View Europe and Possible EC Membership," *Current Sweden*, Swedish Institute, June 1991.
Malmström, Victor H., "Inequality in Sweden: Has the Spatial Dimension Been Annihilated?" *Focus,* Fall 1992.
Maremont, Mark, "Abuse of Power: The Astonishing Tale of Sexual Harassment at Astra USA," *Business Week,* May 13, 1996.
Marklund, S., "The Decomposition of Social Policy in Sweden," *Scandinavian Journal of Social Welfare,* July 1992.
McIvor, Greg, "Waiting in the Wings for the Wallenberg Throne," *The European,* July 14, 1995.
Melcher, Richard A., with Sains, Ariane, "The Wallenbergs' Troubled Empire," *Business Week*, July 19, 1993.
Meyerson, Per-Martin, "Where Is Sweden Heading?" *Viewpoint Sweden,* Swedish Information Service, New York, January 1992.
Moore, Stephen D., "Scandinavian Paper Firms Wrestle With Price Declines," *The Wall Street Journal,* Sept. 5, 1996.
Ohlsson, Per T., "Election Year '94: Back to the Future," *Current Sweden,* Swedish Institute, June 1994.
Olsson, Ulf, "The Nordic Countries and Europe in the Twentieth Century: An Introduction," Oslo: *Scandinavian Journal of History,* Vol. 18, No. 1, 1993.
Prokesch, Steven, "Swedes' Disaffection With 'Big Brother,'" *International Herald Tribune,* Sept. 14, 1991.
Rexed, Knut, "Swedish Labor During the 1990s," *Viewpoint Sweden,* Swedish Information Service, New York, November 1991.
Skog, Rolf, "Foreign Acquisitions of Shares in Swedish Companies," *Current Sweden,* Swedish Institute, May 1992.
"Survey: Sweden," *Financial Times,* Oct. 23, 1991, Dec. 21, 1993, and Dec. 15, 1995.
Sains, Ariane, with Dwyer, Paula, "The Wallenbergs' Flagship May Cross the Ocean," *Business Week,* March 4, 1996.
Samuelson, Paul, "The Failure of the 'Swedish Miracle': Toting Up the Victories—and Problems," *The New York Times,* Aug. 30, 1987.
Schneider, Steve, "Stockholm's Pleasure Island," *Travel & Leisure,* May 1987.
"Serene in Sweden," *Travel,* June 1994.
Stein, Peter, "Sweden: From Capitalist Success to Welfare-State Sclerosis," Cato Institute, *Policy Analysis,* Sept. 10, 1991.
"Stockholm: Hot IPOs and Cool Clubs in Europe's Internet Capital," *Newsweek,* Feb. 7, 2000.
Strom, Stephanie, "In Sweden, A Shy Dynasty Steps Out," *The New York Times,* May 12, 1996.

"Swede Sees Major Effort to Help Baltic Nations' Transition," question-and-answer interview with Carl Bildt, *International Herald Tribune,* Sept. 9, 1991.
"Sweden Means Business," *Europe,* September 1995.
"Sweden: Still in Convalescence," *The Economist,* Oct. 14, 1995.
Taylor, Robert, "The Economic Policies of Sweden's Political Parties," *Current Sweden,* Swedish Institute, June 1991.
Vågerö, Denny, "Women, Work and Health in Sweden," *Current Sweden,* January 1992.
Weiss, Jonas, "Björn Ulvaeus and Benny Andersson," *Europe,* April 1996.
"Whither the Wallenbergs?" *The Economist,* Dec. 25, 1993.

Index

Aalders, Gerard 199
Åberg, Alf 29
Acheson, Dean 194
Adolf Fredrik 60
Adolf Fredrik of Holstein-Gottorp 55
af Chapman, Fredric Henric 60
Åhrén, Uno 158
Åkerlund, Erik 202
Albrekt of Mecklenburg 34
Almström, Robert 146
Alströmer, Jonas 50, 51, 56, 57, 58, 132
Alwall, Nils 203
Anckarström, Johan Jakob 61
Anckarsvärd, C. H. 70
Andersdotter, Grudd Anna 137
Anderson, Bengt 281, 282, 284
Andersson, Gunnar 262
Anger, Per 195
Armstrong, Neil 213
Asplund, Arne 204
Asplund, Gunnar 182
Ax:son Johnson, Axel 133
Ax:son Mörner, Antonia 261
Bachmanson, Andreas 50, 55
Bagge, Gösta 155, 159, 192
Bagge, Jonas Samuel 123
Baird, Robert 140
Barnevik, Percy 243, 246, 278
Beardmore, W. 100
Beijer, Carl Gottreich 102, 228
Belfrage, Erik 247
Bell, Alexander Graham 105
Bellman, Carl Michael 60
Benedicks, Michael 197
Beowulf 29
Berch, Anders 58
Berg, Jan O. 273
Berg, Rudolf F. 104
Berggren, Hinke 157
Bergman, Carl Otto 114
Bergman, Ingmar 230
Bernadotte, Folke 195
Bernadotte, Jean Baptiste 62
Bessemer, Henry 67
Betulander, Ansgar 106
Bierman, John 197, 198
Bildt, Carl 72, 234, 248, 271, 276
Birgersson, Jonas 23, 269
Björkstén, Ingmar 288
Blomström, Magnus 273
Boberg, Ferdinand 137
Bøe, Alf 184
Boheman, Erik 191, 194
Bolinder, Carl 64, 66
Bolinder, Jean 66
Bonde, Peder 220
Bonnie Prince Charlie 131

Bonnier 191
Bonnier, Karl Otto 136, 158, 180
Börlin, Jean 134
Branting, Hjalmar 100, 116, 146, 150, 151, 153, 154
Broman, Gunnar 252
Broms, Gustaf 114
Broström, Axel 133
Broström, Dan 133
Bruce, Pierre 264
Bruchfeld, Stéphane 201
Calissendorff, Rolf 200, 220
Campbell, Colin 52, 53, 131
Carl XVI Gustaf 216
Carlander 117
Carlson, Allan 160
Carlson, Curtis L. 144
Carlson, Oscar 146
Carlsson, Ingvar 250
Carlsson, Lars-Börje 252
Carlsson, Sten 55, 59
Carnegie 131
Carnegie, George 131
Cassel, Ernest 114, 138, 165
Cassel, Gustav 158, 159
Catherine the Great 60
Cedergren, Henrik 105
Cederlund, F. 136
Chalmers 131
Childs, Marquis 13, 156, 177
Clary, Desirée 62
Cleveland, Grover 138
Clinton, Bill 276
Crafoord, Clarence 110
Crafoord, Holger 202, 203
Cromwell, Oliver 65
Cronstedt, Carl Johan 60
Czar Alexander 62
Dahlbäck, Claes 175, 222, 244, 245, 246
Dahlberg, Erik 47
Dahmén, Erik 231
Dalén, Gustaf 110
Danielsson, Carl Ivan 195
Danius, J.H. 182
Daun, Åke 279, 281, 282, 283
Davidson, Wilhelm 135
de Geer, Carl 220, 222
de Geer, Hans 130, 147, 148, 153, 154, 161, 210, 211, 213, 236, 238
de Geer, Louis 41
de Geer, Louis Gerhard 71, 150
de Laval, Gustaf 108, 109, 110
de Maré, Rolf 134
de Miranda, Francisco 132
de Montesquieu 279
Delors, Jacques 242
Dickson, James 66
Dietrichson, Lorentz 180

Dulles, John Foster 200
Dyer, Robert F. 287
Edén, Nils 153
Edison, Thomas 109
Edström, J. Sigfrid 108, 144, 162
Ehrenkrona, Olof 71, 243
Eidem, Erling 190
Eisenhower, Dwight 178
Ekeblad, Claes 57
Ekeblad, Eva 57
Ekéus, Rolf 288
Ekman, C.G. 154
Ekman, Carl Edvard 99
Ekman, Gustaf 67, 107
Eleonora, Ulrika 46, 49
Eliasson, Jan 288
Elizabeth 202
Elofsson, Peter 33
Engelbrektsson, Engelbrekt 34
Engellau, Gunnar 224, 225
Engström, Odd 238, 239
Ericson, Estrid 183, 184
Ericson, Nils 64, 102
Ericsson, Anne-Marie 183, 184
Ericsson, John 64, 96
Ericsson, L.M. 285
Ericsson, Lars Magnus 104, 106, 107
Erik of Pomerania 34
Erik XIV 38
Erikson, Sven 68
Eriksson, Herman 201
Eriksson, Magnus 30, 34
Erlander, Tage 190, 207, 209, 213, 215, 233
Erskine 131
Ersman, Nina 241, 288
Eugén 137, 180
Fälldin, Thorbjörn 230, 231, 232
Fant, Kenne 97
Feldt, Kjell-Olof 233
Ford, Henry 121
Francke, David Otto (D.O.) 102, 112, 132
Fränckel, Eduard 102
Franco, Francisco 230
Frängsmyr, Tore 56
Frank, Josef 183, 184
Fränkel, Louis 95, 165
Fraser, Donald 64
Fray 29
Fredholm, Ludvig 107
Fredrik of Hesse 46, 49
Friedrich II 13
Frisinger, Håkan 240
Gabrielsson, Assar 118, 224
Gahn, Johan Gottlieb 123
Gallé, Emile 180
Gate, Simon 181, 182
Gates, Bill 23
Geijer, Erik Gustaf 37, 139
Göransson, Göran Fredrik 67
Göring, Hermann 122
Gripenstedt, Johan August 70
Gromyko, Andrei 198

Gustaf 146
Gustaf II Adolf 38, 41, 43, 52, 61, 100
Gustaf III 59, 60, 61
Gustaf IV Adolf 60, 62, 70, 150
Gustaf V 118
Gustavson, Carl 105, 124, 131
Gustavson, Carl 288
Gyll, Sören 240
Gyllenborg, Carl 55
Gyllenhammar, Pehr 172, 219, 223, 225-228, 240, 241, 244, 247
Hadenius, Stig 213, 231
Hageberg, Thorleif 259, 261
Hagstrom, Marion 288
Håkansson, Olof 59
Hakélius, Johan 288
Hald, Edward 181
Hall, Christina 132
Hall, John 132
Hambro, Charles 200
Hammarskjöld 152
Hammarskjöld, Dag 15, 184, 212, 272
Hammarskjöld, Hjalmar 151, 212
Hammarskjöld, Michaël 15
Hansen, Signe 136
Hanson, Henry 286
Hansson, Joseph 59
Hansson, Per Albin 127, 155, 190, 206, 215
Haring, Keith 253
Harold Godwinsson 28
Hasselblad, Victor 193
Hatje, Ann Katrin 160
Hay, Bernhard 124
Hayes, Geoff 252
Heckscher, Eli 32, 53, 67, 155, 159, 189, 277
Hedin, Adolf 149
Hedin, Sven 152
Hedlund, Gunnar 209
Hellner, Johannes 199, 201
Henry the Lion 31
Herlitz, Gillis 282
Hermelin, Samuel 113
Hierta, Lars Johan 69, 158
Hildebrand, Karl-Gustaf 125, 127
Hindenburg 190
Hirsch, Leo 224
Hitler, Adolf 18, 188, 189, 191, 195, 197, 279, 281
Hjärne, Harald 146
Hopstock, J.S.K 105
Horn, Arvid 54
Hull, Cordell 189
Hult, Jan 64
Ibsen, Henrik 149
Jansson, Erik 141
Jarl, Birger 30
Jedvardsson, Erik 29
Johan III 38
Johan, Karl 62
Johansson 117
Johansson, Alf W. 192, 194
Johansson, C.E. 120
Johansson, Mats 271, 287

Johansson, Sven Olof 244
Johnson, Axel 133
Johnson, Herschel 198
Josephine of Leuchtenberg 113
Josephson, Anna 136
Josephson, Gunnar 191
Kåge, Wilhelm 182
Kaiser Wilhelm I 152
Kamprad, Ivar 173, 203
Karl IV Johan 140
Karl IX 38, 39
Karl X Gustaf 44, 45
Karl XI 45, 46
Karl XII 46, 49, 52, 55
Karl XIII 63, 64
Karl XIV Johan 63, 64, 70, 113, 135, 150
Karl XV 70, 150
Karleby, Nils 155
Karlsson, Bert 248, 249
Keiller, Alexander 133
Kempe, Carl 101
Kempe, Frans 101
Kempe, Henrik 101
Key, Ellen 180
Keynes, John Maynard 156
Kistner, Erik 116
Kjellberg, Oscar 115
Knutsson Bonde, Karl 35
Knutsson, Torgils 30
Koblik, Steven 188, 195
Kockum, Frans Henrik 134
Kolff, Willem 203
König, Henrik 52, 53
Koskull, Anders 179
Kreuger, Ivar 16, 106, 108, 123, 125, 126, 144, 155, 170, 185, 239
Kristian August of Augustenborg 62
Kristian II 35
Kristina 39, 40, 43, 44
Kristoffer of Bavaria 35
Ladulås, Magnus 30, 33
Lagergren, Fredrik 108
Lagerlöf, Selma 33
Lagerman, Alexander 64, 124
Lagerström, Magnus 57
Lamm, Emma 138
Lamm, Jacques 109
Lamm, Oscar 109
Lamm, Uno 204
Langlet, Valdemar 195
Larsson, Carl 180
Larsson, Gustaf 118, 119, 224
Larsson, Janerik 287
Lauer, Kálámán 197, 198
Lefeld, W. 109
Leissner, Maria 261
Leksell, Lars 265, 266, 267
Leksell, Laurent 23, 265-268
Lenning, Christian 68
Leutwiler, Fritz 243
Levine, Paul 195, 198
Levine, Paul A. 201

Lewis, Richard 251, 252, 253
Lidman, Sven 129
Liedman, Sven-Eric 58
Liljegren, Henrik 288
Liljenroth, Frans 220
Liljevalch, Carl Fredrik 114
Lind, Sven-Ivar 183
Lindén, Ulf G. 228
Lindgren, Astrid 230
Lindgren, Håkan 187
Lindmark, Lars 251
Lindstrand, Vicke 184
Linneaus, Carl 56, 57, 59, 96
Ljungberg, Erik Johan 113
Ljunglöf, Robert 201
Ljungström, Birger 110
Ljungström, Fredrik 110
Louis XVI 61
Lübeck, Sven 161
Lundberg, Per 223
Lundgren, Bo 276
Lundgren, Wilhelm 134
Lundh, Lennart 287
Lundhqvist, Gustaf Aldolf 112, 144
Lundström, Carl 123, 124
Lundström, Johan 123
Luther, Martin 35, 140
MacLean, Rutger 65
Madame Chatelet 57
Magnus the Good 27
Malmros, Lars 240
Malmsten, Carl 183
Malthus, Thomas 157
Mannheimer, Theodor 95, 114, 165
Margareta 34
MasOlle, Helmer 119, 120
Mathsson, Bruno 183
Meidner, Rudolf 233, 237
Minuit, Peter 40
Mitterrand, François 241
Moberg, Anders 203
Moberg, Vilhelm 41, 258
Möller, Gustav 158, 206
Moncrief, Jo Anne 288
Mond, Alfred 161
Moore, Roger 225
Morgenthau, Henry 198
Morger, Kersti 15, 33
Morse, Samuel 104
Morton, John 40
Munters, Carl 122
Muthesius, Hermann 181
Myrdal, Alva 157, 158, 272
Myrdal, Gunnar 157, 191, 207, 272
Myrdals 157, 158, 159
Napoleon 62, 113, 270
Nicolin, Curt 20, 111, 172, 234, 236, 237, 243, 273
Nilsson, Göran B. 73, 169
Nilsson, Måns 36
Nisser, Marie 15, 33
Nixon 215, 216
Nobel, Alfred 96-98, 100, 103, 110, 205, 285

Nobel, Brita 96
Nobel, Emanuel 235
Nobel, Immanuel 96
Nobel, Ludvig 96
Nobel, Robert 96, 98
Nobelius, Olof Pärsson 96
Nordencrantz 50
Nordström, Kjell 271
Nordström, Paul 116
Norman, Torbjörn 192, 194
Norrby, Marianne 288
Nycander, Curt 251
Nystedt, Olle 195
Nyström, Anton Dr. 145
Odhner, Clas-Erik 154
Odhner, W.T. 103
Odin 29
Ohlin, Bertil 191, 209
Olai, Petrus 96
Öller, Anton Henric 104
Ollers, Edvin 181
Olsen, Ivar C. 198
Olson, Kjell 286
Olsson, Ulf 13, 125, 205, 221, 244
Oskar 70, 97, 113
Oskar I 66, 70, 113
Oskar II 151, 196
Östberg, Gustaf Fredrik (Dick) 146, 148
Owen, Samuel 269
Oxenstierna, Axel 38, 40, 44
Palm, August 145
Palmblad, Vilhelm Fredrik 142
Palme, Olof 19, 171, 215, 217, 219, 229, 230, 233, 238, 247, 248, 250, 272
Palmer, Potter 138
Palmstierna, Jacob 239
Palmstruch, Johan 43
Pasch, Gustaf 123, 124
Paulsson, Gregor 181, 182
Penser, Erik 100
Persson, Göran 276
Petersson, Magnus 260
Phillips-Martinson, Jean 278
Pilo, Carl Gustaf 60
Pirenne, Henri 27
Polhem, Christopher 46, 58, 60
Ramquist, Lars 272
Rausing, Gad 202
Rausing, Ruben 170, 202
Reagan, Ronald 276
Rising, Adolf 116
Rockefeller, John D. 98
Roesdahl, Else 26
Röhss, Wilhelm 68
Romert, Lars 26
Romert, Lars 287
Roosevelt, Franklin D. 122, 156, 184, 197
Rothschild 98
Roux, Michael 252
Rudbeck, Olof 96
Rudbeck, Wendela 96
Rurik 28

Rydbeck, Oscar 185
Rydén, Bengt 239
Sahlgren, Niclas 52, 53, 132
Sahlgren, Nils Persson 52
Sampe, Astrid 183, 184
Sandemose, Aksel 13, 280
Sandemose, Axel 285
Sandström, Birgitta 137
Scheele, Carl 123
Schough, Robert 114
Schumpeter, Joseph 231
Schwan, Johan Gustaf 71
Scott, Franklin 45
Scott, George 140
Sefeldt, Nils 224
Segerstedt, Torgny 190
Sergel, Tobias 60
Shand, P. Morton 183
Shirer, William L. 189
Siewert, Karl 103
Silfversparre, Arent 99
Sillén, Gunnar 68
Singer, Al 251
Skötkonung, Olof 29, 37
Smith, Lars Olsson (L.O) 139, 251, 252
Smitt, J.W. 97
Sobrero, Ascanio 97
Söderblom, Nathan 161
Söderlund, E.F. 277
Söderlund, Gustaf 162, 169
Sohlman, Ragnar 100
Sontag, Susan 283
Sörlin, Sverker 57
St. Erik 29
Staaf, Karl 150, 151
Stalin 192
Stare, Jacqueline 288
Stejdie, Astrid 281
Stenbeck, Jan 269
Stewart Gardner, Isabella 138
Strindberg, August 131, 149
Sture, Sten 35
Stuyvesant, Peter 40
Sundel, Martin 139
Svanholm, Bert-Olof 22, 241
Svärd, Berit 262, 263, 264
Svedberg, Elias 183, 184
Taft, William Howard 138
Taylor, Bayard 131
Tegnér, Esaias 63, 70, 141
Telford, Thomas 64
Tham, Vollrath 114
Thiel, Ernest 109, 129
Thiel, Signe 129, 137
Thunborg, Anders 287
Tingvall, Karl 113
Toll, Paul 125
Tor 29
Tragos, Bill 252
Triewald, Mårten 51, 56
Truman, Harry 122
Turner, Graham 252

Uddhammar, Emil 151
Ullgren, Clemens 124
Ullsten, Ola 231
Usselinx, William 52
Valdemar 30
Varman, Kai 270
Vasa, Gustaf 15, 35, 36, 37, 40, 44, 135, 150, 179
Verne, Jules 267
von Dardel, Fredrik 197
von Fersen, Axel 62
von Hayek, Frederik 207
von Holstein, Bogislaus Staël 179
von Höpken, Daniel Niclas 52
von Platen, Baltzar 63, 67
von Platen, Baltzar Carl 122
Wachtmeister, Ian 12, 248, 249
Wall, Anders 172, 228
Wallenberg 13, 17, 20, 21, 73, 95, 102, 104, 106, 108, 109, 118, 133, 136, 144, 162, 178, 185, 186, 196, 203, 219- 223, 227, 228, 234
Wallenberg, André Oscar (A.O.) 73, 102, 112, 114, 143, 196, 285
Wallenberg, Ebba 220
Wallenberg, Gustaf 143, 144, 196, 197
Wallenberg, Jacob 21, 116, 175, 187, 196, 199, 200, 201, 220, 222, 226
Wallenberg, K.A. 103, 109, 114, 134, 136, 198
Wallenberg, Marc 219, 222
Wallenberg, Marcus 20, 108, 175, 200, 204, 234, 235
Wallenberg, Marcus Jr. 106, 136, 199, 220, 221, 223, 228
Wallenberg, Marcus Sr. 103, 196, 197, 198
Wallenberg, Peter 222
Wallenberg, Raoul 11, 143, 178, 195, 196, 197, 198
Walling, Anna 96
Warhol, Andy 253
Weguelin, Christopher 114
Wehtje, Ernst 104
Wehtje, Walter 220
Weibull, Jörgen 37, 47, 49, 141
Welander-Berggren, Elsebeth 182
Wenner-Gren, Axel 121, 122, 126, 221
Wenström, Georg 107
Wenström, Wilhelm 107, 108
Werthén, Hans 122
Wessberg, H.G. 287
Westerberg, Henry 119
Westholm, Carl Johan 13
Westman, K.G. 190, 191
Wettergren, Erik 181
Wicksell, Knut 157
Wiebes, Cees 199
Wieselgren, Per 140
Wigforss, Ernst 155, 158, 207
Wihlborg, Clas 212
William the Conqueror 28
Wilson, Thomas 133
Winquist, Sven 117
Wising, Mai 196
Wycis, Henry 266
Zetterberg, Christer 240
Zetterberg, Hans 231
Zinin, Nikolaj 97
Zorn, Anders 137, 138, 180
Zorn, Leonhard 137